*The Impact of Publicity
on Corporate Offenders*

SUNY Series on Critical Issues in Criminal Justice
Gilbert Geis and Donald J. Newman, EDITORS

The Impact of Publicity on Corporate Offenders

Brent Fisse
Reader-in-Law,
University of Adelaide, Australia,
AND
John Braithwaite
Director,
Australian Federation of Consumer Organizations

State University of New York Press
ALBANY

Published by
State University of New York Press, Albany

© 1983 State University of New York

All rights reserved

For information, address State University of New York
Press, State University Plaza, Albany, N.Y. 12246

Library of Congress Cataloging in Publication Data

Fisse, Brent.
The impact of publicity on corporate offenders.

(SUNY series on critical issues in criminal justice)
Includes bibliographical references and index.
1. Criminal investigation—United States—Case studies. 2. Corporations—United
States—Corrupt practices—Case studies. 3. Corporations—Corrupt practices—Case
studies. 4. Publicity—Social aspects—Case studies. 5. Crime prevention—United
States—Case studies. I. Braithwaite, John. II. Title. III. Series.
HV8073.F525   1983   364.1′68′0973   82-19643
ISBN 0-87395-732-6
ISBN 0-87395-733-4 (pbk.)

Contents

34650

Preface

This book was animated by the uncertainty which surrounds the use of publicity as a means of controlling corporate crime. On the one hand, many are quick to agree with Louis Brandeis' famous dictum that sunlight is "the best of disinfectants; electric light the most efficient policeman." On the other, the view is prevalent that what happens within companies is so shrouded in fog that the glare of public scrutiny quickly is reduced to a flicker.

Our aim has been to look beyond the rhetoric by utilizing some prisms of corporate experience. We have undertaken a qualitative inquiry, based mainly on interviews at the corporations involved in 17 publicity crises. The result is a collection of vignettes and conversations, with their implications for reform. Whether or not the reforms we suggest can command any political support, we hope at least that others can draw upon our data when formulating hypotheses for their own research or putting forth ideas for reform.

We are indebted to many people for their generous cooperation and assistance. Above all, the project could not have proceeded without access to the companies which agreed to interviews. With few exceptions, their representatives responded to our inquiries cheerfully and openly, and remained cooperative despite the often unflattering content of the case studies that emerged. The standard disclaimer must of course be made that we alone are responsible for any of the views expressed here.

Many individuals assisted in other ways. Terry Speed reviewed chapter 1, eliminating much overblown methodological justification. Norman Bowie, John Byrne, John C. Coffee, Jr., David Ermann, Louis Schwartz, and Christopher Stone offered helpful suggestions on a number of points. Gil Geis gave us full access to his research materials on the electrical equipment conspiracies; Christopher Stone did the same in the case of Allied and Kepone; and Andrew

Hopkins similarly assisted with the Appin disaster. A cast of hundreds went out of their way to answer questions arising from our interviews and draft case studies. Behind the scene, Anna Davie, Jacqui Elliott, Leonie Farrell, Mary and Ernest Mathieson, and Scott Starry provided copious research assistance, and two of the best stunt experts in the business, Sandy Manno and Evelyn Jacobsen, performed the bulk of the typing. For the final production we are most grateful to Gil Geis, Susan Suarez, and Malcolm Willison for their sprightly editorial assistance.

We also acknowledge with appreciation the contribution of our corporate sponsors, the University of Adelaide Law School, the Australian Institute of Criminology, and the Center for the Study of Values, University of Delaware. Both of us wish to disclose small shareholdings in one subject of our case studies, BHP.

Our work should be regarded entirely as a joint and equal venture. Each of us felt the other's name should appear first, a question resolved only by resort to the entrails of that luckless football team, the University of Delaware Blue Hens.

Brent Fisse
John Braithwaite

CHAPTER 1

Introduction

Corporate Crime Control through Publicity

The value of publicity as a means of controlling harmful business behavior is often proclaimed, but insufficient attempt has been made to explore its potential.[1] This book describes the various impacts of adverse publicity in a number of major corporate crises and, in light of this information, suggests how publicity could be used more effectively to control corporate crime.[2]

Adverse publicity is highly valued for its capacity to expose and thereby to police unwanted behavior.[3] As Joseph Pulitzer put it so well:

> There is not a crime, there is not a dodge, there is not a trick, there is not a swindle, there is not a vice which does not live by secrecy. Get these things out in the open, describe them, attack them, ridicule them in the press, and sooner or later public opinion will sweep them away. Publicity may not be the only thing that is needed, but it is the one thing without which all other agencies will fail.[4]

Moreover, public approval has traditionally been prized for its capacity to reward and thereby to encourage desirable conduct. These general advantages aside, publicity as a technique of social control may have special merit where corporations are the targets.

First, many corporate offenses cause harm so surreptitiously that public notice is necessary to provide an adequate alert.[5] As Ralph Nader has stressed:

> The *style* of violence and fraud that flow from corporate activities enhances their perpetuation without countercorrection. Unsafely designed automobiles, pollution, harmful food additives, and other con-

taminants embody a silent kind of violence with indeterminate, unpredictable incidence per victim. That impact does not provoke immediate sensory response of pain or anguish directed at the source of the harm. Such harm does not depend on its motivation for its impact. And it does not come in the anthropomorphic form that is apparently so necessary to motivate action. Corporate-induced violence illustrates in compelling fashion the biological obsolescence of human beings toward machine, chemical, or other injurious exposures emanating from the technology of corporate groups. Our sensory apparatus, adapted to cruder and older forms of visible hazards, cannot detect carbon monoxide or radiation until it is too late. Soon, this widening gap between the obsolete mechanisms of man's physiology and the multiple, cumulative impacts of his technology may mark the confines of the struggle for planetary survival . . . .The mind of man must abstract what is happening more rapidly, for the body of man provides few early alert signals.[6]

Second, community blame and resentment[7] now tend to be weak constraints upon corporate crime because corporateness obscures blameworthiness. For one thing, individual accountability is easily masked where collective blame is also in the offing; where all are responsible collectively, no one is responsible individually.[8] For another, corporate blameworthiness is a less familiar concept than individual blameworthiness; indeed, some even go so far as to deny that corporations can be treated as blameworthy agents.[9] Were publicity used to highlight individual and corporate responsibility, the veil of corporateness would be much less likely to confound the usual communal reactions of blame and resentment.

Third, it is hypothesized that publicity will catalyze enforcement action which would not otherwise occur, because of the difficulty of investigating and proving corporate crime. Enforcement agencies, squeezed for resources as they are, typically take the line of least resistance, obtaining consent agreements from defendants wherever possible.[10] This strategy of compromise is often justified, but there is an obvious danger that serious cases will not be treated seriously enough if relegated to a routine and largely informal bargaining process. Where serious cases are publicized, as by investigative journalists, enforcement action is driven out into the open, thereby prompting formal proceedings or more rigorous bargaining.

Fourth, publicity may offer some hope for improving the array of sanctions available against corporate offenders.[11] Many have doubted whether corporations can be sanctioned effectively, usually on the ground that conviction and fine are relatively innocuous when compared with jail in the case of human offenders. However, as we will see in the final chapter, infliction of loss of prestige by means of court-ordered adverse publicity conceivably could provide a more potent weapon.

Despite these potential advantages, only sporadic attempts have been made to explore or harness the power of publicity as a sanction,[12] whether formally by court order, or informally via consumer activism, investigative journalism, and other channels of public redress. This limited attention stems largely from diffidence as to the impacts which publicity is likely to have.[13] Indeed, the reaction frequently has been pessimism,[14] as illustrated by Herbert Packer's doubt as to the impact of stigmatization upon a corporation:

> Sociologists . . . talk about corporate recidivists, but there is very little evidence to suggest that the stigma of criminality means anything very substantial in the life of a corporation. John Doe has friends and neighbors; a corporation has none.[15]

But neither pessimism nor optimism should prevail until more is known about the impacts which publicity has in practice.

To this end we have undertaken a series of case studies revealing what happened in the wake of corporate exposure to serious adverse publicity. Speculation about the sanction of publicity can thereby be laced with data, data derived not only from news media and other publicly available sources[16] but also from interviews with corporation executives.

Cases Studied and Persons Interviewed

Empirical analysis in this book is limited to the impact of adverse publicity on large transnational companies. The smallest corporation subjected to case study is G. D. Searle, which, at the time of its adverse publicity crisis, was number 268 on the Fortune 500 list of the largest industrial corporations in the United States. Only companies which suffered adverse publicity crises since 1960 were included. In fact, only two of the cases occurred during the 1960s — the General Electric price fixing conspriracy, and the General Motors Corvair episode; these proved to be the most difficult data-collecting ventures because memories had faded with the passage of time. Several companies were still exposed to adverse publicity campaigns at the time of our interviews; in these cases the respondents were predictably more on the defensive.

With the assistance of other "corporate crime watchers," we drew up a list of the most severe adverse publicity crises experienced by large U.S. and Australasian companies where the publicity stemmed from allegations of gross misbehavior; allegations of criminal behavior were not involved in three of the cases (GM, IBM, and the BHP coke oven case), but in all cases the misbehavior alleged was sufficiently gross as conceivably to warrant criminalization as a matter of reform.[17] There was no requirement that the allegations be true or false for the case to be considered for inclusion. The resulting sample is calculatedly non-random, our intention being to select extreme rather than average or representative cases. In addition to the 17 cases which appear in the book, the following were on the list but could not be included, for want of cooperation:

Hooker Chemical: the Love Canal toxic wastes tragedy.

United Brands; Gulf Oil; and Northrop: the foreign bribery crisis.

Westinghouse: the heavy electrical equipment price-fixing conspiracy.

Firestone: the tire safety scandal.

B. F. Goodrich: the product safety revelations of whistleblower Kermit Vandivier.

Occidental Petroleum: the occupational health skirmish.

Olin: the convictions for false filings with the government over kickbacks in Asia, illegal arms shipments to the Union of South Africa, and mercury discharges into the Niagara River.

Nestlé: the infamy stemming from the promotion of infant formula in the Third World and the distribution of salmonella-infected formula in Australia.

We cannot discern any systematic pattern of bias among the companies that refused to talk to us: Three companies agreed to interviews about the foreign bribery crisis, three refused; General Electric agreed to discussions on the electrical equipment price-fixing conspiracy, Westinghouse refused. A clear majority of the companies approached agreed to interviews. Nevertheless, it must be conceded that there may be hidden differences that systematically distinguish the cooperating and non-cooperating companies. Moreover, it has to be granted that other observers would have included different cases on their list of the most severe instances of corporate adverse publicity. Our selection procedure being rough and impressionistic, we can only repeat that random sample selection is not critical to the methodology adopted for this study.

For each case study we wrote to the chief corporate executive officer asking if we could speak with him and a variety of other senior executives about the crisis. In only four cases did we actually speak to the chief executive, but in all cases he passed us down to very senior lieutenants. In three instances we were granted an initial interview with only one senior officer, while in all the others we were given a fairly free rein to speak with a variety of officers. The maximum number of interviews with insiders was 14 at BHP, where we spoke with top management at the corporation's head office in Melbourne, with top management of the Australian Iron and Steel subsidiary at Port Kembla, with senior officers at the AIS Collieries head office in Wollongong, and with personnel at the coal face of the Appin Colliery. Initial interviews were usually supplemented by follow-up interviews, often with other officers, once our draft chapter had been circulated within the company.

In addition to soliciting information from insiders, we sought the reactions of union officials in those case studies that involved alleged offenses against workers. In many cases we also interviewed officers from government regulatory agencies, disgruntled employees who had left the company, competitors, outside accountants, government prosecutors, public interest activists, judicial officers, stockbrokers, and other experts. Data from these outsiders were more important in the cases where insiders were less cooperative.

Note on Qualitative Methodology

Empirical research on corporate crime is still in its infancy. We hope that one of the contributions of this book will be to show how useful empirical research on corporate law-breaking can be conducted.[18]

The strengths of qualitative empirical research [19] have been succinctly captured by Matthew Miles:

Qualitative data are attractive for many reasons: they are rich, full, earthy, holistic, "real"; their face validity seems unimpeachable; they preserve chronological flow where that is important, and suffer minimally from retrospective distortion; and they, in principle, offer a far more precise way to assess causality in organizational affairs than arcane efforts like cross-lagged correlations (after all, intensive fieldwork contains dozens of "waves" of data collection, not just two or three). Furthermore, their collection requires minimal front-end instrumentation. Qualitative data also have attractive qualities for their producers and consumers; they lend themselves to the production of serendipitous findings and the adumbration of unforeseen theoretical leaps . . . .Finally, there are many reasons to believe that qualitative data can very usefully be played off against quantitative information from the same organizational setting [20] to produce more powerful analyses than either sort of information could have produced alone.[21]

Qualitative research only enjoys these advantages to the extent that it is unstructured: Totally structured work puts blinkers on the field worker and can impose a reality on phenomena which is totally meaningless to the actors involved. Nonetheless, a certain amount of structure is essential to a successful research enterprise: Totally unstructured work may produce a flood of serendipity but only a trickle of relevance to established theory and real public policy dilemmas; "An incoherent, bulky, irrelevant, meaningless, set of observations may be produced, which no one can (or even wants to) make sense of."[22]

Our interviews were unstructured but goal-directed. There were not set questions. Yet by the end of each interview we ensured that we had elicited the respondent's views on a predetermined range of issues. These issues are discussed broadly in the next section and set down in detail in the summary chapter. Our unstructured methodology provided multiple "waves of data collection"; we would for instance, telephone back to respondents, checking the accounts given in interviews against the accounts presented at public hearings or in company documents, and test the accounts of insiders against those of outsiders.

The problem with such a variegated methodology, however, is that it does not incorporate formal guarantees against self-delusion. What are the assurances that any dynamic, rich, serendipitous, holistic findings are not, in fact, *wrong?* [23] Here there is no test of statistical significance according to a set of conventions that, at least in principle, cannot be tampered with. There is no standard measuring instrument that could be used in the same way by another scholar in an attempt to replicate the findings. When we decide to do qualitative research, we are, if we are good scholars, making a conscious choice to sacrifice reliability for the sake of validity.[24] We choose to provide a moving-picture description of reality rather than a snapshot, even though we know that with the snapshot we (and others) would be able to put a ruler on the photograph to reliably measure a limited reality. More formally stated, the trade-off between reliability and validity is as follows:

Certain kinds of reliability must be intentionally violated in order to gain a depth of understanding about the situation (*i.e.,* the observer's behavior must change from subject to subject, unique questions must be asked of different subjects . . . . There is an inherent conflict between validity and reliability — the former is what fieldwork is specially qualified to gain, and increased emphasis on reliability will only undermine that unique function.[25]

Having decided upon that sacrifice of reliability for validity, there is still the need to build in safeguards to keep research honest. But how can this be done when we make a virtue of non-standardization? In publishing qualitative studies of alleged violations of law by identifiable corporations, there is at least one built-in assurance of validity which other more anonymous types of qualitative research do not have — the law of defamation. Bankruptcy is not one of the consequences of slipshod research that the social science researcher need normally consider. Nor is the gruelling experience of hours of cross-examination by counsel of the caliber which transnational companies can afford to hire. On another occasion, one of the authors was asked by a publisher's law firm to indicate whether he would be in a position to prove to the satisfaction of a court of law some 300 assertions about empirical reality; by answering this question in the affirmative, the author laid himself wide open to a suit by the publisher for indemnification in the event of defamation. Both of us have been chastened by that experience, but even so our caution has not always been enough to avoid the threat of defamation; in relation to two of the case studies we found ourselves forced to approach our solicitors. In light of this experience, we would venture to suggest that qualitative corporate crime researchers undoubtedly drop more conclusions from their research reports because they could not be validated in a court of law than do quantitative criminological researchers as a result of the imperfect validity of their instruments of measurement.

A second safeguard of validity built into the present research has been the submission of draft case studies to the companies interviewed with a request for their comments and criticisms.[26] In those case studies where the alleged offense was against employees of the company, we also circulated the draft for comments by the unions concerned. This advance notice provided respondents with an opportunity to stop publication in the courts, and therefore reinforced the first guarantee of validity mentioned above. A further precaution in the case of larger companies was to send the draft to the chief executive officer as well. This resulted in the draft being circulated to different constituencies whose members often perceived events differently from the other insiders previously interviewed. Our undertaking to the companies in this feedback process was not to guarantee adoption of suggested changes, but to take considered account of them.

Circulating drafts to officers within the company generated an enormous amount of further data. In one case study, the initial interview with the chief executive officer was of two hours' duration, while the follow-up interview to discuss the draft lasted more than four hours. Written comments on the drafts were also generally voluminous (up to 20 typed pages) and incorporated the criticisms of several staff. J.P. Stevens was the only company that declined the opportunity for comment; its letter in reply concluded: "Apparently, you chose to disregard the extensive information we sent to you and under the circumstances we must disassociate ourselves from your project." A number of other companies criticized us strongly, but at least were willing to keep a constructive dialogue flowing. For example, useful further discussions were held with ITT despite this seething initial reaction: "[The draft] falls far short of the serious scholarship I would have expected from someone with your professional affiliations and which was the basis for granting you extensive interviews of ITT executives." On the debit side, it should be pointed out that at times this safeguard can actually reduce validity. There are occasions when researchers get the truth on a first encounter while the defenses are down: When presented with an actual dossier, respondents sometimes try to "rewrite history" for self-protective reasons.

A third safeguard was the fact that almost 90 percent of the initial interviews were conducted jointly by the authors. Braithwaite experienced this as an important advance over his earlier qualitative study, *Corporate Crime in the Pharmaceutical Industry*. As we dictated from our notes into a tape recorder immediately following each interview, one of us would frequently challenge interpretations or misunderstandings of the other. When we could not agree, we would go back to the company for clarification. In proceeding in this way, we were mindful of the lesson about interaction between fieldworkers which Miles had previously drawn:

> We also learned that much analysis was going on in the mind of the fieldworker. Each one developed a fairly rich set of working hypotheses about what was going on in his or her site, along with a fairly retrievable store of specific anecdotes and incidents supporting the hypotheses.

But without interaction with colleagues, the hypotheses went unchallenged and usually untested, and the anecdotes remembered were only those in support of the hypotheses.[27]

To this it should be added that, with interviews on a topic as sensitive as corporate crime, superior rapport and data recording can be achieved with two interviewers in contrast to just one. When a respondent reveals inside information, one researcher can get this down verbatim while the other puts his note pad away and works busily at maintaining eye contact and sustaining the flow of questions.

A fourth safeguard of validity in qualitative research is for researchers to make their field notes freely available to other researchers. Unfortunately, this is not possible with the present research because of confidentiality problems. However, there are many sources of raw data in our files which are freely available; these include the extensive press cuttings which underpin our statements about the nature of the adverse publicity in particular cases, and plots of stock market prices which underlie our conclusions about stockmarket impacts. With the exception of confidential material, our files are open to all bona fide scholars.

Nevertheless, because our data are "soft," a fundamental problem we have in this book is essentially the same as one confronted every day by courts of law: Does the set of circumstances about one particular case justify a certain inference about that case? Decisions about whether A caused B (e.g., does the fact that Japan cancelled defense contracts with Lockheed in the mid-1970s justify the inference that Lockheed lost sales because of the foreign bribery crisis?) are not made on the basis of a correlation coefficient between A and B from a sample of observations, but on the facts surrounding one observation of concern.

Our inductive process is straightforward. We make a common-sense presumption, then attempt to rebut it from as many different angles as possible.[28] The best way of arriving at presumptions and locating angles for rebuttal is to talk to as many key actors as possible and to read as many documents as are available. Out of this process many presumptions emerge for which there is no line of rebuttal. For example, no one is likely to challenge the presumption in the Sharp case that the recall to Japan of all the senior Japanese executives in Sharp's Australian subsidiary was caused by the conviction of the company for misleading advertising — there simply is no other reasonable explanation.

The path of induction may have more twists, of course, as in the James Hardie case. There, we attempted to rebut the presumption that one reason why James Hardie removed asbestos from its building products was the health scare over asbestos or, stated more positivistically, that the health scare over asbestos was a cause of James Hardie's removing asbestos from its building products. The presumption is reasonable because common sense tells us that large companies, when confronted with a threat to their livelihood, are likely to adapt and innovate to avert the threat. Moreover, we note that it was during the late 1970s when the asbestos health scare hit Australia, and not in some other period, that James Hardie made the decision to invest millions of dollars in a research and development program to remove asbestos from its products. However, during the period when this decision was made, asbestos also was becoming increasingly expensive. Perhaps, then, it was cost-cutting which caused James Hardie to get out of asbestos rather than the health scare. After considering various possible alternatives, this was the one which continued to challenge seriously the presumption. Our ultimate conclusion was that the evidence that the health scare was a cause remained stronger than the evidence that it was not. Both the health scare and the escalating asbestos costs were contributory factors. One important reason for adhering to the original presumption was that the health scare was itself a cause of the rising costs of asbestos, because it forced heavier regulatory and workers' compensation burdens on asbestos mining companies.

There is another sense in which causal inference in qualitative case study research is different from inference under the quantitative models of the physical sciences. The mechanistic conceptions of causality which social scientists inherited from the early physical sciences do not take account of the fact that human beings, unlike atoms or rocks, make choices. Human actors are often capable of making choices consciously to counteract the causal forces which might otherwise determine their behavior.[29] Corporations also exhibit intentionality, although of a special collegial form.[30]

The choices of individual executives or, where relevant, corporate intentionality, can be a basis for causal inference in the kind of research within this book. If the chief executive officer says that he decided to do B (remove asbestos from company products) because of A (the asbestos health scare), then this might warrant the inference that A caused B. Before making this inference, however, lines of rebuttal must be assessed. In this case, the lines of rebuttal consist mainly of the standard caveats against fieldworkers accepting the reasons given by informants as the "real" reasons.[31] And of course one should insist on verification that *B* really was done. For example, if a company claimed it had a new, more stringent, policy, we asked for a copy of that policy. If it claimed it had reduced emission levels for carcinogens, we asked for a copy of the data on which that claim was based and then checked the information against that collected by government inspectors.

Because the economic activities of corporations and their senior executives are guided by rational choice, asking them why they made certain choices, if they will tell the truth, is apt to prove a reliable source of confirmation. And getting at the truth about past scandals (if not current ones) is more possible than the uninitiated researcher might assume. In all large organizations, be they universities or the Ford Motor Company, there are always disgruntled individuals who are willing to be critical of the organization. Or at least there will be individuals who, while they might identify with their subunit goals, are not enraptured with the overall goals of the organization. Then, of course, there are people who want to be loved or at least approved of, even by researchers they have just met for the first time. Such people enjoy impressing researchers with their sophisticated understanding and helpfulness, so they divulge secret knowledge. There are others, however, who enjoy leading researchers up the garden path by telling falsehoods. The art of qualitative research is to catch these falsehoods by shrewd trap-setting and cross-checking.

A considerable proportion of the inferences in this book deal with changes which were directly the result of conscious choice by top management. Decisions to establish a new vice-presidency for environmental affairs, to invest in modernized pollution control technology, or to recall senior executives to Japan, are clear manifestations of managerial and corporate intentionality. To the extent that the impact of adverse publicity is mediated by such intentionality, then persuasive causal inference is possible in a study such as this. Indeed, where we find transformations responsive to managerial edict, our qualitative methodology is at its strongest.

However, not all important impacts are directly under management control. Since managers cannot control stock market prices for example, we cannot discover whether an adverse publicity crisis caused stock prices to tumble by asking them. Stock market prices are so beyond the control of anyone's intentionality, and are so complexly determined by a multitude of economic variables, that quantitative multivariate techniques of measurement might also be useful.[32] Even so, however, if we were asked to make a choice, we would go to a stockbroker who is an expert on qualitative market intelligence rather than to a statistician.[33]

Plan of Book

The bulk of this book is made up of 17 case studies. Each follows the same pattern of presentation. In the first section the allegations against the company are described, together with convictions and other legal outcomes that ensued. The next section within each case study describes the nature of the adverse publicity suffered and whether the company itself mounted any form of counter-publicity campaign. Then the financial impacts of the crisis — on sales and stock market prices in particular — are assessed. The following part proceeds to review non-financial impacts, especially upon corporate prestige and employee morale. Last, there is a résumé of reforms resulting from the crisis in question, with particular emphasis on corporate reforms, whether organizational and/or technological, or in the form of discipline or retraining.

The three final chapters bring the work to a conclusion. Chapter 19 summarizes the main findings of the 17 case studies and considers how the conclusions might have been different had different types of cases been studied. Chapters 20 and 21 then build upon the case studies by exploring ways of extending and improving the use of publicity as a means of corporate regulation, chapter 20 being devoted to informal publicity, and chapter 21 to publicity which is formal in the sense of being ordered by a court or independent tribunal.[34]

CHAPTER 2

Labor Relations Violations
at J.P. Stevens

The Alleged Offenses

J.P. Stevens and Company is the second largest company of the textile industry in the United States, with sales of $1.4 billion, 45,000 employees and 85 plants. From the commencement in 1963 of a campaign to unionize J.P. Stevens mills in the South, the company, until 1980, was continually in violation of the National Labor Relations Act (NLRA). In 136 cases, J.P. Stevens has been found guilty of violations of the NLRA by the National Labor Relations Board.[1] The U.S. Court of Appeals has upheld virtually all of the many findings made by the Board against Stevens. Three appeals to the Supreme Court have also gone against Stevens.

The most common kind of offense committed by the company has been the firing of union supporters during union organizing drives. There have also been many instances of relatives of union sympathizers being dismissed or threatened with dismissal. A variety of illegal forms of harassment, surveillance, and victimization of individuals has been employed. Union supporters have been coercively interrogated, spied on electronically, prohibited from distributing union literature, and threatened with physical harm. In one case, in a small Georgia community, the local police chief was enlisted to assist in illegal surveillance of union organizers and workers.[2] J.P. Stevens unquestionably has been the most notorious unfair labor practices offender in the United States in recent decades. Even when courts have ordered it to desist from certain practices, it has on occasions ignored them and been held liable for contempt.

13

The Impact of Publicity on Corporate Offenders

Publicity and Counterpublicity

J.P. Stevens' repeated defeats in court over NLRA violations did not normally attract significant adverse publicity at the time they occurred. For example, an important decision against them on January 25, 1980, in which, among other things, they were ordered to rehire workers allegedly dismissed for union activity, attracted one column inch on page 36 of the *New York Times*. The snippet was headed, "STEVENS LOSES 22D LABOR CASE."[3] The important adverse publicity did not follow from normal reporting of court decisions; it was created by activists.

The best known publicity against the Stevens harassment of Southern union supporters was the 1979 film, "Norma Rae," which won Sally Field an Oscar for her portrayal of a Stevens textile worker, Crystal Lee Sutton. Amalgamated Clothing and Textile Workers Union members across the country distributed pamphlets on the "Real Norma Rae" to patrons filing into the movie. At the time the film was publicizing Stevens' harassment of unionists, Crystal Lee Sutton was keeping Stevens in the press through a public speaking tour. Prominent clergy, politicians, and civil rights campaigners such as Coretta Scott King were also enlisted in the public speaking campaign against Stevens. Church groups across the United States carried resolutions condemning the firm.

Churches which had monies invested in Stevens put up stockholder resolutions to change the company's labor relations practices. The Amalgamated Clothing and Textile Workers Union organized 4,000 marchers to protest outside the March 1977 annual stockholders meeting, an event which attracted considerable publicity. The next year the meeting was shifted from its normal venue in New York to Greenville, South Carolina, to avoid a recurrence of the public demonstration and attention.

The next element of the campaign was a consumer boycott. Church groups in particular rallied to the cause of boycotting J.P. Stevens products. Campaigns were also run at the major retail outlets for Stevens products (e.g., Woolworth's and Macy's). Union tactics to persuade retailers to reduce the Stevens stock in their stores and to cut back on advertising of Stevens products skated close to illegal secondary boycott activities. Some Woolworth stores were subject to sit-ins at their lunch counters during which union supporters occupied all the seats without purchasing any food.

The final aspect of the union strategy was the "corporate campaign." This targeted certain key Stevens board of directors members for personalized adverse publicity and efforts to unseat them.

The corporate campaign will be described in detail in the section on non-financial impacts.

Adverse publicity about J.P. Stevens' labor practices also attracted attention in regard to occupational safety and health, racial discrimination against black employees, and civil liberties abuses. Workers who had been victims of horrifying industrial injuries and diseases became celebrities of the anti-Stevens campaign. The Stevens case study and the General Motors one which follows were unlike any of the others in that the adverse publicity against the corporation was orchestrated by an interest group rather than being spontaneous. The effort put into the consumer boycott and the corporate campaign by the Amalgamated Clothing and Textile Workers Union was extraordinary. At its peak, 40 full-time organizers were employed on the campaign across the country. The union's budget for the campaign was $4 million in 1979.[4] Most resources were spent on the consumer boycott rather than on the corporate campaign which only had a staff of three.

J.P. Stevens also spent a great amount on a counterpublicity campaign. It widely disseminated a pamphlet, "Straightening Things Out," detailing its side of the story. Media representatives were constantly fed copy from the J.P. Stevens Public Relations Department. Special counterpublicity campaigns were directed at Stevens' main customers. Members of Congress were recruited to defend the company on the floor of the House and Senate. Prominent clergy were found who could fire salvos at church groups backing the boycott. Organizations consisting mainly of J.P. Stevens employees, "Stevens People" and "Friends of Freedom," gave strong support to the company. (Labor and Justice Department subpoenas calling on these organizations to disclose whether they were backed financially by J.P. Stevens were thrown out by a U.S. District Court.[5]) Much was made of the fact that in the overwhelming majority of unionizing ballots, J.P. Stevens workers had voted against union representation. It was also forcefully pointed out that the company was not alone in having violated the NLRA—the union had also done so on occasions.

Financial Impacts

In spite of the considerable resources thrust into the adverse publicity and boycott tactics by the union and church groups, the financial impacts upon J.P. Stevens of these parts of the campaign were only modest. Indeed, the company was contemptuous of them;

15

it acted in the belief that the benefits of breaking the NLRA were greater than the costs of being caught in violation. This attitude, that non-compliance was economically rational, prevailed at least until after the relatively biting injunction of 1977.[6] The fact that J.P. Stevens had viewed the costs imposed by the courts as a bearable license fee to break the law moved the U.S. Court of Appeals in 1971 to utter the following lament:

> In fact, one of the employees so discharged had been illegally terminated before, was reinstated by our prior order, but was then illegally discharged again. We regard this pattern of flagrantly contemptuous conduct most seriously. Our system of justice cannot survive if litigants are seized with the notion that they can ignore the lawful orders of a court simply because they may disagree with them. In addition, the record here strongly justifies the inference that these respondents deliberately took their chances in ignoring our decrees because they thought it profitable for them to do so.[7]

In a 1977 civil contempt case, the same Court remarked:

> This case, perhaps destined to be bleakly denominated as Stevens XVIII in the long list of Stevens litigation, has been a troubling one not only because of the violations of the rights of the employees involved, but also because it raises grave doubts about the ability of the courts to make the provisions of the federal labor law work in the face of persistent violations. It is now a decade since first we decided Stevens I and Stevens II. Since then, the Company has twice been held in contempt of our prior orders, and a third NLRB petition charging contempt has been filed.[8]

The intransigence of J.P. Stevens and the expertise of its lawyers in using appeals and other delaying tactics neutralized legal threats. It could be said that while the courts failed totally up until 1977 to impose costs of not complying commensurate with the benefits of non-compliance, the adverse publicity and consumer boycott campaigns at least caused J.P. Stevens management to question whether intransigence was economically rational. The union turned to the boycott campaigns out of disenchantment with a situation where dismissed workers went hungry while the course of litigation dragged on impotently.

Modest successes for the consumer boycott included announcements by some major buyers of textile products that they would cease purchasing J.P. Stevens goods. Among these were the state governments of Maine and Michigan and the Los Angeles Board of Public Works. Some retailers were persuaded to cut the percentage of their stock purchase from J.P. Stevens in order to placate unionist customers and as an investment in the maintenance of good labor relations.

There can be no question, then, that J.P. Stevens lost some business as a result of the boycott. Whether this was enough to put a serious dent in the corporate bottom line is another question. While the company was warning its employees in the South that the boycott could cost them their jobs through plant shutdowns, it was at the same time telling Wall Street that sales were higher than ever and unaffected by the boycott. An informant in the company also claimed that some customers who admired Stevens' anti-union posture increased their purchases as an act of solidarity. The company was unwilling to provide details of these increased sales.

At best, the boycott could have a limited impact. Only a third of Stevens sales are through retail outlets. This is, nevertheless, fairly high for a large corporation. (Imagine attempting a boycott against Lockheed, virtually none of whose sales are retail.) The third of J.P. Stevens sales that are retail, however, take place under a plethora of brand names and designer labels, such as Yves St. Laurent and Suzanne Pleshette. Very few of the products are sold under the Stevens name. The boycott sought to educate consumers as to the brands under which Stevens products were sold. But this was a difficult task. According to Gene Carol, National Campus coordinator for J.P. Stevens workers: "The highest level of effectiveness that ever existed in a boycott was roughly 10 percent— so 10 percent of one third of Stevens products means less than five percent of their total product line."[9]

It is J.P. Stevens home furnishings division which manufactures the sheets, towels, and other products sold through retail outlets. During the twelve months between 1978 and 1979 when the consumer boycott was at its peak, the earnings of the home furnishing division were down from 34 percent to 29 percent of total corporate earnings. During the same period, by contrast, Stevens' aircraft rental division more than doubled its sales. This raises the interesting question whether conglomerates which are threatened in one area of their business can simply switch their emphasis and energies to redirect capital investment into areas untouched by the crisis.

Stevens' stockholders certainly became nervous in mid-1980 when President Carter's domestic affairs chief, Stuart Eizenstat, and the Secretary of Labor, Ray Marshall, began devising a Presidential directive which would have banned the company from receiving federal contracts. J.P. Stevens struck a truce with the union before this threat materialized. If it had not, J.P. Stevens with $65 million in sales to the Federal Government in 1979, would have been in real financial trouble.

Overall, Stevens' sales moved slowly upward throughout the campaign. The union pointed out that the increases reported were substantially lower than those of Stevens' main competitors.[10] Consistent with this analysis, J.P. Stevens stock prices showed a continuous downward slide after the commencement of the consumer boycott in July 1976. In contrast, 1975 had been a year of rising prices for Stevens stock. The company's earnings were fairly steady between 1976 and 1979, falling sharply in 1980; a loss was recorded for the fiscal year ending 31 October 1981.[11] It could well be that the corporate campaign discussed in the next section did more to undermine confidence in Stevens stock than the consumer boycott. However, there is no way of separating out the effects of these concurrent prongs of the attack. There can be little question that overall the stock market was impacted. After the October 1980 agreement in which the union dropped the corporate campaign and consumer boycott, J.P. Stevens stock jumped sharply upward for the final quarter of 1980.[12]

Non-Financial Impacts

The most innovative and effective part of the struggle against J.P. Stevens was the "corporate campaign."[13] According to its chief strategist, Ray Rogers, "personalizing the enemy" was the fundamental precept of this campaign: "When we confront Stevens, we should not think of it as 83 plants, 44,000 employees and a multinational corporation with endless Wall Street connections. We should view it as 13 men—the Stevens Board of Directors. . . ." The corporate campaign made life difficult for those men. The 13 were not targeted all at once. The strategy was to pick them off one or two at a time. The outside directors targeted would receive a massive volume of mail, petitions, and telephone calls complaining of their association with J.P. Stevens; this was a softening up for putting the squeeze on them.

The corporate campaign really opened at the March 1977 annual stockholders meeting when union supporters attending the session retaliated with intimidation of directors against what they saw as intimidation of workers. Board members were put on notice that unless they cut their ties with J.P. Stevens they would be fair game for the tactics of the broad coalition of community and union groups which were putting their support behind the campaign.

All large corporations draw a considerable portion of their strength from their links, through interlocking directorates, to other members of the corporate and financial community. A company which needs to draw on banks or finance companies for loans to expand will place a banker or senior finance executive on its board. A wholesaler dependent on retailers selling its products is likely to put retailers on its board. The corporate campaign set out to sever J.P. Stevens' links to the wider financial and corporate community.

The first victory was in March 1978 when James D. Finley, Chairman and Chief Executive Officer of J.P. Stevens, admitted that union pressure had forced him to leave the board of the Manufacturers Hanover Trust Company, America's fourth largest commercial bank. The lever the union movement used to push Finley out was the fact that Manufacturers Hanover held more than $1 billion in union trust and pension funds. At the same time, a second Stevens Director, David W. Mitchell, stated that he would not stand for re-election to the Manufacturers Hanover Board, but gave the pressure of other duties as the reason. The union, nevertheless, claimed credit for this second resignation as well. Its claim seemed to be confirmed when, two weeks later, Mitchell, Chairman and Chief Executive Officer of Avon Products Inc., resigned from the Stevens Board. What factors caused Mitchell to cave in to the union pressure? According to Mitchell, "There was only one: when it became apparent to me that my membership on the Stevens Board was becoming detrimental to Avon, I had to get off; that was the only factor."[14] Mitchell said he was influenced by church groups writing to him complaining of Avon's association with J.P. Stevens. He became worried when an employee first showed him a pamphlet advising union members to "boycott Avon products, tell everybody about my being on the Stevens Board, and so forth."[15]

We have an interesting question here. J.P. Stevens was being subjected to the same adverse publicity that caused Mitchell to protect Avon by resigning from the Stevens Board. Why should Avon be more willing to submit to this pressure than Stevens? The difference is that J.P. Stevens had a lot to gain by riding out the adverse publicity (i.e., cheap labor), while all Avon had to gain was a link to a company smaller than itself and of only limited use to it. The link was not important enough for Avon to risk becoming a bête noir of the union movement, to have its corporate image besmirched by reputable church groups, and for Mitchell to put up with personal abuse and distraction from his Avon responsibilities. The corporate campaign was effective because the union picked on interlocks which benefitted Stevens more than the other party.

Next to leave the Stevens Board was Ralph Manning Brown, Chairman and Chief Executive Officer of New York Life Insurance, who resigned in September 1978. At the same time, Stevens chief, Finley, was forced off the New York Life Board. New York Life held $600 million in union pension funds and many union insurance policies. Yet it was another quite innovative type of leverage which clinched the New York Life campaign. The union moved to put up candidates to contest the election for the New York Life Board. Uncontested board elections are the norm in the insurance industry. Running a ballot among 6 million policyholders is an expense which any cost-conscious company would like to avoid. In resigning from the J.P. Stevens Board, the New York Life Chairman issued this statement:

> For some months the Amalgamated Clothing and Textile Workers Union has been conducting a campaign in connection with its boycott of J.P. Stevens to force me to resign from the Board of J.P. Stevens and to force James D. Finley, the Chairman of Stevens, to resign from the Board of New York Life Insurance Company. That campaign has now resulted in an effort by the union to obtain from New York Life a list of its about six million policyowners and to subject New York Life to the very expensive and burdensome statutory procedures which a contested election to its Board of Directors would entail. . . .
>
> The union's involvement of New York Life in the Stevens controversy places me in a position of conflict between the interest of New York Life and Stevens. Under the circumstances, I must consider the interests of New York Life to be paramount. Therefore, with deep regret, I am resigning from the Board of J.P. Stevens. I am equally regretful that Mr. Finley has felt compelled to resign from the Board of New York Life. He has acted because his sense of duty and responsibility to New York Life left him no alternative.[16]

The fact that the two Stevens board members who resigned were replaced with an attorney and a college professor convinced the union that the company was unable to obtain persons of prominence in the financial community. At the end of 1978, the target on the Stevens Board became E. Virgil Conway, Chairman and President of the Seamen's Bank for Savings in New York.

Unions were encouraged to threaten withdrawal of their funds from the bank, and lobbying began for a change in New York State law which would have challenged the autonomy of the chief executives of banks like the Seamen's. These executives had always been unaccountable in their own fiefdoms. The changes would have had the effect, in the election of trustees, of giving each depositor in a bank one vote for each account, regardless of the size of the account. Charges of "red-lining"—taking money out of poor areas while refusing to return any of it to these areas in loans—had been made against the Seamen's Bank. The corporate campaign began to exploit such allegations. Backing was given to community groups who opposed a license for the Seamen's Bank to open a branch in Nassau County because of its alleged history of red-lining. About 600 United Church of Christ ministers and lay leaders signed a petition requesting that Conway be removed as a trustee from the United Church of Christ pension board.

At the time of the termination of the corporate campaign it had still not succeeded in dislodging Conway, whose removal had proved unnecessary for victory. The union also was putting pressure on a major Stevens lender, the Metropolitan Life Insurance Company. The threat was the same as that previously used so effectively against New York Life—to run two dissidents against Metropolitan's nominees for its Board of Directors. Richard Shinn, the Metropolitan Chairman, moved to save his corporation the expense ($5 to 7 million) and embarrassment of an election. He arranged a meeting with the J.P. Stevens Chairman for some behind-the-scences maneuvering. The *Wall Street Journal* provided a delicate account of what happened at the meeting:

Mr. Shinn says he applied "absolutely no pressure" on Mr. Stevens. "I merely wanted to find out how the negotiations with the union were going", he says. "It was an exchange of information."

But overt pressure undoubtedly wasn't necessary. Metropolitan last year held $97 million of the textile company's $226 million in long-term debt, public records indicate.

"Without my ever having to say anything," Mr. Shinn says, J.P. Stevens "realized that if in the course of good business dealings they could settle with the union, it would minimize our election problems" with the textile workers.[17]

J.P. Stevens succumbed and agreed to an historic contract with the union. Appropriately enough, a unique condition in the contract was that the union abandon its corporate campaign. In this remarkable union victory, the company agreed to a contract for the 10 plants where the union had previously won representation and at any of the 75 other plants where the union subsequently might win elections. Stevens also agreed not to use legal delaying tactics to stall union recognition after such elections. At the time the campaign was terminated, the union was also beginning to mount an assault on the interlocks between Stevens and the Sperry Corporation and was also starting to work on J.C. Penney. The severing of these links was not needed. Stevens had had enough.

The confidence of Ray Rogers in the corporate campaign strategy was thus vindicated. It is possible, of course, that the power elite may regroup to ensure that they are never humbled in this way again. However, this conclusion was rejected by Rogers in an analysis provided long before the campaign had succeeded:

People have asked me if Corporate America, banks and insurance companies, won't band together to put a stop to the Corporate Campaign. I'll tell you why they can't. You have to understand the nature of power relationships in the corporate community. Up until now the banks and insurance companies in Corporate America have been an impenetrable bastion of power. There is no doubt in my mind that when Manufacturers Hanover was being confronted by the union that all of the other banks got together and said, "Look . . . don't you give into those damn unions. Don't get rid of the directors on your board, because if you do you are going to set an awful precedent. Nobody has ever been able to confront us successfully and we don't want it to happen now." I have no doubt in my mind that the Manufacturers Hanover board of directors said, "Don't worry because we will never give in." Manufacturers Hanover was figuring that the whole thing would blow over. But they soon realized that it wasn't going to blow over.

I never asked any labor union or anybody else to threaten to boycott or to pull a penny out of Manufacturers Hanover. But when the labor unions realized these intimate links existed between Manufacturers Hanover and J.P. Stevens, they did what they thought they had to do. *Newsweek* and other publications mentioned that the bank was facing a $1 billion pullout of union funds. That is raw economic power. It is confronting power with power and that is what unions have to do with these big financial institutions.

Manufacturers Hanover officials got to a point where they said to themselves: "Even though J.P. Stevens is an important and profitable relationship for this bank, it is only a pebble on the beach compared to our overall business." They recognized that their image, reputation, and creditability were being seriously jeopardized in large segments of the population that were important to their *overall* growth and prosperity. They were not about to put the well-being of a $38 billion institution on the line for J.P. Stevens when they could get rid of the Stevens' directors . . . .

Manufacturers Hanover got to the point where they said to all the other banks (Citibank, Morgan Guaranty, all of them), "You are telling us not to set a precedent, not to give in; allright but you also must realize now that we are facing a $1 billion pullout. Some unions are already taking deposits out. You tell us not to give in; but we say to you that if our money is going from our bank it is going into yours. You tell us not to give in, but we are getting the hell kicked out of us in this thing—and you are all benefiting from our losses. So if you don't want anyone to give in, then don't you give in. Right now we are getting out of this thing."—and that is exactly what they did.[18]

History is littered with examples of the use of divide and conquer tactics by the ruling class against workers. The Stevens case is unusual in that workers turned these tactics against the ruling group. The strategy was built on the reality that the interests of the power elite are not always unified and that interest groups can replace puny jabs against the jaws of power with a ju-jitsu which turns the strength of the power elite against itself.[19] As the *Los Angeles Times* commented, the campaign was victorious partly because of "the union's success in turning many other corporate leaders against Stevens for giving all business a bad name."[20] This case study is unlike any of the others in this book in that the significant adverse publicity was not mediated by the reactions of the general public, suppliers, or customers, but by the impact on the business elite itself.

It is hard to say how much of the effectiveness of the Corporate Campaign was due to its financial impact and how much to the fact that it exposed hitherto faceless men who were so accustomed to exercising their power anonymously that personal public criticism was an embarrassment they could not handle. Corporations may have been relatively immune from public attacks in the past because of the anonymity of the collectivity and the diffusion or deflection of individual exposure. On the other hand, we heard reports of persons targeted by the campaign who, far from being embarrassed, bragged about the fact to their cronies and characterized others who caved in as "chicken." Unfortunately, the interview data from J.P. Stevens is the weakest of all in our case studies, and we are not in a position to establish whether bravado or embarrassment was the more common reaction.

In addition to the effects on targeted individuals, we were told by one J.P. Stevens executive that the Stevens loss of *corporate* reputation due to the campaign had been more important in wringing out its concessions than the financial impacts. The decline in employee morale that accompanied the loss of corporate prestige was also reported to have been a significant factor.

Reforms

Before the Stevens campaign achieved union recognition, it contributed a great deal to the premature retirement of the company's Chairman, and architect of its uncompromising industrial relations policy, James D. Finley. The departure of the hardline anti-unionist helped pave the way for the settlement.

The October 1980 agreement commits J.P. Stevens contractually to fair and legal labor practices. Inevitably, harassment of union supporters still happens as individual managers act out their prejudices. However, harassment is no longer company policy and the company has committed itself to stamping out such practices. The contract also provides for the union to designate two members of each plant's five-member health and safety committee with the right to file public minority reports. In the strongest health and safety clause in any Southern textile union contract, the union also has a right of access to relevant company information and documents.

Another upshot of the J.P. Stevens campaign was the introduction in the House of Representatives of a 1977 Labor Reform Bill, which some dubbed the "J.P. Stevens Bill." The chair of the House Subcommittee on Labor-Management Relations described Stevens as "one of the major inspirations for this Bill." The proposed legislation sought to cut delays in the processing of unfair labor practices cases in order to stop tactics (such as used by J.P. Stevens) of interminable hold-ups and appeals while workers who had been victimized languished on no pay. It also sought to strengthen remedies and sanctions so that the costs of violation would no longer be less than the economic gain from crushing unionizing campaigns. After the Bill was passed in the House, however, an unprecedented business lobbying effort painted it as "the all-time great power grab for unions," and it lapsed in the Senate for want of one vote.[21]

The October 1980 agreement in effect provides the same kind of protection specifically for J.P. Stevens workers as was sought generally in that congressional Bill. The company's capitulation was a major reform, and it was a reform brought about partly through adverse publicity. However, it was not reform in the sense of organizational changes to prevent recidivism through checks and balances in regard to compliance with the law. It was a capitulation which made continuing violations of the NLRA unpracticable. Publicity therefore helped in removing the root cause of the pattern of offending rather than, as in other cases (e.g., Lockheed), by strengthening compliance systems.

Internal compliance systems had been strengthened by Stevens back in 1978, but this had little, if anything, to do with adverse publicity. This reform was compelled by the Second Circuit Court's contempt adjudication of 1977.[22] J.P. Stevens was forced by the Court to commence an education campaign to ensure that management, supervisors, and factory workers understood the rights of employees under the NLRA. Similarly, several dismissed union activists were reinstated because this was ordered by the Court, while union organizers were granted greater access to employees on job sites.

Another policy change that occurred in 1978 was that the company prohibited supervisors from speaking with employees about union affairs. The new corporate policy required supervisors to answer questions about unionization with the exact words: "I appreciate your asking me this question and I will be happy to get you an answer." A standard written reply worded in the company's head office would subsequently be provided. The policy was accompanied by clear guidelines as to what disciplinary action would be taken against supervisors who continued to speak with employees on union matters. This was a reform which reduced the harassment of union sympathizers by supervisors. But the main reason for the directive was to increase the credibility of supervisors in court when they denied allegations of harassment. In motivation, it was a self-protective measure rather than a constructive reform.

Also in response to the 1977 judgment against them, J.P. Stevens set up a corporate compliance committee to hear and seek out complaints from employees about unfair labor practices. The committee consisted of the Vice-President of Manufacturing and representatives of the corporate industrial relations and legal departments. There is no way of knowing how effective a compliance function this committee has performed, but it has been credited by one executive with having improved the awareness of senior

25

management of actual or potential unfair labor practices occurring in the corporation's far-flung operations.

In summary, there were some significant, although hardly major, organizational reforms during the campaign which probably prevented some further offenses. These reforms were not caused by adverse publicity, but by the 1977 court order. Adverse publicity played a significant role, however, in the 1980 capitulation that eliminated the root cause of most of the labor relations offenses at J.P. Stevens.

CHAPTER 3

General Motors — The Corvair

The Corvair Controversy

Early in the 1960s, General Motors Corporation responded to the market threat of the German Volkswagen with an American rear-engine car — the Corvair. Loaded with panache and slung on a semi-swing-axle rear suspension, the Corvair initially proved to be very popular. After numerous serious accidents involving spins and rollovers, however, the 1960–1963 Corvairs acquired a reputation for unsafe handling characteristics. Foremost among the critics was Ralph Nader, who chose General Motors and the Corvair as the first target of *Unsafe at Any Speed,*[1] a vitriolic attack upon the United States auto industry. Indeed, so vitriolic was the attack that, in the case of General Motors, even the far safer 1965–1969 models of the Corvair suffered a servere downturn in sales.

Nader contended that General Motors had knowingly marketed a dangerous product. He indicted the company on three main counts: (a) designing and manufacturing the 1960–1963 Corvair with an unstable weight distribution and rear suspension; (b) failing adequately to warn customers of the danger inherent in the Corvair's design; and (c) failing to rectify the danger of the 1960-1963 Corvair by providing appropriate suspension modifications free of charge.

The first of these counts alleged that the 1960-1963 Corvair was inherently prone to skid out of control, often to the point of rolling over. To begin with, the weight distribution was biased towards the rear, allegedly creating an unsafe pendulum effect on the tail of the car. More important, the rear suspension consisted of an independent swing-axle which, it was claimed, caused wheel "tuck-under" and hence instability during hard cornering. Nader cited

27

numerous accidents involving the Corvair, including more than 100 which had resulted in civil litigation.[2]

The second count alleged a deliberate failure to advise Corvair owners of the danger created by these features of the car's design. The only warning given in the owner's manual was that "over-steer problems may . . . be encountered with incorrect [tire] pressures. Maintain the recommended inflation pressures at all times."[3] No indication was given as to the meaning of "over-steer" (a car which over-steers points inside the radius of a turn when pushed to the limit of tire adhesion in cornering, whereas a car which under-steers points outside the radius.) Worse, said Nader, no mention was made of the risk of over-steer causing spins or rollovers.

Third, it was charged that although General Motors had substantially improved the suspension of the 1964 and 1965 Corvairs (the 1965 Corvair was given essentially the same fully independent rear suspension as that used on the General Motors sports car, the Corvette), it had failed to recall and refit the 1960-1963 Corvairs. The cost of such a recall was put at $25 million, less than a half-day's gross sales or five days' net profits after taxes.[4]

Most of the civil claims against General Motors as a result of Corvair handling-related accidents were settled out of court, the company winning all but one of the cases which went to trial. The major victory for General Motors was *Drummond and Lyford v. General Motors Corporation*,[5] an action for wrongful death in which a California Superior Court decided that the suspension and handling charateristics of the 1960 Corvair were within the band of acceptable manufacturing design. In the opinion of the court, drivers were to blame, not General Motors:

> The only reasonable conclusion the Court can draw from the evidence is that when average drivers approach the limit of a car's control by driving a curve too fast, it creates a dangerous risk of harm irrespective of whether the car be a Corvair, a Falcon, a Volkswagen, a Dodge, a Cadillac, or any other make or model of automobile . . . .
> The Court is convinced from the evidence that the 1960 Corvair when driven at normal speeds and within normal driving ranges is not defective. The claim that the 1960 Corvair develops suddenly, and without warning, a treacherous and unpredictable over-steer characteristic is not established by the evidence. The Court is convinced from the evidence that normal driving in transient maneuvers does not produce any dangerous over-steer or other objectionable handling characteristics. If a driver is driving within the normal speed range, the over-steer characteristic in the Corvair will not be reached at all.

If, however, a driver is accelerating at a high rate of speed upon entering a curve, the over-steer characteristic could be achieved suddenly. The sudden reaching of the over-steer characteristic in such a situation, however, is due to the driver's dangerous method of handling the car, rather than any characteristic of the car itself.[6]

However, the court did level strong criticism at the vague advice in the owner's manual that "over-steer problems may be encountered with incorrect [tire] pressures":

None of the engineers of General Motors could explain what this language meant. This is preposterous. Why was such language used? Certainly the average purchaser would have no conception of what was meant . . . . If in fact a wide variation in tire pressures from those recommended in the Owner's Guide would make the automobile difficult to handle or unsafe, this language would not adequately warn the driver of this.[7]

As it happened, the failure of General Motors to provide a clear warning about tire pressures was irrelevant to the facts of the case because there was no evidence that the tires of the Corvair involved in the accident were inflated otherwise than in accordance with the figures recommended in the manual.

Some four years later, much to General Motors' surprise, the Corvair safety question was raised by Nader again. In a letter to the Secretary of Transportation, he claimed that General Motors had "misled" the court because key proving-ground data had been suppressed.[8] The letter contended that:

GM proving ground tests and films back in 1962–63 conclusively proved the Corvair to be uniquely unstable with unprecedented rollover capability unlike any other American car. (Such characteristics were known by GM engineers when the Corvair was in its design stage back in the late Fifties. But the cautions of the more concerned were overridden by management which refused to adopt a much safer suspension system then available.) None of this information was ever offered or disclosed in response to court orders to produce such or any other requests from federal and state officials. On the contrary, in a consistent posture of suppression and prevarication the company declared the Corvair as safe as any other car and asserted that any claims to its lack of safety were false.[9]

Nader also addressed a complaint to Senator Abraham Ribicoff claiming that the Senate Subcommittee on Executive Reorganization had been misled on the same question in 1966 when the matter had arisen peripherally during hearings into General Motors' investigation of Nader's private life.[10] In light of this allegation the Subcommittee decided to conduct another inquiry.

After a two-and-a-half-year study, the Subcommittee concluded that General Motors had not previously misled it.[11] Given a favorable evaluation of the 1960-1963 Corvair in a detailed report completed in 1972 by the National Highway and Traffic Safety Administration,[12] General Motors was considered to have met its obligation to produce a car "reasonably safe for driving on American roads" (the Subcommittee expressly refrained from expressing any opinion on "the technical questions relating to the ultimate safety of the car").[13] Moreover, the Subcommittee declared there was no corroborated evidence that any engineer, lawyer, or executive within General Motors thought the Corvair was unsafe when it was developed and produced.[14]

The Subcommittee's findings were denounced by Nader as "an uncritical reiteration of both General Motors rationale for its actions and of the Department of Transportation's incompetent and deliberately distorted report exonerating the Corvair's handling and stability defects."[15] Later, a Nader staff memorandum described the Subcommittee's report as "a presumptuous whitewash" marred by "faulty methodology, technical incompetence and inaccurate assertions."[16] Exception was taken to the secrecy of the Subcommittee's staff investigation (public hearings were not held, the view of Senator Ribicoff being that the inquiry was a preliminary one) and to the non-disclosure of unfavorable Corvair proving-ground reports (reputedly known within General Motors as "hot documents").[17]

Although Nader thus continued to fan the embers of the Corvair controversy, it was a burnt-out case: The first Corvair had appeared on the market 13 years earlier, almost four years had elapsed since the sell-out of the last model, and the much-improved 1965-1969 models had already become collectors' items.

Publicity and Counterpublicity

The Corvair controversy began and ended amidst widespread publicity in the press.[18] However, it was Nader's book, *Unsafe at Any Speed,* which captured the imagination of the American public. By March 1966, 27,000 copies had been sold. (Nader, pointing out that Truman Capote's *In Cold Blood* had sold 279,000 copies and

Jessica Mitford's *The American Way of Death*, 90,000, commented, "And I could have used either title for my book.")[19] By mid-July 1966, *Unsafe* had climbed to eighth position in the *New York Times* General Best Seller List.[20]

One reason for the success of *Unsafe at Any Speed*, gravity of allegations aside, was the engaging mode of Nader's discourse; in one reviewer's eyes, it was charismatic scientism:

> In his often impassioned efforts to arouse his audience to a fighting pitch, the author employs a style not dissimilar at times to soap box oratory in the grand tradition . . . . Who could resist becoming intrigued upon learning of the "acceleration overshoot" and "bottoming effect" aspects of conventional seatbelt design, or the "rear leafspring wind-up" that has spelled disaster during many a sudden stop?[21]

Another relevant factor was timing. According to the General Motors executives we interviewed, *Unsafe at Any Speed* followed immediately in the slipstream of two major legal developments which had already brought the Corvair to public attention. To begin with, a strong plaintiffs' bar had emerged since the mid-1950s, largely organized under the banner of the American Trial Lawyers Association. Members of that association had played a very active role in bringing Corvair-based suits against General Motors, and in 1966 had published their own manifesto, a booklet entitled *Stop Murder by Motor*. Second, early model Corvairs appeared at a time of radical expansion of product liability in the United States, a movement led by the Supreme Courts of California and Illinois.[22] Given this development, coupled with the incentive of the contingent fee system, the plaintiffs' bar had campaigned against the Corvair with a view to winning "at any speed."

What really brought *Unsafe at Any Speed* home to ordinary folk, however, was General Motors' ill-fated attempt to investigate its author's private life, a countermove which backfired in a spectacularly embarrassing way.[23]

After the publication of *Unsafe at Any Speed* in November 1965, General Motors general counsel engaged an attorney to look into the possibility of Nader's involvement in numerous damage suits pending against the company. When no link was found, arrangements were made by the attorney for an inquiry by a detective agency. The inquiry had continued for over two months when Nader complained of acts of harassment and even attempted seduction.[24] The Senate Subcommittee on Executive Reorganization thereupon launched investigative hearings.[25] At the hearings, top

31

General Motors executives, including the president, James Roche, were grilled at length about the nature and purpose of the detective inquiry.

Some idea of General Motors purpose emerged from the detective agency's description of the assignment:

> [Ralph Nader] is a freelance writer and attorney. Recently he published a book, *Unsafe at Any Speed*, highly critical of the automobile industry's interest in safety. Since then our client's client has made some cursory inquiries into Nader to ascertain his expertise, his interests, his background, etc. They have found out relatively little about him . . . . Our job is to check his life and current activities, to determine "what makes him tick," such as his real interest in safety, his supporters, if any, his politics, his marital status, his friends, his women, boys, etc., drinking, dope, jobs — in fact all facets of his life.[26]

The assignment outlined had cost General Motors $6,700.[27]

General Motors insisted that it had no knowledge of the intrusive prying into Nader's personal life, and denied implication in any acts of harassment or attempted seduction. However, the general public found it difficult to believe that the detective inquiry was confined to Nader's possible involvement in civil suits arising from accidents involving Corvairs. In the absence of any clear evidence as to the actual purpose of the investigation, the suspicion remained that it was undertaken with a view to counterattack Nader or subject him to blackmail. As the *New York Times* editorialized, it was a piece of "shabby snooping."[28]

Although General Motors maintained throughout that there was no cause for suspicion, its president made a public apology, conceding that the inquiry was "most unworthy of American business."[29] In response, the chairman of the Senate Subcommittee, Senator Ribicoff, revealed that the inquiry had turned up nothing detrimental to Nader, adding that "You and your family can be proud. They [the detectives] have put you through the mill and they haven't found a damn thing wrong with you."[30] Subsequently, without admitting any wrongdoing, General Motors paid Nader $425,000 in settlement of a civil action for invasion of privacy. (The money was allocated by the Nader organization to "continous legal monitoring of General Motors activities in the safety, pollution, and consumer relations area.")[31]

All of the General Motors staff with whom we spoke were of the view that the revelation of the company's investigation of Nader, plus the humiliating apology before the Senate Subcommittee, had "blown everything out of proportion." Moreover, as one observer of the Senate Subcommittee hearings commented, "It was a great show, but it didn't make the cars any safer."[32]

Financial Impacts

The adverse publicity surrounding the Corvair's safety did not materially affect General Motors' profits, although it did substantially abet the demise of the Corvair. Stock prices were little affected, but product liability cases and Senate inquiries involved considerable costs.

The effect of *Unsafe at Any Speed*, together with the competitive edge of Ford's Mustang, was to cause almost a 100 per cent drop in the sales of 1965 and later Corvairs;[33] production was abandoned in May 1969. However, the impact on General Motors profitability was very slight, because at best the Corvair accounted for only 350,000 units out of a total annual output of approximately 4 million. Moreover, the Chevrolet plant "never missed a stroke," because the production of the new Nova, then in high demand, was stepped up to compensate for the loss of Corvair production. Indeed, it was conceivable that the quicker switchover from full Corvair production to full Nova production had actually increased profitability. However, it was pointed out to us that it would be a different story if such a crisis occurred today. The decreased saleability of U.S. automobiles in recent years has denied companies the flexibility to manage a problem car in the same way; as one executive reflected, "If it were happening this year, we'd be tearing out our hair."

Because General Motors' overall profitability remained substantially unaffected by the decline and fall of the Corvair, GM stock market prices appear to have suffered only a very minor degree of slippage. After the publication of *Unsafe at Any Speed*, there was a slight dip from 104 ⅜ (November 26, 1965) to 103 ⅛ (December 3, 1965), the Dow Jones Industrial Average having also dropped (from 948.16 to 946.10); for the rest of December, the GM stock remained steady (on December 31 it closed at 103 ½, the Dow Jones average having increased to 969.26). After Roche's apology to the Senate Subcommittee on Executive Reorganization there was also a drop, from 96 ⅞ (March 22) to 92 ⅞ (March 30), the Dow Jones average having fallen from 934.42 to 919.76. Throughout April 1966, the stock hardly wavered,there being no appreciable decline until May, a time when industrial stocks generally fell away.

Subjectively, a more favorable picture may have impressed itself upon GM executives: As one senior interviewee recollected, "There was not even a blip."

The product liability suits, prompted by criticism of the Corvair in the media, took a greater toll. General Motors won all but one of the cases which went to trial. In the one case lost (in 1974), General Motors was found only 12 percent responsible, but had to pay $880,000 because the driver held primarily to blame was insolvent.[34] Even in relation to the cases won, the defense of General Motors proved to be expensive, partly by reason of the time taken (we were told that the Corvair litigation group tied down 15 to 20 people in the company for over two years), and partly by reason of the expense of conducting special tests for use as evidence. More significantly, 285 cases were settled out of court, at a cost of approximately $2.5 million.

Finally, it was remarked that a heavy commitment of time and resources had been made in order to respond to the inquiries made by the Senate Subcommittee on Executive Reorganization. In all, the Subcommittee's investigation into whether General Motors had previously given misleading evidence about the safety of the Corvair had extended over a period of two and one half years. Moreover, the allegations in issue (those made by Nader to the Secretary of Transportation) went deeper than product liability claims because General Motors' management had been accused of egregious public deceit.

Non-Financial Impacts

The Corvair affair had three main non-financial impacts — loss of corporate prestige, loss of individual prestige, and decline in morale. At the level of corporate prestige, our respondents emphasized the damage done by the president's apology about the investigation into Nader's private life. We were told that General Motors had always prided itself on a keen team spirit, that the position the president adopted was highly demeaning, and that the degradation thereby inflicted upon the company had caused people to wince. However, the assault upon General Motors' image was now seen as only "transitory."

Individual prestige also suffered. Apart from the subjection of the president and other top executives to personal challenge and attack in the 1966 Senate inquiry, those back in Detroit saw their own reputation suffer in the community. One senior engineer told us that he "felt bad at breakfast time" when he read about the Corvair in his morning newspaper, although the adverse publicity "didn't make you go to pieces." Outside the company, however, the impact of adverse publicity had been more difficult to keep out of mind: The Corvair affair had provided neighbors and friends with a relentless topic of conservation.

A third non-financial impact was attenuation of morale. In particular, Nader's attack upon General Motors engineering integrity had been deeply resented. For one thing, the consumer warlord had "killed the wrong car" (i.e., the 1965–1969 Corvair, which had a superior fully independent rear suspension). Furthermore, many within the organization were unhappy about the lack of recognition given to what the company had achieved in the area of safety (e.g., development of an energy-absorbing steering column, crash simulators, and laminated windshields). Again, however, it was stressed that the impact had been transitory.

Reforms

Soon after the Corvair crisis, the U.S. auto industry became subject to a new Congressional Act providing for extensive regulation of safety standards. General Motors, for its part, increased expenditure on safety research, improved its reporting procedures on product defects, and strengthened its decision-making structure.

The major reform was one affecting all auto manufacturers: the National Traffic and Motor Vehicle Safety Act of 1966. This Act, largely a legacy of *Unsafe at Any Speed* and the hearings of the Senate Subcommittee on Executive Reorganization, established the National Highway and Traffic Safety Administration (NHTSA) and, for the first time in the United States, made provision for comprehensive federal vehicle safety standards.[35] *Unsafe at Any Speed* did much to set the stage for this legislation and the Senate hearings into General Motors' investigation of Nader's private life brought down the curtain; as Elizabeth Drew observed at the time:

> The hearings were a sensation, and did as much as anything to bring on federal safety standards. "It was that Nader thing," said one senator whom I asked how it had all come about. "Everybody was so outraged that a great corporation was out to clobber a guy because he wrote critically about them. At that point, everybody said the hell with them." "When they started looking in Ralph's bedroom," said another

Hill man, "we all figured they must really be nervous. We began to believe that Nader must be right."[36]

Ironically, no government standard has ever been prescribed for vehicle handling characteristics, the central subject of the Corvair controversy; it remains to be shown that any useful workable minimum standard is possible.

Reforms have also occurred within General Motors, the first being increased investment on safety research. In 1965, Robert Kennedy attacked General Motors for spending only one percent of profits on safety research.[37] No cost breakdown of the company's safety research today is available, but some indication of the increased expenditure is apparent from the fact that $100 million was spent on research and development for inflatable restraints (air bags) alone. However, the adverse publicity resulting from *Unsafe at Any Speed* was thought to have played little role in this development. Ever since the late 1950s, increased attention to safety had been spurred by the dramatic rise in the scope of liability for product defects. Moreover, the consumer movement had steadily gained momentum throughout the 1960s; Nader had been a major but by no means single-handed force behind that movement. Above all, there had been many breakthroughs in safety research, particularly the work of Colonel John Paul Stapp on human tolerance to crashes,[38] and to the development by General Motors of realistic dummies for use in crash-testing. At least for the engineering staff at General Motors, the increased spending on safety research had primarily a technical rather than a legal or political genesis.

General Motors also took steps to improve its procedures for internal reporting of product defects, although again this was not seen as a response directly attributable to the publicity surrounding *Unsafe at Any Speed*. The main change was to make "loop-closing" more formal and a matter of higher priority.

When a question is raised about the safety of a product, the "loop" thereby opened should be closed by a written answer either resolving the problem or denying that a problem exists. It was explained to us that "loop-closing" is essential for engineering personnel. As professionals, it was noted, they tended to be perfectionists and were often highly critical of programs, policies, and products; put another way, they would not be doing their job properly unless they submitted a flow of critical reactions.

In order to avoid "a welter of unjustified litigation," it was considered essential for the company to maintain a well-documented action file. This strategy had been implemented primarily in response to the threat of product liability (as augmented by liberal civil discovery rules), but it was also seen as a tool of cost-efficient administration and sound, responsive engineering. When asked whether loop-closing tended to result in concealment of bad news, General Motors officials replied that concealment would be counterproductive: first, expensive product recalls could be avoided by timely prevention; second, an uncorrected small defect could cause expensive problems (e.g., a faulty 75¢ switch could cause a $250 electrical or mechanical failure); and third, quick corrective action demonstrated good faith, which was important from the standpoint of both public relations and minimizing the risk of ordinary or punitive damages in civil litigation. True enough, but a cover-up can still be the best way of dealing with a corporate scandal.

Much more substantial were the steps General Motors took to improve its decision-making, partly in order to manage the demands of the National Traffic and Motor Vehicle Safety Act. Since 1967, decisions as to the necessity for product recalls have been made a joint divisional and corporate staff function. Under the new administrative arrangements, as further revised in 1974, each division has a product problem evaluation committee consisting of representatives from the engineering, manufacturing, reliability, and service departments of the division, together with a corporate representative from the head office. The corporate representative has discretion to take any safety or other decision to a product investigation group at headquarters, and the product problem evaluation committee is required to report any problems of a defined level of seriousness to the divisional management committee. By thus providing a double-track mechanism for reporting trouble up the line, General Motors has attempted to avoid the risk of safety recalls latent in its emphasis on decentralized profit centers. The motivation was put succinctly by one spokesman: "The corporation is sued, not Chevrolet."[39]

Another step towards improved decision-making was the introduction of new vehicle model project centers. During the development of a new car, these centers coordinate all engineering inputs, including safety, one aim being to build safety into a car from its inception. Cross-fertilization had previously existed among the various divisions but, by rationalizing the range of models and using one body-platform as the basis for all General Motors cars of comparable size, basic points of design are now completely united.

A further major change was the establishment of two staff committees, the automotive safety committee, and the safety review board. The task of the automotive safety committee, in part, is to review matters arising under the National Traffic and Motor Vehicle Safety Act and to make suggestions about the quality and safety of the products of every corporate division. The safety review board, composed of higher-level personnel, provides an opportunity for a "focused evaluation" of safety issues. Since this is a top-level committee (the president is a member), those in charge of day-to-day compliance regarded it as their "ace in the hole."

The Corvair episode forms at least part of the background to the company reforms outlined, and was a strong catalyst behind the National Traffic and Motor Vehicle Safety Act. Yet was the controversy a costly and deplorable mistake by Nader? In *Free to Choose*, Milton and Rose Friedman have suggested that it was:

> Ralph Nader's attack on the Corvair, the most dramatic single episode in the campaign to discredit the products of private industry, exemplified not only the effectiveness of that campaign but also how misleading it has been. Some ten years after Nader castigated the Corvair as unsafe at any speed, one of the agencies that was set up in response to the subsequent public outcry finally got around to testing the Corvair that started the whole thing. They spent a year and a half comparing the performance of the Corvair with the performance of other comparable vehicles, and they concluded, "The 1960–63 Corvair compared favorably with the other contemporary vehicles used in the tests." Nowadays Corvair fan clubs exist throughout the country. Corvairs have become collectors items. But to most people, even the well informed, the Corvair is still "unsafe at any speed."[40]

However, even if Nader were totally mistaken in his attack on the 1960-1963 models of the Corvair, it does not follow that a system of "free," supine consumer choice would be superior to one in which consumer choice is assisted by consumer activists. On the contrary, there is little option but to have a system in which suspect products are brought to light by consumer representatives, and then, in the event of reasonable suspicion, evaluated by means of informative, independent, and timely public inquiry.

To begin with, it is unrealistic to expect individual consumers to gather their own data on peformance characteristics, accident rates, or other indications that a product may be unsafe. As Kenneth Arrow has argued:

> The seller is bound to know considerably more about its properties than all but a very few of its buyers. In order to develop the car, the producer has had to perform tests of one kind or another. He knows the outcome of the tests. Failure to reveal this knowledge works against

the efficiency of satisfying consumers tastes. The argument of course applies to any aspect of the quality of a product, durability or the ability to perform under trying circumstances or differing climatic conditions. Perhaps we are most concerned about the safety features of the automobile. The risks involved in the use of automobiles are not trivial, and the kind of withholding of safety information which has been revealed to exist in a number of cases certainly cannot be defended as a socially useful implication of profit maximization.[41]

Moreover, even if all the information relevant to the safety of a product under suspicion were available, most individual consumers do not have the time or competence to assess it. This being so, consumer preferences are exercizable on the basis of:

(a) uninformed choice;

(b) choice informed by reliance on corporate advertising or advice of friends, neighbors, relatives and consumer representatives or research groups;[42]

(c) choice informed as in (b), subject to feedback from product liability litigation; or

(d) choice informed as in (c), subject to feedback from official inquiries launched by administrative agencies or congressional committees.

Of these bases of choice, (a) may be rejected as non-rational, (b) as prone to bias, and (c) as crippled by the long delays typical of litigation.[43] Basis (d), by contrast, looks to official inquiries to overcome these limitations by providing an informative, independent and timely assessment of product worthiness.

In the case of the Corvair, consumer preferences were exercized not on basis (d) but on basis (c) (at best): No attempt was made to provide any adequate official inquiry into the safety of the Corvair until almost 10 years after the last questionable model had been produced. For this there are many targets of blame. NHTSA might have acted sooner, on the basis of Nader's allegations in *Unsafe at Any Speed*. Perhaps consumers themselves should have lobbied much earlier for a National Traffic and Motor Vehicle Safety Act; in complex matters of vehicle safety, they were unfree to choose wisely. Above all, however, the Senate Subcommittee on Executive Reorganization focussed upon the right of Nader to privacy rather than upon the ability of consumers to assess any dangers of the

Corvair; sensational revelations were underscored at the expense of leaving a serious question of consumer safety unresolved. To sum up, publicity there was, in plentitude, but the political system failed to move beyond muckraking to demanding and monitoring reform.

CHAPTER 4

Ford—The Pinto Papers

The Pinto Trial

Prevalent as corporate "violence" is,[1] corporations are rarely prosecuted for homicide or assault. The Pinto trial in Indiana provided a dramatic exception, for it involved the spectacle of one of America's largest corporations, the Ford Motor Company, being charged with reckless homicide, not by knife or gun but by fire.

The trial arose from an accident in August 1978 in which three young women were fatally burned when their 1973 Ford Pinto burst into flames after being rear-ended by a Chevrolet van. The fuel tank of the Pinto ruptured in the collision, gasoline entered the passenger compartment as the car crumpled, and fire exploded instantaneously.

Grand jury proceedings were launched, there being much doubt as to the safety of the Pinto fuel system. Over the previous year the media had criticized the location of the fuel tank, which was positioned six inches forward of the rear bumper. As a result, the National Highway and Traffic Safety Administration had initiated defect proceedings in April 1978, and in June Ford had announced a voluntary recall of all Pintos manufactured between 1971 and 1976.[2] Moreover, these events aroused product liability actions against Ford, most notably the *Grimshaw*[3] suit in which damages of $128.5 million were awarded, including a record $125 million in punitive damages (later reduced to $3 million). Although the suit in *Grimshaw* was civil, the award of punitive damages depended upon a finding of corporate knowledge about the danger of the Pinto fuel tank location, and this in turn suggested that Ford might be found at fault in criminal proceedings for unlawful homicide.

The grand jury returned three indictments of reckless homicide, an offense recently enacted under Indiana's criminal code.[4] A pre-trial skirmish ensued wherein Ford attacked the indictments on a variety of grounds, including the application of the reckless homicide offense to corporate persons[5] and the constitutional difficulty raised by the allegations of reckless conduct by Ford at times prior to the creation of the offense. The indictments stood. It was held that corporations could commit reckless homicide under Indiana law and unconstitutional retroactivity was avoidable if the recklessness alleged was deemed to be that Ford had knowingly failed to rectify the Pinto danger after the new offense became law.

The resulting trial revolved around three issues. First, had Ford been aware of an unjustifiable danger in the design of the Pinto? Second, had Ford failed substantially to rectify any such unjustifiable danger? Third, in any event, was the closing speed between the van and the Pinto low enough that a small car could reasonably have been expected not to leak fuel? For the prosecution to succeed, each of these questions had to be resolved affirmatively beyond reasonable doubt.

The main obstacle confronting the prosecution on the first issue was the non-admission of much evidence. Many of the so-called "Pinto Papers"— internal documents about engineering and safety matters—were ruled inadmissible, some because Ford refused to stipulate their authenticity, others because they related to the 1971 and 1972 Pinto and not the 1973 car in which the victims had suffered their fatal burns.[6] The most critical document excluded was a highly unfavorable NHTSA report of fuel leakage rates from crash-tested Pinto and GM Vegas, the ground of exclusion being that only 1971 and 1972 Pintos had been tested, whereas some improvements had been made for the 1973 model (according to Ford, these improvements raised the speed of barrier-crash survivability from "around" 20 m.p.h. to above 20 m.p.h.).[7] Surprisingly, the prosecution never asked NHTSA to perform tests on the 1973 model (Ford has suggested that this possibly was because the results were expected to be unfavorable to the prosecution's case).[8]

The prosecution also ran into difficulty over the second issue. Had Ford failed substantially to rectify any danger in the design of the Pinto? To begin with, the relevant time span was the 41-day period between the commencement of the new reckless homicide offense and the date of the fatal accident subject to prosecution; the diligence of Ford prior to that period was not in issue. Furthermore, during the two months between Ford's recall announcement and the accident, NHTSA had been regulating the recall and there was no evidence of undue delay or neglect on the part of Ford.[9]

Third, was the closing speed between the van and the Pinto so high that no small car could reasonably have been expected not to leak fuel? The contention of the prosecution was that the closing speed was no more than 35 m.p.h. (several eye-witnesses so asserted) and that this speed was insufficiently high to cause fuel leakage in a small car of adequate design. Late in the trial the defense produced two witnesses who testified that, just before the driver of the Pinto died in hospital, she had mentioned stopping just before the crash occurred.[10] If this were true, the closing speed would have been approximately 50 miles per hour, a speed of impact that no small car fuel tank could be expected to withstand. To highlight the point, the defense showed films of specially arranged crash tests in which a similar van hit a 1973 Pinto and other makes of cars at 50 m.p.h. All of the cars struck suffered substantial fuel leakage.[11]

After 25 hours of deliberation stretched over four days, the jury returned a verdict of not guilty. Its members' reasons for acquitting Ford were aired at a press interview arranged by the trial judge at the conclusion of proceedings. Although there was no consensus as to the safety of the Pinto or the closing speed of the vehicles at the time of the accident, it was agreed that the prosecution had not proven reckless failure by Ford to rectify any danger which may have existed in the Pinto's fuel system.[12]

Publicity and Counterpublicity

The Pinto trial attracted intensive media coverage, partly because there had been much advance publicity, and partly because the idea of a corporation committing reckless murder was no longer merely political rhetoric but living law.[13]

The adverse publicity began in earnest with "Pinto Madness,"[14] an award-winning article by Mark Dowie in the September 1977 *Mother Jones* magazine; this, Ford executives lamented to us, was "the real watershed." The article claimed that internal company documents (the "Pinto Papers") showed that "Ford has crash-tested the Pinto at a top-secret site more than 40 times and that *every* test made at over 25 m.p.h. without special structural alteration of the car has resulted in a ruptured fuel tank." It also contended that none of the protective modifications tested had been incorporated in production-line Pintos, reference being made to an internal cost-benefit study[15] in 1973. The gist of this particular study was represented as follows:

$11 VS. A BURN DEATH
Benefits and Costs Relating to Fuel Leakage
Associated with the Static Rollover
Test Portion of FMVSS 208

BENEFITS

Savings: 180 burn deaths, 180 serious burn injuries, 2,100 burned vehicles.
Unit Cost: $200,000 per death, $67,000 per injury, $700 per vehicle.
Total Benefit: (180 × $200,000) + (180 × $67,000) + (2100 × $700) = $49.5 million.

COSTS

Sales: 11 million cars, 1.5 million light trucks.
Unit Cost: $11 per car, $11 per truck.
Total Cost: (11,000,000 × $11) + (1,500,000 × $11) = $137 million.[16]

The implication was that Ford had deliberately chosen not to make "an $11-per-car improvement that would prevent 180 fiery deaths a year."[17] These were the allegations which stuck in the mind of the state trooper at the scene of the Elkhart accident, and prompted him to take active steps toward prosecution.[18]

Soon thereafter the *Grimshaw* suit was decided. A "major spout" of adverse publicity resulted from the record award of $125 million in punitive damages and, more significantly, from the evidence relied upon to establish that Ford had consciously and willfully disregarded the safety of Pinto owners. As a result, the Pinto became infamous, even overseas.[19]

Then came the much-publicized NHTSA defect notice in May 1978.[20] After completing an initial investigation into the Pinto (an investigation provoked by the *Mother Jones* article), NHTSA advised Ford that there has been "an initial determination of the existence of a safety-related defect" in the 1971–1976 Pintos.[21]

It was the trial, however, which drew the most publicity. The horrific nature of the deaths, the sinister reputation of the Pinto Papers, the novelty of the charge of corporate homicide, and the flamboyance of chief counsel on both sides made the event a theatrical occasion. Throughout the two months of the trial a group of about 50 reporters, producers, cameramen, and technicians stayed on location to cover the proceedings. Their output was prodigious, largely because prosecution and defense supplied them with an abundance of newsworthy lines, including the prosecution's chilling opening allegation that Ford "deliberately chose profit over human life" and "totally disregarded" repeated warnings from its engineers.[22] Ultimately, the trial became the subject of a book by Lee Strobel, a reporter who covered the event for the *Chicago Tribune.*[23]

A notable feature of the publicity about the Pinto trial was that a *corporate* defendant held the limelight. As was repeatedly stressed in the media, it was the first case in which a corporation had been charged with unlawful homicide in the context of product liability,[24] and the indictment for reckless homicide as opposed to merely manslaughter added an additional element of novelty. Moreover, no Ford personnel were tried with the company itself, the prosecutor's explanation being that "Ford Motor Co., the corporation itself, was all that Elkhart County could handle. To go further, and take the next step, which may be individuals, [would have to be taken by] somebody with far more resources than we have. . . ."[25] Accordingly, those who followed the trial were presented squarely with a question of corporate blameworthiness.[26]

Despite the acquittal of Ford in the Pinto trial, adverse publicity continued. Although the decision was generally considered to be correct, given the particular facts of the case, it did not resolve the basic doubts surrounding the safety of the Pinto. Thus, in one widely-publicized comment on the jury's verdict, Clarence Ditlow, a leading critic of the motor industry, revived the issue of blameworthiness:

> In view of the judge's restrictions against the introduction of supporting evidence, but letting in the Ford crash tests, I felt the decision was preordained. However, in the next case, with a better judge or with a different striking vehicle, I feel sure Ford or any other manufacturer would be convicted.[27]

Faced by the adverse publicity outlined above, Ford became involved in three counterpublicity exercises of note: a press release in response to the *Mother Jones* article, a voluntary recall in response to the NHTSA defect notice, and the trial itself.

In response to the *Mother Jones* article, Ford issued an eight-page release. The main counterclaims stressed in this press release were threefold:

(a) statistically, the Pinto was not involved in an unusually high proportion of fire-related deaths;
(b) internal Ford documents (i.e., the Pinto Papers) relied upon by *Mother Jones* related neither to the Pinto models subject to criticism nor to rear-end impact protection, but concerned either later models or prospective federal vehicle safety standards; and
(c) autos and their makers should be judged by the standards applicable at the time, rather than in light of ideas for future improvements.

In conclusion, it was urged that:

> the Ford Pinto does not pose any undue hazard to its occupants as [*Mother Jones*] tries to contend. Although absolute travelling safety cannot be guaranteed in any car, [government statistics] show that the performance of the Pinto's fuel-tank system in actual accidents appears to be superior to that which might be expected of cars of its size and weight.[28]

A second counterpublicity measure was the recall of the 1971–1976 Pintos shortly after the NHTSA defect notice. The press release announcing the recall indicated Ford's disagreement with the NHTSA finding that the Pinto was unsafe, but nonetheless offered the promise of "modifications" designed to "reduce significantly" the risk of fire if the cars were hit from the rear. As one executive testified at the Indiana trial, the recall was seen as an important public relations exercise:

> The corporation had been subjected to allegations of a problem unique to the Pinto, and this obviously was damaging our public reputation, and the attitude of the public. It had become a critical problem for the company, a reputational problem. . . . On balance, it was felt that if we could reach an agreement with NHTSA [on a recall], it would reassure the owners and the public of the company's good intentions in the matter.[29]

In effect, although not by admitted intention, the recall avoided a full-scale NHTSA hearing and reduced the obvious risk of further adverse publicity (however, the recall did provoke Nader into issuing a press statement vilifying Henry Ford II).[30] At this time, it should be remembered, Ford had no other small car to offer in the immediate future; in the words of one of our respondents, "we had to keep the Pinto alive for two years."

Subsequently, the Pinto trial provided Ford with a far better opportunity to defend itself publicly, and full advantage was taken of it. As an initial precaution, an opinion poll was conducted to test the reaction of potential jurors in the areas where the accident occurred;[31] the results being unfavorable, a change of venue was obtained (from Elkhart to Winamac, Indiana). When the trial began, a senior public relations officer was assigned to follow press reactions, to keep reporters abreast of Ford's stand, and to tackle those "not giving us a fair break."[32] Above all, Ford staged a showcase defense, meticulously prepared by a team of lawyers and brilliantly presented by James Neal, an accomplished trial counsel of Watergate fame. As well as winning over the jurors at the trial, Neal's presentation was deliberately aimed at the general public. It repeatedly portrayed Ford as an All-American institution which, far from being an inhuman reckless murderer, was peopled by executives who not only were sensitive to the issue of safety, but also were prepared to provide Pintos for the use of their own families.[33]

After the acquittal, Ford considered mounting a public relations campaign, but no serious steps were taken in this direction, largely because the media was believed to be preoccupied with immediate events; "news a day late is no news." This belief, we were told, was founded partly on experience: some information had been provided to reporters without evoking any sign of interest. Accordingly, Ford let the matter rest with a statement by its new chairman, Philip Caldwell, that "there must be responsibility on the part of those who use products as well as on the part of those who manufacture them."[34] Others, however, were quick to come to Ford's side. Most notably, General Motors issued a congratulatory press release, and one of Ford's defense counsel for the trial published a sympathetic series of articles in the *National Law Journal.*[35]

Looking back over the Pinto trial, the Ford executives with whom we spoke regarded being prosecuted as a blow which could have been struck against any company in the auto-manufacturing business and, indeed, many companies in other industries as well. They resented the difficulty they experienced in getting Ford's side of the story into the media, especially the company's position that the cost-benefit study related to a proposed federal safety standard, and not to the actual design of the Pinto. It was said that Strobel, the author of *Reckless Homicide: Ford's Pinto Trial,* had written a distorted account because he had never approached Ford to check out the facts. These reflections ended on a sweeter note, however, because *Fortune* had smiled. A recent article in the magazine had excluded Ford from its list of 100 leading corporate criminals, presumably because the company had been vindicated by the acquittal at Winamac.[36]

Financial Impacts

The adverse publicity before and during the Pinto trial did have an impact on Ford's sales and profitability, and stock prices may also have suffered. Sales of the Pinto dropped sharply at first but later recovered. As a result of the "Pinto Madness" scare in 1977–1978, its share of the market was cut from 11–12 percent to 6.7 percent.[37] The car was then facelifted for the 1980 model year, and an advertising campaign stressed the price advantage the Pinto had over imports. The share of the market then climbed back to 9.7 percent.[38] We were informed that the path back had not been blocked by any criticism of the Pinto by competitors ("they were rooting for us on the footing that, but for the grace of God, there go I") or by any bans on government purchases (the last 4,000 Pintos were bought by the U.S. government for the Postal Service). At the same time, the recovery had not really been Ford's doing alone; the crisis in Iran had resulted in an upsurge in demand for small cars generally. Within 30 days of the onset of that crisis there had been a significant switch in consumer preference from large to small cars (in 1980 the number of Pintos produced increased by 125,000 to 325,000). This being so, why had the Pinto been discontinued in 1980? Contrary to rumor, it was insisted that the production of the Pinto had not been stopped as a result of the publicity about safety, but because the car had come to the end of its planned 10-year cycle.

Despite overall sales of 2.9 million, however, the Pinto was not a profitable car. As Ford's chairman recently bemoaned in corporates: "I just wish we had been able to get a better balance between the incomings and the outgoings."[39] Apart from loss of revenue through a fall in sales, and the cost of the 1978 recall, considerable legal costs were incurred in the criminal trial and in civil damages actions. The legal costs associated with the criminal trial were never disclosed by Ford, but the figure often guessed was $1 million;[40] the amount paid out in civil damages remains confidential. By no means can all of these costs be attributed to the adverse publicity surrounding the Pinto, but that publicity did induce Ford to spare no expense in staging its defense at the criminal trial and undoubtedly contributed to the onset of civil claims and to Ford's willingness to settle them. It is noteworthy that Ford's associate counsel in charge of litigation felt that the publicity about the deaths of three young women in the homicide case "made it very difficult for us to get a fair trial almost anywhere on a Pinto case."[41] After the acquittal in the criminal trial, the flow of civil claims dropped to a trickle and a case proceeding to trial in December 1980 was won by the company.[42]

Apart from the impact upon the sales and profitability of the Pinto, the effects of the publicity were felt generally in the market share of other cars sold by Ford. During the period of the trial, Ford sales declined 30.6 percent whereas General Motors and Chrysler suffered smaller declines of 7.2 percent and 26 percent respectively.[43] At least part of this decline was attributed to the adverse publicity. As one spokesman informed us, "management here believe that the Pinto adverse publicity has raised questions about our product quality generally and is one of the reasons for our declined market share in the last two years."

The impact on stock market prices was far more difficult to gauge. We were told by one senior executive that "the general reaction is that nobody knows what the hell the stock market is doing; I can't remember anyone saying that the market went up or down in response to the acquittal or the indictment." He also said that he could not remember any impact, favorable or unfavorable, of the *Grimshaw* case.

We then spoke to Ford's investor-relations officer. Ford's stock had generally traded in the range of $40–$50 during the 1960s and 1970s but more recently there had been a precipitous drop to the $22 mark. Throughout 1980 and late 1979, Ford stocks consistently traded well below the prices prevailing during the previous four years. However, there had been no apparent connection between any attacks on Ford during the Pinto trial and any drop in the price of Ford stock on particular days. The market was so irrational that it was impossible to explain particular changes in stock market prices except where the causes were blatant. He pointed out that Ford's stock price had dropped on the day of the acquittal in the Pinto trial whereas it had gone up after the announcement of a quarterly loss and a substantial reduction in dividend. Nonetheless, the Pinto publicity was considered to have had an adverse effect over the period during which Ford's stocks had dropped in price. "It had an effect on our image and therefore on our ability to sell cars and trucks; in turn, it affected our profitability and hence had an effect on our stock price."

These financial impacts should be seen in perspective. All of the executives with whom we spoke stressed that the loss threatened by the sudden switch in preference from large to small cars (a switch precipitated by the crisis in Iran) had transcended any of the other problems facing the company, especially since Ford then had no car to match the Japanese subcompacts. Adverse publicity, particularly as extreme as that in the Pinto case, is much less likely than fines to be written off as a minor cost of doing business, but it can be pushed into the background by a force majeure.[44]

Non-Financial Impacts

The adverse publicity leading up to and surrounding the Pinto trial had four main non-financial impacts: tarnishing of Ford's corporate image, lowering of personal reputation of executives, creating worry about possible longer-term effects on sales, and arousing concern about legislative implications.

The image-blackening effect of the Pinto trial and the prior adverse publicity was considerable. Numerous newspaper accounts of the Pinto story spoke explicitly of its detracting from Ford's corporate reputation,[45] and then pressure to save that reputation in large part accounted for the effort which the company put into defending itself against the reckless homicide charges. Just how great that pressure was is apparent from the results of one survey of consumer opinion undertaken soon after the indictments: 38 percent of the persons surveyed had heard that Ford cars were unsafe (cp. 6 percent re GM cars; 4 percent re imports; and 1 percent re American Motors cars) and 47 percent of those under 35 years of age had heard or read negative comments.[46] Moreover, there was Henry Ford II's famous quote: "The lawyers would shoot me for saying this, but I think there's some cause for the concern about the car. I don't even listen to the cost-figures—we've got to fix it."[47]

The attack upon Ford's corporate image radiated out to executives. This is how Strobel saw the impact:

Even though no executives were formally charged, prosecutors had to present evidence that the car had been defectively designed and that the corporation had been reckless in failing to warn consumers. A corporation acts through its executives, and so the prosecutors, in effect, would be trying individual members of Ford management for their decisions regarding the Pinto. Ford executives, accustomed to

50

receiving community respect commensurate with their high social status and lucrative salaries, cringed at such a degrading possibility. Even if they felt they had done nothing wrong, the idea of undergoing public interrogation and being the target of a prosecutor's allegations and insinuations was a humiliating thought.[48]

"Cringed," however, is much too strong a word, for although the executives felt themselves assailed (for example, the chief engineer felt under an obligation to explain to his family why he considered Ford not to be a murderer), their attitude was described to us as being one of willingness and anxiety to have the opportunity "to set the record straight." Furthermore, the reflection was offered that persons working for auto-makers in Detroit were essentially members of one big family, whereas personnel employed by Lockheed during the bribery scandal had far less collegiate insulation; unlike the car industry in Detroit, aerospace has no real home.

Also significant was the worry occasioned about long-term sales. Shortly after the indictments, Ford's associate general counsel for litigation admitted that "publicity has called into question the design of the Pinto and that has a tendency to rub off on other areas as people are apt to wonder: 'If there's a problem with the Pinto, there might be a problem in other areas.'"[49] Ford's sensitivity on this issue was particularly acute since its executives worried that adverse publicity from the Pinto trial could trigger sales resistance to the new Escort, a car essential to the company's recovery in the early 1980s; in the words of Henry Ford II,

> Everything hangs on the success of that car—it sure does. It has to do *everything* by itself for 1981 and 1982. We'll have to sell every one we can make to . . . support the profitable end of the line.[50]

Moreover, it was feared that a dramatic downturn in Pinto sales would increase Ford's fleet fuel economy average above that required by the Energy Policy and Conservation Act of 1975, thereby forcing the company to restrict sales of its new full-size models.[51]

A further non-financial impact was concern about legislative implications. Although no safety standard governing resistance to rear-end collisions resulted from the Pinto trial or the publicity which inspired it (a new standard had been introduced in 1977 prior to that publicity), the Pinto case was relied upon to support a federal Bill requiring corporate managers to disclose life-threatening defects in any of their company's products.[52] The statute proposed was not enacted, but the prospect was anathema to business because of the possibility of severe individual criminal liability and the danger of being forced to provide information which could provoke costly civil damages claims.[53]

Reforms

Shaken by the adverse publicity over the Pinto, Ford instituted several reforms in the areas of safety and legal self-protection. No changes were made in the fuel storage system of the Pinto after the recall for modifications in 1978, and the fuel tank of the new Escort, a front-wheel drive car, had always been planned to sit ahead of the rear wheels. As to law reform, Ford's acquittal muffled any calls for change.

In the area of safety, it was felt within Ford that one contributing factor in the Pinto crisis had been the pressure placed upon the design and engineering staff by the then president, Lee Iacocca, that the car had to weigh under 2000 pounds and cost less than $2,000.[54] The edict, according to one executive we interviewed, was the toughest Ford had ever experienced with a new vehicle. There was also limited time for design and retooling. Today, these areas are covered by a major policy directive of June 1979: "Targets will be selected in sufficient time for all company activities to achieve the desired DQR [Durability, Quality, and Reliability] end result."[55] This policy directive was backed by considerable pruning and grafting of decision trees within the organization, the aim being to ensure that management would look beforehand at points of no return. In addition, there was an increase in engineering and research staff, and several positions were upgraded.

The document setting out the new policy directive, Policy Document F 1, sought to establish the importance of durability, quality, and reliability by stressing the relevance of these goals to how Ford fared competitively. It was explained to us that the problem within the organization was to convince people that there was no justification for sacrificing safety in the name of profit. The real solution to this problem was to elevate safety to a high level, "DQR" being a designation which minimized the risk of association with Ford's unsuccessful "Life Guard" campaign to sell safety in the 1950s.

It was readily conceded by those with whom we spoke that the new policy directive was subject to the pressures of time, cost, and survival. Time was always a problem in the planning, design, and manufacture of cars. Consumer preferences were fickle, whereas car production was necessarily governed by routine. In the car industry, flexibility had always been delicately balanced against rigidity and certainty. Admittedly, the Japanese had adjusted to this tension by opting for long-term planning and sticking to their plans, but in the American context that was considered to be a recipe for disaster. In terms of cost, it was stressed that mammoth expenses were involved in retooling and that, once a car had been put on the market, there was little room to adjust the trade-off between safety and profitability. Above all, the first aim of the company was to survive. It was all very well talking about safe cars, but there was no future in losses; the business of automobile manufacturers was not to make "museum pieces."

The other significant area of organizational reform was that of legal self-protection. The main impact of the Pinto trial, according to product liability specialists at Ford, was to ignite their desire to provide effective legal protection against exposure to liability. A new procedure was instituted for recording the background to safety and engineering decisions; the aim of the fuller documentation was to enable the company to defend itself more adequately in any future litigation.

Although the Pinto was a rough ride for Ford and led to some internal revisions within the company, legislative reform did not ensue. Calls for tougher regulation of auto safety were muted by the acquittal at Winimac.[56] It cannot be said, however, that the trial provided the public with the information required to made an informed choice about the need for reform.

The Pinto trial, although widely heralded as a passion play about the riskiness of Ford engineering and design, turned out to be a great disappointment. The relevant offense was defined in terms of recklessly causing death, and the trial therefore necessarily focused on issues directly connected with the particular deaths subject to prosecution. This meant that information about the safety and engineering decisions behind the Pinto was irrelevant unless it related to the 1973 Pinto involved in the death of the three young women. Moreover, any question of reckless engineering or non-rectification of faults was overshadowed by the question of whether the closing speed of the van that struck the Pinto was so high that the fuel tank of any small car would have been ruptured. As a result, the rights or wrongs of the Pinto Papers were never effectively canvassed at the trial.

Not surprisingly, the trial confused rather than clarified lay perceptions of the dangers of Ford's policy and the safety of the Pinto. For instance, after Ford had been acquitted, the foreman of the jury disclosed that "We just felt that the state never presented enough evidence to convince us that Ford was guilty," but added that he wouldn't buy a Pinto himself, although he would not be averse to a gift of one. "I wouldn't feel safe but I'd drive it."[57] So, from the standpoint of community education or sociodrama[58] the trial was a dismal flop. It failed to clarify, much less resolve, the issues that should have been of real concern to the public.

This bears out the point that criminal trials and their attendant publicity inadequately inform public choices about corporate decision-making if the focus of attention is an offense defined in terms of causing harm as opposed to taking an unacceptable *risk*.[59] Harm-causing offenses are oriented towards idiosyncratic results rather than underlying problems of risk-taking. Guido Calabresi has made this clear in his discussion of road-accident compensation policy:

> The effect of case-by-case decisions is to center on the particular or unusual cause of an accident. If one asks, as case-by-case determinants tend to do, "What went wrong in this case?" the answer will most likely center on the peculiar cause. Yet here is a very good argument for the notion that the cheapest way of avoiding accident costs is not to attempt to control the *unusual* event but rather to modify a recurring event. It may be that absentmindedness is a cause of one particular accident, too much whiskey the cause of another, and drowsiness the cause of a third. But it may also be that a badly designed curve or inadequate tires are causes of each of these as well. The fault system, because it centers on the possible *particular* cost avoider, is very likely to ignore the recurring cost avoider and hence fail altogether to consider some potential cheapest cost avoiders such as highway builders or tiremakers.[60]

In the absence of an offense defined in terms of manufacturing an unjustifiably dangerous product, questions of acceptable risk of the kind raised by the Pinto Papers will rarely be the central subject of inquiry in the context of corporate offenses against the person. This is unsatisfactory, not only because of the danger of a serious underlying risk being concealed from society, but also because it may do more harm than good not to face up to the need for studies of the costs of improving product safety in matters such as that for which Ford was pilloried.[61]

CHAPTER 5

Ford—The Emissions-Testing Fraud

The Emissions-Testing Offenses

A much publicized pollution case of the 1970s was Ford's violation of the emissions-testing requirements of the Clean Air Act.[1] Ford was charged with making false statements in order to obtain certification of its 1973 engines. Many of the tests run by the company in 1971 and 1972 were invalid because the engines tested had been tampered with (e.g., by changing spark plugs or substituting "gold-plated" parts). When the tampering was discovered by Ford's senior management, the Environmental Protection Agency (EPA) was notified within five days.[2] An inquiry by the General Accounting Office (GAO) was then commissioned by the Air and Water Pollution Subcommittee of the U.S. Senate. Ford's engine and foundry division was found to have "routinely performed unauthorized inspections, tests and maintenance on the 1973 prototype vehicles" without notifying either the company's automotive emissions office or the EPA.[3] Indeed, the GAO found that there had been 442 instances of unauthorized maintenance on test vehicles. Subsequently, the EPA recommended that criminal proceedings be taken by the Justice Department. The explanation given by the EPA Administrator, William D. Ruckelhaus, was as follows:

> This commendable action by top corporate management cannot, in our judgment, make lawful the action of Ford employees who were responsible for the conduct of recording of emission tests required by Federal law.
> To condone unlawful practices by responsible employees at the operating level of the corporate hierarchy would entail a serious risk to the integrity of the procedures by which compliance with Federal automobile emission standards is determined.[4]

The charges were settled without trial. Ford agreed to pay a criminal fine of $3.5 million and a further $3.5 million in civil penalties. Moreover, the company undertook by consent order to keep written records of emission-testing procedures and to notify the personnel concerned of their legal obligations and the consequences of non-compliance.[5] These requirements applied for ten years, from February 13, 1973.

Publicity and Counterpublicity

Ford's violation of the Clean Air Act was widely publicized by newspapers around the country, the leading accounts being those published by the *New York Times* and the *Wall Street Journal*. The *New York Times* ran three front-page stories, the last of which gave a particularly comprehensive picture.[6] Under the headline, "COURT FINES FORD $7 MILLION IN SUIT ON POLLUTION TEST," this account gave a blow-by-blow description of all stages of the proceedings, the case being described as another round in a continuing struggle between the Federal Government and the auto industry over emission standards.[7]

The *Wall Street Journal* covered the events in a series of lengthy news items.[8] The most striking of these reported the findings of the GAO inquiry under the heading, "GAO SAYS FORD FIXED TEST CARS 442 TIMES WITHOUT TELLING EPA."[9] Moreover, the *Wall Street Journal* rekindled the adverse publicity six years later when it interviewed Harvey Copp, a former Ford executive who had brought the illegal testing procedures to the company's notice. In Copp's view, the violations had resulted from pressure upon middle managers to get the 1973 engines certified: "If they failed, it would have been impossible for Ford to meet its ambitious production and earnings goals that year."[10]

Ford's public response to the emissions-testing crisis was restrained — there was no denying that a blatant contravention of the Clean Air Act had occurred. Nonetheless, the company's reputation was defended, notably by means of voluntary disclosure, apology on television, and lobbying for relaxation of auto-emission standards.

Ford's voluntary disclosure of the false test reports was partly a public relations exercise. Although the initial source of adverse publicity, this disclosure took much of the sting out of the offenses. In particular, Ford was able to congratulate itself for cooperating with the EPA and for "reassigning" four employees who had withheld information about "unscheduled, unauthorized maintenance" on test cars.[11] Moreover, by taking the initiative, Ford was able to elicit praise from the EPA.[12]

Negative publicity from the emissions fraud was also countered by making a public apology. Henry Ford II appeared on television to explain the company's position. In the course of the interview he remarked, in heartfelt tones, that the case was "the worst thing that has ever happened to us."

This confession entered, Ford took the offensive against any tightening of auto-emission standards. When Engelhard Minerals announced a promising new catalytic converter designed to meet the 1975 auto-emissions standards, Ford issued a press release claiming that the device had been inadequately tested because the car equipped with a prototype of the device had been subject to adjustments forbidden under EPA emission-testing procedures.[13]

Ford also made concurrent attempts to lobby against the 1975 auto-emission standards. On May 11, 1972, the day that top Ford executives became aware of the emissions-testing fraud, Henry Ford II inveighed against the 1975 standards, claiming that they were too strict and, if enforced, would lead to plant shut-downs.[14] Furthermore, immediately in the wake of settlement of the emissions prosecution, Ford proposed a plan to relax emissions standards.[15] Although these countermeasures were fired expressly against the standards proposed for 1975, their smoke formed a haze over the offenses Ford had committed.

Financial Impacts

We were informed by Ford that the emissions-testing offenses and their adverse publicity had not resulted in loss of sales or any perceived drop in share prices. However, there had been much agitation about the implications of delayed certification for the 1973 models.

The main financial impact of the emissions fraud was the $7 million paid in fines. This was the largest fine yet imposed for pollution (Allied Chemical was later fined more than $13 million in the Kepone case),[16] although for Ford the amount was far from crippling. As its position was explained to us, Ford was then financially buoyant, whereas in more recent years the company's profitability had dropped to such an extent that a fine of $7 million today would be very significant indeed.

Despite Ford's ability in 1973 to absorb a large fine, however, there had been considerable disquiet about the possibility of prejudice to Ford's competitive position, especially in the event of public condemnation. The main source of concern was that the appearance of the 1973 models would be substantially delayed if the EPA, riding a wave of public criticism, were to insist upon a complete rerun of the engine tests (which would have taken four months).[17] For the chairman, Henry Ford II, the position seemed particularly grim: "We're in one hell of a lot of trouble."[18] For his key troubleshooter, Donald Jensen, certification would be miraculous; "I pray a lot," he said.[19]

As it happened, Ford managed to negotiate a compromise solution involving substantially shortened test procedures; one week's delay in the introduction of the 1973 models resulted.[20] Even so, the company was worried that the 1973 models could earn a poor reputation. We were informed that the driveability of the 1973 cars had suffered as a result of the time wasted on fraudulent testing, and the rush to obtain certification was a matter of public knowledge.[21]

The impact on Ford's stock prices was far less significant. When news of the fraud broke towards the end of May 1973, Ford's shares increased from 58 ⅛ on May 23 to 62 ⅜ on May 24, and then dropped to 60 ½ on May 25. (The Dow Jones closing average for these days was 895, 924, and 931 respectively.) Not until November and December was there any marked fall, the market preoccupation with respect to industrial stocks then being the crisis over the supply of oil on the U.S. domestic market. The executives to whom we spoke could not remember any stock market impact; in the words of one respondent, "I don't recall any concern about sales or shares. The real concern was whether anyone was going to end up in jail."

Non-Financial Impacts

The non-financial impacts of the emissions-testing case and its attendant publicity were primarily loss of corporate and individual reputation, agitation about the possibility of increased levels of enforcement, and demoralization. Repute, corporate and individual, was threatened by the emissions-testing offenses. As the media made plain, the offenses disclosed by Ford involved not merely pollution, but fraud. Moreover, the GAO inquiry had cast some doubt on the innocence of senior executives at Ford by reporting that General Motors, Chyrsler, and American Motors were all of the view that senior management in their organizations would be aware of any irregularities in testing procedures.[22] Nonetheless, many Ford personnel, we were told, viewed the emissions fraud as an isolated incident. "The people upstairs," however, were very sensitive about the matter. In the case of Henry Ford II especially, the discovery of the fake tests came as a severe blow, partly because of his pride in the company and family name, and partly because of his standing as an opinion leader in U.S. business (e.g., after the electrical equipment conspiracies, it was Ford who led the call for a moral rearmament among U.S. corporations).[23] We were informed that "Mr. Ford was appalled and personally aggrieved that the company was involved in flagrant violation of the law." Accordingly, Ford felt obliged to apologize on television, secular society's confessional box.

The assault upon the company's image was revived seven years later in the unusual context of reliance upon a prior conviction to impugn corporate credibility. During the Pinto trial of 1980, the prosecution fell back upon the emissions-testing violations in an attempt to destroy the veracity of evidence given by Ford personnel.[24] Although this tactic was successfully parried by Ford on the basis that "[b]laming Ford's 500,000 employees because four or five people cut corners would be like blaming every person in Pulaski county because a few people tried cutting corners,"[25] it did introduce an additional element of embarrassment into the proceedings. Indeed, in a television interview about the matter, James Neal, Ford's lead counsel at the trial, felt driven to respond that, given the voluntary disclosure of the fraud to the EPA, the emissions violations "may have been Ford Motor Company's finest hour."[26]

Second, there was agitation over the prospect of increased levels of enforcement of the Clean Air Act. Although widely proclaimed as a major legislative measure against pollution, it had been only weakly enforced, partly because of the limited resources of the EPA.[27] The proceedings against Ford, however, foretold a different future. To begin with, it was conceivable that the EPA would be given additional resources to try to control auto emissions — this was the explicit wish of Senator Muskie, chairman of the Senate Subcommittee on Air and Water Pollution, and main proponent of the GAO inquiry into Ford's emissions-testing procedures.[28] Worse, it was likely that Ford would be pressed into a consent decree that would impose stringent check points, and transfer much of the burden of enforcement onto the company's shoulders. It turned out that EPA enforcement of emissions-testing procedures was strengthened,[29] but the consent decree imposed less exacting obligations than had been feared. As one spokesman described the reaction within the company to us, Ford was relatively happy with the consent decree and the $7 million fine because neither posed any threat to the timely and hence competitive certification of Ford's engines.

Perhaps the most significant non-financial impact, however, was personnel demoralization. Apart from the ripple caused by Henry Ford II's sensitivity about the fraud, there was uneasiness as people "waited for the sword to fall," anticipated being called as witnesses at the trial (hundreds of engineers were involved in the testing procedures), or worried about the problem of getting the 1973 cars into the showrooms on time (as it happened, Ford was able to persuade the EPA to allow cars to be supplied to dealers in anticipation of certification).[30] The uncertainty, we were told, was very unsettling. Management therefore resolved to overcome the problem as soon as possible. A special task force of 30 lawyers and engineers was appointed to steer the company through the mine-field. This task force, it was said, worked for three months, seven days a week, and 16 hours a day, aided throughout by an unlimited budget. As well as negotiating with the EPA, the task force prepared a special investigative report which preempted the need for a stringent consent decree. Eventually morale was restored, an accomplishment which earned the leader of the task force the bionic nickname, "the seven million dollar man."

Reforms

Ford's encounter with the emissions-testing offenses led to corporate reforms in four areas: internal discipline, certification procedures, compliance auditing, and company policy. These reforms were certainly significant, but the company stopped short of radically engineering its way out of trouble.

Internal discipline was imposed against four persons directly involved in the emissions-testing fraud (two were middle managers, one a supervisor, and the fourth an executive engineer). Initially, these people were reassigned. After the settlement of the case with the Justice Department, they were formally demoted. We were told that all four are still with the company today although they had not gone "as far up the ladder" as would otherwise have been expected.

We asked whether there was any resentment within the organization about the non-application of internal discipline to senior management.[31] It was replied that lower level personnel felt that "management must have known we were bending the rules" because there was a very tight schedule and inadequate resources to meet it. However, the task force inquiry had not found any evidence to support the allegation. The response of management was to concede that those down the line in the emissions-control program had been given a tough task, and yet to insist that no one had authority to break the law. Those who had resorted to faking results, it was said, should have stood up for themselves and asked for more help from above.

A second major area of corporate reform was engine-testing certification procedures.[32] To begin with, tighter documentation was introduced, with particular emphasis upon a vehicle "Bill Book" which had to be signed off by all persons responsible for different phases of the emission-tests required under the Clean Air Act. Thus, in order to guard against the possible use of "gold-plated" components, each part of a car delivered for testing had to be certified as being randomly chosen to assure representativeness of the model under test. Physical controls were also improved; for instance, engine hoods were locked to prevent tampering. In addition, testing procedures were modified by providing two persons at recording points, one to record, the other to observe and confirm.

To tie these new procedures to an independent backbone, Ford separated the testing function from that of design. At the time of the emissions-testing fraud, the functions had been integrated, creating an organizational risk that the testing people would be co-opted and compromised by the more senior design personnel. Under the revised system, testing was insulated from design by making the former a staff function under the control of a new unit, the Environmental and Safety Engineering Central Staff.

Despite these changes in certification procedures, it was pointed out that a problem could still arise as a result of conflicting loyalties. We were asked to consider the position of a Ford representative negotiating with EPA for engine certification. On the one hand, such a person was under a definite obligation to Ford to act according to the rules. On the other hand, however, "a lot of people would be pushing to ensure that the company succeeded."

Ford's system for auditing compliance was also strengthened as a result of the emissions-testing offenses. Four notable changes were made. First, the auditing program was extended to cover legal obligations as well as financial controls. Second, a procedure was introduced under which problems of compliance could be reported to management on a no-names basis. Third, personnel management instituted confidential surveys, again with a view to encouraging the "bubbling up" of bad news. Fourth, a Stationary Source Environmental Control Office was set up, together with the Environmental and Safety Engineering Central Staff mentioned earlier; "Mr. Ford" had decided that if a problem of compliance could arise in one area, like auto-emissions, "we're not going to let it happen in another."

It was urged that these changes were not formalistic but had been accompanied by a change in attitudes within the organization towards complaints about non-compliance. One interviewee was particularly outspoken about previous reluctance at Ford to speak out about actual or suspected difficulties; in his view, bottling up adverse news had been rife, largely because headquarters then had a record of scapegoating. By contrast, a freer, more open atmosphere was said now to prevail—the emissions-testing fraud had demonstrated the pitfalls of allowing the company to be led down secret paths of illegality.

A fourth corporate reform was Policy C-3, relating to standards of corporate conduct. Although this policy was not introduced until May 1976, the view expressed to us was that it manifested not only a contemporary uneasiness about bribery scandals,[33] but also a lingering concern about the emissions-testing offenses. The relevant policy letter, over the signature of Henry Ford II, reaffirmed the importance of having a good corporate reputation, amplified the company's policy directives against illegal and unethical practices, and warned personnel that, "An employee who knowingly violates the policies and guidelines of this letter shall be subject to disciplinary action, including demotion or dismissal."

Although Ford's measures of internal discipline and rectification of certification procedures were compelled by the necessity to avoid harsh penalties or remedies, it is to the credit of the company that it took additional steps, especially in relation to compliance auditing. However, it must also be said that those additional steps were defensive. It was apparent that the technology-forcing provisions of the Clean Air Act were anathema to the engineering staff at Ford, the perceived evils being undue cost to consumers, inefficient bureaucracy, and excessive interference with corporate freedom.[34] Yet the fact remains that Ford chose to lobby against the proposed 1975 emissions standards rather than to engineer its way out of difficulty.[35] By contrast, Honda developed its praise-winning anti-pollution CVCC engines,[36] and produced a latter-day Model T.

CHAPTER 6

Kepone and Allied Chemical

The Kepone Offenses

The Kepone case arose from offenses against nature. A large quantity of wastes from the manufacture of Kepone, a pesticide akin to DDT, had been discharged into the waterways of Virginia. The discharges came initially from a plant of Allied Chemical Corporation, a leading manufacturer of chemicals, and later from the factory of Life Science Products Company, a small firm which had been formed by two former Allied Chemical employees to manufacture Kepone for supply to Allied Chemical. Although Kepone wastes had passed into the James River and its tributaries for many years (from 1966 to 1974), these discharges did not result in prosecution until 1976, after many workers at Life Science Products had complained of severe shakes and other symptoms of Kepone poisoning stemming from appalling conditions at the Life Science plant.[1]

Two indictments were returned by a federal grand jury in May 1976. The first charged Allied Chemical with 940 counts of violating the Refuse Act and the Water Pollution Control Act by discharging Kepone and other toxic materials without permits, and also one count alleging a conspiracy with five of its employees to violate pollution control laws. The second charged Allied Chemical, Life Science Products, two managers of Life Science Products, and the City of Hopewell on 153 counts of water pollution arising from Life Science's discharge of Kepone into the Hopewell sewerage system.

The conspiracy count against Allied Chemical under the first indictment was dismissed on the ground that a corporation cannot be criminally liable for conspiring with itself.[2] However, Allied Chemical did not contest the 940 counts of water pollution in the first indictment. Trial did proceed on the 153 counts of water pollution under the second indictment, but Allied Chemical was acquitted because it had not been proven that Life Science Products was an agent for whose conduct Allied could be vicariously liable, and because there was insufficient evidence of intent to establish liability on the alternative basis of complicity.[3]

Sentencing Allied Chemical on the water pollution counts, Judge Merhige of the Federal District Court initially imposed a maximum fine of $13.25 million, subject to the rider that the sentence would be reconsidered in light of any action taken by Allied to alleviate the offenses.[4] Subsequently, the fine was reduced to $5 million after a submission by Allied Chemical that account be taken of its expenditure of $8 million to establish the Virginia Environmental Endowment, a new non-profit corporation which would "fund scientific research projects and implement remedial projects and other programs to help alleviate the problem that Kepone has created . . . . and . . . . enhance and improve the overall quality of the environment in Virginia. . . ."[5]

Publicity and Counterpublicity

The Kepone offenses exposed Allied Chemical to a barrage of adverse publicity before, during and after trial and sentence. The adverse publicity was understandable. Large quantities of Kepone residues had been dispersed throughout the James River, extending into Chesapeake Bay. Kepone was suspected to be a cancer-producing agent.[6] Fish and wildlife had been contaminated by it.[7] Fishing in the James, a river notable for its abundance of shad and oysters, had to be banned.[8] And removal, let alone safe disposal, of the Kepone residues was impractical: the costs of cleaning up the James were put as high as $2 billion and, in any event, disturbing the river bottoms where the residues lay might have made the situation worse.[9]

Another attention-getting factor was the size of the fine imposed upon Allied Chemical.[10] A fine of $13.25 million was conspicuously large given the relatively small fines traditionally imposed for corporate crimes. Moreover, it nearly doubled the previous record fine of $7 million for pollution offenses which had been imposed against Ford in 1973.[11] Admittedly, Allied won a tax deduction of $4 million by donating the $8 million to establish the Virginia Environmental Endowment, but the tax deduction itself attracted some adverse publicity.[12]

The press, particularly on the East coast, persistently followed the Kepone story. The more pastel commentaries included a series of articles by Thomas J. Bray in the *Wall Street Journal.*[13] In particular, Bray drew attention to the widespread dispersal of Kepone in the James River and Chesapeake Bay, the major blow to Virginia's fishing industry struck by the closure of the James River to most types of fishing, the slack pollution control measures adopted by Allied Chemical and Life Science Products, and the need for a Toxic Substances Control Act. There was also more lurid reporting, notably Brian Kelly's 15-part series in the *Washington Star* between September 19 and October 3, 1976. The flavor of Kelly's stories is readily apparent from their headlilnes: "THE JAMES RIVER: VIRGINIA'S GREATEST MAN-MADE DISASTER," "HOW KEPONE BECAME A NAME FOR ENVIRONMENTAL DISASTER," "THE DEADLY DUST," "LIFE AMONG THE SMOKING STACKS," "HOW ONE GOVERNMENT AGENCY AFTER ANOTHER FUMBLED KEPONE," "IF A BLUEFISH COULD THINK, HE'D WONDER . . . WHERE HAS MAN GONE?," and "ENTIRE KEPONE TRAGEDY IS VERY, VERY HARD TO BELIEVE." Although Kelly's criticisms and innuendoes were aimed partly at enforcement agencies, the city of Hopewell, and the managers of Life Science Products, the arch-villain was Allied Chemical, creator of Kepone and pay-master of Life Science Products.[14]

This extensive press attention went hand-in-hand with coverage by other media. The Kepone story attracted much initial notoriety as a result of television exposure on the CBS "Sixty Minutes" program.[15] Soon thereafter, two congressional enquiries (one by the Senate Subcommittee on Agricultural Research and General Legislation of the Committee on Agriculture and Forestry, the other by the House of Representatives Subcommittee on Manpower, Compensation, and Health and Safety) provided further embarrassment.[16] One of the main questions pursued in those avenues of inquiry was the link between Allied Chemical and the Life Science Products Company. Thus, during the Senate Subcommittee hearings, William Moore, president of Life Science Products, was asked if Allied Chemical was trying "to get rid of a hot potato" by encouraging the creation of a separate firm to produce a dangerous chemical. He replied: "The way it turned out they sure did. I had my hands burned from the potato."[17]

Confronted by this formidable wave of adverse publicity, how did Allied Chemical respond? A conscious decision was made not to wage an aggressive counterpublicity campaign but rather to "hunker down," as one executive described it, and to devise a superior environmental compliance program. To some extent this decision was influenced by the political climate: The Kepone case occurred at the time of extensive debate about the Toxic Substances Control Act.[18] Although an aggressive counterpublicity campaign was not waged by Allied, the company did resort to a number of defensive measures.[19]

First, throughout the congressional enquiries, Allied repeatedly maintained that it had no legal connection with or responsibility for the conduct of Life Science Products.[20] However, moral responsibility for rectifying the injury or damage caused by Kepone was not denied (Allied Chemical spent $300,000 to detoxify the Life Science Products plant and $62,000 to assist Kepone-eradication research at the Medical College of Virginia).[21]

Second, Allied Chemical sought to defuse the indictments with this press release:

The Company's general record on environmental and safety policies has been excellent. . . . The scope of the criminal actions was unwarranted and unprecedented. The extreme reaction shown by the indictments appears to reflect official frustration over failure of regulatory agencies to coordinate their activities and perform their duties with respect to the events which took place at the Life Science plant . . . .[22]

Third, in achieving a reduction in fine from $13.25 million to $5 million by paying $8 million to set up the Virginia Environmental Endowment, Allied Chemical gained not only a tax deduction of $4 million but also the goodwill flowing from an apparent act of public benefaction.

Fourth, after being sentenced and fined, Allied Chemical defended its corporate image by advertising a lengthy "Message to the People of Virginia." After expressing disappointment but contrition at its sentence, Allied Chemical spelled out what the company meant to the quality of life in Virginia:

The Kepone problem, unfortunately, has given most people a distorted view of Allied Chemical. The 3,800 Virginians who run our plants in Hopewell and Chesterfield County know us as a company that plays a vital role in American industry, a company they can be proud to work for. On behalf of those employees, we would like to tell you some things you probably don't know about Allied Chemical.

First of all, we've been doing a great deal to improve environmental control in our Virginia plants. Since 1970, we have carried out air and water pollution control projects costing $15 million, and we are spending $40 million more in environmental improvement over the next three and one-half years in Virginia.

A going, growing business means jobs for Virginians. Our annual payroll in Hopewell-Chesterfield County is $53 million and going higher. And there are other economic benefits to the community. We pay $2.8 million in taxes annually to local communities and the Commonwealth of Virginia — money that helps finance the services Virginians expect from their governments. We spend about $90 million on goods and services purchased from local sources. This is money that enables other Virginia businesses to provide jobs, pay salaries and earn profits.

Allied Chemical has been steadily increasing its investment in eastern Virginia by adding to capacity. We have spent $119 million on new and improved facilities since 1970, and our fixed investments now total $300 million. We're currently spending $32 million on a new Hopewell facility to produce specialty oximes, which we will sell to other chemical companies for use in manufacturing safe, biodegradable pesticides.

Just as important as our economic contributions, we think, are the contributions of time and effort made by Allied Chemical employees in programs to improve the quality of life in their neighborhoods. They take part in virtually every worthwhile community activity in the Hopewell-Chesterfield area. They provided leadership to help establish the John Tyler Community College. In a cooperative program with Virginia State College, they helped set up an unusual new program of graduate-level economics education for high school teachers. Our people have been prime movers in planning and funding the Hopewell Regional Wastewater Treatment Plan, an ultra-modern sewerage facility now under construction. The company supports these employee efforts by regular contributions of funds to nine institutions of higher learning and 28 community and charitable projects.

We in Allied Chemical are proud of the Virginians who run our Hopewell-Chesterfield facilities. We are also proud of the community of which we are a part. We think the Hopewell-Chesterfield area is a good place to work and live. Allied Chemical and its 3,800 Virginia employees will do their best to keep it that way.

John T. Connor
Chairman[23]

Fifth, Allied Chemical later distributed to a "handful" of interested persons a booklet, *Allied Chemical Corporation and the Kepone Problem,* published in 1978.[24] This booklet, published "in the interest of setting the record straight," denied any sinister connection between Allied Chemical and Life Science Products, accused Life Science Products of gross irresponsibility, drew attention to the various preventive and remedial measures taken by Allied, and claimed that the offenses proven against Allied were "technical," on the ground that, although the company had discharged some Kepone wastes without specific approval from the EPA, a wastewater discharge permit had been obtained and would have covered those Kepone wastes had specific application been made.

Finally, in the dying stages of the crisis, Allied Chemical lent its assistance to *Fortune* magazine in the preparation of a sympathetic article, "Allied Chemical's $20-Million Ordeal with Kepone."[25] In the words of one Allied executive, "we put a lot of work into that."

As publicly manifested by these defensive measures, the reaction within Allied Chemical was that the Kepone affair had been blown up out of all proportion. The incident had arisen on the front doorstep of the East Coast media. Had it occurred in "a place like Mississippi" the story would have been on the back page, whereas the Eastern news corridor was noted for young journalists trying to win Pulitzer prizes for front-page scoops. Given this accident of bad location, the executives at Allied were thankful that the company had already equipped itself to manage such a problem (an environmental affairs department had been in operation since 1970). By contrast, Hooker Chemical appeared to have been caught napping: After the Love Canal scandal broke, it had been necessary to create the position of environmental affairs manager, a position which had long existed at Allied Chemical.

Financial Impacts

Massive as the adverse publicity about Kepone was, the impact upon Allied's stock prices and sales was minimal. However, the company was placed under pressure to settle civil claims and there were also miscellaneous costs of significance.

The price of Allied's shares on the market fluctuated only slightly during the period of adverse publicity. For instance, after the fine of $13.25 million was announced, Allied's shares dropped from a closing price of 37 ½ on October 5, 1976 to a closing price of 36 ⅛ on October 6. (The Dow Jones average over this period dropped from 966.76 to 959.69.) By October 17, the date of publication of the advertisement by Allied quoted above, the price had climbed back to 39. (The Dow Jones average also climbed, to 979.06.)

In accounting for the Kepone debits in the 1976 *Annual Report*, Allied Chemical offered shareholders the following reassurance:

The Company cannot predict what, if any, liability or damages may be adjudged against it as a result of [civil suits] or other proceedings that might arise out of the Kepone affair. It is believed, however, on the basis of available legal defenses, insurance coverage and the speculative nature of the damages alleged, that any loss ultimately sustained in the suits now pending will not materially affect the company's financial position or results of operations.[26]

Subsequently, Allied found it necessary to concede that the extent of liability could be material,[27] but within the company the impact of the Kepone affair was not regarded as significant. As far as management was concerned, "the general feeling" was that the stock price was depressed by only several points. Admittedly, the stock market analysts had paid special attention to Allied during the crisis, especially at the beginning. However, they had gradually lost interest when it became apparent that the total cost of the Kepone ordeal would be kept below $100 million and, eventually, below $30 million.

More important, even though the adverse publicity had made some impact, it was short-term and minor. What mattered in investment circles was keeping management intact and avoiding over-commitment of managerial time and mental effort to coping with a crisis lest business operations suffer and new entrepreneurial opportunities slip by. The solution adopted by Allied was to set up a separate management unit to deal with the Kepone affair and, according to the executives interviewed, this had worked well, not only as a means of conserving managerial resources for normal activities, but also as a way of responding to public criticism quickly and yet authoritatively. So, when Hooker Chemical sought the advice of Allied about what they should do to deaden the pain of Love Canal, a key piece of advice was that Hooker should set up a task force along the same lines.

Allied's overall sales increased substantially during the publicity over Kepone, the relevant turnover figures for the years 1975–1978 being $2,333, $2,630, $2,923 and $3,268 million. The absence of any discernible setback is hardly surprising, since Allied Chemical sells almost all of its products to other corporations, a marketplace governed more by economic considerations than by ethical preferences. Overall sales aside, what was the impact on sales of Kepone? Allied withdrew the product, but thereby incurred only a small loss because, even in the best year, Kepone sales had accounted for profits of only $600,000. However, account should be taken of loss of prospective earnings from Kepone. The demand for the pesticide in Europe and other foreign markets was growing, the demand was inelastic, and Allied enjoyed a monopolistic position.[28] Accordingly, Allied could well have enjoyed not only larger profits, but also greater opportunity to pass on at least some part of the Kepone fine by charging higher prices for the product.

It is much more difficult to assess the impact of adverse publicity upon the extent of civil liability. Many claims were made against Allied Chemical, resulting in a total pay-out of approximately $15 million (including a $5.25 million settlement with the Commonwealth of Virginia and the City of Hopewell).[29] It is impossible to say just how influential the Kepone publicity was in prompting these claims, but it helped to foment at least one suit by fishermen, seafood dealers, and others affected by the closure of the James River to fishing; the suit, eventually settled for $500,000, became a bandwagon.[30] Moreover, Allied representatives expressed the view that some claims had been settled more favorably to plaintiffs than might otherwise have been the case: The company wanted to settle quickly "to end the whole sordid chapter."

There were also miscellaneous costs. In-house research was conducted on methods of identifying and retrieving Kepone pollutants.[31] Many Virginian farmers came to Allied wanting blood tests to be done on their cows and other animals suspected of Kepone poisoning. Official agencies, including the EPA, asked the company to assist in the task of toxic-assessment. And numbers of private researchers clamored for assistance. It seems reasonable to assume that many of these requests would have been made and granted in any event: Allied Chemical possessed a unique laboratory capability with respect to Kepone. However, there is little doubt that the effect of adverse publicity was to stimulate requests for expert advice and virtually to guarantee their acceptance. No figure has been put upon these and other miscellaneous costs by Allied, but they were regarded by the officers with whom we spoke as "considerable."

Non-Financial Impacts

The non-financial impacts of the Kepone publicity were more important. The main non-financial impact was loss of corporate prestige, in the sense of corporate standing, over and above financial well-being. Allied Chemical, long recognized as a blue chip corporation, had been stigmatized as a polluter extra-ordinary. So it was that a survey in preparation for criminal trial revealed that most potential jurors in Virginia would be strongly prejudiced against the company. To add national insult to local infidelity, the *Smithsonian* magazine refused on moral grounds to accept Allied's institutional advertising.[32] As Richard C. Ashley, president of Allied's chemicals unit, later observed, the adverse publicity "knocked out any degree of respectability we had."[33]

Apart from loss of corporate prestige, many personnel felt that their individual reputation had been impugned. The typical reaction of outsiders at social gatherings, for example, was to say, "So you work for that mob." For the man at the top, John J. Connor, the fate was much harsher: Kepone blotted a distinguished career in government and business.[34]

Concern was also expressed about the working pressures generated by the Kepone publicity. Survival and getting through the day were said to be more of a problem than the financial impact. As one executive put it, "We were not sitting around biting our nails over the stock market, we were just worried about surviving." This impact of adverse publicity provided a further reason for setting up the special managerial task force mentioned earlier.

Another consequence was increased reluctance to proceed with environmentally risky ventures. Thus, having spent $25 million to develop air bags as crash-protection devices for motor vehicles, Allied Chemical retreated from further development, partly because the type of air bag likely to win bureaucratic and marketing approval would be pressurized by sodium azide, a toxic gas which could leak.[35]

A further non-financial impact was the additional effort needed to retain insurance at favorable rates. In the wake of the Kepone case, Allied's compliance programs were closely scrutinized by underwriters. Although there is no evidence that Allied suffered adverse ratings as a result of the Kepone publicity, it was subjected to more testing scrutiny than would otherwise have been the case; adverse publicity as extreme as that given to Kepone highlights risk so dramatically that insurers crave extra reassurance. Some indication of the pressure thereby generated was given by one Allied spokesman who recounted that his performance at an underwriters' inquisition had been described by one observer as "worthy of a Baptist minister."

Reforms

The uproar over Kepone led to a variety of reforms on the part of Allied Chemical. Federal and state legislative action also followed.

Spurred on by the adverse publicity over Kepone, Allied reappraised and substantially revised its environmental compliance program.[36] In the words of one EPA administrator, "the shock caused them to look around and tighten things up. They have accomplished that."[37]

An initial step was to upgrade the position of environmental affairs manager to the vice-presidential level. This was not an exercise in routine promotion, but a conscious, Kepone-induced move to place environmental compliance on the agenda of top management. As a result, more attention has been paid to the capacity of plant managers, who carry the day-to-day burden of compliance. Some have been replaced, Allied's comment being that "[Our] internal reviews are more rigorous than those of the Federal agencies. This thicket of regulations hits hard at the work place and you have to have people who are trainable to respond."[38]

An Energy and Environmental Policy Committee of the Board of Directors was also established. This committee is chaired by an outside director, whose position has been compared to that of a junior partner in a big law firm. The committee has a small task force and calls upon an outside consulting firm, Arthur D. Little, Inc., for assistance. The task force conducts on-site inspections of Allied's various plants and has direct access to the Board. The main intention behind this change is to ensure that there are no surprises at the top of the organization:[39] It should be remembered that Allied's Board denied any knowledge of Kepone prior to the revelations of poisoning of workers in the Life Science plant; indeed, even the environmental affairs manager reputedly had not heard of the product. According to John Funkhouser, an Arthur D. Little organization specialist, Allied's managerial coverage of safety standards has since more than doubled.[40]

We were shown examples of the reports made to the Board by the Energy and Environmental Policy Committee. These were not very detailed; they recorded only the broad nature of the problems which had arisen, together with a brief indication of the action taken. However, two points were stressed about these reports: First, the function of directors was to direct and that of managers to manage; the Board had to know that an effective compliance system was in place, a need which did not require that the Board be buried in paper. Second, the Energy and Environmental Policy Committee had an active role to perform in satisfying the Board, assisted by a well-qualified director of environmental surveillance. It was emphasized that "You can't insulate the Board by sending a non-knowledgeable person [to answer their questions]." The implication was that other companies avoid exposing their boards to environmental problems by interposing technically inexpert senior managers as filters between the board and top technical people.

A further important change has been the introduction of a Toxic Risk Assessment Committee, partly in response to the Toxic Substances Control Act of 1976, and partly in memory of Kepone. This committee is composed of a vice-president for medical affairs, a senior attorney, and a wide range of personnel from various relevant disciplines (e.g., toxicology). All operating plants must submit a monthly report indicating whether or not there has been an environmental risk situation in the plant during the previous month. If there has been a risk situation, the details must be set down on a special form. Moreover, all personnel, irrespective of rank, have an obligation to fill out a special pink sheet detailing any risk situation they believe to be substantial. A supervisor has no authority to stop pink sheets from going up the line to the toxic assessment officer, a person far removed from the subunit subject to inquiry; cover-up is thereby rendered difficult. The risk assessment official then refers the pink sheet to the Toxic Risk Assessment Committee or deals with it personally. Once an assessment is made, it is communicated back down the line. In practice this system is said to result in many unfounded complaints, but it was firm corporate policy that all complaints be received and answered, and that full documentation be kept on file. It was said that "You never destroy a complaint, no matter how frivolous or ridiculous."

In another move, Allied Chemical introduced an incentive scheme designed to motivate personnel to improve their efforts towards compliance. Executives are set non-financial as well as financial goals. Generally, a third of the bonuses of executives relates to environmental compliance, safety, antitrust, civil rights, and other non-fiscal goals.[41] The amount of the bonuses depends on the level of the executive (at the top, bonuses for financial and non-financial performance can be as high as the base salary). The bonus is quantified partly on the basis of objective criteria, namely incidence of violations and injuries and amount of financial loss from civil or criminal judgments and settlements (violations and losses are booked against the division responsible). More enterprisingly, account is also taken of self-perceived, self-set, non-financial goals. For example, inspection of 20 plants might be set as a goal for the year by a member of the environmental surveillance director's task force and feedback from other personnel then used to judge the success of those missions. This reflects the underlying advice from Arthur D. Little that:

> Environmental risk management is most effective when it is an integral part of the overall corporate business strategic planning and management processes. In this way, corporate resources for dealing with environmental issues can be appropriately allocated and managed in the context of corporate goals, objectives and values.[42]

Contrary to the conventional wisdom, Allied claimed that in practice quantifying performance under such an approach had not proven difficult.

The foregoing organizational reforms have been supported by a variety of reinforcing and monitoring devices. A manual, *Compliance with the Environmental Laws*, provides a readable and comprehensive summary of federal and state environmental laws governing Allied's operations. It also proclaims that every employee "is expected to adhere to the spirit as well as the letter" of the company policy to avoid unacceptable risks to human health or the environment, and to devise internal standards where existing regulation is inadequate; this proclamation is posted on bulletin boards in all plants.

These measures are complemented by a program of seminars, lectures, films, and workshops. Videotapes are used for in-house training to show personnel exactly to whom they should report suspected environmental problems and to highlight the legal and internal disciplinary implications of failing to make due report. For senior officials, business ethics seminars are often held (at Pleasantdale Farm, a company retreat); typically, these seminars revolve around a well-chosen case study; one example we sighted was the Kepone case under faint disguise.

As well as educative procedures, Allied also relies upon an environmental legal status report, which originated pre-Kepone in 1971. This provides a running account of where the company stands on environmental compliance, in much more detail than the standard reports that go to the Board from the Energy and Environmental Policy Committee; it is a managerial rather than a Directors' tool. Circulated regularly to a lengthy list of senior executives, the report is aimed at "bubbling up" potential as well as actual problems of compliance. Plants are commonly named and by implication criticized in this report, a practice said to be much feared because "people don't want their plants to be spotlighted negatively in a report that goes to top management."

But was anything done to guard against the risk of being associated with sloppy contractors of the kind exemplified by Life Science Products? Allied's response to this risk was to tighten up its procedures for outside contracts, one of several steps taken under a Product Responsibility Program designed to reduce the hazards of products during their development, manufacture, distribution and use. This precaution involves investigative review of supply contractors rather than supervision of their operations: To supervise the plant operations of a contractor like Life Science would be to attract the application of civil or criminal vicarious liability in the event of wrongdoing by that party, whereas a hands-off approach confined to careful selection and review attracts the protection of the general rule of non-liability for the conduct of independent contractors.[43]

Allied's environmental compliance program, as rebuilt in the wake of Kepone, has received widespread acclaim. Thus, Funkhouser of Arthur D. Little has advised us that "Independent of our work with Allied, I can affirm that I believe Allied Corporation has demonstrated leadership in the environmental management area, including environmental auditing. Their environmental review program is soundly based, well managed, and is serving a very useful function for the corporation."[44] A head of the EPA Enforcement Section regarded Allied as a leader in compliance programs, noting that the company had done a great deal to assist the EPA in formulating effluent standards and other regulations.[45] That opinion is shared by Allied's peers: Several companies have sought its advice and assistance.

Much more visibly, the steps taken by Allied Chemical to improve its environmental control capacity were the subject of a congratulatory article in the *New York Times*.[46] Soon thereafter, the same newspaper published this editorial tribute:

PRAISE FOR AN EXPOLLUTER

Only a few years ago, Allied Chemical Company was an industrial polluter of the public-be-damned type. One of its satellite companies that manufactured the pesticide Kepone turned out to have been unbelievably careless. It let workers become coated with hazardous dust that sickened them. Allied itself despoiled the Virginia countryside by illegally dumping the toxic chemical into a tributary of the James River. That forced health officials to ban fishing; dangerous residues may remain for decades. Ultimately, Allied was hit with one of the stiffest pollution fines ever levied. It had already paid out more than $15 million in fines, donations and claim payments, and a major class-

75

action suit is still pending. The damage to Allied's reputation was also serious.

But sinners can repent and old dogs learn new tricks; it is a pleasure to report that Allied seems to have been converted into an environmental good guy. As reported in *The Times'* business pages the other day, Allied has overhauled its safety and environmental programs. A high corporate officer is now in charge. Plant managers are rewarded for good safety records and replaced if they can't handle their new responsibilities. A committee of experts assesses the potential hazards of everything Allied produces; several risky products have been abandoned or delayed.

Federal regulators are delighted. The Environmental Protection Agency praises the caliber of Allied's new safety managers and the company's cooperative spirit. The agency even touts Allied's committee for risk assessment as a model for other companies. Allied's once dismal record of injury and illness is now far better than the industry average.

No one can guarantee that there won't be another major mishap. But Allied Chemical deserves recognition for an impressive corporate turnabout.[47]

There was also a turnabout legislatively. The federal Toxic Substances Control Act of 1976,[48] a pioneering statute which radically strengthened regulation of pesticides and other noxious materials, was very much force-fed on Kepone. As Thomas Bray observed in the *Wall Street Journal,*

The Kepone aftermath underlines in human and economic terms the destructive potential of many of the chemicals that find their way into the environment every year. The case also emphasizes the difficulty of dealing with the problem on an after-the-fact basis. For those reasons, the Kepone case gave added impetus to the drive for a Toxic Substances Control Act.[49]

At the state level, Virginia enacted tougher pollution laws conferring new enforcement powers, including the power to stage surprise checks at plants making toxic substances.[50]

In the end, however, it must be wondered whether the root cause of the Kepone crisis has been effectively treated. Most of the harms caused were occasioned by Life Science Products, a legally independent company but one linked symbiotically to Allied Chemical through a production contract. Because Life Science Products was too insubstantial a company to meet its civil and criminal liability in respect of Kepone, and because the connection between Allied Chemical and Life Science Products was so close, most of the blame settled upon Allied. Was this allocation of blame justified? Allied Chemical denied that it was, but its attempts to point the finger at Life Science Products were unconvincing because the independent legal status of Life Science Products seemed spurious. Until the law faces up to the problems of two-bit companies being used to conduct hazardous enterprises,[51] there may be many imitators of Life Science Products. Moreover, if the law fails to provide a clear and realistic allocation of responsibility betwen corporation and an "independent" contractor, the risk of scapegoating one or the other is aggravated.

CHAPTER 7

Coke and Cancer at BHP

The Workers Rebel

BHP (Broken Hill Proprietary Company Limited) is Australia's largest corporation and one of the world's top 100. In addition to extensive oil and mineral investments, BHP totally monopolizes the manufacture of steel in Australia. BHP's largest steelworks are at Port Kembla on Australia's east coast. The steelworks are run by BHP's Australian Iron and Steel subsidiary (AIS). Carcinogenic emissions from coke ovens at Port Kembla were the subject of an extraordinary series of industrial disputes between 1979 and 1981. Local unions (the Federal Ironworkers and Amalgamated Metalworkers and Shipwrights) accused BHP of putting profits ahead of the safety of its coke oven workers through intolerable levels of emissions of dangerous gases.

A crucial stage in steelmaking is the conversion of coal to coke of sufficient quality to charge the blast furnaces. Coke is made by cooking coal in batteries of ovens arranged in rows. At Port Kembla there are five batteries, each with between 66 and 101 ovens. Many of the gases driven out of the coal by the coking process are captured and sold as by-products. However, some of these gases also escape from the doors at the side of the huge ovens or from the lids on top. The emissions are a complex mixture of small particles, vapor, and gases. They include such gases as carbon monoxide, hydrogen sulphide, benzene, and hydrogen cyanide, as well as other carcinogens such as benezopyrene and coal tar. There is voluminous evidence from North America, Europe, and Japan indicating an association between the products from the carbonization of coal and cancers of the skin,[1] lungs,[2] and bladder.[3] After reviewing this evidence, the U.S. Occupational Safety and Health

Administration (OSHA) described the support for the conclusion that coke oven emissions are carcinogenic as "overwhelming."[4]

In mid-1977, the unions representing Port Kembla workers became concerned about the health risks their members working at the coke ovens were facing. On August 30, 1977, the New South Wales Labor Council requested a conference with BHP to discuss the issue. Following that meeting, the company reported back to the Labor Council on November 30, 1977, with plans to improve the situation. But by 1978 it was the local Port Kembla branches of the unions that were running the campaign. After being sent OSHA material on coke ovens by the United Steelworkers of America and the International Metalworkers Federation, they wrote to BHP asking to be informed whether the company accepted the standards laid down in the OSHA regulations, and if it did not, the reason why not. A campaign began for the application to BHP of the OSHA prohibition against exposing workers not wearing protective equipment to coke oven emissions of benzene-soluble particulate in excess of 0.15 milligrams per cubic meter of air. The company openly admits emission levels that reach more than six times the OSHA maximum.[5] In fact, company records for 1980 revealed emission concentrations at the worst locations of over 100 times the OSHA standards.[6] There is no New South Wales or national legislation mandating a legal limit to coke oven emissions. The Australian National Health and Medical Research Council promulgated a voluntary standard of 0.2 milligrams of benzene-soluble particulate per cubic meter. BHP's Port Kembla ovens, in addition to its ovens at Newcastle and Whyalla, are routinely in excess of this voluntary standard. A central plank in the union's campaign was to persuade the New South Wales government to enact legally enforceable limits on the emissions.

Many more specific reforms were also sought. These included:

(a) Air-conditioning and air-filtration of the cars which travel up and down the ovens filling them with coal and pushing the coke out once it has been cooked.

(b) The employment of additional lidsmen to work on top of the ovens. The lidsmen are responsible for sealing the lids with clay to cut down the escape of fumes. With more lidsmen, a better sealing job could be done, and it would be possible to give existing lidsmen more time in air-conditioned rest rooms to recuperate from the hellish heat and fumes.

(c) The installation of the air-conditioned rest rooms and the introduction of the relief time mentioned in (b).

   (d) Annual medical examinations paid for by the company with the results to be made available in writing to the workers.

   (e) Provision by the company of lockers and laundering for workers' clothes so that there would be no necessity to take these home. There is evidence that such carcinogens carried home in workers' clothes pose a potential threat to their families.[7]

   (f) Washing time prior to breaks to allow workers to clean carcinogens from their hands prior to eating food.

   (g) Worker education and training on the dangers of coke oven emissions.

Steve Quinn, of the Amalgamated Metalworkers and Shipwrights Union, described the attitude of BHP management to the initial 1977 campaign as "intransigent."[8] The company response was said to be "Don't get things emotional and the workers stirred up." The unions turned to their elected representatives for help. A government backbencher, George Petersen, castigated BHP in the New South Wales parliament, and as a result the government sent a team from the Health Commission to report on conditions at Port Kembla.

An inspection led by Dr. W. Crawford of the Health Commission took place on December 19, 1979. The team concluded that emission levels "exceed the National Health and Medical Research standards in nearly all the assays undertaken by the company" and that "the employees are at a considerable risk to health by the physically and chemically hostile environment in which they must work." A variety of reforms was recommended, including the employment of addition lidsmen, the provision of lockers and industrial laundering for the work clothes of oven employees, and a speeding up of engineering improvements to reduce the emissions.

Four months after the inspection, the contents of the report were revealed to the company. Between the receipt of the report in April 1980 and September of that year the company introduced no changes in response to the recommendations of the report. By September, the unions were wondering why they had heard nothing about the results of the Health Commission inspection. When they were told that the government had informed the company of the contents of the report five months earlier, but not the unions, the 1,000 coke oven workers went on strike for four days.

The government responded by setting up another working party to determine the action necessary to implement the Crawford Report. This was an interdepartmental working party with officers from the Departments of Industrial Relations and of Health. An inspection took place on September 15 and 16, 1980. The resulting report adopted a softer line than the earlier report on the rate at which leaking oven doors would have to be replaced, although there were other respects in which tougher recommendations were made. The Minister for Industrial Relations requested the company to act on the recommendations.

The company, among other reforms, had already agreed to provide lockers and industrial laundering for workers employed on the ovens, and these reforms were implemented. This did not satisfy the unions; they wanted the same benefits to apply to workers in the vicinity of the coke ovens—mainly in the coal washery (which washes the coal prior to its being fed into the ovens) and in the by-products plant (which processes the gases extracted from the ovens). At the request of the unions, Dr. Crawford was brought in for another inspection to ascertain whether his recommendations with respect to workers on the ovens should also apply to those around the ovens. In this report, Dr. Crawford exacerbated the dispute with the ambiguous conclusion that extending the same recommendations to the 320 by-products and associated workers would be "desirable" but not "essential." Bitter dispute between management and employees as to whether these workers should get the same benefits as those on the ovens continued until the entire coke plant work force struck on May 15, 1981, and stayed out until May 28. On November 26, the Industrial Commission of New South Wales decided in favor of the company that laundering and locker benefits not be extended beyond workers actually on the ovens.[9]

Publicity and Counterpublicity

Throughout the 1979–1981 period, the coke ovens saga was reported on many occasions on the front page of the local Port Kembla newspaper, the *Illawarra Mercury*. The Sydney and national press also devoted more limited attention to the problem. Some of the headlines seemed to be damaging for BHP: e.g., "BHP MEN IN CANCER PERIL AFTER GOVT ERROR";[10] "CANCER KILLING COKE WORKERS."[11] One front-page story was headlined "AIS CANCER RISK COVER-UP CLAIM."[12] This reported statements in the New South Wales parliament by George Petersen that the company had settled two coke oven compensation cases out of court so that there would be no evidence on which to establish a precedent for future claims. BHP issued a press release denying that this was its motivation in settling the cases. But as in some of the other case studies in this book, allegations of cover-up can draw stronger fire than the material concerning the offense itself. The worst publicity came in union journals. *The Metal Worker* (circulation 640,000), for example, headed one story: "DEATH ON THE COKE OVENS—BHP STYLE: KEMBLA CHALKS UP 13 KNOWN CANCER DEATHS."[13]

Contrary to the complaints made to us by BHP management, not all the press coverage was negative. There were a number of articles giving the company's side of the story: e.g., "BHP DEFENDS HEALTH AND SAFETY PROGRAM";[14] "COMPANY REFUTES CANCER CLAIMS: AI&S DEFENDS HEALTH POLICY."[15] The Health Minister was reported as saying that the coke oven workers were "being well looked after" by BHP in a story headed "BHP TREATS MEN WELL."[16] In addition, there have been a variety of newspaper articles lauding safety improvements made to the coke ovens: e.g., "AI&S ACTS ON CANCER REPORT,"[17] "AIS TELLS OF PLANT IMPROVEMENT."[18] However, none of these were front-page stories.

The industrial confrontation aspects of the problem generated much of the media coverage. For example, when Dr. Crawford and his team inspected the ovens on December 17, 1979, the company was at first not agreeable to union representatives accompanying him on the inspection. In response, a stop-work meeting was held and a television crew from Channel 10 in Sydney arrived to film the action. The company backed down and gave permission for union representation during the inspection. However, Channel 10 was refused permission to enter the steelworks itself and was forced to film from outside the gates.

Adverse publicity over the occupational health problem led to a limited amount of snowballing into publicity over related issues. The main example was pollution from the ovens drifting into the suburbs of Port Kembla and Wollongong. Steve Quinn, the union leader, believed that the company "likes to give the image that they are good for Wollongong." So, when Nationwide Television took their cameras to the plant in the early hours of the morning to film the fumes emitted at that time, the company was not pleased. Coke oven workers had long alleged that when the company falls behind with its production targets, it is the night and early morning shifts that are required to cook "green ovens"—coke which emits excessive green fumes because it has not been cooked for long enough. At 2 a.m. there is less risk of billowing fumes alarming members of the public (or government inspectors). The company categorically denies these allegations and in its defense showed us a memorandum of February 19, 1979 from the General Superintendent to battery foremen instructing that:

1. No oven is to be pushed unless it is coked (no matter what the coking time).
2. No oven is to be pushed under minimum coking time.

Another related risk which was the subject of some adverse publicity in the *Illawarra Mercury* and in a speech to the State Parliament by Petersen was that "Escaping fumes from the vats of by-product liquid materials cause sleepiness and watering of the eyes of operators."[19]

BHP did not run a counterpublicity campaign. It was averse to "feeding the hand that bit us" by paying for advertisements explaining its position in the press. However, when we visited Port Kembla, M.J. Burns, the Manager, Coke and Sinter, could not meet us because he was taking a course at the head office in Melbourne on handling media appearances and public relations.

Financial Impacts

The financial consequences of the emissions struggle for BHP were minor. Neither objectively nor subjectively in the minds of management could the problem be viewed as having any impact whatsoever on BHP share prices. From late 1980 to mid-1981, when the struggle reached its climax with the plant-wide strike, BHP shares were trading at three times their 1978 prices. The period was one of a consistent climb in BHP share values.

Since BHP is a monopolist in Australian steel, there was little chance of reduced production resulting in competitors seizing a slice of the market. It is doubtful if there was any diminution in ultimate steel production as a result of the strikes by the coke oven workers.[20] Coke is stockpiled, and at no point was the stockpile expended. During the strikes, the ovens, run by the supervisory and management staff, continued to operate at about 70 per cent capacity. (Coke ovens cannot be shut down because their life will be reduced if their temperature is not kept at about 1,000 degrees Centigrade). Undoubtedly, however, the disruptions to other working functions by pulling people out of their normal responsibilities had certain costs in inefficiency and aggravation of management problems.

The total capital costs of improvements, from new oven doors to lockers for workers' clothes, could reach a total of US$6 million. However, as we will see in the section on reform, many of these monies might eventually have been spent without the extra impetus of the union campaign,[21] and publicity was only a small part of that impetus. Another cost was in the double handling of coal during the strikes. Instead of coal being dropped straight into bins on railway tracks at the pit-head ready to be transported to the ovens, it had to be trucked elsewhere and picked up after the strike. Finally, it is possible that the publicity and antagonism aroused by the campaign may well provoke some victims of coke oven emissions into damages litigation against the company. According to the unions, there have been 13 cases where BHP has settled out of court for payments, running up to US$30,000, to the families of deceased coke oven workers.

Whatever the total costs, they will not loom large when compared with BHP's US$5 billion in annual sales. Moreover, BHP in the past has usually managed to employ its monopoly status to pass on to consumers whatever extraordinary costs it incurs in its steel operations, although in recent times Australian protectionism has not been sufficient, given the world steel glut, to shield BHP from growing import competition.

Non-Financial Impacts

The adverse publicity to which the company had been subjected was certainly cause for considerable dejection and concern over loss of corporate prestige among the executives with whom we spoke. Because of some hostile coverage, primarily in the *Illawarra Mercury*, the company's repute in Port Kembla and Wollongong undoubtedly suffered as a result of the affair. However, individual executives were not singled out as villains in this press coverage. Consequently, our senior informants did not report loss of personal prestige to match the damage to corporate prestige. Employee morale was also reported as having suffered. One executive expressed concern that wives who had been washing their husbands' work clothes for years were now being told that by doing this they had been putting their families at risk of cancer. Hence, there was a belief that the morale of the work force was also being debilitated through family involvement in the issue.

Another adverse consequence of the affair for the company, although this could not be attributed to the bad publicity, was a deterioration of already poor industrial relations. On May 13, 1981, when the workers started work late because of a gate meeting to consider the company's replies to a number of claims on cancer and emissions, they were forbidden their normal morning tea break, docked an hour's pay, and, according to the unions (although denied by the company), told to handle the same number of ovens they would push in a full eight-hour shift. It was this kind of event which badly soured industrial relations at the plant.

Avoidance of publicity was a consideration in many important management decisions. For example, after being told that the National Health and Medical Research Council standard for coke ovens was unrealistic, we asked why management had not complained to the Council with a view to setting a "realistic" standard. We were told that appeals against medical judgments on the grounds of "practical considerations" would only result in public attacks on the company for putting dollars ahead of lives.

Reforms

Numerous technological and other emission-control measures were introduced during 1977–1981. Machine-operated door and frame cleaners have replaced manual cleaning on all batteries, thereby eliminating one of the jobs with the highest exposure. Fifty additional workers have been engaged as door adjusters and for sealing the lids on top of the ovens. Water seals have been introduced on the standpipes which take gases to the by-products section. There has been extensive machining of oven lids to improve their seal. Stage one of the program, which involved the installation of air-conditioning and air filtration equipment on charger cars (which move up and down the battery dropping coal into ovens) and establishment of air-conditioned and air-filtered oven-top rest cabins was completed in mid-1979. However, the government inspection of September 15–16, 1980 found that the air–filtering systems on two of the charger cars were not functioning properly. The cabins of the rams which push out the red hot coke still have to be air-conditioned, although testing of suitable equipment is under way. A new videotape has been made to explain the dangers of coke ovens and means of minimizing risk to employees. Workers are now given five minutes' washing time before tea and meal breaks.

The most important engineering improvement will be the replacement of the existing leaking doors with a new Japanese spring–loaded self-adjusting model. There are over 700 doors on the ovens. Dr. Crawford erroneously concluded in the report of his December 1979 inspection that "New oven doors are being installed at a rate of 10 per week." Moreover, the report concluded that this rate of replacement was not fast enough. In fact, as of May 26, 1981, only 13 doors had been replaced. The company has no intention of replacing the doors on two of the five batteries. On one of these, the investment is not regarded as justifiable because the battery is to be closed down in two years. On the other, the ovens are so warped that fitting new doors is not regarded as feasible, given that the cost could reach US$50 million.

The unions' view is that the reforms have not gone far enough fast enough. However, considerable amounts of money have been expended on a variety of measures. There have been a number of technological repairs and other changes mentioned above. When they are all catalogued in the company's public relations handout, they appear to be an impressive list of improvements. They are not trivial reforms. However, the question remains whether emission levels have measurably improved.

Only two sets of figures for emissions are publicly available, one for 1978–1979 and another for September 1980. These figures were the subject of some discussion before the Industrial Commission of New South Wales on June 4, 1981. As Bauer J. pointed out at the hearing, the two sets of figures indicated that, if anything, emission levels had worsened.[22] There was certainly no evidence of an improvement up to September 1980. When we visited the company in 1981, we asked whether it had any data suggesting an improvement since 1978. We were informed that it did not. We were then told that if one looked at the whole decade to take in the total program of upgrading, improvement would definitely be evident.[23] When we asked for evidence from systematic recording of emission levels throughout the period to substantiate this, we were informed that no such data existed.

It is likely that, when the door replacement program is completed, significant improvements will be demonstrable. However, the ameliorative reforms that have been introduced since 1977 do not seem to have measurably improved the situation. BHP has stopped short of the drastic action which would be needed to create a low-risk environment at the Port Kembla coke ovens. The oldest and least productively efficient battery, No. 1, is due to be closed down and replaced by a new oven in the near future. However, the unions argue that it is the second oldest battery, No. 3, which should be shut down because its design results in excessive emissions. The structural defects of No. 3, it is claimed, cause it to emit more dangerous fumes than No. 1. But management has opted for closing the least efficient battery rather than the most dangerous one.

Little of the credit for the reforms which have been introduced by BHP can be given to the New South Wales Government. Witness the fact that no new initiatives were introduced between the communication of Dr. Crawford's report to the company in April 1980 and its discovery by the union in September. Things started to happen when the unions flexed their industrial and political muscle.

For the same reason, not much of the credit for the reform can be attributed to adverse publicity. While the publicity undoubtedly helped the workers in their cause, the change in the pace of reform was primarily attributable to industrial agitation. Two managers with whom we spoke, while adamant about the unions' not forcing them to do anything they would not eventually have done of their own initiative, expressed the view that the industrial threats, backed by adverse publicity, had quickened the progress of reform. In responding to our draft, however, the company rejected any interpretation that it has been forced into more rapid reform by the use or threatened use of the strike weapon. Its position was that reform should be interpreted in terms of a self-motivated corporate desire to improve health on the job.

In this case, in summary, adverse publicity played a relatively minor role in ushering in relatively minor reforms of company practices. Perhaps more significant was the part that adverse publicity played in jolting governmental authorities into action. In 1979, Dr. Crawford of the Health Commission was quoted as saying that the Port Kembla coke ovens had a good pollution monitoring and filtering system.[24] By June 4, 1981, in giving evidence before the Industrial Commission, Dr. Crawford could be heard to describe emissions from the same ovens as "dangerously high" and "frightful."[25] In fact, Bauer J., in his Industrial Commission judgment, found that a previously lax approach of the government to monitoring coke oven emissions had now been replaced by a new, appropriate level of concern:

Whilst it might reasonably be said that there was a long delay in the commencement of detailed inspections and formation of recommendations after the responsible departments had been or ought to have been seised (sic) of the seriousness of the problems of industrial exposure to coke oven emissions and other industrial substances, the present position appears to be that the problems are being treated by these departments in a manner commensurate with the risks.

Furthermore, whilst disquiet might also reasonably be expressed at the delay in implementing the overall programme, the commendable vigilance of the unions will no doubt ensure that the departments continue their supervision of the amelioration of the problems. . . .[26]

Notwithstanding this improvement, the New South Wales Division of Occupational Health has pointed out that its staff resources are still insufficient to conduct a comprehensive survey of emission levels at the Port Kembla ovens.

Recently, the Australian House of Representatives Standing Committee on Environment and Conservation has strongly criticized both BHP and the health authorities for the tardiness of their responses to the coke-and-cancer problem at Port Kembla.[27] Unless the scandal is more vehemently pursued in the media, however, this latest admonition seems destined to fall upon deaf ears.

CHAPTER 8

BHP—The Appin Mine Disaster

The Explosion

On July 24, 1979, there was an explosion of methane gas from combustion of coal dust at the Appin Colliery near Sydney, Australia. Fourteen men died. Coal from Appin is used to fuel the coke ovens at Port Kembla, the subject of the last case study. The mine is owned by BHP through its Australian Iron and Steel subsidiary.

Two comprehensive inquiries were held into the disaster—the first by the Court of Coal Mines Regulation under Judge A.J. Goran,[1] the second by the Coroner, J. Hiatt.[2] Both inquiries attributed the explosion to inadequacies in the mine's ventilation system, which had permitted a dangerous buildup of methane gas. The primary source of ventilation at Appin was an exhaust fan which drew air out of the mine's tunnels. Clean air enters by an intake tunnel and is directed through the maze of mine workings by barriers located at strategic tunnel intersections until it is drawn out of the mine by the exhaust fan. As extensions are driven further into the coal seam, dead-end tunnels are created until such time as connecting tunnels are hewn. It was in such a dead end that the explosion occurred. Dead ends pose the most difficult problems of ventilation, since fresh air cannot simply be forced through them. Auxiliary fans are used in these areas to supplement the main exhaust fan by pulling air from the work face.

During the shift before the explosion, a changeover in the ventilation system was to have taken place. By erecting new barriers at certain locations (in some places plastic partitioning, or brattice, and in others, solid walls), the airflow was to be reversed near the coal face concerned. This ventilation changeover was carried out by persons who did not fully understand the implications of what was being done and who consequently did not implement it as they should have. Most important, one brattice from the old ventilation system was not pulled down as soon as it should have been and may not have been pulled down at all. Without the removal of this brattice, the air flow needed under the new system was blocked.

Deputy Schuster, whose job it was to remove the critical brattice during the pre-explosion shift, did not do so because he ran out of time before the end of the shift. At both inquiries Schuster was subjected to considerable questioning about why he had left the mine without completing the changeover when pulling down the brattice would have taken only three to four minutes. At one stage he said: "Subconsciously, of course I did not want to miss the transport. If you are not there, bad luck for you, mate." Both Judge Goran and Coroner Hiatt partially excused Schuster's neglect on the grounds that the implications of his duties had not been adequately explained to him. Judge Goran: "It is difficult to avoid the conclusion that at the time Schuster knew very little about the method of changing over the ventilation. He was told to do specific things which brought it about. He was not told the theory behind it, simple though it was."[3]

Schuster claims that he informed the Deputy on the incoming shift, Rawcliffe, that the brattice had yet to be removed. However, both inquiries found Schuster to be an unreliable witness, and it seems quite likely that he was lying in order to pass the full blame for the disaster onto the deceased Rawcliffe. There is no way of knowing whether Rawcliffe discovered the brattice during the change of shift and before the explosion.

Apart from the question of this brattice, there were other important deficiencies in the way the ventilation changeover was implemented. A new brattice was stapled onto the wrong side of the supports holding it. Another brattice was loose as a result of a flap being raised to drive a shuttle car and other traffic through it. A solid "overcast" was incomplete and leaking—holes in it being filled with brattice instead of mortar. The devastation following the explosion made it impossible to assess the relative contributions, if any, of these various ventilation system deficiencies to the methane accumulation.

Once a high concentration of methane has built up in a mine, the second necessary element for an explosion is an ignition source. The most likely source at Appin was the spark emitted when an auxiliary fan was turned on. A defective fan was worked on by an electrician during the shift in which the explosion occurred. The electrician switched off the fan and opened the flameproof metal box which encloses the wiring. After rectifying the trouble, he apparently checked his work by running the fan. But rather than tighten all 24 bolts necessary to secure the flameproof box over the wiring, he merely closed the door, inserted one bolt and gave it two turns. The spark from the test start or stop of the fan was the probable source of the ignition.

By switching on a fan not in a flameproof condition, the electrician, who was killed by the explosion, clearly violated the New South Wales Coal Mines Regulation Act. The deceased Deputy Rawcliffe also violated the Act, as both inquiries concluded that Rawcliffe was present when the electrician did the testing and must have condoned the offense. As Coroner Hiatt concluded:

> No matter what else happened it is indisputable that Deputy Rawcliffe was in charge when a flame-proofed enclosure was opened with power on and in a gassy place. The evidence reveals this to be a breach and of course there is no reason why other breaches would not occur such as failure to comply with the General Rules as to inspection for gas.[4]

However, the Coroner was unwilling to conclude, as was Judge Goran, that it was a spark from the fan which ignited the explosion. This was because Coroner Hiatt felt unable on the evidence to eliminate another possible source of ignition—Deputy Rawcliffe's lamp. While the Coroner concluded that lamps at Appin were generally well maintained, investigations revealed 19 defective lamps to be in service at the colliery.[5] Rawcliffe's lamp had a double flint, which was in contravention of the regulations.[6]

Other violations of the Act were revealed in the course of the inquiries. One related to circumventing safeguards built into the continuous mechanical miners which actually win the coal. Gas-monitoring devices are attached to these miners; they automatically switch the machine off when gas concentrations reach dangerous levels (2%). It was common practice for these devices to be set into "defeat," by-passing the cut-off switch, so that mining could continue without the interruptions arising from the machine "tripping out." The evidence at the inquest showed that on the day of the explosion a continuous miner was operated in "defeat" for a considerable period of time.[7] Moreover, despite the machine being in "defeat," the required half-hourly checks of gas concentrations at the face were not always done on the day of the explosion.[8] However, this placement of machines into "defeat" was not found to have occasioned the explosion.

Further serious violations of the Coal Mines Regulation Act arose from a lax attitude toward continuing work while methane concentrations forbidden by the Act prevailed in intake airways. It was commonplace to continue production in the presence of methane concentrations in intake airways of more than twice the percentage proscribed by the Act. Judge Goran did not conclude that this resulted in coal being cut in the presence of high concentrations of gas at the face, since illegal concentrations in the intakes do not necessarily build up to dangerous levels at the face. However, the Judge was critical of the attitude that the law could be ignored when those involved felt it was safe to do so.

> What in fact was allowed to happen was the growth of a philosophical attitude towards methane as a fact of life. It was a nusiance, it could hold up production in working places, but it was not a matter of great concern in standing places where the possibility of ignition was remote. The officials had their own view of when methane gas was permissible. It differed from the standard of the Act.[9]

Even more disturbing was the fact that Mines Department inspectors were aware of these violations and allowed them to continue. Government inspectors testified that Appin and perhaps four other gassy collieries in New South Wales could have been forced to close had they enforced strict adherence to the statutory limits.[10] The Appin Colliery Manager, Fisher, testified that he felt the inspectors allowed them to violate the Act because "We were doing everything within our power" and "as far as reasonably practical" toward ameliorating the dangers.[11]

The official view of the union, the Miners' Federation, was that management was not doing everything possible. However, employees at Appin must be criticized for tolerating a situation where they were frequently being asked to enter work sites with methane concentrations beyond the legal limit. The rejoinder which the District President of the Miners' Federation presented to us in defense of his members was that the workers find themselves in a situation in which they have an incentive to work in dangerous conditions. Miners are paid bonuses according to the tonnage of coal produced by the whole mine each week. Appin miners could earn up to US$40,000 a year under this system, and deputies considerably more. In many of the most productive weeks of the year, Appin miners earn about as much from bonuses as they do in base pay. Consequently, employees can be as loath as management to slow down production until safety problems are rectified.

In addition to tolerance of violations of the Act, Judge Goran found a lax approach to the reporting and recording of potential dangers: "[Management] believed it could ignore a categorical General Rule of the Act which dealt specifically not only with the safety of inflammable gas in a part of the mine, but with the reporting of it."[12]

Tolerance of illegality and sloppy reporting of dangers were compounded by a third problem—poor communications. If everyone concerned had fully understood what was going on in the ventilation changeover, the disaster might not have occurred. Judge Goran summarized the situation neatly. On management's side, "There is always a tendency for those who issue instructions to believe that those who obey them are in as good a position as themselves in understanding the instructions."[13] On the side of those who received the instructions, "They were also victims of their own belief that they understood—either that or they were too proud to ask questions and so betray their lack of knowledge."[14]

The Miners' Federation believed that both the company and a number of its officers should have been prosecuted for the violations of law surrounding the disaster. Both Judge Goran and the Coroner conceded that such violations under the Act had occurred, but because a causal link between specific offenses and the 14 deaths could not be proved, neither was willing to recommend prosecution.[15] For example, if ignition was by the fan, then here was one specific violation of law which was a direct cause. If ignition was by the lamp, then another specific violation was a direct cause. Since these were the only two possible sources, one violation of law or another was a direct cause. However, at least according to the Coroner, there was no way of establishing which one of the two was the culprit.[16] Another factor disposing both the Judge and Coroner against a recommendation for prosecution may have been that so many of the deviations from the standards of the Act took place with the knowledge and tacit approval of the government.

Publicity and Counterpublicity

An interesting feature of Judge Goran's report is that bouquets as well as brickbats were dispensed. Several mine managers (namely Matcalfe, Strong and Viljacik) were singled out for praise for their organization of the rescue effort.[17] Extraordinary praise was also conferred on Deputy Wilmott in Judge Goran's report:

His actions showed cool resourcefulness and calm courage in a situation of high danger. His care for his men and his leadership demonstrate the high level of dedication which marks a good deputy. I might add that as a witness of intelligence and truth he set an example that some others might well follow. I have made these remarks because of my belief that Mr. Wilmott's conduct and character should be acknowledged publicly.[18]

But the bad publicity outweighed the good. Because the Coroner's inquiry did not begin until Judge Goran's was completed, the media were fed negative copy from the testimony of a string of witnesses for the best part of a year. The judicial inquiry attracted much more publicity than the later inquest. During most days of inquest hearings only a journalist from the *Illawarra Mercury* was present. The most damaging publicity came from two separate exposés on the nationally syndicated Australian television program, "60 Minutes." One of these dramatically personalized the disaster when the widow of a killed miner complained that company witnesses had suppressed the truth of corporate negligence before Judge Goran's inquiry. BHP was the sponsor of "60 Minutes" and its executives expressed some annoyance to us that they had so little influence over the program's content. In fairness to BHP, it should be pointed out that the widow did not make such allegations at the inquest.

BHP did not run a significant counterpublicity campaign. This was undoubtedly a wise decision, since most people outside the local area probably did not even identify the corporate giant as the owner of the Appin Colliery. On the day of the disaster, the public relations officer from the Port Kembla steelworks was sent to the pit to handle the press. The company also made a US$118,000 donation to an appeal for the victims' families run by the *Illawarra Mercury*. The company rejects any suggestion that the decision to donate this money was made partially with an eye to the possibility of good publicity. Nevertheless, the donation did result in a favorable front-age banner in the *Illawarra Mercury*, "AIS GIVES $100,000 TO APPEAL."

Financial Impacts

We do not know the sums involved in out-of-court settlements of damages claims against the company by the families of victims. However, the total probably did not exceed $3 or $4 million. The mine was completely shut down for six weeks after the disaster. However, worse loss of output was yet to come. Production was only resumed for a short time, until the existing longwall was worked out; it was impossible to go on to the next longwall without disturbing the section of the mine that was the subject of the judicial inquiry. Production was effectively shut down for 12 months. While this would have been a significant financial setback for a smaller company, it was not important enough to affect BHP share prices in the slightest. For the 18 months following the disaster, BHP share prices showed a constant upwards movement, almost doubling in value until the market-wide discounting of late 1981 took its toll.

To the extent that there were significant financial impacts on the company, none of these could be attributed to the adverse publicity. Adverse publicity certainly did not keep the mine shut down any longer than would have occurred in its absence. No customers could be lost since all sales of Appin coal were intra-company, to the Port Kembla steelworks.

Ultimately, there may be a reverse twist in the financial impact of the disaster. The reader will recall that Mines Department inspectors were reluctant prior to the disaster to enforce the letter of the law lest this make it impossible for the mine to operate. Prior to the disaster, the Mines Department had urged the company to experiment with methane drainage before expanding the mine further. Methane drainage is a technology of drilling holes into the coal (either down from the surface or directly into the coal face from the underground tunnels) from which the gas is extracted prior to mining. In response to union demands that BHP turn its innovative skills to safety as well as production, the government became insistent after the disaster that new mine sections could not be opened up without provision for methane drainage.[19]

Methane, of course, is a marketable commodity. Lo and behold, what should we find on opening our newsaper of June 27, 1981 but a front-page banner reading "BIG SOUTH COAST GAS FIND." The story in the *Weekend Australian* opens:

A big discovery of methane gas with the potential to become an alternative NSW power source and to lift the strain off the Snowy Mountains hydro-electric scheme has been found in sedimentary basins around Sydney.

95

The find, on coal areas owned by BHP in the Wollongong area, is being investigated by the Sydney gas supplier, the Australian Gas Light Co. Ltd., in association with the international oil producer, Occidental.

Now it may be that the initial fanfare of publicity for these methane discoveries resulting from the drainage program was greatly exaggerated. Only time will tell. And certainly the technology of methane drainage from coal seams, even in countries such as Japan that have been working on it for a number of years, is still relatively undeveloped. Yet it is a sad irony that an enforcement of strict statutory standards which was eschewed because it might shut a mine down can now be seen as a prospective source of profits. The gases which cost 14 lives before they were brought within publicly acceptable limits might now be harnessed for private gain. It does raise the question of whether government regulators should take with a grain of salt industry claims that law observance will bring financial ruin.

Non-Financial Impacts

It is doubtful whether BHP's corporate prestige suffered in any notable way as a result of the disaster. The authors have yet to meet anyone living outside the Illawarra region who recognized BHP as the owner of the mine. In any case, most, although not all, of the adverse media coverage pointed the finger of suspicion at individual mine officials rather than drawing attention to any element of corporate fault. The weight of press coverage was bound up with regret and sympathy for the personal tragedies of the victims and their families rather than with attributions of blame.

For individual miners and mine officials, the days in the witness box under cross-examination were days of anguish. However, only one of the 370 Appin mine employees resigned because of the disaster. Nevertheless, management did notice some drop in morale among the miners following the incident. For a time after the disaster there was naturally a feeling, "Is it going to happen to me some day?" However, neither management nor the miners with whom we spoke attributed this short-term drop in morale to the adverse publicity. It was the tangible reality of death in the mines which disturbed them, not the newspaper stories.

Reforms

Management at the Appin mine and at AIS Collieries headquarters in Wollongong provided us with very little evidence of reform since the disaster. Moreover, events since the disaster have hardly been reassuring. While Judge Goran's inquiry was still running, on October 1, 1979, there was an incident at the mine which ultimately led to the prosecution and acquittal of an assistant electrical engineer. Power to a 415-volt transformer had been switched on in the mine without authorization and before gas checks had been completed. The District President of the Miners' Federation, Les Ohlsen, felt that the attitude towards safety violations had not changed among many of the management people at the mine. On one occasion since the disaster, Ohlsen had personally observed excessive gas in an area of the Appin mine during a visit on union business. When he questioned an under-manager about the deputy's report that the area was clear of gas, it transpired that the deputy had written his report without going into the area. He had only proceeded as far as the crib room (where the miners relax during their breaks) in testing for gas.

Then, in June 1981, the company faced an embarassing 48-hour strike over what the miners saw as a lack of concern for safety by management. The episode began when an auxiliary fan broke down. The regulations require auxiliary fans to incorporate a cut-out device, so that a failure of the fan results in power being cut off to the machinery at the coal face. On this occasion the fan stopped, but power continued to flow to the mining machinery. Angry miners demanded an investigation into why they had been exposed to working at an unventilated coal face. It was discovered that at some unknown time in the past a diode had been placed in the fan in a position which prevented the automatic cut-out from working. Because de-activating the cut-out would eliminate a frequent source of interruption to work, some of the miners accused management of inserting the diode to increase production. However, a much more likely explanation is that an electrician, after working on the transformer, negligently forgot to remove the diode which he had used in testing the mechanism. The investigation failed to pin-point such a culprit.

Irrespective of the cause, the Miners' Federation point out that a simple standard operating procedure could ensure that such an incident would not recur. Prior to any work shift beginning in a gassy area, the fan could be turned on and off to check that the cut-out to the mining machines worked—a two-minute operation.

Mine management admitted that this "could and probably should" be done, but that because the Mines Department did not require it in the regulations, it was only done in special circumstances.

BHP has an institutionalized system of private enforcement of internal discipline in its mines. It is common for miners to be fined $10 to $20 for violations of all manner of company rules. No one was fined as a result of the Appin disaster; the company decided to leave recommendations for sanctions in the hands of the judicial and coroner's inquiries.

One reform which did occur even before Judge Goran's inquiry was completed was the issuing of methanometers to all mine deputies. Previously only under-managers were in a position to measure methane concentrations accurately with methanometers; deputies relied on the much cruder indication provided by oil-flame safety lamps. Quality control checks on the safety of lamps were also tightened up.

Both Judge Goran and the Coroner identified poor communications from more senior officers to middle and junior persons in the mine as a fundamental cause of the disaster. Specifically, assistant under-managers did not attend the meeting at which the ventilation changeover was planned; they were later given minutes which outlined what had to be done, but which did not provide reasons why it had to be done. The deputies who directly supervised the alterations received no written instructions, although the minutes were posted up for them to read if interested. Oral instructions clearly had their limits in an area where a diagram showing airflows would have been worth a thousand words. The response of management to the recommendation that lines of communication be a subject of corporate reform has been to contend that both Judge Goran and Coroner Hiatt were mistaken in their analysis on this point and that there has therefore been no need to make changes. In comments on the draft chapter, the company described the last sentence as a "mis-statement." However, we were not provided with any information on what the company had done to restructure its communications, but only with a non-specific claim on training: "Both the company and industry generally have spent considerable time on reviewing and upgrading training procedures, particularly for officials connected with the day to day activities of the mine." Management's view is that it was the personal failings of individuals that explained the defective implementation of the ventilation changeover; the system of communications "was and still is" regarded as satisfactory.

All in all, there have been only minor changes to procedures which might improve safety. One senior company officer was candid enough to concede: "I don't think anyone would say where we've done anything to improve basic safety." However, he did go on to point out that a response of many individuals had been to adopt practices which would ensure, should there be a recurrence, that the finger could not be pointed at them. For example, there would be witnesses to the fact that a particular instruction had been given.

One area where important changes have been occurring, however, is in the technology of methane drainage. It is uncertain at this stage how much of a reduction in methane levels will be achieved by new technology. But there are grounds for guarded optimism. Small experimental methane drainage programs at Appin and another mine on the New South Wales South Coast had been tried before the disaster. Since then, largely in response to Mines Department insistence, BHP's investment in methane drainage has accelerated markedly, growing to a total of US$7 million in the two years following the explosion. If the extracted methane is in commercial quantities, as it generally has been in West Germany, where about a third of coal faces have methane drainage,[20] then this investment can be expected to grow even faster.

Much more dramatic than the changes in corporate ways have been the impacts on governmental practices. The Southern District President of the Miners' Federation used the disaster as an opportunity to highlight the staggering costs of mine accidents in New South Wales. He pointed out before the Goran inquiry that in 1978–1979 there were 10,000 compensated injuries in the NSW coal fields, adding "It is a disturbing number of injuries when you consider there are only 15,000 people working in NSW collieries and that includes surface and underground workers."[21] Compensation payouts to NSW miners in 1978–1979 were US$30 million and insurance payments represented 9.7 per cent of gross wages paid.

A year after the disaster the Minister for Mineral Resources issued a statement detailing how all 27 recommendations of Judge Goran's report would be implemented.[22] In fact most of the undertakings to "implement" the recommendations were vague, being in the nature of "directing the Chief Inspector to investigate" means of implementation. However, certain specific recommendations to change the Coal Mines Regulation Act have been made as part of a total rewriting of the Act which was already underway before the disaster. And the inspectorate has been increased by over a third in line with the Judge's recommendation. The disaster certainly gave impetus to the rewriting of the Act and, beyond Judge Goran's suggestions, probably prompted some substantive changes, such as giving the Chief Inspector power to require methane drainage in a mine.[23]

Critics from the industry, such as R.D.G. Reed, the Manager of Mining Services at BHP,[24] claim that, in the words of the *Australian Financial Review*, "The thrust of this bill is to facilitate prosecution on behalf of the Department and to make it easier for the department to establish a prima facie case."[25] While the new Act does require managers and owners to "ensure" that more things are done, and while they no longer have the escape hatch of having to ensure only that they are done "as far as is reasonably practicable," the Minister has forcefully rejected the proposition that, as a package, the Act will ease the burdens of proof on the state in mounting prosecutions. At most, he argues, it may make it easier for the prosecution to determine whose obligation it is to comply with a provision.[26]

However, there have been administrative changes favoring a more prosecutorial stance by the Department of Mines. For most years in the 1970s there were no prosecutions initiated by the Mines Department under the Coal Mines Regulation Act. A maximum of four persons were prosecuted by the government in any one year. However, in the 1980–1981 fiscal year nine persons were charged with 16 offenses. Apart from this quantitative increase, the union is convinced that, since Appin, qualitatively the Mines Department has been more stringently enforcing the letter of the law. The union as well as the Department of Mines is persuaded that gas concentrations beyond statutory limits in mines like Appin are now rarely tolerated by government inspectors on the ground that enforcing the law might cause the closure of the mines. No mines have been closed as a result of this apparent change in administrative policy.

CHAPTER 9

James Hardie Industries
and Asbestos

The Allegations against James Hardie Industries

In Australia, as in all Western societies, the second half of the 1970s saw the dangers of asbestos dust become a heated social issue. Most of this Australian heat was directed at James Hardie Industries which, after taking over CSR's Wunderlich subsidiary in 1977, monopolized the Australian asbestos products industry. Hardie's asbestos-containing products include building materials of various types, asbestos cement pipes, and brake linings.

Working in an environment which contains asbestos dust increases the risk of contracting at least three diseases: *asbestosis*, a form of pneumoconiosis (dust disease of the lung); *lung cancer*; and *mesothelioma*, a cancer of the lining of the chest or abdominal cavity. Awareness in the United States that asbestos is a severe health hazard can be traced back at least to the 1930s. The story of how the U.S. asbestos industry covered up the dangers of asbestos for so many years to forestall dust control regulations has been well documented elsewhere.[1] It was the ultimate realization of the size of the problem in the United States in the early 1970s that led to the Australian anti-asbestos campaign of the late 1970s. U.S. Secretary of Health, Education and Welfare, Joseph A. Califano, summarized the enormity of the catastrophe in 1978 with the estimate that 67,000 people would die from cancer each year in the United States for the next 30 to 35 years as a result of exposure to asbestos.[2]

James Hardie executives admit to some regret over the atrocious conditions which existed for many years at their Baryulgil asbestos mine near Grafton in northern New South Wales. The company sold the mine in 1976. One critic described conditions in the mill attached to the mine as follows:

> In the mill, the dust was shovelled by hand into bags and sometimes it was so thick that the shoveller could not even see the man who was holding open the bag—and he was less than a metre away. Until as recently as 1972, years after such practices would have been outlawed in the company's more visible operations in the capital cities, hessian bags were being used and re-used for the asbestos dust. Men shook out the bags, standing in a cloud of asbestos dust.[3]

In 1972, the New South Wales Division of Occupational Health recorded a dust reading of 280 fibres per cubic centimeter of air at Baryulgil. This compares with the current level permissible in Australia of 2 fibres per cc. The mine employed almost exclusively Aboriginal labor, leading to allegations that Australia's dirty work was being done by its most oppressed group.

Much safer conditions prevail at James Hardie's largest manufacturing plant at Camellia, Sydney. However, there have been at least ten inspections of this factory by the New South Wales Health Commission since 1972 that have reported dust concentrations in excess of the asbestos standard under the New South Wales Factories Regulations. None of these reports resulted in prosecution, even though in some cases dust concentrations of more than 20 fibres per cc. were reported. The legal limit until 1977 was 4 fibres per cc., and from 1977 on, 2 fibres per cc. However, higher concentrations are permissible if workers wear respirators in the area. Even though, as we shall see later, considerable improvement in asbestos levels was achieved by the company throughout the 1970s, as recently as 1980 a New South Wales Health Commission inspection report on the Camellia plant indicated that "approximately 20 per cent of [work] positions tested were found to have excessive exposures indicating a need for remedial action." Three inspections in 1980 concluded that the Factories Regulations had been violated.

A third area of public exposure for James Hardie during the asbestos scare concerned its dumping of asbestos waste. Broken and reject scrap had been used over the years as filling for driveways, parking lots, paths, and for many other purposes. The Camellia plant alone was revealed to have 19 known major tip sites. Public concern rose when many of these sites were found to have surface exposure of asbestos in places frequented by the general public.

In addition to mining, manufacturing, and dumping practices, a fourth area of criticism centered upon the lack of warnings given to the public over the dangers of asbestos. Regulatory agencies have expressed concern to James Hardie from time to time. For example, on December 3, 1979, the New South Wales Health Commission wrote to James Hardie about the labelling of its "fire-rating board":

> The present label states "This product contains a small percentage of asbestos bound firmly into it by cement and other materials." The approximately 45 per cent asbestos content of FR Board cannot be considered to be "a small percentage." Also the asbestos in the FR Board is not "bound firmly into it" in the manner of your asbestos cement products. The information on the label in fact infringes the Trade Practices Act.
>
> Accordingly, I suggest a more suitably worded label should be prepared for this product forthwith.

The company retorted that the asbestos content of the FR board was not 45 per cent but only "approximately 20%." Nevertheless, the company agreed to change its label to: "Caution. This product contains asbestos. Breathing asbestos dust can damage health. Keep dust down."

Critics have been most concerned with statements from the company which might be called subtly misleading, in the sense of playing down the problem. One example which attracted some unfavorable comment was the final sentence of James Hardie's "Asbestos and Health" pamphlet: "Asbestos cement products have been used in Australia for 75 years by tradesmen, builders and handymen and to our knowledge these people have suffered no ill effects." An earlier (1968) company statement read: "Asbestos is by no means alone in having suspicion directed at it of being a possible health hazard. There are hundreds of substances as mundane as fuel oil, charcoal-grilled steak and iron rust which are known or suspected of being cancer-causing agents under certain experimental conditions."

Publicity and Counterpublicity

One morning in December 1979, two large brass plates reading "Asbestos House" were removed from the facade of James Hardie's Sydney headquarters. The renaming of the office building as "James

Hardie House" followed the dropping of "Asbestos" from the former company name, James Hardie Asbestos. While the company did not run a massive counterpublicity campaign over the asbestos scare, these two actions were testimony to the fact that the company believed that it had an image problem.

James Hardie was not a tailor-made corporate villain for the media, the workers' health action groups, and the unions. Throughout the campaign it remained open, always willing to talk to the press, and to have critics look over its plants. On one occasion, a television camera crew trespassed onto the Camellia plant by climbing a fence. When this was discovered, the manager invited the cameras into the plant, an offer which was declined on the ground that the journalist did not want to have his independence compromised by the company! There was some downright misrepresentation by critics who did not avail themselves of the company's open-door policy. For example, a film on Baryulgil suggested that when the company sold this mine, it opened another in Indonesia. James Hardie owns a manufacturing plant in Indonesia but not a mine. The company contemplated legal action against the misrepresentations by some of its critics, but decided that the aggravation and further highlighting of the problem would be counterproductive.

Probably the most influential component of the anti-asbestos campaign in Australia was a series of broadcasts in 1977 by the Australian Broadcasting Commission (ABC) current affairs radio program, Broadband. While the series did not enjoy high ratings, its detailed treatment of the asbestos problem provided a springboard for many follow-up stories in the popular press and on television (the most significant being a three-part series, "THE FATAL DUST", in the *Sydney Morning Herald*).[4] The Broadband program provided some favorable as well as unfavorable recognition for James Hardie. Presenter Matt Peacock stated on the July 21, 1977, program: "Most authorities I've spoken to point to them [James Hardie] as models of good behavior so far as occupational health goes . . . ." Nevertheless, the program went on to hammer James Hardie through quotations from internal documents, such as the following:

Half dust respirators should as a rule only be issued where it has been shown, or where commonsense suggests there is good reason to believe, that exposure exceeds 4 fibres per millilitre per shift. Heretofore it has generally been the practice to issue a respirator to any man requesting it. This practice is now contrary to policy. It is desirable that the new policy should be introduced as quickly and as completely as possible. However, discretion should be used. If a man requests the issue of a respirator despite the fact that his exposure is below 4 fibres per millilitre per shift, every effort should be made to persuade him that he has no need of the respirator, and it may be useful to seek the help of officers of the State Government Health Departments in this endeavour. On the other hand, the matter should not be allowed to develop into an industrial dispute, and if this seems a possibility, a respirator should be issued. Even where such an issue has been made under duress all efforts should continue to be made to relieve the man of his respirator either by continuing to persuade the man that he has no need of the respirator in his present job or by moving him to some other job in which he manifestly has no need of such a respirator. The aim is to ensure that no man has a respirator who has no need of it but that any man who has need of a respirator has a respirator of the appropriate kind and that the same is properly cared for and maintained.[5]

The point made by the Broadband program was that, because no level of exposure to asbestos is completely safe, a policy which in certain circumstances encourages employees not to wear masks is indefensible. At any level above zero, "there will be some risk associated with the exposure to asbestos."[6] Even when the dust concentration is down to 4 fibres per cc., a worker will inhale about 32 million fibres that are longer than five microns in a working day.[7] The company no longer discourages the wearing of masks in any circumstances.

At the 1978 annual meeting of the company there was a demonstration, spraying of graffiti on "Asbestos House," and a motion that a proportion of the dividend for the year be directed towards the compensation of an Aboriginal victim of the Baryulgil mine.

Adverse publicity did not follow from the many unfavorable reports on factory and mine conditions by the various state occupational health authorities. Improvements were always negotiated privately, without exposing any alleged violations to public airing in a court of law. James Hardie have a reputation with regulatory agencies for a reasonable and cooperative approach to rectifying deficiences reported by inspectors. The company has paid for overseas study trips by Australian health officials on asbestos hazards. While the company justifies this as part of its policy of helpfulness and openness with health authorities, its critics have attacked it as "buying off" the officials.

James Hardie did not run any counterpublicity campaign of paid advertisements to answer its critics. In this they differed from the

British asbestos industry which carried out a vociferous and well-funded campaign against the "unwarranted, biased and inaccurate" asbestos scare.[8] However, they did change their name and their image—from that of a specialized asbestos cement company to that of a diversified firm. A certain amount of corporate image advertizing on "James Hardie—the name behind the names" was used to foster this diversified image. The company also went to considerable lengths to ensure that their own employees were briefed and given literature[9] to counter the publicity which was seen as undermining the stature of the company.

Financial Impacts

The financial impacts of the asbestos campaign have been nowhere near as severe for James Hardie as they have been for Johns-Manville in the United States. In 1981 Johns-Manville financial statements for the previous two years were qualified by their accountants until such time as they could reasonably assess the ultimate costs of its growing asbestos litigation.[10] This has not been a problem for the Australian asbestos companies. None of them has been the target of a successful common law suit to recover damages for a deterioration in health as a result of occupational exposure to asbestos.

James Hardie has taken the unique step of voluntarily making workers compensation payments to employees totally disabled by an asbestos related disease; they have received these payments in excess of their normal workers compensation entitlements. Only workers with a number of years' service to the firm come under the scheme. In accepting the additional $ US 20,000 the employee does not forego his or her right to a common law action against the company for damages. To date only about 20 payouts have been made under this scheme.

The amounts involved have been small. However, one critic of Hardie has claimed that they have "made at least two near hundred thousand dollar settlements to senior staff members killed by the asbestos who threatened to make highly embarrassing public disclosures about what they knew."[11] A company spokesperson denied that these settlements were made because of threats of embarrassing public disclosures, and in any case he said such settlements were normally handled by the company's insurers.

James Hardie has certainly lost some important sales as a result of the campaign. Some of the government authorities whose workers were the victims of the most dangerous uses of asbestos as insulation materials have now, in response to union pressure, introduced an outright ban on the use of asbestos in their organizations. Many of the safer applications of asbestos which James Hardie is still successfully marketing have been caught up in these bans. For example, after it was found that raw blue asbestos fibre was used on railways rolling stock, the New South Wales Public Transport Commission, in response to union demands, issued a policy prohibiting the purchase of any product containing asbestos. Similar circumstances have led the State Electricity Commissions of New South Wales and Victoria to end the use of asbestos cement sheeting in their cooling towers.

Some architects refuse to specify any asbestos-containing product on major city buildings lest their clients run into industrial trouble from building unions which refuse to work with asbestos or which demand danger money for such work. Customers have also opted out: In one example a single director vetoed the purchase of Hardie asbestos building materials by his company, saying that they would be used "over my dead body ." Likewise, a number of local government engineers had adopted a play-safe approach by recommending steel or plastic pipes rather than asbestos cement pipes.

Few of the lost sales could be attributed to exploitation of the asbestos scare by competitors. James Hardie management were aware of one case where a competitor in the building sheets market placed a poster in several of its shop windows with a skull and crossbones to denote the alleged dangers of James Hardie products. Management of the company responsible was horrified when told of the posters and James Hardie fully accepted their explanation that they were made by "overzealous sales people."

While lost sales were never sufficient to jolt James Hardie's steadily rising earnings, there can be little doubt that the asbestos campaign created some buyer resistance to the purchase of James Hardie shares. As one commentator summed it up: "The health scare is not something that investors will suddenly stop associating with James Hardie."[12] Hardie share prices were on an upward climb until the end of 1976, but from 1977 until the end of the decade, against the general trend of the market and in spite of the company's strong financial performance, James Hardie share prices showed a marked decline. The period of the decline coincided perfectly with the worst period of adverse publicity. While top management admits that the health scare may have been a factor in the decline of the late 1970s, they point out that there were other factors as well. There was a lack of shareholder confidence that James Hardie could make its massive 1978 takeover of Reed Consolidated work. Questions were asked about whether James Hardie could be as financially successful as a diversified company as it had been as a more specialized asbestos manufacturer. Also the company had its first-ever stock-option issue.

In 1981 James Hardie shares recovered almost to their 1976 peak. There is no way of knowing how much of the decline of the late 1970s was attributable to the asbestos scare, and there is no way of knowing how much the recovery of the early 1980s can be explained by the shift out of asbestos which will be described later. But few observers of the market would disagree that changing investor concern over the health problems of asbestos played some part in both the fall and rise of James Hardie.

Non-Financial Impacts

The adverse effects of the asbestos campaign on corporate prestige have been amply demonstrated. The decision to change the company's name clearly evidenced a desire to keep the corporate image clean even though the Managing Director claimed that they were "not so much pulling down James Hardie Asbestos as . . . building James Hardie Industries." The company's official line is that the change of image and structure to a diversified company had to do with the positive virtues of diversification rather than with countering the stigma of asbestos. We think it was a bit of both, and, informally, management conceded as much.

The adverse impact on corporate prestige was combined with a rather complex effect on employee morale. Personnel management described three stages in the impact of the asbestos campaign on the morale of the work force. In the first phase there was a strengthening of morale as a backlash against the initial Broadband publicity. After this initial rallying of employees to the flag, phase two, the "siege mentality", depressed employee morale for about two years in the late 70s. The second phase drop in morale was said to be most noticeable among more senior people. It was pointed out that the adverse morale impact of sickness in the workplace is fundamentally different from what would be expected from a problem with a defective product which affected only outsiders: "You know the people who got sick, you saw them on television, and those feelings radiated out into the homes of workers." One executive reflected: "Mrs. Jones had always been proud to say that her husband was a factory manager at James Hardie, and now this pride was called into question." By the end of the decade, a third stage had been reached. By this phase the company had pulled through the morale problem. The widespread view among employees became that the attacks had been unfair, and that due recognition had not been given to the fact that the company was a leader in occupational health innovation in Australia. The very real program of reform by James Hardie, to be discussed in the next section, undoubtedly gave impetus to a return of employee confidence.

A further non-financial impact of the publicity was that it prompted a more activist interest in occupational health matters among the unions which represented James Hardie employees—primarily the Miscellaneous Workers Union. During the 1960s, workers' health was generally something about which management approached the unions rather than vice versa. For example, when James Hardie sent an executive to an overseas conference on asbestos and health, one of his or her duties on returning would be asked to brief the union officials on what had been learned. In the 70s, however, management increasingly found the unions initiating disputes and discussions on health hazards.

Reforms

Management claims that in the mid-1960s it foresaw that the health dangers of asbestos would ultimately cause serious difficulties and became genuinely concerned about the need for greater control over exposures. From then on the policy has been to "engineer our way out of the problem." Improvements which occurred in the second half of the 70s must be viewed as more than simply a reaction to the adverse publicity of the period, but also as a continuation of a program of reform which started 10 years earlier. Equally, the reforms of the late 60s and early 70s must be viewed in part as changes made *in anticipation* of the adverse publicity of the late 70s.

James Hardie has made great progress towards engineering its way out of the problem. The dangers of dumping hazardous wastes have been largely removed by capturing dust and waste within the factory and recycling it back into the production process. Since the mid-60s over US$20 million has been spent on dust control technology by the company. In recent years the average asbestos dust exposures of James Hardie workers have declined significantly. Graphs supplied to us by the company show that for the 1976–1977 financial year, 0.9 per cent of its work force in Australia and New Zealand had time-weighted average exposures in excess of the current Australian standard of 2 fibres per cc. The next year this figure dropped to 0.5 per cent and in the two following years to less than 0.1 per cent. Over the four years, the percentages of the work force above the company standard of 1 fibre per cc. were 6.1 per cent in 1976–1977, 2.0 per cent in 1977–1978, 3.3 per cent in 1978–1979, and 1.7 per cent in 1979–1980.

There are three major reasons why we consider that these company data, if anything, understate the reduction in the dangers to which James Hardie workers were exposed over the recent period. First, the technology for detecting fibres has improved, so that fewer would be slipping through the net today than in the past. Second, the fibres counted today, as in the past, include many non-asbestos fibres. The procedure specifies that fibres of a certain length, width, and length-to-width ratio will be counted as asbestos fibres, even though in some cases non-asbestos fibres will happen to conform to these dimensions. Because James Hardie has reduced the percentage of asbestos content in its products over the period, one would expect an increase in the proportion of fibres counted as asbestos that are not in fact asbestos. Third, in earlier periods dust counts were not always made as rigorously as they are today. Previous testing might have been concentrated in places that would produce lower readings, while avoiding the trouble spots. Such dishonesty obviously could still go on today, but there are reasons for believing that the testing is now done more scientifically. For one thing, government testing is more frequent today, so spurious company figures have less chance of passing unnoticed. Also, the unions are now retaining independent consultants to come into plants to measure dust levels.[13] Cheating might still go on, but it's a lot harder.

The recorded readings in the files of the New South Wales Health Commission are consistent with this picture of marked improvement in recent years, although we must be mindful that those files also indicate that violations of the law were still occurring, as of 1980.[14] It should also be mentioned that many of the 99.9 per cent of workers who over the 12-month period have *average* asbestos exposures of less than 2 fibres per cc. may have exposures in excess of the standard for one week of the year, or two weeks, or even 20 weeks. A 99.9 per cent average exposure of less than 2 fibres per cc. over 12 months does not mean 99.9 per cent compliance with the standard. Further data provided confidentially by the company, however, show that only a tiny fraction of the

99.9 per cent are outside the standard for any prolonged period. Whatever the data mean in absolute terms, they certainly show to our satisfaction a substantial improvement in relative terms.

The reforms at James Hardie have been technological rather than organizational. Safety managers, hygienists, and physicians have not been granted any additional powers to overrule decisions made by managers concerned primarily with production and marketing. The company did not have a formal written corporate health and safety policy before the publicity on asbestos and still does not have one at the time of writing.[15] One notable change, however, has been the establishment of employee/management safety committees. These committees, and the worker representatives on them, have access to dust counts. Management and the union are jointly considering the feasibility of a dust count register that would be available for scrutiny by all workers and union officials as well as government inspectors who come into the plant. The company is therefore moving towards greater accountability to its work force for safety performance. On the debit side, however, a review of the company's occupational health program conducted by Noel Arnold, an industrial hygienist, concluded: "Union members did not, in general, feel that they were an integral part of safety committees."[16]

The heightened openness is part of a wider change of approach which can largely be attributed to the impact of the adverse publicity. Until the mid-70s, the attitude of the company had been that it was doing everything it reasonably could to abate the dust problem and that there was no point in alarming employees. Once the publicity broke, there was no choice but to communicate with the work force about the dangers, because workers now were asking questions. One executive described the new attitude of the company as: "To hell with the press: Whatever they say will be distorted. But let's explain it ourselves to our own people." The old attitude is illustrated by a section of a letter from Hardie's medical adviser to the Health Commission on April 30, 1968: "The company employs a large number of people whose mastery of the English language is negligible. Among such groups it is impossible to be sure that an attempt to arouse proper concern will not result in a quite implacable alarm." The best evidence of the new attitude is an audio-visual program on the dangers of asbestos, and how to minimize them, which is shown to all new employees. The sound track is available in six languages. According to a senior personnel manager, the new openness and frankness had "resulted in a healthier attitude with the workforce."

The new openness is also manifest in the approach of the company's doctors in dealing with sick workers. The old practice had been for the company doctor not to worry workers with details of their condition unless they were positively diagnosed as suffering from asbestosis. Now employees are told in a fairly detailed fashion about any changes in their lungs that are likely to have been caused by asbestos, even if those changes are giving rise to no symptoms. There are today two full-time company doctors instead of one.

Now that the work force has a clearer understanding of the risks of asbestos, preventive programs can be expected to get a better reception. These include programs to persuade workers to use their respirators properly, to report dust leaks, to wet down dust before sweeping it up with a broom (or to vacuum), and to refrain from wearing work overalls home. Because smoking and asbestos exposure may combine to multiply the risk of cancer, James Hardie has experimented with a variety of anti-smoking campaigns for the work force. At its newest plant, the company tried to ban smoking on the job, but this ran into opposition from employees. The compromise was to draw lines around certain parts of the plant which became non-smoking areas.

Critics of James Hardie claim that while there has been reform at home to deal with the dangers of asbestos, the company has resorted to exporting the problem to Indonesia, a country not noted for the stringency of its legislation to protect the health of workers. Indonesia has no regulations concerning asbestos dust, although late 1981 saw its government announce plans for the introduction of an asbestos standard. The Australian Prime Minister, Malcolm Fraser, opened a new US$22 million James Hardie asbestos products plant in Indonesia in 1976. The building materials and pipes made in the factory are exported throughout the Pacific basin. Top management contends that anticipating the problems of continuing asbestos manufacture in Australia was not a consideration in the decision to commence some manufacturing off-shore. Rather it was a move to expand market opportunities. Further, we were told that the company's dust control procedures and standards are applied with equal force in all countries. Contrary to the view of top management, a middle manager said to one of the authors that anticipation of the asbestos scare and of the enormous costs of compliance with new regulations was indeed a factor in the Indonesian move.

In any event, James Hardie has now come up with a solution superior to moving off-shore—it is moving asbestos out of its products. This solution is available to James Hardie in a way that it is not to the vertically integrated European and American asbestos companies—for the latter, shifting manufacturing off-shore is the preferred solution because the output from their asbestos mines must be consumed.[17] James Hardie has no mines and therefore no vested interest in clinging to asbestos usage.

A crash US$3 million research and development program since 1978 has found a replacement for asbestos in the building products which comprise 55 per cent of James Hardie sales—a form of cellulose fibre. The C.S.I.R.O., a government-funded research institute, and several other research institutions assisted the company with basic research in developing a sound method of fibrillating cellulose fibres to give them the required tensile and ductile properties. Retooling production lines to produce the asbestos-free building materials is costing a further US$12 million. In spite of these enormous costs, it is expected that the investment will be more that recouped in the long run because the replacement of raw material is cheaper than asbestos. For this reason, the research and development and the retooling costs have not been included under the heading of financial impacts.

The advent of asbestos-free building products will be the culmination of a more gradual transition in the 1970s by which Hardie building products have been reduced from an average of 14 per cent to 4 per cent asbestos. By the time this book goes to press, all James Hardie building products sold in Australia will be asbestos-free.

A major motivation of the shift out of asbestos has been the threat of increased regulation—not so much in-factory regulation as tight control over the use of asbestos on building sites. Customer unwillingness to put up with these regulations, plus building workers' resistance to using asbestos materials would have resulted in increasing losses of sales.

The removal of asbestos from James Hardie's building products was as much motivated by rising cost as by this consumer resistance. However, the rising cost is itself attributable in part to the more stringent regulation of asbestos mining.

Considerable research has also been done on removing asbestos from the company's second major line of business—asbestos cement pipes. So far this has been unsuccessful. The only alternative raw materials with anything approaching the tensile strength of asbestos are more than twice as expensive. So the company has also begun to test various coatings for its pipes to totally lock the asbestos in. To date this too has proved unsuccessful. James Hardie has also innovated with asbestos-free brake linings; 25 per cent of sales in this product are asbestos-free.

Hence, as time passes, James Hardie grows further away from its roots as an asbestos company. Years ago it moved totally out of the most dangerous area of asbestos application—insulation. By the end of the 70s, it had abandoned asbestos mining, with the sale of the Baryulgil mine and its 12 per cent share in a Canadian asbestos mine. And by 1982 it had removed asbestos from the building products which until 1978 had provided over 80 per cent of the company's sales. Today James Hardie no longer deserves to be called an asbestos company.

This then is a case study in which publicity played an important role in fostering change. In addition to the impacts on James Hardie mentioned above, the Australian Broadcasting Commission, on the occasion of publishing the 1977 Broadband transcripts as a book, with some justification made the following claim:

> Within months of the first program the Australian asbestos standard was halved to two fibres per cubic centimetre and the N.S.W. Government had introduced its first asbestos regulations. . . . As this book goes to press the Asbestos Association of Australia is discussing the introduction of an asbestos warning labelling scheme.[18]

The Commission might also have pointed out that prior to that first program only two of the six Australian states had any asbestos regulations; today they all have. Now the National Health and Medical Research Council is urging another halving of the uniform state standard, from two fibres to one. Its urgings may well succeed because of the wide public support for asbestos regulation which the publicity against James Hardie generated.

CHAPTER 10

Sharp Corporation —
The Microwave Exposure

The Microwave Offenses

The enactment of the Trade Practices Act in 1974 was much vaunted as a sign of the coming of a New Deal in Australian consumer protection. For Lionel Murphy, then Attorney-General and one of the most zealous of the antipodean New Dealers, the occasion called for a show-case prosecution.[1] He was soon presented with a promising script — a case of blatantly misleading advertising by Sharp Australia, the local subsidiary of a multinational, the Sharp Corporation of Japan.

In 1975 Sharp advertised its microwave ovens to Australians on a national basis. Under a general blurb, "Microwave Cooking is Here!," it claimed that "every Sharp microwave oven is fully tested and approved by the Standards Association of Australia." This claim was misleading in at least two respects: First, the Standards Association of Australia (SAA) had not tested and approved Sharp microwave ovens, and second, any such testing would not have been for every microwave oven but only one or two samples of the model.

The company was prosecuted on ten charges under the misleading advertising provisions of the Trade Practices Act. It pleaded guilty, the advice of its solicitor being that the fines would be approximately US$40,000.[2] The fines imposed, however, totalled US$134,000 (the maximum fine possible was US$675,000). In the opinion of the court,[3] the offenses were far from trivial. Contrary to the company's claim that they resulted from "just a simple mistake," Justice Smithers regarded the matter as one of deliberate deceit:

I am not of the opinion that this was carelessness. I think it all bears the marks of too much construction. We would be very naive indeed to think that when this trouble was gone to by this company to put the trade mark [of the Standards Association of Australia] there, to wrongly state the certificates, when any persons connected with the certificates at all in that institution would have known that two years' work had been undertaken by the corporation in an effort to get the certificates not from the Standards Association of Australia but from the Electricity Authority of New South Wales, and that so far as this particular microwave oven was concerned, no applications had been made to the Standards Association for any approval whatsoever.[4]

Another member of the court, Justice Joske, went even further in his condemnation of Sharp's conduct: For him the company had made "a gross and wicked attempt to swindle the public of Australia."[5]

Publicity and Counterpublicity

So pungent were the judicial criticisms of Sharp at the time of sentence that the microwave story became front-page news in Australia. The case also received some attention in the Japanese press.

Two leading Australian newspapers, the *Sydney Morning Herald* and the Melbourne *Age*, announced the news of the sentence on page one.[6] The *Sydney Morning Herald* account, headlined "$100,000 FINE FOR 'ATTEMPT TO SWINDLE'," emphasized Justice Joske's denunciation of Sharp and the size of the fine.[7] The Melbourne *Age* story drew attention to the fact that Sharp Australia had continued to claim SAA approval for its microwave ovens despite receiving a letter from SAA's technical director that the association had not established any standards for microwave ovens and hence had not approved them in any way.[8]

Subsequently, a number of adverse postmortems were undertaken by the Australian press, notably in the *National Times* and the *Broadcasting and Television Advertising, Marketing and Media Weekly*. The *National Times* published a lengthy leading article, "How NOT to Fall Foul of the Trade Practices Act: Sharp's Case History,"[9] which, although doubting that Sharp Australia had engaged in willful deceit, alleged a woefully negligent breakdown in communication between the marketing and technical units in Sharp's organization. The *Broadcasting and Television Advertising, Marketing and Media Weekly*, however, was far less charitable: it reported that

Sharp had not received much sympathy within the advertising industry, the consensus being that the experience would "serve them bloody well right."[10] The adverse publicity somewhat snowballed later in 1975 when Sharp Australia was convicted under the Trade Practices Act on a charge of resale price maintenance.[11]

The Sharp case also made news in Japan, brief accounts appearing in leading newspapers, including the *Nihon Keizai Shimbun* and *Asahi Shimbun*.[12] It may seem surprising that the Sharp case was newsworthy in Japan. However, one must remember that in Japan company-watching has become almost a national pastime.[13]

Sharp made some attempt to ward off adverse publicity over the microwave offenses, but never engaged in a direct counteroffensive. Initially, the company tried to minimize adverse publicity by making a public apology to SAA for misrepresentation.[14] A degree of camouflage was then attempted at the trial: The company avoided full inquiry into the question of fault by pleading guilty and then, in mitigation of sentence, claiming that the offense was due to a simple breakdown in communication, a breakdown readily avoidable in the future. When this tactic failed to appease the sentencing court, Sharp managed to tell its side of the story in a leading article that appeared in the *National Times*.[15] These public relations exercises, however, were rather half-hearted. The firm believed that vigorous counterpublicity would result only in adverse public reaction (the company did not bother to call in a public relations firm). Moreover, Sharp Australia traditionally had not been oriented towards public relations, although recently the company has indulged in some corporate image advertising.

Despite the absence of any direct counterpublicity, Sharp did engage in an extensive brand image campaign in Australia between 1977 and 1980. A great deal of money was spent on national advertising, the image projected being of Sharp as a manufacturer of quality products. This campaign, we were told, did not result from the microwave crisis, but was part of a move by the parent company in Japan to market aggressively in Australia. Nonetheless, so bright was the polishing of Sharp's image and so alluring the display of its products that by the late 70s the public tarnish of the microwave offenses was virtually gone.

Financial Impacts

Immediately after the Sharp conviction and fine, the microwave oven market in Australia contracted significantly. Sharp Australia had maintained its share of the market (it was top-seller at the time and has remained so ever since), but this was cold comfort. As the market leader, it appeared that Sharp was dragging its microwave competitors down with it. On a confidential basis, we have been provided with figures which show that the reduction of the microwave market in 1975-1976 was quite substantial.

The reason for the drastic drop in oven sales was attributed to the scare about leakage of radioactivity which the publicity about the microwave offenses had revived. The reaction of the average housewife, as perceived within the company, was that there was "something smelly" about microwave ovens. That the public was highly sensitive to the potential danger of these ovens was confirmed in 1979 when sales dropped in response to an ABC "Four Corners" television documentary about the safety of microwave cooking.

Overall sales for Sharp Australia, however, blossomed during 1976–1977, sales for that fiscal year being well over double those for 1974-1975. The main factor behind this upsurge was Sharp's success in the color television market. As the company was happy to relate, this market had soared in Australia after microwave sales had dived.[16]

Significant as the color television boom was in boosting Sharp's sales figures, the company also believed that the publicity surrounding the microwave offenses had ultimately worked to the corporation's advantage. As the crisis abated, the impression within the company was that "Sharp" had stuck in people's minds, while the memory of the US$134,000 fine had faded. Like everyday words, company names can undergo a radical transformation in meaning: "prestigious" no longer refers to deception, illusion, or legerdemain (as the Oxford English Dictionary would still have us believe), and "Sharp" has become prestigious. In fact, not only have Sharp microwave oven sales recovered to the levels before the scandals, the sales figures we have seen indicate that they have gone on to much higher levels.

Nonetheless, the microwave offenses and their attendant publicity did affect the profitability of Sharp Australia between 1975 and 1977. We were informed by one senior executive that the losses incurred by the company during that period were partly attributable to the Trade Practices prosecution and the resulting public notoriety. Moreover, that notoriety had contributed to the other main cause of the overall losses, unsatisfactory management: A severe decline in morale and hence in efficiency had resulted from this poor management. The subsidiary did not return to profitability until 1978, after most of the management team had been replaced.

No figure was put on the loss of profit inflicted by the microwave crisis, but the costs of the fine and legal expenses, US $335,000, were regarded as only a small part of the total losses resulting from the decline in morale following the scandal.[17]

By contrast, the microwave offenses had no apparent impact on share prices, which continued to move upward during both the year of the scandal and the year after. This is what one would expect, given that Sharp Australia contributes only 3 per cent of Sharp's turnover. However, some within the Australian subsidiary felt that a ripple on the Japanese stock market was always possible, though hardly probable, because financiers and other powerbrokers in Japan not only regard credibility and honor as highly important but also base their assessments on meticulous information-gathering; "they are great report readers," it was said.

Non-Financial Impacts

The adverse publicity caused by the microwave offenses had a variety of non-financial impacts upon Sharp: loss of corporate and personal face, consternation about the future of Sharp in Australia, and disquiet about the possibility of prejudicing trading relations between Japan and Australila.

The major non-financial impact was loss of corporate and personal repute, in Japan as well as in Australia. In describing this impact to us, a Sharp executive pointed out, somewhat ruefully, that respectability at both a corporate and personal level was far more important in Japanese than in American companies. It was emphasized that "There's a level of respectability we've got to maintain; personal and company loss of face are very significant." For this very reason, the Japanese manager of Sharp Australia was unhappy about our inquiry; the episode was a highly regrettable past event about which he did not want himself or others to be reminded.

As to corporate loss of face, the shock to Sharp Australia was severe. There was profound nervousness among subsidiary executives over how their superiors in Japan would take this loss of face. The concern was that in Japan the offense would be seen as affronting the company's long-standing business credo of "Sincerity and Creativity" (Sharp's handouts to employees and customers proclaim that "[b]y devoting ourselves to [these] two ideals our work will bring genuine satisfaction and joy to people and provide a meaningful contribution to society"). One Japanese manager in

Sharp Australia is reported to have said at the time, "Our parent in Japan feels shameful about this. It spoils our reputation. It is against our philosophy of sincerity."[18]

Personal loss of face was also acute: Those working within the company at the time were well aware of Sharp's reputation in the business community as the company that had been exposed to the first prosecution under the Trade Practices Act. Most of the Japanese executives in Australia were recalled to Japan and they did not remain long with the company, although, in a couple of cases Japanese executives of Sharp Australia who bore no responsibility for the offense gained subsequent promotions. Moreover, personal shame was experienced even among personnel who had been in Japan during the events giving rise to the Australian offenses. As already mentioned, the new manager of Sharp Australia was highly sensitive about the subject, despite the healing power of six intervening years.

Apart from loss of face, Sharp went through much soul-searching as to the future of the company in Australia. The microwave offenses took the parent company by surprise, and the ensuing adverse publicity rubbed salt in the wound. Subsequently, a team of executives was sent to Australia to determine whether Sharp Australia should be saved or scrapped. After an extensive review, it was decided to continue the Australian operations and to install an almost completely new management team. This decision, we were told, was not taken lightly, the view being expressed that "Sharp would not exist in Australia if it had a major problem like that again."

There was also agitation about the possible effect of the microwave offenses upon trading relations between Japan and Australia. Japan at that time was recovering from a severe economic recession, and recovery depended in part on the ability of Japanese manufacturers to exploit overseas markets.[19] In Australia, the unfavorable balance of trade with Japan was a vexing political issue, there being much clamor for additional tariff protection and increased import duties. Discussions between the Australian and Japanese governments over trade coincided with Sharp's microwave sentence. Given the publicity which followed that sentence, there was disquiet within Sharp that the Japanese national interest may have been prejudiced. Trade discussions were at a delicate stage and it was believed in some quarters that the example made of Sharp "could have an adverse effect on those relations."[20]

Reforms

Four main corporate reforms resulted from the adverse publicity suffered by Sharp for the microwave offenses: internal discipline, revision of advertising practices and procedures, introduction of training and auditing programs, and realignment of bureaucratic politics.

The measures of internal discipline taken by Sharp were slow but sure. Since the Australian subsidiary had been slow to report the crisis to headquarters, the parent corporation had been unable to take quick action with a view to avoiding prosecution. That being so, it was decided to leave the Japanese executives of Sharp Australia on location "until the case had been fought out." After the company's sentence, however, most were withdrawn to Japan. At least five senior executives of Sharp Australia were eventually replaced as a result of the crisis, including the managing director. It was pointed out to us that the replacement of these executives was a clear indication of the gravity with which the microwave offenses were viewed by the parent company, for banishment is highly unusual in the family-like culture of Japanese companies.[21] The message for employees, we were told, was plain: In the event of any intentional violation of company policy, they would be dismissed.

A second major reform was the revision of advertising practices and procedures. To begin with, a rule was imposed that all microwave ovens, television sets, and certain other products be approved by the Standards Association of Australia before being put on the market (the oven model involved in the microwave offenses was in fact subsequently approved by SAA). It was also laid down that no mention be made of approvals by SAA or similar authorities, and that advertisements should be cast in more general terms (e.g., "one of the best" products on the market, as opposed to "the best").[22] Furthermore, a checking procedure was introduced. All advertising material became subject to mandatory review by technical staff, several of whom are now stationed in the marketing section; this integration of technical and marketing functions was aimed specifically at avoiding the type of communication breakdown which led to the 1975 offenses.[23] In the case of new products, the monitoring procedure involves a checklist covering a wide range of matters, ranging from sales tax to compliance with the Trade Practices Act. Before any advertisement is published, there is a meeting at which a decision is taken as to whether the advertisement needs to be scrutinized by the company's lawyers or the relevant trade association to guard against infringing the rights of competitors. It is also worth noting that after the conviction, Sharp's advertising agency, F.P. Leonard, introduced a new policy of having a solicitor examine all the agency's ads.[24]

Thus, substantial safeguards against a repetition of the 1975 offense have been introduced. Nevertheless, our attention was drawn to the difficulty of providing equally effective safeguards in the area of cooperative advertising, where a wholesaler such as Sharp subsidizes advertisements run by a retailer. Assiduous as the company tried to be in checking cooperative advertisements as they appeared in the media, the system was not foolproof, since it operated after initial publication. Prior to publication, Sharp's state managers were required to use their influence to keep retailers in line, a control mechanism that was obviously imperfect, particularly where the retailer was larger and more powerful than Sharp. Risk in this connection appeared to have been accepted as inevitable by the company.

Another reform directly attributable to the microwave debacle was the adoption of new training and auditing programs. Training sessions for sales people were introduced, partly for the purpose of educating them about the Trade Practices Act, and partly to enable managers to monitor the types of sales and marketing practices being used in the field. In addition, Freehill, Hollingdale and Page, a leading Sydney commercial law firm, was engaged by Sharp, at considerable expense to the company, to conduct regular compliance reviews, with particular emphasis upon Trade Practices.

Finally, and most important of all, the microwave publicity induced Sharp radically to alter the balance of power within its Australian subsidiary. At the time of the microwave offenses, an atmosphere of bitterness was said to have prevailed between factions of the subsidiary's executives, primarily over questions of financial management. When the parent company sent in a team to investigate why the company had fallen foul of the Trade Practices Act, it discovered that the profit recorded for 1974–1975 was only a paper gain and that the company had in fact suffered a very substantial loss. As a result, the Japanese executives were replaced by a new Japanese team, and the Australian faction had its sphere of independent action curtailed to the point where its members began to resign.

In a previous study of Sharp's reactions to the microwave prosecution one commentator has stressed that the changes made in the company's monitoring methods conform to a "standard operating procedures" model of corporate decision-making;[25] according to this model, corporate crime attributable to defective standard operating procedures can be controlled by punishing corporations in order to induce procedural change. As far as it goes, this interpretation of the microwave case undoubtedly is correct. However, Sharp did much more than modify its standard operating procedures: It purged its Australian bureaucracy. Accordingly, the prime model of corporate decision-making exemplified is not that of "standard operating procedures," but of what Graham Allison and other political theorists have termed "bureaucratic politics"; under the "bureaucratic politics" model, corporate decision-making is "a bargaining game involving a hierarchy of players and a maze of formal and informal channels through which decisions are shaped and implemented."[26] The microwave offense and the resulting adverse publicity became an occasion for the Japanese elite to realign the power structure within the Australian subsidiary. This realignment eliminated a managerial faction that had brought about corporate conviction for crime and handed power over to a team that presumably would be more responsive to head office expectations. A purge of the delinquent management was undertaken because it suited head office plans for increasing the profitability of the subsidiary.

CHAPTER 11

ITT and Covert Actions in Chile

The Allegations

The first allegations against ITT (The International Telephone and Telegraph Company) efforts to prevent Marxist Salvador Allende from election to Chile's Presidency were made by *Washington Post* columnist, Jack Anderson, on March 21 and 22, 1972. Anderson had obtained some 80 pages of internal memoranda from ITT executives in Chile and New York. These documents led to allegations about ITT plots to foil Allende's election; they confirmed regular discussions between ITT and the United States Central Intelligence Agency concerning the role of American transnational corporations in creating economic chaos within Chile to push the country to the right. The documents also mentioned discussion of the feasibility of an American-backed military coup as a way of thwarting the electoral will of the Chilean people. They even revealed an offer by ITT Chairman, Harold Geneen, to contribute "up to seven figures" to the CIA to stop Allende. While the offer was rejected, ITT did subsequently admit to giving $575,000 to anti-Allende Chilean political parties and to conservative Chilean newspapers in 1970 and 1972.

ITT had a variety of investments in Chile that it was afraid would be threatened by an Allende victory. The most important of these was its 70 per cent ownership of Chile's telephone system. ITT claims that while it supported conservative Chilean political forces in legitimate attempts to protect its investments, it did nothing illegal. President Allende disagreed. Already four executives of Chilean companies controlled by ITT had been placed by him under arrest in late 1971 on fraud charges (they were later acquitted). After the 1972 scandal surfaced, Allende broke off negotiations on compensation for nationalizing ITT's telephone company. In a December 1972 address to the United Nations General Assembly, he drew thunderous applause when he accused ITT of plotting to overthrow the constitutionally elected government of Chile. ITT, he charged, had "driven its tentacles deep into my country, and proposed to manage our political life. I accuse the ITT of attempting to bring about civil war."[1]

In fact, while the secret ITT documents show much evidence of plotting and planning against Allende and for disrupting the Chilean economy, they could not sustain a case that ITT actually *did* anything illegal. Nor did subsequent United States Senate Subcommittee hearings chaired by Frank Church prove any violations of either U.S. or Chilean law by ITT.

Allende was overthrown in a military coup in 1973. The new President, Colonel Pinochet, announced that "there will be no elections in Chile during my lifetime nor in the lifetime of my successor." There were allegations that ITT continued covert political activities with respect to Chile years after the military coup. For example, an unrelated lawsuit against the Chicago Police Department in 1975 over the activities of its so-called "Red Squad" turned up allegations of ITT spying against an anti-Pinochet group. The *Washington Post* took up the story:

—On February 7, 1975 a bus chartered by the Chile Solidarity Committee of New York left for a conference near Chicago with 19 passengers aboard.

—One of them was a spy for the International Telephone and Telegraph Corp.

—An ITT photographer secretly took pictures of a number of the travellers as they boarded the bus. The spy then accompanied the group to the two-day meeting, which ITT's "manager of major investigations" later summed up as "a radical summit conference with a central theme of fascist oppression, crimes and atrocities in Chile as an object lesson for the United States."[2]

These accusations caused ITT immediately to issue a statement asserting that it "has never maintained a program of political spying and infiltration." The company added, however, that its facilities since 1972 had been the subject of

more than 90 terrorist threats, bombings and attacks . . . . The company cooperated with law enforcement agencies investigating such crimes in an attempt to protect its personnel and property from further terrorist activities. ITT also followed, through available sources of information, the activities of groups seeking to organize a boycott as a protest against the corporation.

Asked whether "available sources of information" included the assignment of infiltrators, an ITT spokesperson said that "no officer or director of ITT authorized any infiltration of a domestic organization." The information that turned up in Chicago was "obtained by an ITT employee . . . from a source known only to him."[3] John H. Coatsworth of the Chicago Committee to Save Lives in Chile retorted that, "None of the organizations victimized by ITT spying has ever discussed, planned or engaged in any activities that could remotely cause ITT to fear for the security of its property or the safety of its employees." Coatsworth maintained that ITT was trying to disrupt efforts "to aid the victims of a bloody dictatorship" that the company "helped to install" in the first place.

The scandal broke again in the late 1970s when it was charged that the CIA and ITT conspired to conceal the truth from Senator Church's Senate Foreign Relations Subcommittee. Former CIA director, Richard Helms, was allowed to plead "no contest" in late 1977 to charges of providing misleading testimony under oath. He was fined $2,000 and given a suspended two-year jail sentence. The first ITT executive to be charged was Harold V. Hendrix, the company's former Latin American public relations director and a Pulitzer prize-winning journalist. Hendrix pleaded guilty to withholding information from the Senate concerning communications he had with CIA employees in Santiago. His light one-month suspended sentence and $100 fine may have been a factor in enticing Hendrix to cooperate with the Justice Department in trying to build a perjury case against ITT Chairman, Harold Geneen, and other senior ITT executives. The investigation, however, did not lead to any charges being laid against Geneen. The former U.S. ambassador to Chile, Edward Korry, accused the Justice Department of a cover-up over its failure to prosecute Geneen. Korry claimed that the decision not to charge Geneen was made because "he knows too much" about the CIA's relationships with U.S. corporations around the world.[4]

However, charges were laid against two other ITT executives, Edward J. Gerrity, Jr., a Senior Vice-President, and Robert Berrellez, a more junior executive from ITT's Latin American operations. A variety of charges were made, including conspiracy to obstruct the proceedings of the Senate subcommittee, perjury, inducing another ITT official to lie, and making false statements before a 1974 arbitration board considering ITT insurance claims on confiscated property in Chile. In early 1979, the Justice Department finally dropped all charges against the two executives. The prosecutor, John T. Kotelly, included the following statement in his motion to dismiss the charges against Gerrity: "The reason for dismissal is to protect classified national security information from public disclosure. The government believes that to proceed any further would risk the disclosure of information that the government must take every reasonable, appropriate step to avoid."[5]

ITT was seen by the press as pioneering a new defense tactic which was dubbed "graymail."[6] Defense attorney, Patrick A. Wall, was reported as saying: "One of the defenses in this case is that through at least one, if not more, of its agents the Central Intelligence Agency in effect assisted and requested that Berrellez give the testimony [which was now the subject of perjury charges]."[7] Such revelations led journalists like Jack Anderson to allege that the offenses were committed at the behest of the CIA and that the charges had been dropped to save face for the CIA:

> The official excuse was that secrets revealed in open court might endanger "national security," though it seems more than likely that the real reason was to avoid embarrassing the CIA and ITT. At any rate, Berrellez' attorney shrewdly refused to keep the government's secrets inviolate at trial and the case was dropped.
>
> It was a solution that left all parties to the decision satisfied: Berrellez got off, the CIA was spared embarrassment and the Justice Department, after wrapping itself in the flag, could claim at least it had made the old college try. The workings of justice apparently had become a game in which all the players wound up winning.
>
> The only loser in this exercise was the American public, which was denied information about the misdeeds of its spy agency in collusion with a giant corporation.[8]

Publicity and Counterpublicity

The adverse publicity directed at ITT was enormous, even though its basis was a plethora of unprovable allegations. This case is a classic illustration of how bad press from one crisis begets more adverse publicity on other problems dug up once the company is in the spotlight. ITT's bad press had begun in February 1972, before the Chile allegations, when Jack Anderson got hold of secret memos from an ITT lobbyist suggesting that the company may have used campaign contributions to buy support from the Nixon White House to have the Justice Department drop a major antitrust action against it.[9] Then came the Chilean scandal, with its follow-up "Red Squad" and perjury publicity. Close on the heels of the initial Allende revelation involving ITT, newspapers took up allegations of insider trading against senior ITT executives who sold ITT stock just before an antitrust divestiture settlement became public. This led to formal Securities and Exchange Commission charges in June 1972 against ITT and one of its executives. The charges were settled in a consent decree in which the defendants agreed in effect that "they didn't do it, but they won't do it again." Senator Edward Kennedy took ITT to task for paying no federal income tax for 1971. Senator George McGovern, in turn, used this in his Presidential election campaign. Anthony Sampson captured the atmosphere when he said: "The press were having an anti-ITT festival."[10]

Jack Anderson's initial Chilean stories in March 1972 at first created more press interest in Europe and Latin America than in the United States. The full text of the ITT memos was first published in Britain and Chile, and only much later in the United States.[11] However, the peculiar nature of American political institutions gave the story more staying power in the United States. The Senate Foreign Relations Committee decided to set up a Multinationals Subcommittee with Senator Church in the chair to investigate ITT's alleged covert activities in Chile. It was a full year after the Anderson exposés (March 20, 1973) that the first Congressional hearings were held. The articulate Senator Church went to town on the ITT witnesses; ITT General Counsel, Howard Aibel, described the hearings as conducted "in a circus atmosphere." It was a many-ringed circus: ITT's annual stockholder meetings became lively affairs, with religious and public interest groups advancing stockholder resolutions condemning what they saw as the company's unethical practices.

There were considerable ironies about the adverse publicity directed at ITT. In spite of the fact that ITT was one of America's top 10 companies, it had not been well known by the general public. The ITT brand name is not to be seen in stores; ITT is the quintessential conglomerate, selling everything from telephones to lawn mowers to insurance under a proliferation of trading names. Some confused folk were even blaming the more visible American Telephone and Telegraph (AT&T) for ITT's misfortune.

ITT decided to run a counterpublicity campaign, which proved to be an enormous success. In the end, ITT had moved from an obscure conglomerate to a household name, indeed one with a highly favorable image. Through a process which one ITT executive described as ju-jitsu, the publicity was harnessed to become a plus rather than a minus for the corporation.

The first element of the counterpublicity campaign was to release a press kit in Spanish and English replying to the allegations against the company. From then on, the campaign, primarily of television advertisements around the world, was aimed at creating a corporate image. The message was simple: ITT is a company which is "helping people." Each advertisement focused on ITT technological breakthroughs which were of benefit to mankind. One featured experimental machines to alleviate a form of blindness, and another, technology to help doctors diagnose heart failure. The campaign action statement was:

> No urgency line or "do it now" phrase is included in the copy. Immediate response which is often demanded in retail advertising is seldom found in corporate messages. The implied request for action is: "When our name comes up, think positively about who we are and the good things we do."[12]

John Lowden, ITT Vice-President of Corporate Relations and Advertising, explained: "We're trying to humanize ITT and let the public know that part of our research and development budget goes toward creating products that will help make life better for everyone. We also believe it's important to speak out now in order to bank the good opinions of the public in case the issues that affect big business ever come down to a Congressional showdown. You could call it preventive medicine."

The campaign was nothing short of brilliant. It won a string of advertising and television awards and even a Special Effects Award at the Cannes Film Festival. Admittedly, it cost a lot of money— over $10 million each year. However, it was a tax-deductible expense.

At the start of the campaign, ITT's public opinion research had shown, as Lowden explained: "There were too many people out there—prosperous, relatively well-educated people—who didn't know what ITT was or did. They were voters, people who might be potential buyers of our stock, college students who are influentials of tomorrow, and so on. . . . And lacking knowledge about us, they were ready to believe anything about us." At the end of the campaign this was no longer true. Interestingly, ITT only interviewed persons earning over $15,000 a year in its national public opinion surveys. By October 1976, 80 to 90 per cent of survey respondents recognized ITT as "one of the largest companies," "very profitable," "leader in technology," and making "quality products." Seventy-two per cent of respondents even rated ITT as a "good stock to buy or own," a rise of 20 per cent over the three years of the campaign. This was a remarkable feat, since ITT stock was in the doldrums during this period. There were equally dramatic increases in the proportions of respondents who felt that ITT "cares about its customers" and "cares about the general public." In other words, through advertisements which focused narrowly on socially useful technological innovations, ITT was able to improve its corporate image on 25 out of 25 dimensions, ranging from "working to curb pollution" to "fair to employees of all races." The tracking studies also show that, over the period, ITT accomplished the most consistent improvement in its image of any of eight major corporations in the study.

Some ITT executives we interviewed claimed that the campaign was introduced to deal with the scandals of the early 1970s, others that it was not. The latter, while admitting that corporate image advertising underwent a quantum leap in 1973 with the first international television campaign,[13] point out that ITT had used the print media for image advertising for some time. Whatever the motivation of the campaign, the important empirical finding is that it more than neutralized the effects of the adverse publicity.

Financial Impacts

There was little evidence that the scandal cost ITT any sales. As a highly diversified conglomerate, ITT was well insulated from that. Most consumers would not know, for example, that in patronizing Sheraton Hotels, they were supporting an ITT subsidiary. Certainly big institutional customers were too financially hardheaded to be affected by the publicity. Throughout the Chilean allegations, negotiations continued smoothly to secure some major deals with the Soviet government. Outside Chile itself, the anti-ITT political backlash did no harm to financial ties with left-wing governments.

However, the publicity did great damage to ITT's negotiations over the nationalization of its Chilean telephone company. In early 1972, progress was being made towards obtaining reasonable compensation for the telephone nationalization. A February 11, 1971, confidential memo from Senior Vice-President Gerrity to Chairman Geneen revealed a shrewd plan. Sampson outlined this strategy:

They realised that Allende would expropriate the copper companies (as he did) without compensation, and that this would provoke world criticism. ITT therefore would approach Allende directly, suggesting that if he gave *them* good terms, "he can point to us as an example of how a fair deal can be completed if both sides approach the matter sensibly." In other words, ITT would benefit from the disasters of the copper companies, and leave them in the lurch.[14]

Negotiations broke off in March 1972 as soon as Jack Anderson had published the first stories based on the secret ITT memos. Allende thereafter nationalized the Chilean telephone company without compensation. This was not an unmitigated disaster, because ITT had already lodged a claim for $92 million under expropriation insurance with the Overseas Private Investment Corporation (OPIC). However, the terms of this insurance made it possible for OPIC to refuse to pay if it could be shown that the expropriation was the result of provocation by the investor. At the conclusion of the Senate Subcommittee hearings, OPIC announced that ITT's $92 million claim would be denied. An arbitration hearing subsequently reversed this decision, and with the return of a pro-American government in Chile, OPIC was reimbursed by Chile. ITT nevertheless suffered a net financial setback from the episode—it was ultimately compensated for only 80 per cent of the value of the investment, without interest.

Along the way, ITT had a rough row to hoe financially. During the Senate hearings, ITT stock fell five points, presumably because it had become increasingly apparent that ITT might lose its insurance coverage because of evidence of its provoking the nationalization. After a bad year in 1970, ITT stock had recovered in 1971. But from 1972 to 1975 prices fell disastrously, to less than half the levels prevailing in the late 1960s. After 1975 there was a partial recovery but it still left the stock over a billion dollars short of its highest previous value.

The *long-term* slump in ITT stock prices cannot be explained by the Chilean nationalization experience, because the company did not lose very much in the end as a result of that episode. Whether any of the slump can be attributed to a loss of confidence in the stock from the run of adverse publicity in the early 1970s is impossible to say. Top management of the company was disrupted by the retirement of Geneen and the dismissal of his replacement by the Board after less than two years in the job; such dislocation at the top can sap stockholder confidence, even if profits remain stable. Although earnings went up and down during the 1970s, they were reasonably steady in the years when there was the most severe discounting of ITT shares. Another significant factor in share prices was that ITT was forced by the Justice Department to divest some subsidiaries during this period.

The four senior executives we interviewed, two of them Senior Vice-Presidents, granted that a decline in ITT stock values coincided with the adverse publicity over Chile; however, no causal connection was perceived. The executives claimed to have given a lot of thought to whether the publicity had adversely affected share prices. Their conclusion was that the period was a bad one for conglomerates generally (although ITT did fare worse than most). Irrespective of whether the executives' perception was accurate or not, the fact that they *perceived* their stock to be dropping in response to market-wide forces rather than to the bad press is significant from the standpoint of the regulatory power of adverse publicity.

One direct financial cost of the adverse publicity to the company was the tens of millions of dollars spent to counter it. However, this was anything but money down the drain. We have seen how the company harnessed its new-found public prominence to make sure that ITT was not only remembered, but that it was favorably remembered. Successful ju-jitsu notwithstanding, the executives we interviewed were adamant that they would rather not have experienced the adverse publicity. Whatever the upshot, "you wouldn't voluntarily go through it again." Executives do not take the view that all's well that ends well. They prefer a smooth ride to a bumpy one.

A financial benefit of the counterpublicity campaign, in addition to the favorable public image, was more people wanting to apply for jobs at ITT. ITT became in this period a company "where everything was happening," and in the end, a company with a favorable image for prospective job applicants. For a company that employs 375,000 people, anything that attracts more and better applicants is an important plus. One informant also argued that the heightened visibility also gave ITT salespeople a foot in the door of many customers during the scandal. Because ITT was in the news, prospective purchasers of ITT equipment were interested in chatting with someone from the company.

Finally, on the negative side, the adverse publicity made ITT a bête noir of certain extremist groups. The company was the target of more than 90 terrorist threats and attacks, including a 1973 explosion at ITT world headquarters in New York and a 1974 storming of the annual stockholders meeting in Seattle. As a consequence, ITT drastically increased its expenditure on security.

Non-Financial Impacts

The executives we spoke to did not feel that there was an adverse impact on morale within the organization from the publicity. They did find that employees sought the reassurance of facts with which to reply to friends who were critical of ITT. After such facts were provided, it was believed that the effect on morale was not notable. The executives with whom we spoke found that the adverse publicity provoked a fair amount of discussion at cocktail parties they attended in the early 1970s. However, they described it as "more an entrée to cocktail party conversations than a stigmatic experience."

They did concede non-financial costs which were real and telling, however: "For a little while the top management who feel they are subject to unfair publicity get very aroused. There's a psychic cost, a lot of lost energy." The Senate Subcommittee hearings were a gruelling experience for executives, from Geneen on down, who were subjected to cross-examination. There was also a kind of stigma. Two executives who appeared before the Subcommittee complained of being "grilled under bright lights" (a consequence of the presence of television cameras). The lights were so bright that Howard Aibel, Senior Vice President and General Counsel, wore sunglasses, despite jocular comments within the company that this gave him the appearance of a Mafioso.

Reforms

In his book on ITT, Robert Sobel has suggested that the string of publicity crises discussed earlier, of which the Chile scandal was the most important part, contributed to Harold Geneen's early retirement as chief executive officer. According to Sobel, "insofar as public relations were concerned, Geneen had become a liability, in large part because of the bad press he had received from the time of the ABC conflicts through the Chilean episode."[15] It is difficult to say whether a desire to remove such a supposed public relations problem had anything to do with Geneen's withdrawal, but it must be said that the fact that ITT did not suffer materially from the public relations problem is inconsistent with this interpretation.

As a direct result of the Chilean affair, ITT introduced a policy prohibiting contributions to any political party or candidate in any part of the world. It remains acceptable, however, to contribute to non-election campaigns over issues which directly affect the corporation. For example, the corporation recently threw its support behind a campaign against a referendum to ban the use of nuclear energy. Corporate financial support was based on a belief that having the referendum would be contrary to the best interests of both the United States and ITT, since ITT make high pressure pipes used in nuclear power plants.

Certain senior executives must now provide a signed statement to the chief executive officer indicating that the political contributions policy has been complied with inside their divisions. The chief executive officer, in turn, makes an annual statement to the Board on compliance with the program. The political contributions policy is one of twelve compliance policies now overviewed by a committee of the Board.[16] A "compliance officer" has also been appointed to the legal department; he has unrestricted access to the chief executive officer. Sanctions available for violations of these policies include the cancellation of stock options and bonuses and the stretching out of salary increases. The strongest sanction available is dismissal. We were told that since the political contributions policy had been introduced, no violations had been detected and therefore no sanctions imposed. We asked Senior Vice-President and General Counsel Aibel how many employees had been dismissed for violations of the other eleven compliance policies. The answer was: "I don't think I have the authority to tell you that." However, we know that two Austrian ITT executives were dismissed in connection with the payment of bribes to win hospital construction contracts for ITT-Austria.[17]

The Chilean scandal triggered a series of more general investigations by a special committee of the ITT board on the use of "questionable payments" to increase corporate political influence.[18] These questionable payments investigations revealed that, although new policies on political contributions, slush funds, and payments through intermediaries had been introduced, compliance during the late 1970s had been less than perfect. The second report of the ITT special committee was critical of the steps which had been taken to implement the new policies:

. . .until the present top management of ITT took office, signals from headquarters to foreign managers may not have been as clear and firm about enforcement of the Policies as with hindsight one might wish.

We found that . . . senior management did not succeed in conveying to the rest of management its determination on the subject of the Policies. The highest levels of the Corporation were aware of the reluctance of foreign managers to accept what many of them viewed as exported American morality.[19]

The compliance system, although strengthened in recent years, has not been foolproof. We found instances of inadequate supervision, inadequate documentation and violations of the Policies in some ITT subsidiaries.[20]

In short, the program of reform at ITT was half-hearted compared with the effort made by Lockheed, Allied and indeed most of the other companies included in the present study. One probable reason is that ITT succeeded in using counterpublicity to outflank the scandal to which it was exposed.

CHAPTER 12

Drug Testing at Searle

Reincarnated Rats

Since the thalidomide disaster,[1] there has been concern over the problem of pharmaceutical companies fraudulently rigging drug safety testing experiments to show their products to be safer and more effective than in fact they are. A series of drug-testing frauds culminated in protracted investigation of the problem between 1975 and 1977 by the Senate Judiciary Committee, Subcommittee on Health chaired by Senator Edward Kennedy. The company which was subjected to more vilification than any other before the Kennedy Subcommittee was G.D. Searle & Co., one of America's largest pharmaceutical transnational corporations.

Kennedy and the U.S. Food and Drug Administration (FDA) were convinced that both fraud and incompetence were widespread in the Searle safety-testing program of the early 1970s. FDA head Alexander M. Schmidt testified to particular concern over the testing of what was to become Searle's top selling line, Aldactone:

This report clearly indicated a dose-related increase in the frequency of liver and testicular tumors and recommended that these findings be analyzed for statistical significance.

Although FDA regulations require "alarming findings" to be submitted to the Agency promptly, this had not been done.

In the course of our review of the 78-week study on rats, we have found a variety of other problems and questionable practices. For example, tissue masses were excised from three live animals during the study, and the animals were allowed to continue in the study. Two of these tumors were malignant and were not reported to FDA.

It is disconcerting that even today, after three separate reviews by Searle personnel of the same data from the 78-week rat study, we are continuing to discover errors that complicate review of this study.

Review of a 104-week rat study on Aldactone conducted at Hazleton Laboratories [a subcontracting laboratory] also revelaed problems. Only 70 percent of the tissues scheduled for histopathological examination in the protocol were actually examined. In addition, some animals with gross lesions which, according to the study protocol, required histopathological examination, were not so examined.[2]

Another Searle top seller, Flagyl, which had been the subject of a concerted campaign by Nader's Health Research Group seeking its withdrawal from the market on the grounds of alleged carcinogenicity, also had a dubious testing record. In a stinging criticism, Commissioner Schmidt alleged that the company had resorted to biased selection of data:

Among additional major findings of the investigation of this study are: (1) For several of the animals, it was noted that the microscopic examination of tissue slides had been conducted by two different pathologists at Searle who reported different findings. Rather than submitting both reports, or having a third pathologist review slides on which the first two disagreed, Searle submitted only the second pathologist's report, which in our view appears substantially more favorable to the drug; and (2) Searle employees were unable to explain many of the procedures by which microscopic findings were recorded, edited and verified prior to the inclusion in the report of this study; most records of observations of microscopic findings were not dated or signed. They were also unable to account for the differences in raw data and the final reports submitted to FDA.[3]

Similar allegations were made by Schmidt with respect to the sweetening ingredient, Aspartame:

Our investigators found that a pathologist's summary was edited in such a manner as to alter, generally in a favorable direction, some of the pathologist's summarized findings. The original report was not submitted.[4]

In a similar vein, it was also implied that tests which progressed unfavorably had been abandoned. A 46-week hamster study on Aspartame was "discontinued because of 'wet tail' (a disease of hamsters), but none of the symptoms of the disease are reflected in daily observation records."[5]

Myriad other FDA allegations against Searle are spread over thousands of pages of testimony before the Senate. Thus, in a rat study of the drug Norpace, there were alleged to be "inadequate antemortem observations: e.g., animals reported in good condition were actually dead, inadequate reporting of tissue masses."[6] The most serious problem which the FDA claimed to be common in many Searle studies was that: "Because of the perfunctory nature of the observations, tissue masses come and go and animals die more than once."[7] In fact some rats listed as dead later were recorded as alive, then dead, then resurrected once or even twice more. Searle's former principal pathologist, John W. Sargatz, testified that in 1968 and 1969, over his objections, he had been instructed to write reassuring comments on post-mortems of rats which died in 1967, before he joined the firm.

The FDA General Counsel's office was of the view that Searle should be prosecuted criminally for its pattern of conduct with respect to drug testing. The Justice Department, however, equally strongly believed that a criminal case should not proceed. Its opinion was that the scientific complexity of the case would be an excessive burden on limited government prosecutorial resources, and that while it might be possible to convict a few low-level company operatives, guilt on the part of senior executives could not be demonstrated beyond reasonable doubt. The Justice Department was averse to a result which might lay all blame at the door of junior scapegoats. Moreover, the Department considered that Searle's alleged misdeeds were not clearly definable specific acts, but rather constituted a cumulative pattern of conduct. Indeed, the FDA itself had admitted as much in the report of a task force appointed to investigate Searle's animal studies:

> While a single discrepancy, error, or inconsistency in any given study may not be significant in and of itself, the *cumulative* findings of problems within and across the studies we investigated reveal a pattern of conduct which compromises the scientific integrity of the studies.[8]

The investigations resulted in a reputedly close grand jury decision not to return an indictment against Searle or any of its executives. The company felt vindicated and was able to claim, as one Searle executive put it: "While there might have been a little dishonesty here and there, basically it was a problem of incompetence and poor record-keeping among our research staff."

Publicity and Counterpublicity

The Kennedy charisma ensured that a great deal of publicity was generated by the Senate probes into Searle. The press took to stories of experimental animals dying and then being born again with a fervor fanned by the Kennedy flair for making news. A *Wall Street Journal* story quoted Kennedy as saying "These findings [on Searle] must be alarming to every American who takes prescription drugs. The scientific integrity of one of this nation's oldest and most well-known pharmaceutical companies has been seriously challenged."[9] The same story speculated: "The FDA report on Searle is likely to affect the marketing of the drugs involved and also could hurt the company's reputation and credibility." When the Subcommittee resumed sittings in July 1976 and considered other drug-testing scandals as a follow-up to the Searle case, Kennedy was quoted in the *Washington Post*:

> I fear a major American tragedy may be in the making . . . It is beginning to appear that the quality of animal test data in this country is scandalously bad—that the American people are being exposed on a daily basis to products whose safety has been determined on the basis of inaccurate information.[10]

The *New York Times* devoted more than 23 column inches on page 6 to the Searle story when it first broke on July 11, 1975, and followed up with many more articles over the next year, culminating in a front-page story on July 21, 1976, "U.S. AGENCY FINDS DRUG TESTING LAX." The piece described a General Accounting Office report on drug testing in general ordered in the wake of the Searle hearings.

The most poisonous stories came from Morton Mintz of the *Washington Post* under headings like, "DRUG MAKER IS ACCUSED OF FALSIFYING DATA."[11] Back home in Chicago, where Searle has its head office, the *Chicago Tribune* headlines were more encouraging: " 'CHARGES FALSE': FIRM DEFENDS DRUG TESTING."[12]

Searle's response to the adverse publicity was not aggressive. It forcefully told its side of the story at the Senate hearings, but did not run a counterpublicity campaign with paid advertising. Searle cooperated with Senate investigators and avoided fighting back in ways which might have protracted the period during which its drug-testing practices were in the news.

Financial Impacts

It is difficult to assess the extent of the financial impact of the bad publicity from the Kennedy hearings. Searle share values were enjoying consistently rising values during the first four years of the 1970s. This was followed by a considerable decline in the mid-1970s (the period of the crisis) and a plateau at these lower values for the remainder of the decade. Searle profitability began to decline in 1973 and showed a decrease every year until 1977, when the corporation recorded a loss. Most observers seem to agree that the publicity problem with which the company was confronted during this period was compounded by poor management. It would therefore be unwarranted to assume that the Kennedy hearings had a dramatic effect on the corporation's financial performance. Nevertheless, the executives interviewed did perceive some adverse effects.

A good relationship with the FDA is critical to the financial performance of major pharmaceutical companies. The FDA has the power to hold up new drugs for which marketing approval is being sought. If the product is a financial winner, delays of a few months while the agency reevaluates data on the safety of the drug can cost many millions of dollars. Searle's relationship with the FDA deteriorated in the mid-1970s because of its testing problems; key actors in both organizations agree that an attitude of mistrust prevailed for two years. This fact should have led investors to the reasonable expectation that because of extra scrutiny of company submissions to the FDA and consequent delays, earnings might be less than they otherwise would be.

To the extent that publicity played a role in bringing about the disastrous downturn in Searle's earnings and stock prices, it was because of the quality of regulatory relationships more than because of consumer resistance to Searle products. Because the most profitable drugs for any company are those under patent, and because consumers do not make their own choices in the market (doctors make choices for them by writing prescriptions), good will from consumers is not very important for drug companies. If Searle has a patent on the compound which is most effective for a particular set of symptoms, then the consumer will try it. Good will from physicians is important and an erosion of this good will (or a *perceived* erosion by investors) may have been a factor in Searle's financial decline. There is not direct evidence, one way or the other, of an impact of the publicity on doctors' resistance to writing Searle prescriptions.

However, sales of Aldactone and Flagyl, the two drugs most in the spotlight, suffered somewhat. As a result of the Searle investigations, the FDA required new warnings for the two products. Boxed warnings were put on their labels pointing out that animal tests showed the production of tumors (Aldactone) or cancer (Flagyl) and that "unnecessary use of this drug should be avoided." The recommended dose for Flagyl was also reduced by the agency.

Hazelton Laboratories also claims that being named in the Kennedy hearings as having done work on contract for Searle (work which was questioned) cost the small company over a million dollars in business. Other major pharmaceutical companies are naturally reluctant to give contract work to a laboratory that they perceive, rightly or wrongly, as being under a cloud with the regulatory agency that will scrutinize and evaluate the data collected.

Non-Financial Impacts

The nine Searle executives interviewed reported adverse impacts on employee morale as a result of the drug-testing publicity. The worst effects were in the critical new drug research area where scientists for a period of over two years were continually being distracted from their work by the demands of assisting and responding to the government investigations. In this period Searle research virtually ground to a halt. Even afterwards, the confidence of Searle scientists remained deflated by the barrage of criticism. The grand jury investigation and the ordeal of cross-examination by the Kennedy subcommittee will never be forgotten by some Searle executives.

Some informants experienced a degree of social embarrassment at the fact that friends and neighbors were aware that the company's name had been dragged through the mud. Vilification by the Senate Subcommittee was perceived by the executives as having undermined the reputation of Searle as an ethical company serving the public interest through finding new ways of curing disease.

Reforms

A total reorganization of the company was the upshot of the affair. The chief executive officer was replaced by Donald Rumsfeld, one-time Defense Secretary, White House Chief of Staff, and incumbent of other senior positions in the Nixon and Ford administrations. One of Rumsfeld's first acts as President was to attempt to counter Searle's poor compliance record with an edict that staff were to be evaluated for promotion and incentive payments on the basis of their compliance record in addition to the usual criteria.

Searle also gave a blank check to Richard Hamill, lured from Searle's competitor, Baxter-Travenol, to set up a sophisticated corporate compliance group which travelled the world doing compliance audits to ensure that all subsidiaries in all areas of the corporation's operations were meeting both legal and company standards. Hamill's key appointments in the compliance group were also from outside Searle. As Searle's Group Managing Director for the South-East Asian Region complained:

> We have three bosses to work for now, whereas local companies have only one. Firstly, we must follow local laws, like the local Corporate Affairs Commission. Secondly, we have got to have the Securities and Exchange Commission as a boss. And thirdly, we have to have the internal corporation controls which our company has set up since the Kennedy hearings. With three different kinds of checks on our behavior there is far less chance that an American multinational company will break the law compared with an Australian company.

Publicity from the Kennedy hearings had an even more marked effect on the regulatory apparatus itself. The FDA set about drawing up a detailed code of Good Laboratory Practices (GLPs)[13] for drug testers, violation of which could be prosecuted criminally or result in civil remedies such as disqualification of all testing data collected at the laboratory for future new drug approvals. It would now be much easier to convict a company for the kinds of misdeeds alleged to have been committed by Searle. The new GLP regulations set tough standards for equipment design, maintenance and calibration, research protocols, record-keeping, and test article handling and storage. They also require laboratories to have a Quality Assurance Unit which acts as an internal policeman of GLP compliance. One person must be nominated as a study director for each piece of research, and Quality Assurance Unit reports must be placed on his or her desk at regular intervals. The GLP regulations therefore impose a self-regulatory scheme which incorporates accountability and assurances that senior management will have warning or knowledge of violations. At a cost of $16 million, the FDA also set up a Bioresearch Monitoring Program of government inspections to ensure compliance with the GLPs. The impact of the Kennedy Searle hearings has been international, as many developed countries are now enacting GLPs similar to those of the United States.

Interestingly, Searle played a constructive role in drawing up GLP draft regulations, many of which were adopted by the FDA. Perhaps through this cooperative attitude, Searle restored some of the good will it had lost with the regulatory agency. To cap this off, Searle publicly dissociated itself from the Pharmaceutical Manufacturers Association's position that the GLPs should be guidelines rather than sanctionable rules, and insisted that violation of GLPs should be a criminal matter.

Searle in fact reformed its toxicological research procedures to meet the requirements of the new Good Laboratory Practices well before they were introduced. Thus, in this case study, there were three reform impacts: (1) internal compliance reforms and replacement of key personnel by Searle to strengthen its self-regulatory capacity, (2) strengthening of the government's regulatory capacity, and (3) the imposition by the state of stronger self-regulatory mechanisms on all other companies in the industry. These three reforms occurred not because of anyone's being convicted, but because of the heightened visibility of the problem in the aftermath of the adverse publicity.

CHAPTER 13

Bribery at Lockheed

The Payoffs

From the 1950s to the mid-1970s, bribery was an accepted way of doing business in the aerospace industry in general, and by the Lockheed Aircraft Corporation in particular. A Special Review Committee of seven Lockheed outside directors concluded that, for the period 1970–1975, between $30 and $38 million in questionable payments were made to win foreign aircraft sales.[1] Lockheed had been paying bribes to people of influence in the governments of Japan, Germany, the Netherlands, Italy, Indonesia, Iran, Saudi Arabia, and other countries. Recipients of Lockheed largesse included such notables as Prime Minister Tanaka of Japan and Prince Bernhard of the Netherlands.

The Special Review Committee of Lockheed Outside Directors concluded that the pattern of bribery was not an aberration for which relatively junior employees could be blamed. It was a policy for which the corporation's Chairman, Dan Haughton, and its President, Carl Kotchian, were responsible:

The senior management of the Company, in particular Haughton and Kotchian, appear to the Committee to have been willing to distort such a primary principle as integrity for short-term expediency, in order to aid, in their mind, the Company's financial survival. It is obvious to the Committee that they were responsible for the questionable payments and practices. While Kotchian was the architect of the strategy that fostered and allowed the things that have been enumerated herein to take place, at least to the expansive extent that they prevailed from the beginning of the 1970's, Haughton fully supported the program and must share equally the responsibility.[2]

These senior people had systematically prevented an awareness of the bribes from spreading throughout the organization, and most importantly, from reaching the Audit Committee of the Board. When audit reports surfaced at lower levels of the organization suggesting the possibility of impropriety, the bad news was filtered out before it reached those who would demand explanations.[3] Yet there were sufficient people around who sensed that something was wrong to foment the scandal soon to ensue.

The first public whiff of the trouble came with the hearings of Frank Church's Senate Subcommittee on Multinational Corporations. Lockheed's rival, Northrop, was being investigated. The Watergate scandal had uncovered illegal campaign contributions by Northrop, and as the dominos began to fall for them, Northrop Chairman, Tom Jones, testified before the Church Subcommittee in June 1975 that his practices of using consultants to pass bribes were modelled on those of Lockheed. As the press turned their attention to Lockheed in response to the Jones bombshell, the company's auditors, Arthur Young, decided it was time for self-preservation.[4] They requested Kotchian and other senior Lockheed executives to sign a letter stating that to the best of their knowledge and belief:

> All [consultancy] payments are made in accordance with the agreements and are duly recorded on the books of Lockheed . . . . No employee or official of any foreign government, or any director, officer or employee of a customer, is a party to any of the agreements.
> No director, officer, agent or managerial employee of Lockheed or an affected subsidiary has knowledge of the disposition of the payments made to the consultancy.[5]

The executives were not prepared to allow Arthur Young to shrug off all responsibility by passing the buck to them. They refused to sign. Arthur Young, in turn, refused to certify the annual report. A government investigation was then inevitable. Strategic adverse publicity thus flushed out acts of self-preservation by actors who wanted to ensure that they would not be blamed for the bribery. These acts of self-preservation brought on the full crisis.

On April 13, 1976, the U.S. Securities and Exchange Commission (SEC) filed a complaint against the Lockheed Corporation, and against Haughton and Kotchian, alleging bribery.[6] Without admitting any illegality, the three defendants consented to an injunction enjoining them from any activities of the kind described in the complaint, and providing for the establishment of a Special Review Committee of the Lockheed Board of Directors to conduct an investigation into the matters alleged.[7] On May 26, 1977, the committee made public a report which revealed widespread bribery and improper bookkeeping practices. One example of such improper accounting to conceal illegality was: "Utilization of 'shell' corporations to enter into consultant agreements which served as a screen for questionable payments or to provide false receipts for payments actually made to other third parties, such as customer employees."[8]

The Federal Trade Commission issued a cease and desist order against Lockheed on December 21, 1978.[9] The FTC's complaint alleged that Lockheed had undermined free competition in violation of the Robinson-Patman Act by paying kickbacks to secure purchase of their aircraft in preference to those of other domestic American manufacturers.[10] Lockheed was ordered to cease and desist from such practices and to provide adequate documentation in future of all payments which could be questionable (e.g., political contributions, agents' fees).

Meanwhile, the Justice Department was gathering evidence for a criminal prosecution of the company and its two senior officers. Then a deal was made whereby no charges were to be laid against Haughton and Kotchian, and the corporation would plead guilty to criminal charges and agree to a fine totalling $647,000.[11] The plea agreement was attractive to Lockheed because the Justice Department laid charges only for payments to Japanese politicians (including Prime Minister Tanaka) to secure sales of the L-1011 Tristar aircraft in 1972. In return for the guilty plea, the government agreed not to press charges concerning the many other illegalities referred to in the Report of the Special Review Committee of the Board of Directors. Since the bribes predated the Foreign Corrupt Practices Act of 1977, the Justice Department had to rely on other statutes to bring charges. The plea agreement alleged customs violations as a result of transporting 5 million yen in Japanese currency out of the United States without the approval of U.S. Customs,[12] false statements to the Export-Import bank that no uninvoiced discounts or rebates had been made concerning the Japanese L-1011 purchase,[13] and fraud.[14]

Publicity and Counterpublicity

At a number of points in the second half of the 1970s, the Lockheed scandal was front-page news. Even during the periods when it was not, Lockheed executives were informed of stories critical of Lockheed through the company's regular "Domestic and International Media Report." Most large companies have such internal news services that transmit to executives everything that has been said about the company, even in obscure foreign journals. Consequently, adverse publicity that might seem like a ripple to the rest of us can appear as a wave to the executives of the company concerned. Thus the April 23, 1976, issue of the "Domestic and International Media Report" refers to Lockheed bribe stories in newspapers in Great Britain, France, Italy, Holland, and Japan, as well as throughout the United States. A humiliating cartoon in the *Atlanta Constitution* was one item:

ATLANTA CONSTITUTION isn't doing us any favors (largest local industry status notwithstanding)[15] . . . . Cartoon in 4/16 CONSTITUTION portrayed a C-5 as a human penitent, labelled Lockheed, clutching a bible to its chest with one arm and in the other arm holding a sign saying "Repent."

During the crisis, some tour operators included Lockheed's headquarters as an attraction on the regular itinerary of Los Angeles tours for Japanese visitors. Lockheed suffered this misfortune because its offices are located at Burbank airport where flights depart for the tourist mecca of Las Vegas. One executive expressed irritation at having to wind his way past the tripods of Japanese tourists photographing the main entrance to the Lockheed building.

The head of the company's public relations staff said that some people within the company felt at the time that a counterattack was necessary. However, it was decided to try to weather the storm, and to cooperate with enforcement agencies in the hope of getting through the fall-out quickly. The public relations department regarded the main goal as minimizing the length of the "time window" for the scandal. When the company was embroiled in one public event, it became more vulnerable to public criticism for unrelated matters. If Lockheed is news, then the slightest foot Lockheed puts wrong is also news. A public relations executive pointed out that Lockheed was exposed to three weeks of bad press during the bribery crisis because of a relatively minor customs offense. In normal times, this type of problem would not have been mentioned in the newspapers.

Passing consideration was given to insulating operating companies (e.g., Lockheed Electronics, Lockheed Missiles and Space Company, Lockheed Shipbuilding and Construction) by having them drop the

Lockheed name in favor of independent designations. Consideration was even given to changing the Lockheed logo.[16] However, the market research showed that minuses from the scandal were outweighed by the previously accumulated pluses associated with the Lockheed image. Most important, a public relations department survey showed that people still firmly associated the Lockheed name with technical excellence.

The Lockheed case study illustrates how adverse publicity, if it is spicy enough, can feed on itself. As reputations begin to crumble, there are often people with axes to grind who now can exploit the climate of scandal. Particularly crucial in this regard were the revelations by Ernest Hauser of Lockheed's Koblenz office. It was disclosure of the contents of Hauser's diary which began the process by which Prince Bernhard of the Netherlands was judicially investigated and disgraced.

> Hauser's story is that he had a heart attack, and Lockheed, terrified that while under sedation he might let slip some remark that would reveal the pay-off arrangements, tried to transfer him hastily back to the US. He didn't want to go, and a row followed, as a result of which he left Lockheed to set up his own aircraft spare parts business.[17]

Another example came as late as 1980 when the estranged wife of Adnan Khashoggi, infamous middleman in the Lockheed scandal, dragged up new dirt in support of a breach-of-contract suit against her husband.[18] She alleged that executives from Lockheed, Northrop, and Litton Industries had been provided with Swiss bank accounts, prostitutes, and other gifts "worth thousands of dollars" by Khashoggi. This was the first time that Lockheed executives had been accused of *accepting* kickbacks from foreign sales agents. It would appear that some of the $106 million Lockheed paid Khashoggi in commission fees between 1970 and 1975, far from paying foreign bribes, was being kicked back to the Californian executives responsible for retaining his services. Mrs. Khashoggi also alleged that "to bribe a Lockheed executive," Mr. Khashoggi gave a job in one of his companies to the man's mistress.[19]

The Lockheed case may be extraordinary in the way that wave followed upon wave of scandal. Not many scandals have the staying power that comes from the corrupt inolvement of Princes and Prime Ministers.

Financial Impacts

Lockheed's balance sheets for the years of the foreign bribery crisis provide no evidence whatsoever of an adverse financial impact on the company. During the year in which the scandal broke, 1975, and during 1976 when the adverse publicity reached its peak, Lockheed sales were at about the same level as for 1974, and at a much higher level than for any previous year. In 1975 Lockheed earnings almost doubled, and 1976 and 1977 saw earnings continue at a level higher than they had been for a decade.

During the mid-70s Lockheed was beginning to pull out of the worst trough it had experienced in its history. In the early 1970s it was pushed to the brink of bankruptcy by the failure of the L-1011 wide body commercial aircraft program, unwise entry into fixed-price contracts with the U.S. government during a period of high inflation, and the failure of some shipbuilding programs. Any adverse financial impact from publicity over the bribery scandal was bound to be of small consequence compared to these major debacles. Lockheed had been at its lowest ebb, and the only way it could go financially was up (or down into bankruptcy). Any financial impact from the bribery scandal was swamped out by the larger financial realities which governed the future of Lockheed at the time.

Executives we interviewed were not aware of any specific sales lost by Lockheed as a result of the scandal. Interim Lockheed Chairman Robert W. Haack conceded publicly that certain sales were held up because of the crisis: " . . . There are some parts of the world in which marketing decisions have been delayed to let the dust settle and clear up the uncertainty."[20] The most notable examples were pending aircraft contracts in Japan and Canada worth over $2 billion which were shelved for two years until the political heat was off.[21] Naturally, a two-year delay in consummating a deal can cost a company money, and is especially important for a company with liquidity problems. Nonetheless, contracts delayed are nowhere as serious as contracts lost.

One executive explained that while no sales were lost as a result of the adverse publicity, Lockheed had to work harder and wait longer to win contracts. Because governments were cautious about accusations by opposition parties of being on the take if they bought from Lockheed, they were not going to do so until they were convinced beyond a shadow of doubt that Lockheed had the product that was technically superior for their needs. As mentioned earlier, Lockheed's market research showed that potential customers did not have their confidence shaken in the quality of Lockheed products as a result of the scandal. Marketing executives at Lockheed are convinced that customers buy if they think the product is good and reasonably priced, regardless of what they think of the honesty of the company doing the selling.

Neither Lockheed executives nor executives at General Dynamics or McDonnell-Douglas with whom we spoke felt that competitors in the aerospace industry had used Lockheed's foreign bribery problems to advantage in enticing sales away from them. In any case, a large proportion of Lockheed business is not subject to the cruel winds of competition. Lockheed makes Polaris missiles, C-130 Airlifters, and many other products for which defense departments cannot turn to alternative suppliers.

If Lockheed had lost business because of the scandal, one would not expect the decline in sales to show up in the year of the scandal, or even in the years immediately following: In the aerospace industry, contracts are commonly signed for delivery five years into the future. Interim Chairman Haack pointed out, however, that sign-ups for the 12 months when the crisis was at its peak went up to over \$3 billion.[22] By any standards, Lockheed's financial position improved as the bribery crisis worsened. The stock market reflected this. Lockheed stock prices increased steadily and continuously throughout the period. Between the onset of the crisis in 1975 and the criminal conviction in 1979, Lockheed shares had more than tripled in value.

Of course it might have been that, while the bribery scandal did not in any long or medium term sense halt the upward march of Lockheed shares, there were downward slips at various points when the scandal reached new peaks. If this was the case, it was not perceptible to the executive we interviewed who was responsible for stockholder relations for Lockheed throughout the period. It is extremely difficult to interpret the daily fluctuations of share prices, to assess whether Lockheed shares were down for the day because the market generally was down, because an unusually large parcel of stock just happened to be sold on that day, because of a rumor about expected earnings, or because of adverse publicity about the company's foreign bribes. Needless to say, however, if a downward ripple in Lockheed shares was not perceptible to the Lockheed executive responsible for stockholder relations, then one wonders to whom it would have been perceptible. None of the aerospace executives with whom we spoke felt that Lockheed share prices had been adversely affected by the scandal. Nor were they aware of any specialist aerospace market analysts or stockbrokers advising their clients to sell Lockheed shares at the time.

To summarize, the financial impacts of the foreign bribery scandal of 1975–1979 on Lockheed were not major. The costs were limited to delayed sales as opposed to lost sales.

Perhaps a more important type of delay, however, was in the negotiation of the corporation's recapitalization plan with the 24 banks which had kept it afloat during the dark days of 1971–1972: Lockheed still owed them $600 million. It would seem that in early 1976 the banks were adopting a wait-and-see attitude until a consent agreement with the SEC over the foreign bribes was struck. When the consent decree was approved, interim Lockheed Chairman Haack released a press statement:

> CONSENT DECREE WITH SEC
> MAJOR STEP FOR LOCKHEED
> BURBANK, Calif., April 13—Lockheed Chairman Robert W. Haack today described the signing of a consent agreement with the Securities and Exchange Commission as a necessary prerequisite to further proceeding with Lockheed's financial restructuring plan.
> "Obtaining the consent agreement was the pacing factor governing our ability to finalize our recapitalization plan with our 24 lending banks, issue a stockholder proxy statement, and schedule our annual meeting of shareholders," Haack said.
> "We now can move forward with discussions on financial restructuring with our banks and with plans for our annual meeting in June or July," Haack stated . . . .

Non-Financial Impacts

The non-financial impacts of the scandal on Lockheed can only be understood in terms of the affair's impact on the world political system. For one thing, the political fortunes of many who were recipients of questionable payments crumbled.

1. The scandal contributed directly to the fall of a Japanese government. Thereafter, the former Prime Minister, Tanaka, three Diet members, and 13 Japanese company directors were prosecuted for bribery, tax evasion, and foreign exchange violations in connection with the Lockheed payments. Ten of the latter were convicted and sentenced to prison terms or suspended sentences;[23] the other seven trials are continuing. Edwin Reischauer, former U.S. Ambassador to Japan, has said of the fiasco that "the damage has been almost astronomical"

in terms of U.S. foreign relations.[24] Certainly the very powerful Tanaka faction in the Diet sees itself as having an axe
to grind with the U.S. government.

2. On March 10, 1977, the combined houses of the Italian
parliament voted to impeach two former defense ministers,
Luigi Gui and Mario Tanassi. Tanassi was subsequently sentenced to 28 months in jail for his part in Lockheed corruption.[25] Allegations that a Christian Democratic Party Prime
Minister during the late 1960s was the key person in a $1.6
million Lockheed payoff helped the Italian Communist Party
to its best-ever performance in the 1976 elections.[26] On June
15, 1978, Italian President Giovanni Leone resigned after
accusations of tax evasion and kickbacks, including a $2 million
Lockheed bribe.[27]

3. In 1979, the Turkish Deputy Premier, Faruk Sukan, resigned
from the government, accusing former defense minister, Ferit
Melen, of "being directly involved in the bribery case of
Lockheed Corporation in 1975." Sukan also charged that
"former Premier Suleyman Demirel, whose four-part coalition
government of 1975–77 had included Mr. Melen's Republican
Reliance Party, had blocked a parliamentary investigation into
the corruption allegation in order to remain in power."[28]

4. The scandal stripped Prince Bernhard of all his public posts
and almost brought down the Dutch Royal House of Orange.
Queen Juliana could be dissuaded from abdication only by
assurances that her husband would not be prosecuted.[29]

In many other countries there were smaller political crises. A
Spanish air force colonel was dismissed and fined by a court martial
for receiving $200,000 in illegal commissions from Lockheed in
connection with sales to the Spanish air ministry.[30] In Australia,
Opposition Leader Gough Whitlam created front-page news by
accusing a deceased Air Minister of impropriety over aircraft purchases from Lockheed.

Within Lockheed, all with whom we spoke said that they felt
embarrassed by the role of their company in such dramatic events.
One senior officer said: "Executives are always concerned about
your [company's] good name." Another replied that of course it
was acutely embarrassing: "You want to be liked. You want to be
loved . . . . If our peers didn't bring it up, we wondered why.
We wondered, are they being polite?" With respect to acquaintances
within the industry, he continued: "There'd be joshing and winking
from peers from Boeing and Douglas, but it was always easy in
these social confrontations to smile and say, 'Your time will come'.

And it did." With respect to these peers in the aerospace industry, there was no perceived loss of individual prestige because there was no loss of corporate prestige. However, Lockheed executives reported greater discomfort at explaining their company's conduct to family and friends outside the business community. The loss of both individual and corporate prestige for Lockheed was therefore at a general community level, but was not perceived as significant within the business community.

In the face of this decline in repute, the Lockheed families did pull together, according to one insider: "In our company community of Lockheed employees and their families we felt that Lockheed was being made a scapegoat. It hurt." Morale was adversely affected despite this kind of pulling together. Chairman Haack conceded that morale had been low to the point where "People around here felt lower than snakes."[31] Just how much this sagging of morale affected productivity is impossible to assess. One executive pointed out that the deflation was worse among "the engineering and technical people [who] were more shocked because they tend to be more idealists. . . . They felt a little depression because in a sense they felt that their character was being impugned. Some were surprised at the wide scope of the disclosures, but there was still a 'Why us?' attitude."

Chairman Haack was sufficiently concerned about the morale problem to circulate to all employees an explanatory document on the Lockheed Outside Directors' Special Review Committee Report.[32] The first point emphasized in the document was: "*The Lockheed of today is a different Lockheed from that covered in the report, and many of the committee recommendations have already been implemented during the course of the investigations.*" (Italics in original)

Lockheed did not seem to experience a fall-off in the number of people applying for positions in the corporation as a result of the scandal. Nor was there an unusual exodus of people from the company. The only discernible impact of this kind was that some outside public relations consultants became reluctant to take work from Lockheed (in Germany, for example) immediately after the crisis. Their reluctance, however, was short-lived.

Another possible impact of the bribery scandal was the suicide of corporate treasurer, Robert N. Waters, on the eve of the further Senate inquiry in August 1976 into Lockheed's foreign payments. David Boulton, in his book, *The Grease Machine*, contended that Waters committed suicide because of the bribery scandal:

All this was too much for corporate treasurer Robert N. Waters, a moody bachelor who had been with the company twenty-one years. . . . [Waters] was never a member of Haughton's inner cabinet, and though he had been involved in administering some of Lockheed's "off-the-books" payments, his overall responsibility was small. Nevertheless, on the eve of the Proxmire hearings and the Emergency Loan Guarantee Board meeting, Waters cocked his hunting rifle and shot himself dead through the temple. His death was hushed up. Lockheed ascribed the tragedy to "personal difficulties," but a suicide note referred to business problems.[33]

However, executives who knew Waters disputed Boulton's conclusion; they put Waters' suicide down to his generally depressive personality.

Short of causing suicide, the publicity prepared a rack for the infliction of other ordeals. Numerous executives were required to be at the disposal of government investigators who were forever visiting the company. Some had to testify before the Senate. And two were known to have received death threats.

Reforms

Boulton concludes that after the crisis "what Haack called 'the New Lockheed' became perhaps the world's first born-again corporation."[34] This conclusion is reached on the strength of the new *Lockheed Principles of Business Conduct* distributed to all employees in May 1977. The brief statement of principles is full of platitudes, such as, "Ethical conduct is the highest form of loyalty to Lockheed." However, organizational changes at Lockheed have gone beyond platitudes.

Long before the Lockheed Special Review Report that named the Chairman and President as the primarily responsible individuals, both men, Haughton and Kotchian, had been asked by the board to resign (effective March 1, 1976). Both of them retained consultant contracts with the corporation. Haughton's contract provided for payment of $750,000 in consultant fees over a ten-year period, in addition to his annual corporate pension of $65,000. In Lockheed circles, Haughton remains a much revered father-figure who is seen as having acted honorably to take full responsibility instead of passing it on to others.

Some other executives, including two vice-presidents, retired early. The officers we interviewed claimed that this was not the result of any decision by the corporation to force them out, but a voluntary decision undoubtedly influenced by the tension of the period and the realization that prospects for any further advancement had ended for certain individuals. A committee of management and lawyers, including some outside lawyers, decided that no individuals would be disciplined unless they had personally benefitted from their offenses. The evidence gathered by the committee was only strong in one case—a sales executive who received a $100,000 gift from a company consultant in an unidentified foreign country and deposited the money in a Swiss bank account. The executive was suspended without pay in 1976 and soon after resigned.

Haughton was replaced by Haack, a former Chairman of the New York Stock Exchange, selected partly by reason of an impeccable reputation for ethical conduct. He was to be interim chairman only for long enough to set the corporation on a new course. In 1977, Roy Anderson, a senior executive on whom the Special Review Committee placed only a small burden of blame for the foreign bribery, succeeded Haack.

One of the factors contributing to the offenses, we were further informed, was the weakening of Lockheed's internal auditing function. Lockheed had a Board of Directors audit committee from 1967 on. However, the committee failed to function as it should because it was shielded from critical information. Between the late 1960s and 1975, the internal audit group had its staff cut in half. The auditing function tended "to change from a control concept to a trouble-shooting role."[35]

This was altered in the aftermath of the crisis. A new director of auditing was appointed from outside and given a considerably increased staff. The internal audit group's budget has been made independent of the budgets of the operating divisions and subsidiaries which it audits. Whereas previously auditors reported to their local subsidiary or division, their primary reporting relationship is now to the director of internal auditing, who in turn was made to report directly to the Chairman in the years following the crisis. However, in 1980 the requirement that the director of auditing answer to the Chairman was revised. The auditing director now reports to the Senior Vice President—Finance. It will be recalled that one of the factors which made the foreign bribes possible was that reporting relationships that might have channeled adverse audit findings to the board were readily ruptured. The new system, even with the dropping of direct reporting to the Chairman, provides stronger guarantees that bad news will not be contained at lower levels of the organization. The director of internal auditing also now has direct and regular access to the audit committee of the board, without the necessity of going through his superiors. Another fail-safe mechanism is that subsidiaries must now report "unusual financial transactions" to headquarters.[36]

The following recommendation of the Special Review Committee to strengthen the independence of the audit committee has also been implemented:

The audit committee should be expanded to include at least five outside members of the board and its membership should be periodically rotated. In addition such committee should:
- keep full minutes of each meeting with reference to each matter of substance discussed and the action taken with respect to it;
- distribute its minutes to each member of the board and report regularly to the entire board; and
- affirm as its standard that all matters of substance relating to financial affairs of the Company or internal control and audit are to be brought to its attention.[37]

Guarantees of the independence of outside auditors and of the whole board have also been improved. More than two thirds of the board must now be composed of outsiders who are not present or former employees of the company and who do not have other business or professional relationships with the company. The outside auditors' partner attached to Lockheed must now be rotated at regular intervals. Since the foreign bribery scandals, this means of keeping outside auditors honest has become standard practice in American companies.

Perhaps more important, the climate of Lockheed board meetings has changed since the crisis. It is said that now directors ask probing questions and demand more detailed information in audit committee reports that they previously passsed without challenge. To compensate for this extra responsibility, outside directors are now paid more. In spite of this, Lockheed had problems recruiting outsiders with a reputation beyond reproach who would be willing to take on the job of monitoring a company with a checkered reputation.[38]

Various new standard operating procedures have been introduced as extra checks and balances to prevent repetition of corrupt practices. From June 1, 1977, all managerial personnel with financial responsibilities must sign a letter twice a year indicating that to the best of their knowledge the business of that part of the company under their control has been conducted in accordance with Lockheed's *Principles of Business Conduct* and other corporate ethical codes. An executive who has paid a bribe but who through this representation signs that he has not, sets himself up as the person responsible should the matter ever become public. Assurances are also demanded that the executive is not aware of any off-books accounts, that all transactions have been properly described and documented, and that "subject to United States Government security regulations, no material facts or circumstances relating to any transactions were concealed from Lockheed's internal or external auditors . . . ." Since June 1, 1977, no Lockheed employee has been disciplined for violation of the new ethical codes.

Extensive revisions of policies concerning the payment of international marketing consultants have been made. Semi-annual audits of the company's international marketing administration system have been replaced by quarterly audits. Previously, individuals could authorize commission payments to agents; today extensive certification and multiple approvals from officers and committees at various levels of the corporation are required before the payment is made. A Consultant Review Committee and Senior Review Board were established to check the credentials of consultants and the legitimacy of their services:

> The Consultant Review Committee shall include a member appointed by the Senior Vice President—Finance, a member appointed by the Senior Vice President and General Counsel, and two members appointed by the Vice President—International Marketing, one of whom shall be the chairman. The membership of the Committee may be changed from time to time by direction of the Senior Review Board. The Consultant Review Committee shall maintain a record of its activities and shall make periodic reports as directed by the Senior Review Board. The Senior Review Board shall be composed of the Senior Vice President—Business Development (chairman), Chairman of the Board, the President, the Senior Vice President and General Counsel, the Senior Vice President—Finance, and the Vice President—International Marketing. The Senior Review Board shall make reports to the Audit Committee of the Board of Directors. . . .[39]

New policies and procedures improve checks and balances only if they are observed. With Lockheed's bribes the problem was less one of defective standard operating procedures than one of procedures that were ignored:

> Employees learned not to question deviations from standard operating procedures and practices . . . . The Committee was told by several

157

witnesses that employees who questioned foreign marketing practices damaged their chances for career advancement.[40]

There is evidence that Lockheed has made genuine efforts to enforce compliance with its new anti-corruption policies. Annually, the senior vice-president and general counsel, chief counsel, and assistant chief counsel tour all operating facilities to refresh managers' consciousness of compliance responsibilities and to answer questions about law observance. It is unusual in large corporations for the three top lawyers to be given an educational mission as a primary part of their responsibilites: More typically one finds the general counsel's office adopting a reactive rather than proactive approach.

In addition to changes in corporate standard operating procedures, complementary changes have been made to procedures regulating bidding for government business in some of the countries that were revealed in the foreign bribery scandals as hotbeds of bribery and extortion. In the aftermath of the scandals, the Iranian Deputy Minister of War for Armament introduced a requirement that companies bidding for government business swear to certain matters in the presence of a Consular Officer. The affidavit reads as follows:

Neither the Company nor any of its subsidiaries or affiliates, nor any of its officers, directors, employees, or agents has paid either directly or indirectly or incurred liability for, any fees, commissions, bonuses, gratuities, or other payments or considerations to brokers, agents, finders, or other persons or juridical entities (including any official or employee of the Government), whether in or out of Iran (except suppliers or subcontractors as contemplated by and specifically referred to in the contractual arrangements involved in said Business Activities) in connection with the execution or performance of said business activities, or any transactions or contracts contemplated by the Business Activities, except as follows . . . .

I understand and acknowledge that any willful false statements in this affidavit may constitute a criminal offense by me and by the Company under the penal laws of Iran . . . .

I further understand and acknowledge that such willful false statements may also subject me and the company to certain civil liabilities, including the termination, cesssation, or liquidation by the Government of the Business Activities for cause, and the assessment of punitive damages against me and the Company.[41]

Similarly, in 1977 the Saudi Arabian government introduced new service agents regulations.[42] In an attempt to discourage the payment of bribes out of excessive commissions, the regulations set a ceiling of five per cent of the government contract price on agents' fees. Other provisons in the new Saudi procedures include a requirement that, "A committee or more [sic] consisting of at least three persons shall be formed at every ministry or government department to examine bids."[43] This is based on the assumption that it is more difficult to bribe a committee than an individual.

Interviews we conducted at various Japanese companies and government departments indicated that extensive revisions to the Japanese Commercial Code which came into effect in 1982 were in considerable measure motivated by the Lockheed scandal.[44] Broadly, the reforms widen corporate disclosure requirements and increase the independence, powers, and duties of statutory auditors.

Lockheed lawyers point out that the consent decree with the SEC had considerably increased Lockheed's legal exposure to bribery charges. The wording of the consent decree, in restraining Lockheed from "directly or indirectly" violating the Securities and Exchange Act, meant that "any device you use to [pass a bribe], you'll be caught." And so Lockheed requires its sales agents today to complete very detailed written undertakings that they will use their fees only in ways that are approved by Lockheed and that are in accord with local and U.S. law.

No amount of organizational reform can eliminate the possibility of bribery: There are infinite possibilities for finding ways around the most carefully designed compliance systems.[45] Nevertheless, there can be no question that the reforms at Lockheed, even though one of them was reversed in 1980, substantially increase the legal and disciplinary risks for any executive plotting bribery. Bribery therefore becomes an irrational business choice in most circumstances. The changes at Lockheed have been surgical rather than cosmetic. Undoubtedly, their compliance system still has a long way to go. Yet tough decisions were made, not the least of which was asking for the resignation of Dan Haughton, America's "Management Man of the Year" of 1966 and "Marketing Executive of the Year" in 1968.

Lockheed did not enjoy a surge of favorable publicity as a result of the constructive program of reform it undertook in response to the bribery scandal. The public relations staff called a press conference to outline the internal reforms that it believed made Lockheed a leader among American companies in ensuring law observance. Newspapers showed scant interest. Good news is little news.

CHAPTER 14

Bribery at McDonnell Douglas

The Payoffs

In the initial round of disclosures of foreign bribes in 1976, McDonnell Douglas Corporation reported a total of $2.5 million in questionable payments associated with aircraft sales.[1] The SEC was not convinced that this disclosure was full. In 1978, it accused McDonnell Douglas of having made $15.6 million in undisclosed payments to various foreign officials.[2] The Justice Department then opened an investigation which would lead for the first time to individual executives being charged criminally in a foreign bribery case.

A grand jury returned indictments against the corporation and four of its officers on November 9, 1973.[3] The four officers were James S. McDonnell III, Corporate Vice-President and son of the founder of the company, John C. Brizendine, President of the Douglas Division, Charles M. Forsyth, Douglas Executive Vice-President, and Sherman Pruitt, Jr., a Douglas Sales Manager. The indictment charged that McDonnell Douglas had defrauded Pakistan International Airlines by adding $500,000 to the cost of each DC10 aircraft sold to them and paying this to commission agents who in turn agreed to make corrupt payments to Afsar Husain, Planning Director of Pakistan International Airlines, Ashiq Ali Bhutto, the cousin of the then President of Pakistan, and his brother-in-law, Asif Mahmood. In return for his payoff, Husain had also provided McDonnell Douglas with the proposal of a competitor. While the defendants were alleged to have added $500,000 to the price of each plane, they responded to inquiries from the airline by stating that the sales commission was only $100,000. When the airline and the Pakistani Finance Minister protested even the $100,000 commissions, the price of each DC10 was lowered by $100,000, the remaining $400,000 payment still being concealed.

Other counts charged false statements to the Export-Import Bank to conceal payoffs to the two owners of Korean Airlines, the Chairman and Vice-President of Philippine Airlines, three Venezuelans in connection with sales to Linea Aeropostal Venezalano, and to Zaire's Minister of Transportation and the Governor of the National Bank of Zaire to secure sales to Air Zaire. It was alleged that the latter payments were made through a secret account in Belgium. Other payments were alleged to have been laundered through the Bahamas and a Guernsey Island company.

The case had yet to go to trial when the Reagan team took over the Justice Department. With the change of administration the Department adopted a more conciliatory stance toward McDonnell Douglas. In September 1981, the fraud and conspiracy charges against the four executives were dropped in return for a guilty plea by the company to charges of fraud and making false statements. The plea agreement cost McDonnell Douglas a fine of $55,000. In addition, the company agreed to pay $1.2 million in damages to settle a civil suit launched by the U.S. government to recover extra money (i.e. to cover the pay-offs) alleged to have been lent to Pakistan International Airlines by the Export-Import Bank as a result of the fraud.

Charges were not dropped against the most junior of the four executives, Sherman Pruitt, for making false statements to the grand jury when he denied knowing who received some of the Pakistani commissions and how much they received. Pruitt was fined $40,000 and sentenced to six months' probation, six months' suspended sentence, and 200 hours of community service when he pled guilty to the lesser charge of contempt of court. Pakistan International Airlines also continues to pursue its suit against McDonnell Douglas for compensatory damages of $1.6 million plus interest. The Pakistani government has been enthusiastic about the litigation because two of the Pakistanis receiving payments were relatives of the executed former Prime Minister Zulfikan Ali Bhutto.

Publicity and Counterpublicity

The McDonnell Douglas allegations attracted nowhere near the publicity of the Lockheed revelations. By the time McDonnell Douglas made its initial $2.5 million payments disclosure in 1976, the press had already feasted upon several bigger and more spectacular bribery scandals. The newspaper reporting of the McDonnell Douglas disclosure was described by one executive as a "one day wonder." More press attention was directed to the 1979 indictment of senior McDonnell Douglas executives. It was the first instance in which individuals were prosecuted for foreign bribery, but the story was hardly front-page news, although it did attract a modicum of attention. The treatment given by the *Wall Street Journal* was indicative of the gradual tailing off of interest in the case: The grand jury announcement made page 5 of the *Wall Street Journal* (July 6, 1979); the return of indictments made page 8 (November 12, 1979); and the guilty plea page 12 (September 9, 1981).

However, the worst publicity came in June 1981 with the decision of the Reagan Justice Department team not to proceed against the individuals who had been indicted by the grand jury. The decision arose from an unusual meeting in which the Associate Attorney General responsible for criminal matters, Rudolph Giuliani, met with the McDonnell Douglas General Counsel without telling the prosecutors handling the case. The meeting had been arranged by Republican Senator John Danforth, whose brother was on the McDonnell Douglas board. A minor scandal ensued when a letter to Giuliani from the two prosecutors working on the case became public. The letter expressed "shock" and "dismay" that such a meeting could occur without the prosecutors being consulted: "Your action creates an appearance that certain influential defendants have access to senior officials when other defendants or their attorneys do not."

The prosecutors, George Mendelson and Michael Lubin, who subsequently resigned from the Justice Department, were of the view that the individual liability of the four executives had been "bought off" by the $1.2 million settlement. While accepting that plea agreements which result in reduced charges are common, Mendelson and Lubin felt it was extraordinary for charges against individuals to be completely dropped once a grand jury indictment against them had been returned. Moreover, the $1.2 million civil settlement was seen by them as perverse: The civil case rested on a legal basis which the prosecutors thought would be impossible to sustain, whereas victory in the criminal case was regarded as almost certain.

The publicity over the propriety of Giuliani's actions was considerable, making page 1 of the *St. Louis Post Dispatch* three times in one week (June 23, 24, 26, 1981). Senator William Proxmire, architect of the Foreign Corrupt Practices Act, was widely quoted as saying: "The Justice Department's disgraceful behavior on the McDonnell Douglas bribery case shows they cannot be trusted to administer the Foreign Corrupt Practices Act."[4] More bad press for the Justice Department came when the Department decided to withhold commendation awards from Mendelson and Lubin because of what was said to be the intemperate tone of their letter to the Associate Attorney General. The two prosecutors attended the awards ceremony anyway and read statements to reporters afterwards. Lubin said: "I am disgusted and saddened by what I believe is a deliberate attempt to send a message to anyone in the Department of Justice who dares to speak, who dares to criticize impropriety at high levels."[5]

The burst of adverse publicity was short-lived and directed mostly at the Justice Department rather than at the company. St. Louis *Globe-Democrat* reporter, Edward O'Brien, reported the results of some fascinating investigative work on August 6, 1981, but the rest of the nation's press ignored the story; by then the original scandal was yesterday's news. O'Brien found that the day before the meeting arranged by Senator John Danforth between the Associate Attorney General and the McDonnell Douglas General Counsel, Danforth's campaign fund received the first of a number of contributions amounting to $12,000 from McDonnell family members and senior company executives.

McDonnell Douglas did not run a counterpublicity campaign in regard to the foreign bribery scandal in the way that they did with the alleged safety problems of the DC10 during the same period. A plane crash perhaps justifies an expensive television advertising campaign in a way that a bribery allegation does not. This may be because the market is more unforgiving of failures in the quality of a product than it is of failures in the ethics of the people who sell them. Competitors did not exploit the adverse publicity over the foreign bribery in their sales pitches. For example, both General Dynamics and McDonnell Douglas executives agreed that in no sense had General Dynamics used their rival's bribery problems in the intense struggle between them to win a large fighter contract with the Australian Defense Department. On the other hand, the new company Chairman, Sanford McDonnell, believes that in competition for commercial aircraft sales to Egypt Air, "Our competitors have been feeding stories about the crash to the Egyptian press."

Financial Impacts

McDonnell Douglas lost no specific sales as a result of adverse publicity over its foreign bribery. The two years in which the company was exposed to some bad publicity, 1976 and 1979, were years in which both sales and earnings jumped substantially. Stock prices rose for McDonnell Douglas in 1976, followed by relatively steady prices in 1977, and substantial rises in 1978. Prices were down slightly during the middle part of 1979, while plea negotiations were proceeding with the Justice Department. This was matched, however, by an equivalent rise during the fourth quarter, the period in which the indictment was returned.

One vice-president, who claimed to have maintained a close watch over the stock market to see if the adverse publicity was reflected in his company's stock prices, perceived no impact on the market.

Non-Financial Impacts

Notwithstanding the real and perceived absence of impact on stock prices, the same vice-president said that the foreign bribery problems had taken "a heavy toll" of top management. He claimed that his fellow executives were "hurt" by the "soap box treatment" which they received. They felt they had been operating according to rules that always had been regarded as acceptable. The "soap box treatment" was viewed as having deflated corporate prestige and the individual prestige of senior executives. Company morale and drive had also suffered. Dealing with the adverse publicity, responding to queries from journalists and government investigators, and explaining the situation to employees had occupied a great deal of the time and energy of top management. Company Chairman, James S. McDonnell, was interrogated for three full days in his office by the prosecutors between July 10 and 12, 1979. A special review committee chaired by Harold C. Stewart, a Tulsa attorney and former Assistant Secretary of the Air Force, spent one and a half years and 60,000 person-hours looking around the corporation seeking information about the bribery allegations.[6] For a time all this had distracted top management from the business of running the company. Such a "non-financial" impact can easily, of course, have considerable, though non-quantifiable, financial consequences. Who is to know whether top management, distracted by the ordeal of coping with adverse publicity, missed an investment opportunity, a lucrative new market, or a promising takeover?

In summary, then, there were significant non-financial impacts in terms of corporate and individual repute, employee morale, and distraction and worry for management.

Reforms

The scandal did not seem to have generated the will for reform at McDonnell Douglas that it obviously had at Lockheed. No one was dismissed or disciplined as a result of the affair. A vice-president with whom we spoke said that the attitude within McDonnell Douglas was more a feeling of having been unfairly singled out than a desire to right the wrongs of the past. It was believed that the SEC had changed the rules without warning the players beforehand. It was claimed that Lockheed, whose sins had been greater, was being treated more leniently than McDonnell Douglas because the CIA had been informed of the bribes to be paid to Prime Minister Tanaka and others in Japan before they were made.[7] Our attention was resentfully drawn to "legitimate bribes" by foreign governments that compete against McDonnell Douglas on behalf of their local manufacturers. The French government, it was asserted, had used their power over landing rights to secure sales for the Airbus. If the general climate at Lockheed was one of the corporation as penitent, at McDonnell Douglas it was one of the corporation as maligned victim.

In the six years between 1975 and 1981, the McDonnell Douglas internal auditing staff increased by a modest 25 per cent. Cynicism was expressed about the reforms that had taken place at other companies in the wake of the foreign bribery scandals: "Frankly, a lot of it is window dressing." This attitude was reflected in McDonnell Douglas' own *Standards of Business Ethics and Conduct*, a document revised in the wake of the bribery exposures.

The *Standards of Business Ethics and Conduct* is by and large a vague and platitudinous document. In 2,500 words, it covers the following topics: use of company assets; complete and accurate company books and records; conflicts of interest; political contributions; invoicing and payments to customers, agents, and suppliers; cash and bank accounts; employee and representative compensation practices; equal opportunity working conditions; the environment; compliance with securities law; antitrust policies and practices; and disciplinary action. Drawing the attention of the general counsel to the section on "Disciplinary Action," we asked whether any employees had been dismissed or had other disciplinary action taken against them in the last few years under the code. The reply was: "I would rather not answer that question." In exercising their opportunity to comment on the draft of this chapter, the company, through its general counsel, made the following criticism of the previous two sentences: "There seems to be an inference drawn, from our declining to answer a question with respect to discipline of employees, that there has been no discipline. This is an improper inference. What MDC does with respect to discipline of employees is a private matter which MDC does not consider appropriate to discuss with you."

Many corporations responded to the ethical criticisms surrounding questionable payments by banning all political contributions in the company's name. Not so with McDonnell Douglas. The corporate ethics policy permits political contributions so long as they are legal and "approved in writing by the MDC President and paid by MDC check."[8]

There have been changes concerning sales agents,[9] however. To begin with, McDonnell Douglas has established the right to audit the books of sales agents in its contracts with them. While this has value, it is of limited use with an agent who maintains off-book accounts or in situations where McDonnell Douglas does not choose to assert its right. An important advance in standard operating procedures has been that customers must now be notified of the names of sales agents who have been paid to secure the sale. This would put the customer on notice in some situations where monies are being paid to individuals who could be expected to exert improper influence.

As in the case of Lockheed, new policies assure that contracts with foreign sales agents are approved by several senior executives. Agreements with foreign sales agents must be approved at least by the President, a corporate vice-president, and the general counsel. While this reform does not go nearly as far as the detailed investigation of agents by Lockheed's Consultant Review Committee, it is an advance which makes it more difficult for top management to plead ignorance about corrupt relationships with agents. A requirement has also been introduced for executives with financial responsibilities to sign a statement which in effect says that they are not aware of any violation of the Foreign Corrupt Practices Act.

CHAPTER 15

Bribery at Exxon

The Italian Affair

From at least 1963, Exxon's Italian affiliate, Esso Italiana, with approval from corporate headquarters in New York, had been making political contributions in Italy. Almost half the approved donations between 1963 and 1972 went to the Christian Democrats, but all major parties were given a slice of the pie, even the Socialists and Communists. Such payments were legal and were regarded by the company as justified because they would "help bring about a political environment favorable to Esso Italiana's business interests."[1]

Nevertheless, in 1968 Esso Europe became concerned about the size of the Italian political payments and conceived a scheme to reduce them to about $3 million a year. In 1971, they ordered that Italian political donations stop altogether. Trouble surfaced in 1972 after Exxon auditors discovered that the payments for 1971 had been about twice the amount authorized and that this was covered up by a trail of false invoices and 40 secret bank accounts. The Italian chief executive officer, Vincenzo Cazzaniga, could not explain the irregularities to the auditors and was dismissed. Exxon filed suit for damages against Cassaniga in the Italian courts with respect to all expenditures which could not be justified in law. The action is still pending.

The 1972 report on the matter by the Exxon general auditor, H.D. Schersten, was subsequently made public before the Senate Subcommittee on Multinational Corporations, chaired by Frank Church. A major conclusion of the report was that "the internal control system was rendered ineffective" by top management tolerance of shady accounting to conceal political payments: "The principal factor which permitted the irregularities to occur and remain undiscovered for a long period of time was the fact that higher levels of management in both the Region [Esso Europe in London] and in Jersey [actually, headquarters in New York], condoned the falsification of records to obtain funds for confidential payments." The implication was that by allowing executives to use dishonest accounting practices, the corporation was placing itself in danger of being ripped off by these executives.

One of the methods of camouflaging political payments was the issuance of bogus vouchers for purchases so that the company could deduct the payments from its income for Italian taxation purposes. Senator Church later described the practice as "a fraud on the Italian Government."

Following the testimony of Exxon witnesses before the Senate Subcommittee on Multinational Corporations, the Securities and Exchange Commission opened a formal enquiry into questionable payments by Exxon. In September 1975 the company agreed with SEC staff to make a detailed public disclosure concerning the Italian scandal, and then acceded to another such disclosure, following further SEC investigations in 1977. The questionable Italian payments disclosed totalled $46 million; this was the largest amount paid in a single country by any American company that confessed payments to the SEC. There were also relatively minor questionable payments disclosed that had been made in Thailand, the Dominican Republic, Indonesia, Japan, and several other countries. Some legal payments which were improperly recorded in the books were also disclosed. For example, a legal contribution of $12,000 to a political party in Australia in 1972 was booked improperly as legal fees.

In September 1977, the SEC negotiated a consent decree with Exxon which constrains the company from failing to disclose "material information" regarding questionable payments in SEC filings and from making false or fictitious bookkeeping entries to conceal political payments. The decree also prohibited the maintenance of any off-book funds "material in nature, effect or amount," irrespective of the use to which such funds are put.

Publicity and Counterpublicity

Interestingly, the Italian scandal broke as a result of a stock owner asking a question at a shareholders' meeting on May 15, 1975. The Chairman's reply that Esso Italiana had made political contributions in Italy led to press interest, inquiries from the SEC

169

and the Senate Subcommittee on Multinational Corporations, and ultimately to testimony before that Subcommittee.

Because of the size of the Italian payments and because Exxon is the world's largest company in terms of sales, its disclosures attracted more publicity than those of most other firms. The highly visible Senate Subcommittee hearings devoted considerable attention to Exxon and two others of the Seven Sisters of U.S. oil in trouble over bribery, Gulf and Mobil. Religious groups filed three stockholder resolutions in early 1976 requesting Exxon to take a stronger stand against foreign bribery and to implement policies to back that stand. After negotiations in which management gave assurances about policy revisions, two of the resolutions were withdrawn. However, one dealing with foreign political contributions was not withdrawn and was overwhelmingly rejected at the 1976 Annual Meeting. There were also three unsuccessful derivative stockholder suits that alleged that Exxon directors and officers had breached their fiduciary duties and wasted the corporation's assets by failing to prevent the Italian payments.[2] The company did not mount a proactive counterpublicity campaign; it decided to weather the storm by doing little more than answer press inquiries that came its way. Exxon did issue a few press releases, but most communication was directed at keeping employees informed of developments.

Financial Impacts

While sales increased in both years in which the company was subjected to adverse publicity over the Italian pay-offs, 1975 and 1976, earnings were down from the record high achieved in 1974. It would seem that Exxon did not lose any significant business as a result of the revelation of questionable payments from 1973 on. The changes came at a time of oil shortages, when Exxon had no problem in selling all its oil without resort to bribery. One executive claimed that cutting off payments to officials in some Third World countries to secure drilling and prospecting rights had created some difficulties.[3] However, these problems were said to have been dealt with in ways other than the making of payments. Exxon has such an edge in technological sophistication over many competitors that the promise of a higher probability of a significant oil find generally is sufficient to overcome any advantage secured by a competitor's bribe. Exxon stock prices remained steady during 1975, at about the same level which had prevailed in 1974, and during 1976

Exxon stock showed a strong upward surge. Exxon executives did not perceive any downward shift in Exxon shares at any stage as a result of adverse publicity over foreign bribery.

Non-Financial Impacts

We were told, however, that the non-financial impacts had been important. First, there was embarrassment over the allegations: "It was painful to those of us who had a pride in the organization." Corporate prestige and repute were certainly not as severely affected as at Lockheed, and the sensationalism of the Lockheed pay-offs had shielded some of the heat from Exxon. Nonetheless, individual executives were disturbed by their subjective perception that the repute of their company had been tarnished. Second, morale was adversely affected. Insiders pointed out that many Exxon employees began to feel that their own company was not particularly honest, and that hypocrisy had pervaded the mouthing of ethical platitudes by management in the past.

Reforms

Partly as a response to this morale problem, Exxon management became increasingly determined as the 1970s progressed to show that its commitment to business ethics was not hypocritical. The September 24, 1975, *Policy Statement on Business Ethics*, which went from the Chairman to every Exxon employee, laid this on the line:

> An overly-ambitious employee might have the mistaken idea that we do not care how results are obtained, as long as he gets results. He might think it best not to tell higher management all that he is doing, not to record all transactions accurately in his books and records, and to deceive the Corporation's internal and external auditors. He would be wrong on all counts.
>
> We do care how we get results. We expect compliance with our standard of integrity throughout the organization. We will not tolerate an employee who achieves results at the cost of violation of laws or unscrupulous dealing. By the same token, we will support, and we expect you to support, an employee who passes up an opportunity or advantage which can only be secured at the sacrifice of principle.
>
> Equally important, we expect candor from managers at all levels, and compliance with acounting rules and controls. We don't want liars for managers, whether they are lying in a mistaken effort to protect

171

us or to make themselves look good. One of the kinds of harm which results when a manager conceals information from higher management and the auditors is that subordinates within his organization think they are being given a signal that company policies and rules, including accounting and control rules, can be ignored whenever inconvenient. This can result in corruption and demoralization of an organization. Our system of management will not work without honesty, including honest bookkeeping, honest budget proposals, and honest economic evaluation of projects.

Immediately after the dismissal of Cazzaniga as chief executive of the Italian subsidiary, there was reform of the autocratic management style in Italy which, among other things, gave the chief executive sole signatory powers on corporate bank accounts. As Exxon's Special Committee on Litigation reported:[4]

> In the light of what had happened, Exxon turned to a more collegial approach in the management of Esso Italiana, vesting the full executive power in three managing directors, tightened auditing and control procedures and adopted other measures, to prevent a repetition of the unhappy events under Cazzigana.

But the reforms were even more far-ranging. The authors of this book, through a variety of research projects, have become acquainted with the internal law compliance systems of more than 50 transnational corporations. It is our view that Exxon probably has the most impressive compliance system we have seen for preventing financial crimes such as bribery. Assessing how vigorously the system is enforced is difficult, but certainly as a program it is outstanding. Exxon is a leader in its approach to stamping out bribery and related financial abuses, a position it began to assume after 1973. The new Exxon controls, to be described below, were in considerable measure a response to the Italian scandal. Many senior executives were shocked that the control systems were so ineffective as to allow such practices to continue unchecked. This shock and resultant concern to right the wrongs of the past preceded the adverse publicity. It would be a mistake to attribute a great deal of the reform to the adverse publicity of 1975 and 1976, because the major changes began in 1973. Exxon concedes that the will to step up controls was given some impetus by the adverse publicity, but this was only in accelerating a process of improvement already underway.

What we have here, therefore, is a case study in which the outcome of uncovering the offenses was substantial organizational reform, but where this reform was only in a minor way prompted by publicity over the offenses. Of course it could be that Exxon astutely perceived in 1973 a need to preempt publicity that would subsequently occur by adopting the course of putting its house in order. However, we have no evidence that this was the case. Our conclusion is that the proximate cause of the reforms at Exxon was the uncomfortable realization from the Italian affair that financial manipulations by subsidiaries were not under adequate corporate control.[5] The post-1975 publicity was only a contributing factor which accelerated a pre-existing process of change. Let us describe in more detail those reforms and indicate their significance.

Exxon's compliance system was restructured under the direction of the controller, a vice-president. The system was decentralized. Each region (e.g., Esso Europe) has a regional controller, and each subsidiary within the region has a controller. In addition to reporting directly to the chief executive of the subsidiary, the local controller has an important dotted-line reporting relationship through the regional controller up to the controller's office in New York. Even though the local organization is paying for its controller and the local auditing staff, the corporate controller ultimately determines the size of the local controller's work force. Auditors are therefore not tied to the purse strings of those whom they are auditing.

The controller is given responsibility for operational as well as financial auditing. Audits serve the dual purpose of improving operational efficiency and detecting deviations from proper bookkeeping procedures. Control activities, such as inventory, which were formerly independent of the auditing function, are now integrated into a total system of audit and control. Audits incorporate an assessment of whether standard operating procedures adequate to ensure compliance with company policies are in place, and whether these procedures are being consistently followed. An audit of a manufacturing facility includes, for example, an assessment of whether corporate industrial safety policies are being followed. Because of the range of skills which such operational audits demand, interdisciplinary teams which include engineers as well as financial auditors are used. The internal auditing function involves more than 400 people worldwide.

Responsibility for the accounting integrity side of the audit rests with the general auditor who reports administratively to the vice-president and controller. However, the general auditor can by-pass the controller and report directly to the audit committee of the board, which is composed entirely of outside directors. Indeed, the most junior auditor in the most lowly subsidiary is able to report an impropriety up through the general auditor to the board audit committee. If the auditor observes an improper bookkeeping practice, he or she has an obligation to ensure that this gets to the audit committee of the board even if the local chief executive or other superior instructs him or her not to take the matter any further. An auditor who obeyed such an instruction would be in breach of company policy and subject to dismissal. A former Exxon general auditor explained:

> Say, for example—I was an auditor and uncovered something that was unsavory or should have been reported and I told my supervisor and he said to let it go. Well, auditors are briefed that their obligations do not end there. The employee who makes the report knows that his supervisor should report it up the line and that if his supervisor does not, the auditor must. He cannot seek sanctuary, so to speak, just by saying, "It was not my job. I told my boss and that was it." . . . .Much to the consternation, I guess, of some employees perhaps who would say, "Surely the Company does not want me to put this in writing"; and the answer is "yes." We want it to be put in writing, exactly what happened, and we will send it right up to New York to the board audit committee. There is no other way that we know that we can get the message across that we are very serious about this.[6]

The board audit committee makes an annual report to the full board on compliance with the Business Ethics Policy. At the same meeting, independent reports on the same subject are made by the company's external auditors, Price Waterhouse, the controller, the general counsel, and the chief executive officer.

Auditors also have the obligation to report on matters that are not within their area of direct responsibility. For example, auditors in most companies who discovered a letter suggestive of a price-fixing conspiracy would regard this as none of their business. Exxon policies make acting on such a discovery very much the business of the auditor:

> When an auditor reaches a situation where he needs to question whether we have violated antitrust laws, then he needs to go to the Law Department in order to ascertain that. Most of our auditors are not lawyers and they are not qualified to find out whether we have committed a violation. When he does contact the Law Department, he makes a record of the fact that this was turned over to the Law Department and he sends word up through audit channels to New York that he has turned over a situation to the Law Department. The

174

Law Department then sends up through the Law Department channels the fact that they are handling the situation, so the New York Law Department knows that it is not being covered up down in the individual territory someplace. Anything having to do with antitrust is both a complicated and very delicate matter so we make sure it is carried up through the Law Department. We do not let an auditor walk out on a limb and carry something all the way to the board audit committee and then the lawyers shrug their shoulders and say that is not an antitrust violation at all. That is the way we handle things when we are not sure it is a law violation.[7]

As the controller explained to us, effective control means having an organization full of "antennas." All units of the organization have a responsibility not only to report confirmed violations of the "Business Ethics Policy," but also "probable violations." "Probable violations" are defined by corporate policy as "situations where the facts available indicate that a violation probably occurred, even though there is insufficient information for a definite determination."[8] Hence, matters cannot be sat upon on the strength of being "under investigation." However, an obligation to report "probable violations" is a less potent protection than a responsibility to report "suspected violations" as well.

When a violation is reported, there is an obligation on the part of the recipient of the report to send back a determination as to whether a violation has occurred, and if it has, what remedial and/ or disciplinary action is to be taken. Thus, the junior auditor who reports an offense and hears back nothing about it knows that his or her report has been blocked or sat on somewhere. He or she must use the safety valve channel available directly to the board audit committee. To date, this free channel to the top has never been used by a junior auditor. However, the fact that it exists, and that everyone is reminded annually that it does, makes it less likely that it will have to be used. The most effective control system can be one that is never used.

Once the need for remedial action has been decided, it is the responsibility of the controller to check that the remedy is properly implemented. The strength of the Exxon system is in its follow-through. Many companies have systems to enable violations of the law and of corporate policy to be reported, but not many have systems which so effectively feed back responses and corrective action. These reforms to open up communication channels are significant, given the information blockages revealed in the investigation of Exxon's questionable payments: Information was concealed from company auditors, and the general counsel and controller agreed to withhold information from the chief executive because, "Detailed knowledge could be embarrassing to the Chief Executive at some occasion on the witness stand."[9]

A range of sanctions is available for individuals who violate corporate ethics policies. A written reprimand can go into the offender's file permanently. Bonuses and salary increases can be held back. The individual can be demoted or transferred. Then there is the ultimate sanction of dismissal. The controller knew of four or five dismissals under the ethics and conflict-of-interest policies in the last few years. One involved the chief executive of a subsidiary. Other dismissals of more junior employees for ethics violations are dealt with at a local level without reaching the audit committee.

When Exxon is the major participant or operator of a joint venture, it insists that its partners abide by Exxon policies with respect to business ethics, antitrust, and other areas relevant to the joint venture, and that Exxon auditors be able to inspect their compliance with these policies. In cases where Exxon is a minority participant, attempts are made, with mixed success, to convince partners to comply with Exxon policies of proper business practices. This requirement has diffused Exxon's compliance innovation to other major companies, such as its North Sea partner, Shell.

Backing up Exxon's broad corporate policies, which cover such matters as the prohibition of all political contributions, legal or illegal, the banning of off-book accounts, and the like, are more detailed manuals of standard operating procedures issued by the controller. While the auditing of compliance with these standards is tough, it is not inflexible. There is provision for local units to engage in principled dissent from the manuals. Deviations from corporate accounting procedures are allowed, but must be approved "by the appropriate Regional Controller and Regional General Auditor in writing, and will be recorded in a central registry in the regional office, and at the affiliates' offices."[10] A formal internal disclosure principle is therefore used to ensure that deviations from the corporation's operating procedures are made responsibly. Such disclosure is a sensible compromise against an excessively bureaucratic central enforcement of standards, which inevitably becomes unworkable in the unpredictable and ever-changing circumstances characteristic of business environments. Organizations that adopt a formal policy of inflexible adherence to standards may end up in the less desirable situation of having to turn a blind eye to occasional secret deviations.

We will not provide a detailed description of Exxon Standard Operating Procedures for ensuring compliance. However, the basic principles can be outlined quite briefly. The overarching principle is that systems are designed to be automatically self-checking. For example, the problem of diversion of inventory is dealt with by built-in controls so that in simply doing their job, employees are automatically checking that the inventory balances. Periodic counting of inventory is essentially replaced by in-line controls. Fundamental to the Exxon system is the idea that control is a line responsibility. It is not acceptable for employees to think that it is the job of the auditors to ensure that the rules are being followed. As the controller pointed out: "Audit is not the control. Audit is the monitor of the control." At Exxon the audit function is not allowed to be a crutch for line managers who are incompetent at ensuring compliance with corporate standards.

Former Exxon general auditor, Ted Kline, has pinpointed six major control concepts on which the Exxon system is based:

> First—the well known segregation of duties and responsibilities such that no single function, department or employee will have exclusive knowledge, authority or control over any significant transaction or group of transactions;
> Second—the proper documentation of transactions and business events;
> Third—the systematic and thoughtful supervision in documented reviews of managers and other employees' work;
> Fourth—the timely preparation of records, reports and reviews;
> Fifth—control measures designed in such a way that they are responsive to the nature and degree of risk and exposure. . . .;
> Sixth—the various aspects of control should not be so interdependent that a serious deficiency in any one would make other controls also ineffective.[11]

Adequate and consistent documentation is central. Exxon claims that a working principle in the company is: "If you can't book it right, you probably should not be doing it." In a company in which transactions are impeccably booked for exactly what they are, economic crimes are difficult to cover up, and therefore generally entail greater risks than benefits. Of course, we have no way of confirming that transactions in fact are impeccably booked at Exxon, as they claim.

Another underlying principle is that no one is to have unaccountable power. Consider the question, "Who audits the auditors?" This problem is dealt with by peer review. The headquarters auditing group might audit the Asian Regional Auditing Group and the European Regional Auditing Group might audit the headquarters auditing group. Auditors are auditing other auditors all over the world. Perhaps this still does not go far enough—the police are still policing themselves—but it is certainly an advance over the unaccountable accounting one finds in most large corporations.

In addition to formal audits, all subsidiaries have a kind of self-audit in the form of a triennial "business practice review." In this review, managers, after having refreshed their memories of the objectives of corporate ethics policies, assess all their current practices—bookkeeping, bidding, making gifts to customers, expense accounts, the lot—to root out any areas which leave open the possibility of abuse. It is a kind of corporate "cultural revolution," an attempt to keep alive among the masses the fervor to be watchful against unethical practices. Business practice reviews were introduced in 1976 in part as a way of dealing with Exxon's morale problems from the Italian bribery disclosures. Exxon management wanted to make their employees believe in the honesty and integrity of the company. The business practice reviews achieved that goal. By involving middle and junior managers in the campaign to eliminate unethical practices, Exxon convinced its own people that it was serious about its new ethics policy. Some company units found that the reviews were so effective and so good for morale that they involved lower level employees, such as salespeople, in the process. The controller had never really intended that the reviews widely involve these lower levels; but he was happy enough with the result. Quite apart from the other favorable effects, he felt that the reviews had helped managers in the field to understand the reasons for many of the requirements imposed on them, and therefore made the task of the auditors easier. The reviews must also help keep the controller's staff on its toes to ensure that a problem which should have been identified does not surface in a business practice review.

To supplement the business practice reviews, Exxon places great emphasis (just as Lockheed does) on ensuring that employees are aware of their obligations. All employees annually receive a copy of the Business Ethics Policy. Not less than triennially, representatives of the controller's department, often together with members of the legal department, conduct briefings for each department in the corporation on business ethics developments, changes in accounting practices and concepts, and changes in the regulatory requirements imposed by governments. There are, in addition, regular reviews of more specialized areas (e.g., the law department conducts a biennial antitrust review). At Exxon it is hard for a manager who violates corporate standards to say: "I did not really know you didn't want me to do that." Managers above a certain level must certify annually that to their knowledge there have been no unreported violations of Exxon's ethics and accounting policies in the areas under their responsibility. If there have been violations—and in these certifications it is common for minor violations to be reported—they must be detailed and the remedial action taken specified.

It is easy to imagine executives from other companies reading this account of the Exxon system and concluding that only a company with Exxon's massive profits could afford an internal compliance system of this sophistication. Not so, says Exxon's controller. He claims that if he were imposing unreasonable costs on his subsidiary managers he would be getting flak from them. The new systems introduced since the mid-1970s have drawn more praise than criticism from hard-boiled managers out in the marketplace. Many of the reforms involve no costs at all. Having the safety valve of a free route of appeal to the audit committee of the board does not cost anything. Certification by the chief executive of a subsidiary that he or she is aware of all corporate ethics and accounting policies and that they have been followed only costs the time of a secretary to type one letter. Certainly, it consumes the time of executives to assure themselves that the letter can be safely signed. But executives who could not give this assurance would not be doing their job in any case.

Managers in the field do sometimes complain to the controller: "Do we really have to audit this function every 18 months." The controller then says: "Okay, let's look at what we found last time we did this audit." Because the financial audit is also an efficiency audit, findings which are useful in improving the performance of the organization are almost always in the auditor's report. After pointing out the valuable findings from the last audit, the controller then asks the complaining manager if he really wants to wait four years for these kinds of problems to be drawn to his attention again. Typically, on reconsideration, the answer is no. A great advantage of combining the functions of compliance and operational audits is that the compliance side of the audits is not so bitter a pill to swallow: Obviously there is reason for management to cooperate with auditors when productivity is being improved on the strength of their recommendations.

The detailed documentation of transactions demanded by an effective control system is as useful as an aid to business planning and evaluation of past performance as it is to ensuring law observance. As the controller summed up: "If you do all these things you have a damn well-functioning business organization as well. You're not just doing it because you want to claim to be ethical, you're doing it because it's worth money to you."

Exxon auditors are said to save more than the total cost of the auditing function in detecting overpayments to suppliers alone. A good control system that stops bribery and other unethical practices by the corporation also stops unethical practices against the corporation. It can catch the sales manager who fiddles an expense account, the tanker driver or depot manager who diverts oil to a friend or relative, the computer operator who deposits funds in his or her own account. If the accounting system is so out of control that bribes can be paid without this fact becoming widely known, then monies will be ripped out of the system for personal use as well. Hence, mixed in among the Lockheed bribes was the discovery that "In at least one instance, $100,000 of commissions the company paid to a foreign sales consultant were kicked back by that individual to unnamed Lockheed personnel for their personal use."[12]

While the second half of the 1970s saw Exxon dramatically increase its internal audit staff to over 400 persons, the aggregate cost to the corporation did not increase. The integrated nature of a total operational audit meant that some previously independent functions became redundant. For example, some clerks who previously did nothing but count inventory were no longer required. Reconciliation of inventory with the books became an integral part of the audit and of built-in checks and balances.

There are some negative elements to the auditing-control approach found in such a highly developed form at Exxon; these must be balanced against the positive aspects. For one thing, it is not the best approach in every area of self-regulation. Consider occupational safety and health. Audits which assess that procedures are in place and are being followed, even if the audits can be adequately performed by those whose primary training is financial, are not sufficient on their own. Goal-setting might be as important as rule enforcement. Rewarding by bonuses the achievement of a goal of cutting accidents by 20 per cent might do more for occupational health and safety than any number of operational audits. Charging workers compensation payments to the departments that incur accidents might have a similar effect. Not all of the behaviors one would want to improve are readily constrained by rules. Often it is desirable to create an experimental environment using new and creative solutions for performing a task that has defied all previous operating procedures. A new technological "fix," for example, might break all the rules, but provide for better protection of the health and safety of workers than punctillious adherence to existing standard operating procedures.

In other words, the "environment of control," which Exxon has so successfully created, might inhibit lateral thinking toward solutions for improving harm- or risk-prevention. The "environment of control" must be complemented by an "environment of imaginative problem solving." Technical experts in a specialized area must be able to develop new strategies which attempt to reduce the risks of pollution, production of unsafe products, or accidents, through a radical new approach. Goals such as safety and pollution reduction must be approached from other directions which will sometimes be at odds with the rule-following mentality of the auditor. No matter how interdisciplinary auditing teams become through the adding of engineers, they will remain teams of generalists rather than specialists, and teams dominated by the idea of rule enforcement. Specialists who look for creative solutions to the problems which auditors control through rules must be given an independent place. Having auditors who check compliance with an occupational safety policy is no substitute for having a safety department of relevant specialists who monitor plants, often in quite informal ways that would be anathema to the auditor, and who supervise a total plan to make the workplace safer.

Exxon does in fact have groups of the latter type: For the purposes of this research we have made no effort to assess how effectively they operate. These cautionary comments are intended only to check any erroneous inference that the activities of Exxon's controller's office provide a total solution to the problems addressed by corporate self-regulation.

The organizational reforms at Exxon have been substantial and progressive. We do not know how often these policies are winked at in practice. Nevertheless, to demonstrate improved policies and procedures, even if we know little about their implementation, is to demonstrate something of value. The improvements were a direct result of the Italian bribery crisis, but only in a small way did they emerge because of the publicity surrounding that crisis.

CHAPTER 16

General Electric —
The Heavy
Electrical Equipment
Price-Fixing Conspiracies

The Price-Fixing Conspiracies

Tales of corporate crime proliferate, but none has probably captured the public imagination more than the heavy electrical equipment price-fixing conspiracies, the biggest criminal case in the history of the Sherman Anti-Trust Act.[1]

During the 1950s, demand for large-scale power transformers, turbine generators, and other heavy electrical items fell off to such an extent that even the two giants in the industry, The General Electric Company and Westinghouse Electric Corporation, found themselves under pressure to fix prices. They succumbed. In a plot that might have been scripted by a motion picture script writer, sales representatives from General Electric and their U. S. competitors met in secret and agreed to a "phase of the moon" scheme under which bids were submitted in accordance with a pre-arranged code.[2] When the scheme was discovered, a federal grand jury in Philadelphia was empanelled to make a full inquiry. Of 20 indictments returned, 19 named General Electric as a co-conspirator.[3]

General Electric pleaded guilty in relation to seven "flagrant" conspiracies and *nolo contendere* in relation to the remaining 12.[4] The company was then fined $437,500. At the same time, 15 of its executives were fined and three sent to jail as well, most notably William S. Ginn, a vice-president, who was fined $12,500 and jailed for 30 days. Other co-conspirators, including Westinghouse and several of its personnel, were also punished for their roles.[5] In all, fines of $1,924,500 were imposed on 29 companies and 44 of their executives, and 7 persons were jailed for 30 days each.

GE—Heavy Electrical Equipment Price-Fixing Conspiracies

Publicity and Counterpublicity

The heavy electrical equipment conspiracies were of immediate public interest for, as the *New York Times* was quick to sense,

> Here were the classic elements of the great criminal case: charges of the most serious skulduggery, involving vast sums of money; powerful, highly respectable defendants; disclosures raising moral questions not just for the defendants but for society at large.[6]

The media took their cue from Judge Ganey's remarks when pronouncing sentence. For Ganey, the conspiracies threatened the very fibre of American society:

> This is a shocking indictment of a vast section of our economy, for what is really at stake here is the survival of the kind of economy under which this country has grown great, the free enterprise system. . . . It has destroyed the model, it seems to me, which we offer today, as a free world alternative to state control, to socialism and eventual dictatorship.[7]

Worse, the threat came, not from the lower parts of the corporations involved, but from their uppermost management:

> The real blame is to be laid at the doorstep of the corporate defendants and those who guide and direct their policy. While the Department of Justice has acknowledged that they were unable to uncover probative evidence which would secure a conviction beyond a reasonable doubt of those in the highest echelons of the corporations here involved, in a broader sense they bear a grave responsibility; for one would be most naive indeed to believe that these violations of the law, so long persisted in, affecting so large a segment of the industry, and, finally, involving so many millions upon millions of dollars, were facts unknown to those responsible for the corporation and its conduct.[8]

Thus cued, the press relayed the story nationwide.[9] The *Wall Street Journal* opened its account by stressing that never before had severe penalties been imposed on such a wide scale for price-fixing.[10] The *New York Times*, after headlining the jail terms, went into detail, noting that the new Attorney-General, Robert F. Kennedy, had reviewed the cases and considered the crimes "so willful and flagrant that even more severe sentences would have been appropriate."[11] *Life* magazine pictorialized, publishing photos of the executives sent to jail, one from the unflattering angle of prison bars.[12] And, a widely published comment syndicated by Consolidated New Features concluded that:

> All of us were on trial. The national image was also a defendant. What might be called the success formula was a co-defendant. Here were the men who had followed all the rules of how to win friends and influence people. They were living success stories. They were persons who carefully had conformed. They had read and said the right thing at the right time. They had joined the right club, met the right people, been seen at the right places, worn the right clothing, espoused those things which "all right thinking men" espouse.[13]

The publicity was slow to abate. The fire was stoked constantly by the *New York Times*, as with this editorial thrust:

> The primary responsibility for keeping its house clean rests with G.E. We share with Henry Ford 2d, a member of the company's board of directors, the conviction that the best way for all businesses to establish public confidence in their integrity is to set up the most rigorous self-policing machinery to back up their declarations of devotion to the public good. Unhappily little recognition of this responsibility manifested itself at the annual meeting of G.E. stockholders in Syracuse last week. They hooted down the few management critics who called for an impartial investigation and they assailed a complaining union leader with cries of "shut up" and "throw him out."[14]

A lengthy congressional inquiry into the price-fixing conspiracies was subsequently pursued under the leadership of Senator Estes Kefauver, and the hearings generated further adverse publicity (Kefauver was described by a colleague as combining "the gracious manner of a Victorian with the relentlessness of an Apache").[15] Predictably, General Electric, Westinghouse, and other members of the price-fixing gang were much vilified.[16] Although an attempt to show complicity on the part of Ralph Cordiner, chairman of GE, and Mark Cresap, president of Westinghouse, failed, the inquiry did highlight a remarkable failure of top leadership control. The worst inference from the Kefauver hearings was that top management had been willfully blind. Alternatively, the implication to be drawn was that top management were naive, as one vice-president was forced by Senator Kefauver to admit:

> (Kefauver): Mr. Vinson, you wouldn't be a vice-president at $200,000 a year if you were naive.

184

(Vinson): I think I could well get there by being naive in this area. It might help.[17]

At least four books were written about the conspiracies, and many more articles, including Richard Austin Smith's award-winning account in *Fortune*.[18] The episode was ultimately recorded in Ivy League law school casebooks, thereby passing the ultimate test of immortality.[19]

General Electric tried to deflect the adverse publicity towards the executives who had been convicted of conspiracy. This tactic failed, but a few sympathizers in the community offered support.

A lengthy press statement was issued by General Electric upon being sentenced as a price-fixing conspirator. The introduction sought to lay blame at the door of the convicted executives:

> The fines assessed are a result of the company being held technically responsible for the acts of certain employees, even though the acts were not authorized and, in fact, were positively forbidden by written company directive policy. . . . As the record well establishes, the actions of these few individuals were not in conformance with company policy, but a deliberate violation of General Electric directive policy and of the expected high standards of our corporate way of life.[20]

The company's antitrust policy was then held out for praise:

> The company's Directive Policy 20.5, first issued in 1946, is a clear, long-standing, written policy specifically forbidding employee activities which violate either the spirit or the letter of the antitrust laws. This policy is far more stringent than the antitrust laws themselves, and prohibits any employee from discussing prices, terms and conditions of sales or other competitive matters with any representative of a competitor.[21]

This policy had been upheld, it was reported, by subjecting those convicted to severe disciplinary measures, including removal from positions, demotions, reductions in pay, and shifts to work assignments with no responsibility for pricing.

As far as compensating victims was concerned, the reassurance was given that General Electric would initiate cooperative studies with utilities and other industry customers, "to voluntarily determine if recent violations of the antitrust laws by certain employees had been financially detrimental." Ultimately, the company denied that there had been any rip-off:

We believe that the purchasers of electrical apparatus have received fair value by any reasonable standards. The prices which they have paid during the past years were appropriate to value received and reasonable as compared with the general trend of prices in the economy, the price trends for similar equipment, and the price trends for materials, salaries and wages. The foresight of the electric utilities, and the design and manufacturing skills of companies such as General Electric, have kept electricity one of today's greatest bargains. The price of electricity has gone up only 2 per cent since 1939, while the general Consumer Price Index has risen 112 per cent.[22]

This defense, we were informed, "had not gone down very well" among personnel or in the outside world. Some of the internal resentment surfaced at the Kefauver hearings, where several General Electric personnel bitterly gave their side of the story.[23] The external reaction was even more hostile, as in this editorial:

Over forty G.E. managerial employees were involved and seventeen were indicted. Yet listen to the G.E. announcement—the best that one of the finest publicity departments in the country could work up: ". . . The actions of these few individuals were not in conformance with company policy, but a deliberate violation of General Electric directive policy and of the expected high standards of our corporate way of life. The acts were ones of nonconformity and of conspiracy." In short, our high executives are moral men, but a little stupid.

There are compelling reasons for the corporations throwing their hirelings to the wolves of the law. The companies face the possibility of civil damage suits from customers and competitors, in some cases for triple damages. Even so, the cost in prestige for the top officers is high. They may not be as smart as they pretended, but they are not stupid either. All that one can say for them now is that they must have nerves of steel, and a firm belief in the infinite credulity of the public, to have maligned themselves so cruelly and, it may well turn out, to so little effect.[24]

General Electric chose not to mount an active counterpublicity campaign; its "power lines had become overloaded."[25] However, a sporadic, uncoordinated counterattack was undertaken by some sympathizers. On the Western front, a sympathetic flag was waved in a Letter to the Editor of the *Los Angeles Times*:

There are some facts about General Electric and the recent price-fixing trial that haven't been given much space in the press. For one thing the government prosecutor made an "in court" declaration that the government did not imply that GE as a company had any part in the guilt of the men. This statement was not made about any of the other companies.

At the trial the GE lawyers told the judge that any sympathy for the men would be misplaced—that these men not only broke the law, they violated the company's rules. None of the men is now employed by GE.

For several years a part of my contract has called for personal appearance tours during which I speak. I've always chosen my own subject and never once has GE ever interfered.

Last year I criticized a government agency in one of my talks. This particular government department ordered GE to fire me or it would lose $50 million worth of business. GE defended my right as an individual to say what I wanted. I think this shows a great deal of courage.

In these seven years I've found the company to operate with the highest of principles—higher I might add than some elements of government which are so bent on destroying business.

Ronald Reagan,
Pacific Palisades[26]

In the East, the show of support went beyond corporate patriotism. Souls were searched for excuses, as by Arnold Bernhard in a commentary, "U.S. v. Itself," published in *The Value Line Survey*. For Bernhard, the price-fixing conspiracies were the result of illogical law, not blameworthy deviance:

The big fellow in the cyclical industries is on the horns of a dilemma. If he fixes prices or stabilizes them, he may be guilty of conspiracy to violate the antitrust laws. On the other hand, if he observes this section of the law and is governed only by the law of supply and demand, he soon destroys all his competition and emerges as the monopoly power in his field and a violator of section II of the same law. Which horn would Judge Ganey prefer to sit on? Which perch would the Attorney General prefer? Where does the editor of *Life* think would be the moral seat?[27]

However, this explanation was soon summed up for what it was: a forlorn attempt to rewrite the price-fixing scandal as heroic tragedy.

Financial Impacts

Powerful as the surge of adverse publicity was, the impact upon General Electric's sales was slight. However, there was a significant short-term impact upon share prices and the amount which had to be paid out in civil antitrust damages was probably increased as a result of the publicity.

Sales were not affected by the adverse publicity, as far as management could tell. Some salespeople did complain of missing out on deals with public utilities as a result of General Electric's bad standing. However, since "salesmen were always looking for an excuse," these complaints were taken with a grain of salt. Moreover, if American purchasers of heavy electrical equipment were not prepared to deal with General Electric and the other manufacturers involved in the price-fixing conspiracies, they would drop a bonanza in the hands of Japanese industry.[28] No adverse impact was felt upon most of General Electric's other products (the FCC did inform General Electric that the price-fixing conspiracies raised a "serious question" about the renewal of broadcast licenses for its radio and television station at Schenectady, but nothing came of it).[29]

The impact on stock prices was more significant, at least in the short term. Within a week of the announcement of the sentences, GE shares lost over $684 million in paper value, dropping from 69¼ on February 6, 1961 to 62⅛ on February 10, 1961. (The Dow Jones average on the same days was 645.65 and 639.67 respectively.) On February 9, 1961, GE was the first "most active" stock traded.[30] Within General Electric, however, memory of any dramatic drop has long since faded, perhaps because the stocks recovered in the long term: by December 21, 1964, GE shares had climbed to 92 (against a Dow Jones average of 869.74). The company's financial position by then was described by the chairman, Ralph Cordiner, as "the best . . . in history." We were advised that no conclusion could safely be drawn from any fluctuations in share prices, although "it would be dangerous to assume . . . that the electrical cases had no impact." By contrast, the orthodox external view of the stock-market impact of the electric conspiracies is that they precipitated a "selling wave."[31]

By far the worst financial impact suffered was the $198 million paid in civil antitrust damages; in 1964, for example, damages payments reduced earnings by approximately 47 cents a share.[32] Although it is impossible to say exactly to what extent adverse publicity affected the amount of damage claims, the strident public denunciation of General Electric, together with the company's subsequent forced offer to assist victims in recovering their losses, doubtless acted as a catalyst, expanding the number of claims against the company to more than 1800.[33]

GE—Heavy Electrical Equipment Price-Fixing Conspiracies

Non-Financial Impacts

The major non-financial impacts of the adverse publicity occasioned by the price-fixing conspiracies were loss of corporate prestige, loss of individual prestige, diversion, and threat of legislative intervention.

The reputation of General Electric took a battering in the media. In a comment shortly after the company had been sentenced, the *New York Times* observed that,

> For the corporate defendants the immediate effect is a damaging blow to prestige. Despite the protestations of General Electric, for example, that its vice-presidents and other officials involved had acted without the knowledge and against the policy of top management, clearly the company's status as a leader in the councils of American industry has suffered.[34]

Subsequently, an editorial in the same paper reiterated that view:

> Ever since the days of Owen D. Young and Gerard Swope, two great statesmen of industry, the General Electric Company has sought to identify itself with an image of corporate citizenship based on regard for the welfare of the community. The company's admitted participation with other giant electrical manufacturers in a price-rigging conspiracy has put a crack in that image, which G.E. is now trying to repair.[35]

A different interpretation has been advanced by Alan Dershowitz. An examination of newspaper accounts of the sentences meted out to the corporations in the price-fixing ring suggested to him that corporate criminality was remote from popular concern:

> Although this was the largest criminal antitrust prosecution in the history of the United States, and one of the first in which actual prison sentences were imposed, *forty-five per cent of the newspapers in the survey kept the story of the sentencing off the front page.* Fewer than an handful of the surveyed papers mentioned the names of any of the sentenced corporations other than General Electric and Westinghouse, and most of the papers devoted substantially all their headline space and coverage to the executives who received prison sentences. None of the newspapers emphasized that the *corporations* were actually guilty of committing *crimes.* The language of criminality—words like "guilty," "sentences," and "criminal"—was generally reserved for the executives.

189

More neutral language—words like proceedings," "antitrust suits" and "penalties"—was employed in reference to the corporate defendants.[36]

The conclusion drawn was that it made little sense to rely on adverse publicity as a means of sanctioning corporate offenders because the media would protect the powerful companies by using lulling language and euphemistic terms.

The interpretation offered by Dershowitz is not borne out, however, by what happened to General Electric. First, whatever may have been the case as regards other companies, General Electric was repeatedly named in newspaper accounts of the sentencing.[37] Second, it is incorrect to say that no newspaper emphasized corporate criminality; the *New York Times* did, notably in "Trust Case Raises Big Questions," a leading article by Anthony Lewis, a Pulitzer prize-winner.[38] Third, the *New York Times* constantly used the words "sentence," "fines," "indictment," and "conspiracy" in relation to General Electric.[39] Fourth, General Electric was made the subject of a highly critical *New York Times* editorial, part of which has been quoted above.[40] Fifth, opprobrium was not shunted away from the company and lumped upon the convicted individuals; on the contrary, Judge Ganey's allocation of primary blame to the corporations was extensively reported.[41] Sixth, the important reflection about the General Electric case is not what might have happened in the media "had no corporate executives been indicted, or had no prison sentences been imposed," but that the combined proceedings against General Electric and its executives had a strong tarnishing effect because of the opportunity given to the sentencing judge, and later the public, to assess individual and corporate blameworthiness side-by-side.[42] Finally, the General Electric executives interviewed were adamant that a serious loss of corporate prestige had been suffered, a recollection confirmed by the sensitivity shown in many of the company's public statements at the time.[43] We were told that the electrical equipment convictions were still being dragged up by competitors and other antagonists, as in license application hearings. Although the offensive from this quarter never succeeded, it still was felt, even 20 years after sentence.

Individual as well as corporate repute was lowered. Managers thought that the adverse publicity hit home for individuals because of their identification with what had been the good name of their company.[44] Widespread concern and loss of morale resulted, and soreness about the matter was aggravated by criticism at a family and social level. The conspiracies had been difficult to explain away because there were simply too many persons involved for the offenses to be regarded as an aberration. At the same time, the general feeling was that the assault on individual reputations was indirect. The problem had arisen in one particular division of the company, and that division had been operating in a marketplace where the competition had been unusually tough.

Top management at General Electric suffered the worst obloquy, except of course for the executives who went through the trauma of conviction and sentence. The prime target was the chairman, Ralph Cordiner. The University of Massachusetts refused to proceed with the award of an honorary doctorate;[45] far more severe was the pillorying of Cordiner by Senator Kefauver at the widely publicized Congressional hearings.[46] And Cordiner had to resign from the Commerce Department's prestigious business advisory council.[47]

Diversion was an impact distinct from financial cost. After indictment, General Electric offered to assist victims with their civil claims and set up a special litigation group partly for this purpose; it is difficult to believe that this offer would have been made but for the heat of adverse publicity.[48] Much energy was spent in negotiations with the Department of Justice over a civil consent decree. Fortified by its success in the criminal proceedings and the scandal they aroused, the Department sought a consent decree containing some extraordinarily wide terms, including a provision banning "unreasonably low prices." Ultimately, a narrower consent decree was agreed to, but only after General Electric put up determined resistance.[49]

Finally, the price-fixing conspiracies provided so vivid a presentation of the evil of anti-competitive economic behavior that General Electric and the industry as a whole were faced with the threat of legislative intervention.[50] Several bills were introduced to strengthen the antitrust laws. One proposal, that individual criminal liability be imposed for negligent managerial supervision, struck terror into the hearts of many (the intention was to facilitate criminal liability in the event of suspect managerial performance, as alleged against Ralph Cordiner).[51] None of the controversial provisions was ever enacted, but the possibility was a source of considerable agitation.[52]

Reforms

The self-corrective reaction of General Electric to the price-fixing exposé was mixed. Its basic antitrust policy, set out in Policy

Directive 20.5, was preserved. Some minor structural changes were made in the organization without altering the company's scheme of decentralization. The main effort went into internal discipline and compliance procedures.

General Electric's retention of its antitrust policy was non-controversial, but some eyebrows were raised at the decision to preserve a highly decentralized structure. For a number of critics, General Electric's failure to prevent price-fixing was attributable largely to the remoteness of top management from the company's operating divisions.[53] Decentralization also was said to place a heavy burden on each autonomous division to produce profits or be starved of capital and personal bonuses.[54] Despite these criticisms, General Electric remained highly decentralized after the conspiracies, the only structural changes of note being the creation of an audit committee of the Board of Directors and the installation of more staff, especially auditors and lawyers, at company headquarters. It was explained that a breakdown in communication had occurred but that decentralization had been but one of many relevant factors.

Some within the company suggested that anti-competitive practices were born during earlier days of patent protection: Monopoly prices which had been enjoyed under patent protection might have been maintained after patents expired or became invalid; it is sometimes hard for executives to accept that what was once "orderly marketing" is now a crime simply because patent protection expires.[55] If this was so, the task ahead was not to abandon the idea of decentralization, but to ensure that the decentalized units were kept in check by effective internal discipline and appropriate compliance procedures.

The internal discipline exacted by General Electric was severe.[56] All persons implicated in violations of Policy Directive 20.5 were disciplined by substantial demotion long before any of them were convicted. Ginn and others convicted of conspiracy were later asked to resign because "the Board of Directors determined that the damaging and relentless publicity attendant upon their sentencing rendered it both in their interest and the company's that they pursue their careers elsewhere."[57] By contrast, Westinghouse took the radically different course of deciding against disciplinary action, partly by invoking the weak excuse that "anybody involved was acting not for personal gain, but in what he thought was the best interests of the Company."[58]

The disciplinary steps taken by General Electric were criticized on three main grounds. First, it was said to be discriminatory to discipline Ginn and other conspirators but not top management, the claim being that the latter had been at the least negligent in failing to exercise adequate organizational control.[59] Second, it was contended that punishment by criminal law alone was enough for the purpose of deterrence and retribution, and internal discipline amounted to unjust double punishment.[60] Third, from the standpoint of the company and its shareholders, there was consternation that the disciplinary measures would be used as evidence to establish criminal and civil liability.[61] Were these criticisms well-directed?

The first ground of criticism tended to gloss over the distinction between deliberate violation of corporate policy and negligent management. Morally, there is a significant difference between intention and negligence, as is apparent from the limited extent to which negligence is accepted as a sufficient basis of responsibility in criminal law.[62] To raise the distinction is hardly to condone negligent management. General Electric's management was censured not only through the imposition of corporate criminal responsiblity, but also by the stigma of press attack.

Nor was it so obvious that punishment by criminal law alone was enough. Internal norms of behavior typically are more important within organizations than those proclaimed outside, so that external norms may signify little unless clearly reinforced inside.[63] By taking disciplinary action, General Electric sought to avoid anticipated expectations of approval of price-fixing within the organization: It was essential, we were informed, to develop "a climate where people down the line know that if they step out of line, management above would step on them hard." However, it should be pointed out that General Electric decided to force the resignation only of those convicted and sentenced; others implicated in the price-fixing who were immunized by going before the grand jury were left on the payroll.[64]

The third criticism, that internal discipline would backfire against General Electric in subsequent criminal and civil suits, had only a superficial plausibility. There was little difficulty in proving criminal or civil liability against General Electric: Abundant evidence was available from other quarters.[65] To the extent that difficulty of proof might be eased, General Electric believed that a choice had to be made between the flea of facilitating criminal or civil liability and the wasp of sacrificing corporate freedom in the management of internal affairs:

> This system will remain free and competitive only so long as the citizens, and particularly those of us with responsibilities in business life, are capable of the self-discipline required. If we are not capable

of self-discipline, the power of the government will be increasingly invoked as a substitute until the system is no longer free or competitive.[66]

As well as undertaking internal discipline, General Electric revamped its compliance procedures. Changes were made in three main areas: education, reporting up, and checking down.

Steps were taken to improve the level of education about antitrust compliance. The campaign, spearheaded by lawyers, had the full backing of the company's five-star generals. Fred J. Borch, president and chief executive, called 400 senior employees together in 1964 to warn them that those who violated Policy Directive 20.5 would be treated as deserters:

> Success in this area, perhaps even more than in most others, will depend on teamwork. We can expect to be no stronger than the weakest member of the team. One weak, lazy, selfish, or stupid member of the team who tries to cut corners by anything resembling or suggesting collusion is playing Russian roulette, not only with the Company, but with the reputation and the business careers of everybody in this room and thousands of others. Weakness or ignorance in this area must be discovered and corrected promptly. Then, if it can't be corrected, the employee must be removed so that his conduct can't damage the lives of fellow employees or the Company.[67]

Thus, it could no longer be claimed, as several executives previously had, that Policy Directive 20.5 was only for public consumption and not to be taken seriously.[68] To reinforce the point, all executives were required to certify in the presence of a superior officer that they had read and understood Policy Directive 20.5 and that they would comply with it.[69]

In another reformative sortie, attempts were made to find better means of encouraging violations or suspected violations to be reported up the line. The animating concern here was the failure of the price-fixers to "bubble-up" the trouble which arose in the transformer division.[70] Some had attributed the shortage of such indications to the personality of Ralph Cordiner (described by one of our respondents as "a cold cookie and dour"). But this view of the matter was not sustainable, since Cordiner had very approachable senior vice-presidents as lieutenants. Accordingly, modifications were made to the system of communication.

Formally, General Electric implemented what has sometimes been described in the company as the "rat fink" communication theory;

the following "squealer" clause was added to the disciplinary rules accompanying Policy Directive 20.5:

> Experience has indicated (1) that the greatest danger of damage to the Company arises from a course of systematic violations where more than one employee necessarily has at least some knowledge of the violations, and (2) that a substantial violation of the antitrust laws seldom occurs without the knowledge of more than one employee. Because antitrust violations have a serious potential for major harm to the Company's interests, disciplinary action under this Policy will be taken, not only against individuals who authorize or participate in a violation directly, but also against—
> (i) any other employee who may have willfully and deliberately withheld relevant and material information concerning a violation of [Directive 20.5];
> (ii) the violator's management superiors, to the extent that the circumstances of the violation reflect inadequate leadership and lack of diligence.
> Any employee who has any information leading him to believe that this Policy is being, or may be, violated is required to present such information to the General Counsel, or to Company Counsel assigned to his component, who will in turn review the information with the General Counsel. The General Counsel will inquire into the facts reported and advise the appropriate Company Officer of his legal opinion. To the fullest extent practicable, the name of the employee presenting the information will be held in confidence by counsel.

In addition, authority was given to any employee to report to the Chairman of the Board any superior suggesting action contrary to Policy Directive 20.5[71] This was intended to meet the criticism that the single, "one-over-one," channel for communicating complaints, previously in operation at General Electric, was not failsafe.[72]

Informally, attention was paid to the problem of getting personnel to talk to company lawyers (several of the price-fixers had resorted to a conspiracy of silence when questioned).[73] It was accepted that the problem was intrinsically insoluble: There was a basic conflict between the interests of the company and the interests of company personnel, and the normal lawyer-client relationship did not apply.[74] The idea was then mentioned of sidestepping the problem by focusing on future preventive control rather that past misdeeds. Thus, if a complaint were to be made to the general counsel's office, it would be possible to approach the managerial vice-president and say, "We have a problem for which we would like you to pass down a policy, not to draw attention to the specific illegality, but to ensure that they get the message." In other words, "bubbling up" might be achieved without necessarily casting company lawyers in the role of petty informers.[75] It was stressed, however, that this approach did not reflect existing practice.

As regards checking down, General Electric introduced additional auditing safeguards, and an annual compliance review. New auditing rules were devised, and the legal and accounting staff was increased to intensify the probe.[76] Managers in specified positions of authority were required to interview subordinates annually for the purpose of checking whether antitrust violations had occurred.[77] Until recently, a signed declaration of compliance was insisted upon, but this requirement had been abandoned because "people who are not lawyers cannot be expected to know the niceties of anti-trust laws." (They can be expected to know when they are entering dangerous waters, however, and a signed declaration of compliance with organizational rules could be well framed accordingly).

Much skepticism greeted General Electric's revised compliance procedures. Senator Kefauver wondered aloud whether the new program was going to be more effective than the old, particularly in light of the fact that public utilities and cities had subsequently received identical bids on some items of heavy electrical equipment.[78] As subsequently has been shown, however, heavy electrical equipment prices stayed well below the conspiratorial heights of the 1950s (e.g., 1968 prices for oil circuit breakers were slightly over half the prices at the peak of the heavy electrical conspiracy in early 1959).[79]

General Electric's antitrust policy is no longer ambiguous, much less a "Catch 20.5",[80] but the compliance procedures supporting that policy remain open to question on two grounds. First, there is no formal guarantee of feedback down the line after a complaint has been received. Ideally, a response is to be made in writing, but there is no specific system comparable to that which Allied Chemical has installed for toxic risk assessment or that which Exxon has instituted against bribery. Second, compliance is a line rather than a line and staff responsibility. The annual review, for instance, depends on face-to-face interaction between subordinate and superior, not testing by an independent group. Such a system may protect the board against shareholders' derivitative liability suits, yet is far from perfect as a means of unearthing non-compliance.[81] General Electric has decided against attempting to provide a fail-safe system involving outside review on the ground that regular external investigations would be disruptive and cost-ineffective.

CHAPTER 17

Antitrust at IBM

The Monopolization Charges

The dominance of IBM (the International Business Machines Corporation) in the world market for computers and other electronic data-processing equipment has resulted in an ebb and flow of antitrust litigation over the past 30 years; but IBM has never been convicted of any civil or criminal offense under U.S. antitrust laws. Allegations of civil violations of the antitrust laws are still before the courts but IBM has never been charged with criminal violations. Nevertheless, if the public were asked to nominate a company whose name it associated with violations of antitrust laws, IBM probably would be mentioned more often than any of the large companies which do have criminal antitrust convictions. Throughout the 1970s in particular, IBM was the subject of more antitrust publicity than any other company because of the notorious costs of the U.S. government's monopolization case against it, and because IBM's domination of computing assumes proportions that no other contemporary corporate giant can equal. A legally illiterate press and public often presumes that bigness equals badness and that where there is the smoke of civil antitrust litigation there must be the fire of corporate crime. IBM has been the focus of adverse antitrust publicity more because of the magnitude of its dominance that the enormity of its alleged abuses of monopoly power.

It all began in 1952 when the U.S. government brought an antitrust action alleging IBM monopolization of domestic and foreign commerce in the tabulating machines business. A lengthy process of negotiation resulted in a consent decree, signed on January 25, 1956. This meant that the court did not rule on the government's allegations, but that IBM agreed to take certain actions, including the following:

(1) To sell as well as lease equipment without discrimination and at sale prices reasonably related to lease charges.

(a) To disclose prices and terms for sale and lease in order solicitations.

(b) To fill orders without discriminating between purchase and lease customers and, to the extent practicable, in order of their receipt.

(c) To offer purchasers the same services provided without separate charge to lease customers (with certain exceptions).

(d) To offer training to outsiders in or entering the repair and maintenance business; and to sell to them and IBM equipment owners certain technical documents, replacement parts and subassemblies, and instruction manuals.

(e) To allow customers to alter or attach equipment (with certain exceptions) and to provide instruction manuals.

(f) Not to require customers to purchase additional IBM machines or cards in order to get the machine they want.

(2) To license certain data processing patents at reasonable royalties and to limit consultant agreements with inventors and engineers to one year.

(3) To license certain card machinery patents without charge; to sell card machinery under certain cases until 1961; and in 1963 to divest card manufacturing capacity in excess of 50 per cent of total U.S. computer industry capacity. These were met and the requirements have expired.

(4) To transfer its service bureau business to a wholly-owned subsidiary and not to engage in service bureau business on its own nor to furnish tabulating or data processing equipment to its service bureau subsidiary except on the same terms offered to other service bureaus.

(5) To refrain from acquiring used machines except through trade-in or credit against sums payable to IBM and to offer these to secondhand dealers at prescribed maximum prices (with certain exceptions).[1]

In December 1968, the consent decree was resurrected when Control Data Corporation filed a private antitrust suit alleging serious and multiple violations of the decree by IBM. Control Data alleged 34 separate practices by which IBM sought monopoly by eliminating or battering rival firms into submission. The most serious charge was that IBM had sold "paper machines and phantom computers" to deter customers from buying Control Data's CDC 6600. That is, when Control Data began marketing the 6600 in 1964, IBM deflected customers from this advanced machine for a time by announcing that it would soon be releasing an even bigger, better, and cheaper machine—the 360/91. Orders were taken for this new computer, but by 1967 none had been delivered and in the same year the 360/91 project was abandoned. It was announced that the company would only produce enough machines to fill existing orders. IBM memos included descriptions of the machine as "a competition-stopper" which "should be deliberately done as a money-loser."[2] Control Data claimed that in spite of the fact that it had the best computer on the market, IBM's "phantom computer" caused it to show a net loss in 1966.

Control Data had tried to convince the Justice Department to prosecute IBM and only initiated its suit when the Department refused to do so. As Control Data began to discover where IBM's skeletons were buried, the Justice Department became more and more interested, until in 1969, on the last working day of the Johnson Administration, it charged IBM with monopolizing the computer market and with various actions alleged to have restricted competition. The Justice Department had been counting on access to a computerized index, prepared by Control Data lawyers, of 75,000 pages of the most crucial IBM internal memoranda. Then on January 15, 1973, IBM settled with Control Data by agreeing to pay it $101 million over several years and to sell the IBM subsidiary, the Service Bureau Corporation, to Control Data for what amounted to its asset value. On its side, in what may have been the key to the accord, Control Data destroyed the computerized index.

The announcement of the Justice Department suit was front-page news on January 18, 1969 because Justice officials made it clear that they were aiming for a court-ordered breakup of IBM. Thirteen years later, the trial which started in 1975 after five years of pretrial discovery, was stopped when the Reagan Administration dropped the case on January 8, 1982. Both sides sank a small fortune into the contest. Included among the in-house legal gladiators IBM recruited were Burke Marshall, former head of the antitrust division of the Justice Department, and a former U.S. Attorney General, Nicholas deB. Katzenbach. This has led to the criticism that IBM put on its payroll individuals involved in preparing the case against it.

A number of civil cases followed on the coattails of the government suit. In 1973, Telex was awarded $352.5 million in damages (reduced later to $259.5 million) after a U.S. District Court in Tulsa was persuaded that the company had been a victim of IBM's operation SMASH, which amounted to predatory pricing to destroy a competitor. However, a U.S. Court of Appeals in Denver more than a year later reversed this decision. Then there were further IBM court victories in separate civil antitrust suits launched by California Computer Products, Forro Precision, Memorex Corporation, and Transamerica Computer Company. Transamerica and Forro now are appealing their defeats. Two other lawsuits, in which the plaintiffs seek damages aggregating $276 million, remain in the pre-trial discovery stage. The last of 24 private antitrust actions to be settled or won by IBM was an out-of-court settlement in which the Greyhound Computer Corporation was paid $17.7 million in January, 1981, to withdraw its suit.[3]

It seems that as soon as IBM dispenses with one antitrust case, another looms. On December 19, 1980, a 1,000 page "Statement of Objections" was filed by the Commission of the European Economic Community (EEC). The report recommended that the EEC fine IBM up to $2.3 billion for alleged restriction of competition in the European computer market. Such a high fine is possible because of the EEC power to impose fines up to 10 per cent of sales, a power that has never been exercised before. If this case proceeds, it could be the biggest of them all. The EEC brief is based in part on complaints lodged by Memorex, Amdahl, National Advanced Systems, and a fourth undisclosed firm. The brief asserts that IBM Europe has, among other anti-competitive practices, unfairly locked customers into buying its own software (programs) as a requisite for any computer purchase, and has refused to supply its software for use with non-IBM computers. Leading EEC trustbuster at the time, Willy Schlieder, said: "We feel we have a strong case." Another inside source in Brussels has pointed out, however, that "our antitrust staff is no match for IBM's legal resources."[4] The string of successes of IBM lawyers in American courts lends credence to this estimate of the odds. However, IBM lost the first round when the European Court of Justice in Luxembourg refused to consider a request by IBM to stop the EEC investigation.[5]

Publicity and Counterpublicity

The two worst bursts of adverse publicity for IBM during the three decades of antitrust allegations were in January 1969, when the Justice Department commenced its suit, and in 1973 as a result of the Telex defeat. Predictably, while the latter was front-page news, the reversal of the decision by the Court of Appeals in Denver was tucked away in the business pages of most newspapers.

IBM executives have claimed that it was the worldwide publicity over the massive Telex award that prompted the EEC to commence its investigation of IBM.

The executives with whom we spoke at IBM were of the view that, even though many rival computer companies had savagely attacked IBM in court, competitors had not exploited IBM's antitrust problems in their sales pitches.

IBM has run an ongoing counterpublicity campaign against the image of the company as monopolistic. During the 1950s, IBM blasted the Justice Department case in a series of advertisements in major newspapers. Soon after the 1969 government suit was brought, IBM ran full-page newspaper advertisements explaining the company's side of the story. Since then, a frequent theme in IBM advertising—sometimes subtle, sometimes explicit—has been that IBM produces top-quality products because it has formidable competitors breathing down its neck. Some IBM television advertisements have taken what was then the unusual step of flashing the names of a variety of rivals on the screen to suggest the competitiveness of the computing industry.

IBM maintains an opinion survey program to monitor public perceptions of it. These corporate image surveys are conducted on college campuses, in the general community, and among employees. More unusual was the recruitment by IBM counsel of a "shadow jury" with the same demographic and psychological characteristics as the actual jury hearing the California Computer Products antitrust case. Each day, the shadow jury attended the trial as visitors. A University of Southern California Marketing Professor would elicit its members' reactions to the day's arguments and evidence every evening. This feedback was useful to IBM attorneys in evaluating their success in communicating complex antitrust theories to an unsophisticated lay audience. Two months into the trial, the press discovered the mock jury. It attracted so much attention and controversy that IBM disbanded the shadow panel.[6]

At the time of writing, even though the Justice Department suit to break up IBM has been stopped, it continues to generate publicity. Assistant Attorney General William F. Baxter was responsible for the decision to drop the case. In March 1982, Judge David Edelstein, who presided over the IBM trial, publicly attacked Baxter for failure to disclose that in 1976 he received $1,500 from IBM's law firm for acting as a consultant on one of the company's private antitrust cases, and that in 1968–1969 an IBM grant paid all or most of his sabbatical salary.[7] This fact had been brought to the Judge's attention by one of IBM's competitors, Memorex, after

Baxter dropped the case.[8] It was also subsequently revealed that in 1976, as a Stanford University law professor, Baxter had lobbied the Carter administration to dump the IBM case,[9] and that as Assistant Attorney General he had also lobbied the EEC to reconsider its IBM case prior to the dropping of the American charges.[10] A motion by a "friend of the court," Philip N. Stern, to challenge the dismissal of the case is yet to be heard at the time of writing.[11]

Financial Impacts

IBM executives interviewed perceived a temporary downturn in IBM stock values at the commencement of the government's antitrust suit and the initial Telex decision. On 18 September 1973, the day following the Telex decision, IBM stock closed at 270¾, down 14½. The following day it closed at 254½. The effects were certainly short-term, however, as both 1969 and 1973 were generally good years for IBM stock. The Telex decision had an adverse impact on IBM in the stockmarket, because investors realized that other civil suits of the same sort were pending and the company could not afford too many more $353 million damages payments. A factor attenuating this downturn was that one influential market analyst predicted at the time—correctly as it turned out—that the Telex decision would be reversed on appeal. More important than the specific downturns has been the cloud continuously hanging over IBM stock as a result of a fear that the company might be broken up if the Justice Department suit succeeds. *Standard and Poor's* consistently included a warning in its annual stock market prospects report that "Antitrust suits could affect the present dominant market position."[12] Rumors appeared in the press from time to time that the Justice Department was preparing to settle its suit have been associated with improvements in IBM stock prices. Over the past decade stockholders have repeatedly expressed concern at IBM Annual Meetings over the possibility of a breakup's dampening share prices. On the other hand, IBM Senior Vice-President and General Counsel Katzenbach, when we spoke with him late in 1980, held the view that IBM stock prices had for several years incorporated the realistic expection that IBM would ultimately prevail in the suit and be saved from divestiture. Katzenbach felt confident that IBM would in fact win by a comfortable margin if the case ever reached the Supreme Court. His perception of the market was proven largely correct when IBM stock improved only slightly in the days after the dropping of the suit.[13] However, other computer makers, Honeywell, Digital Equipment Corporation, and Apple Computer, recorded sharp drops on the first day of trading after the announcement.[14]

For a corporate giant, IBM is not a highly diversified concern. It has eschewed the policies of growth through takeover which have been characteristic of other top American corporations. There have been suggestions that this reluctance to make takeover bids was a response to the Justice Department suit. At the 1980 Annual Meeting, one stockholder asked: "Does our reluctance to diversify into other business reflect some fear and trepidation about what the Justice Department's reaction might be?" IBM Chairman, Frank T. Cary, replied: "I would expect they might object, and we might have another long legal battle with them. Certainly that does enter into our consideration, although I think the business reasons are the most important."[15]

Another significant cost to IBM has been the sheer legal expenses of fighting the various suits. They would certainly run to an eight-figure sum. Chairman Cary used to joke: "Nick Katzenbach is the only guy at IBM with an unlimited budget . . . and he always exceeds it."[16] The company estimates that the document retention program ordered by the court has alone cost it $3.5 million. There was one IBM office in which 94 million documents relevant to the Justice Department suit were stored. Then, of course, there are the costs of the settlements themselves, which run to a nine-figure sum in the private cases. We cannot give a precise figure because, for most of the 10 or so settlements, the amounts involved were never disclosed.

All the financial impacts—on the stockmarket, on hesitancy to aggressively expand through acquisition, and on legal costs—are impacts of the litigation, but are hardly due to the publicity surrounding the litigation. Indirectly, some litigants may have been stirred to action by the publicity. But there has been no significant direct financial impact from the publicity. Computer buyers do not shy away from IBM because of any perception of it as monopolistic. Shares were discounted because of apprehension of what the courts might do, not of what public opinion might do.

Non-Financial Impacts

None of the seven IBM executives with whom we spoke felt that there had been serious adverse effects on employee morale as a result of the antitrust litigation and its attendant publicity. Some depression in morale was noticed after the Telex defeat, but this was more than matched by a string of boosts to morale with successive company victories in court. IBM has gone to considerable lengths to keep its employees informed of the progress of the litigation. In 1969, for example, a notice was circulated to inform employees that the Justice Department's antitrust suit was not a criminal prosecution and that no individual IBM executives had been accused of breaking the law.

The company has also been concerned at evidence from its own opinion surveys that some bright young college graduates feel a little resistance to being recruited by IBM because of the company's being perceived as an abuser of monopoly power. One IBM informant hastened to point out that this consequence was not of serious proportions, nowhere near as serious, for example, as the problems experienced by Dow Chemical in campus recruiting at the time Dow supplied napalm for use in Vietnam.

The most important non-financial impact has been that, during the past decade in particular, the antitrust litigation has been a never-ending nuisance to top management. Chairman Cary had to produce some 300,000 pages of documents from his files. He was personally questioned at depositions for 53 days and was three days on the stand in the private antitrust trials. As a rule of thumb, IBM General Counsel Katzenbach estimated that one day at deposition for the Chairman cost him five days in tedious preparation. Again, this is an impact of the litigation per se and not of the publicity emanating from it.

Reforms

Katzenbach claimed that since the Justice Department suit commenced in 1969 the company's internal antitrust policies and enforcement have not been strengthened, that IBM had an equally vigilant system prior to 1969. Of course, there are good reasons for him to say this: To admit that antitrust compliance policies are stronger now might imply that they were less than they could have been during the years that are the focus of the continuing litigation. However, there were specific reforms which came immediately in the wake of the Justice Department suit. One of the charges against IBM was that it "impaired" the development of independent service and peripheral companies by maintaining an inclusive price policy for its machines, software, and related materials. In June 1969, IBM responded by "unbundling" its unitary package of hardware-software-services-education, setting separate prices for each element.[17]

IBM now has more detailed and painstaking antitrust policies than any company the present authors are aware of; this detail has been built up during the period of IBM's exposure to antitrust litigation and publicity. Comparable giants that have had their own antitrust problems, such as General Electric and Exxon, do not have the meticulously detailed antitrust compliance policies of IBM. What other corporation devotes over 60 per cent of its business conduct guidelines document[18] to antitrust? It surely is more than coincidence that the company whose name is synonymous with antitrust litigation is the company which communicates the most detailed antitrust policies to its middle and lower managers.

Other commentators on IBM also conclude that the nagging fear of breakup, or another costly round of private antitrust litigation, has made the company peculiarly circumspect on antitrust matters since it became a target for public scrutiny of its marketing practices. Nancy Foy has called it "control by fear":

> I would *not* like to see IBM's almost neurotic fear of governments, unions, and the press cured. I would particularly not like these neuroses to be cured in the classic way—by having IBM actually experience what it fears. I would not like to see IBM broken up by the anti-trust people, for example. But I want the antitrust pressures to continue. The company's fear of being broken up is animal-like, a powerful thing that keeps it relatively well behaved and cooperative, encouraging greater centralization on a voluntary basis. The world doesn't understand IBM's regenerative powers; a broken-up IBM would easily turn into two, five or seven small tigers, afraid of nothing once the ultimate threat had been exercised—able to pounce with invincible ferocity on hapless new market sectors. Most of the competitors are aware of this; very few want IBM to be broken up.
> . . . Nor would I like to see IBM's public image get any more tiger-like and distorted; once this happened the powerful constraint of IBM's self-image would be erased, and the public would be not only less well-informed but also less protected from corporate aggression.
> These fears deserve careful exploration; they are the only real control we have over IBM.[19]

The starting point for understanding the detailed antitrust policies which have been the product of this "control by fear" is IBM's *Business Conduct Guidelines*. All personnel (not just executives and managers) who in any way meet or speak with people outside IBM on behalf of IBM must certify the following in writing each year:

I certify that I have read or reviewed the IBM booklet entitled "Business Conduct Guidelines," Form G506-0001-4, this year and fully understand my responsibility to comply with the guidelines stated in it. I recognize that any wilful violation of these guidelines may be cause for dismissal from the company. I will discuss any questions I have on them with my manager or with an IBM attorney. (If you wish to discuss a question before signing this card, please contact your manager or IBM attorney.)

The *Business Conduct Guidelines* warn that "It's easy to see that large firms must bend over backwards to avoid even the appearance of illegal or unethical conduct. IBM's policy now, as in the past, is to comply fully in letter and spirit with the antitrust laws."[20] The document then goes on to detail in lucid, comprehensible terms the requirements of the Sherman, Clayton, Robinson-Patman, and Federal Trade Commission Acts. It points out that these requirements of U.S. antitrust law must also be followed by IBM employees living and working outside the United States.

Interspersed throughout the Business Conduct Guidelines are also a variety of specific policies to minimize antitrust exposure. For example:

An IBM representative may not attempt to delay a customer decision to order competitive equipment by hinting that a new IBM product is under development.[21]

A firm cannot require "tied" sales, such as insisting that a customer buy IBM typewriter ribbons if it buys IBM typewriters.[22]

In *all* contacts with competitors, IBM employees must avoid discussing such things as pricing policy, terms of sales, costs, inventories, product plans, market surveys or studies, or any proprietary or confidential information . . .. [At trade association meetings] IBM people should confine their discussion to specific items on a meeting agenda. If any discussion is opened on the prohibited subjects listed above, IBM representatives should object and refuse to participate. *If the discussion does not stop then and there, they should leave the meeting in a manner that will be noticed and remembered by others at the meeting.*[23] (italics in original)

You certainly can buy products and services from a supplier who buys products and services from IBM. But you cannot make an agreement to buy from suppliers on the condition that they agree to use IBM products and services. This means, quite clearly, that IBM's decision whether to use a supplier's services and products must be totally independent from his or her decision to use IBM as a supplier. You should not even *hint* to a supplier that, somehow, IBM's purchases from the supplier should be a reason why it ought to do business with us.[24]

IBM internal compliance policies go further than the *Business Conduct Guidelines*. Marketing divisions have internal marketing guidelines and these too are dominated by antitrust concerns. For instance, one division's "General Marketing Guidelines" define a considerable number of "unacceptable activities." Examples include:[25]

Refusing to sell computer programs to customers who do not have an IBM processor. (Note that the EEC's "statement of objections" alleges that IBM has been violating this policy in Europe.)[26]

Threatening customers who do not order IBM equipment with reduced support on their other IBM machines (e.g., refusing installation planning for IBM tape drives because the disk drives will be from another manufacturer).

Implying that resale value will be lower if non-IBM equipment is attached to an IBM machine.

Accepting opportunities to read confidential bids that have been made by competitors to government customers.

The last "unacceptable activity" on this list relates to a particularly important area. Collusion between sellers and employees of the purchaser is a more important threat to competition in the computing industry than collusion among sellers. For example, if an employee of the purchaser is convinced that an IBM computer would be best for his company, or for him personally, he might be tempted to confer with IBM to ensure that the specifications put in the call for tenders are requirements which only an IBM machine could adequately meet. IBM has an array of rules prohibiting collusion by means of tailor-made tenders. Nevertheless, rigging of bid specifications by individual IBM salesmen is an accusation that has been levelled against the giant in the trade press.[27]

Beyond the divisional General Marketing Guidelines, IBM has more specific guidelines for particular areas. These are impressive in the way they define the dos and don'ts of company policy in crystal-clear fashion through providing general principles and then illustrating them with concrete examples. IBM has been kind enough to grant permission to quote the following example from an "Internal Use Only" document—*Data Processing Division Public Sector Marketing Guidelines*:[28]

Sole source procurement

Most procurement regulations require competitive bidding by vendors for government business. However, certain state and local jurisdictions permit sole source procurement in unusal situations, such as emergencies, or when a customer's in-house technical evaluation determines that specific equipment commitments should be made. In addition, some public sector customers do not require competitive procurement.

When rules and regulations permit, IBM representatives may recommend sole source procurement. Be aware that many public sector customers do not have clear sole source standards, and be sure that your marketing efforts do not violate the law or encourage questionable customer activities.

Example: A customer's data processing requirements have increased beyond the capability of his System/370 Model 125. He wishes to upgrade the installation as soon as possible, but procurement regulations require competitive bidding for all data processing equipment or services.

Question: Can the IBM marketing representative recommend an interim System/370 Model 135, pending an RFP?

Answer: Yes. The marketing representative can present the upgrade in an IBM proposal or letter of recommendation. However, he may not recommend that the customer issue a *sole source order*.

Even a legally acceptable sole source order, if not handled with sensitivity and good judgment, can create an appearance of favoritism—resulting in competitive protests, government or judicial review, and damaging public criticism.

In general, IBM accepts sole source orders when it is an acceptable customer practice and when IBM has done nothing to motivate or influence an exception to competitive procurement rules. You should review sole source orders and related marketing activities with branch management.

Be especially careful if a customer decides that valid and compelling reasons exist to sole source, but you think competitive procurement is required. If management review determines that IBM may have influenced the decision, ask the customer to reconsider. Then, if the customer still decides to sole source, you should respond with a letter stating that in accordance with the *customer's* interpretation of his own procurement regulations, IBM will accept his order.

If management decides that IBM did not influence the sole source decision, you may accept the order. Further discussion with the customer is not necessary.

DP Legal and Marketing Practices are available to assist this review.

While IBM was not willing to provide us with detailed figures on the number of individuals who had been disciplined for violations of the *Business Conduct Guidelines*, it was pointed out that employees have been dismissed for flagrant violations. Katherine Fishman's comment in the *The Computer Establishment* is: "Alumni of the branch offices do talk of circumventing the rules, but say that punishment is swift and sure if one gets caught."[29]

IBM representatives do have a sales quota to meet. There is what is called a "100 Per Cent Club" of representatives who have achieved 100 per cent (or more) of their sales quota, and a majority of IBM representatives are in the "100 Per Cent Club". To date, the corporation's market dominance and product quality have made goal attainment relatively easy through legitimate means. It must be pointed out, however, that there is no inevitability about this. IBM could decide to aim for even higher sales by setting its employees tougher targets that could be reached only through ruthless marketing practices. At present IBM has a policy of ensuring that targets are attainable by legitimate means. When times are bad, quotas are readjusted downwards to keep them realistic.[30]

To ensure compliance with its corporate policies, IBM relies heavily on its so-called "contention system."[31] The contention system involves setting up a friendly adversary relationship between staff and line. If the general counsel of a subsidiary raises objections to the subsidiary chief about a marketing practice perceived as contravening company policy, and if that objection is overruled, he or she must report this to division counsel. If the latter agrees with the local counsel, the objection is taken up with the division chief executive to whom the local chief answers. Should the division chief executive support the local chief while the division counsel supports the local counsel, the contention will move up to a higher level of the organization. Ultimately, it might be decided in a discussion between the Chairman and the Senior Vice-President and General Counsel, in which the Chairman will have the final say. Such a formalized contention system between the line and the staff reporting relationships increases the probability that problems will be flushed out into the open.

At the outset, we said that the contention system was friendly. Organizations cannot afford to undermine cooperation by fostering a war of all against all. So certain informal codes of fair play are followed. When a staff person feels compelled to blow the whistle on a line manager through staff channels, good form is to warn the line manager beforehand. This gives the line manager two possible outs. Recognizing that the staff person means business, the line manager can back down. Or, the line manager him/herself can report the problem up through staff channels. The latter protects the line manager from any accusations of trying to cover up problems from staff scrutiny.

Monitoring compliance with the company's antitrust policies is the responsibility of the auditing staff who report to the corporate treasurer. About every three years the auditors check whether all the staff who must sign off on the *Business Conduct Guidelines* have done so. We were not given any evidence of anything more than this clerical chore being undertaken in antitrust compliance audits.

Many of the more impressive features of IBM's antitrust compliance policies emerged during the period of adverse publicity. However, the adverse publicity was only a very minor contributing factor to their development. The elaborate antitrust policies were inaugurated primarily to limit further legal exposure of the company. Being able to fire back at its media critics with the fact that IBM has an excellent control system for ensuring compliance with antitrust laws is an additional reason for implementing the system, but only a minor one.

Two studies by Don Waldman[32] show that the consequence of IBM's more restrained marketing practices under its new antitrust policies was a more competitive computer market.[33] Waldman's first study examined the impact of the 1956 consent decree.[34] After the 1956 decree committed IBM to less predatory marketing practices, a number of new competitors were tempted into the computer market. However, Waldman concludes that IBM's new policies were only a minor factor in encouraging this entry. More important factors were growing demand and technological progress encouraging firms with new ideas to enter the field. By the end of the 60s, the new competitors had made only minor inroads into IBM dominance in the main-frame computer market. However, less retaliatory policies toward competitors in the data card and magnetic tape markets resulted in the entry of many new successful competitors, a dramatic reduction in IBM's share of the data card market, and, in spite of inflation, a 15 per cent reduction in IBM card prices between 1956 and 1966.

The new IBM marketing policies which followed from the 1956 consent decree still left its monopoly of the main-frame computer market barely dented. But the U.S. government's 1969 monopolization suit helped to gradually change that. By 1979, IBM's share of the market, according to one definition, had declined to 35 per cent from the 70 per cent it had enjoyed in the 1960s.[35] In 1975 the competition intensified when Amdahl Corporation introduced a central processor which was plug-compatible with IBM software, yet more powerful and less expensive than the IBM processors. Amdahl's sales grew from $14 million in 1975 to $189 million in 1977.[36] Its successes encouraged others such as Control Data and Itel into the plug-compatible market. And now in the 1980s IBM faces a new Japanese challenge. Waldman points out that without the 1969 monopolization case Amdahl Corporation might never have been formed and that the plug-compatible processor market might not have developed in the 1970s.[37] Amdahl Corporation was formed after Gene Amdahl left IBM, explaining that the company's antitrust troubles would inhibit price-cutting and other retaliation against opponents, and therefore would provide the opportunity for a competitor to sneak in under the giant's guard.

The reduced capacity of IBM to erect and maintain barriers to entry while it was fighting a life-and-death monopolization case permitted a number of other successful competitors to get into the computer industry in the 1970s—e.g., Datapoint, Data General, Computer Automation, and Prime. The peripheral equipment market also saw successful new IBM competitors get under way in the 1970s—Applied Digital Data, Centronics Data, and Storage Technology.[38] Waldman concludes that while rapid technological advance paved the way for much of the new competition, the pace of change in the structure of the computing market was accelerated by the 1969 monopolization case.[39]

Will there be a regression to old practices now that the Justice Department case has been dropped? As IBM's lead outside counsel in the case has pointed out: "There hasn't been a price or product change at IBM for 30 years that hasn't been approved first by a lawyer."[40] Since the 30 years of litigation has virtually ended, at least in the United States, will this continue to be the case? Sy Kaufman, an analyst with Hambrecht and Quist, speculates: "It could become more aggressive in making acquisitions, not only in computer areas but also in communications."[41]

The adoption of the more circumspect, less retaliatory IBM marketing policies which provided room for new competitors in the 1970s can be partly attributed to the 1969 case. It was not the publicity, here, but the fear of losing the case that was the substantial incentive to reform. Ironically, perhaps now that the case has been dropped, fear of adverse publicity will play some part in keeping IBM cautious. When we asked one IBM executive if the company would commence a more aggressive program of growth by acquisition now that the spectre of the suit has been lifted,[42] he replied: "If we started buying out competitors as soon

211

as the government set us free, it would cause a lot of public concern."

A final prospect of reform arises from the publicity surrounding Assistant Attorney General Baxter's failure to declare possible conflicts of interest. In response to motions by Stern and by Nader's Public Citizen group, arguing as "friends of the court" that the case should not have been dismissed, Judge Edelstein opened up the question of the judiciary's power to review the government's exercise of prosecutorial discretion in major antitrust cases. In 1974, the Tunney Act required the Justice Department to tell the public why it wants to settle an antitrust case and gave the courts a role in determining whether a settlement is in the public interest. If Judge Edlestein does successfully review prosecutorial discretion in the IBM case, he will have expanded the scope of judicial review under the Tunney Act to antitrust dismissals as well as settlements.[43]

CHAPTER 18

Air New Zealand—
The Erebus Disaster

The Erebus Allegations

On November 28, 1979, an Air New Zealand Antarctic flight, TE 901, crashed on the lower slopes of Mt. Erebus, killing all 257 people aboard. It was the fourth worst disaster in the history of commercial aviation, and Air New Zealand's first fatal accident on an international flight.

An inquiry under the Civil Aviation (Accident Investigation) Regulations of 1978 was made by the Chief Inspector of Air Accidents, Ron Chippindale. The Chippindale report, although critical of some aspects of Air New Zealand's briefing and other operational procedures for the nonscheduled flight, concluded that the probable cause of the accident "was the decision of the captain to continue the flight at low level toward an area of poor surface and horizon definition when the crew was not certain of their position and the subsequent inability to detect the rising terrain which intercepted the aircraft's flight path."[1]

A Royal Commission then was appointed to inquire into the causes and circumstances of the crash and to canvass its implications for air safety regulation. The report of the Commissioner, Peter Mahon, a judge of the High Court of New Zealand, exonerated the captain from blame: The aircrew had not been advised of a critical change in the flight path that had been fed into the aircraft's computerized navigational system.[2] Rather, "the single dominant and effective cause of the disaster was the mistake made by those airline officials who programmed the aircraft to fly directly at Mt. Erebus and omitted to tell the aircrew. That mistake is directly attributable, not so much to the persons who made it, but to the

213

incompetent administrative airline procedures which made the mistake possible."³

The Report also found that an attempt had been made to cover up the breakdown in navigational procedures. The chief executive, said the Report, had made "one of the most remarkable executive decisions ever to have been made in the corporate affairs of a large New Zealand company"⁴ when he directed the shredding of surplus documents about Antarctic flights:

> An opportunity was thereby created for people in the airline to get rid of documents which might seem to implicate airline officials as being responsible for the disaster, and the whole episode very plainly engendered bitter feelings among the relatives of the dead flight crew and among their fellow pilots . . .⁵

Much worse, the Report alleged that the Commission had been obstructed by a perjurious conspiracy:

> No judicial officer ever wishes to be compelled to say he has listened to evidence which is false. He always prefers to say, as I hope the hundreds of judgments which I have written will illustrate, that he cannot accept the relevant explanation, or that he prefers a contrary version set out in the evidence.
>
> But in this case, the palpably false sections of evidence which I heard could not have been the result of mistake, or faulty recollection. They originated, I am compelled to say, in a pre-determined plan of deception. They were very clearly part of an attempt to conceal a series of disastrous administrative blunders and so, in regard to the particular items of evidence to which I have referred, I am forced reluctantly to say that I had to listen to an orchestrated litany of lies.⁶

To add injury to insult, a substantial part of the costs of the inquiry—$US120,000 out of $US220,000—were awarded against the airline because it had not "put all its cards on the table."⁷

Air New Zealand's chief executive, Morrie Davis, thereupon resigned as a matter of *noblesse oblige*.⁸ Before long, however, findings of the Royal Commission that suggested that there had been a conspiratorial cover-up were challenged in a legal action by Air New Zealand. The action sought various remedies, including a declaration that, in finding "a pre-determined plan of deception" and "an orchestrated litany of lies," the Commission had acted in excess of jurisdiction or in breach of the rules of natural justice.⁹

The New Zealand Court of Appeal unanimously agreed that the findings complained of went beyond the Commission's terms of reference and, in any event, involved allegations that, contrary to natural justice, had been made without fair opportunity to reply.[10] Although declaratory relief was denied (by a 3–2 decision), the $120,000 award of costs was set aside in order to vindicate the reputation of the company, Davis, and other persons subjected in the Report to express or implied accusations of having participated in a conspiratorial cover-up. It should also be pointed out that no charges were laid by the police after their investigation following the Royal Commission's Report.

When the decision of the Court of Appeal was announced, Davis denounced the Royal Commissioner as unfit to remain in judicial office.[11] Justice Mahon proceeded to offer his resignation to the government in the interest of "public confidence in the law," but added that the Court of Appeal had departed from the principles of natural justice by not giving him a chance to speak about the evidence upon which he had relied.[12] Ultimately, Justice Mahon's offer of resignation was accepted, amidst expressions of concern from within the legal profession. An appeal to the Privy Council is now proceeding, there being considerable doubt as to the soundness of the decision made by the Court of Appeal.[13]

The challenge which succeeded in the Court of Appeal did not formally affect the findings of the Royal Commission in relation to the causes and circumstances of the crash. However, in explaining the scope of proceedings before the Court of Appeal, the majority expressed itself in so circumspect a manner as to depreciate the significance of those findings:

> We must begin by removing any possible misconception about the scope of these proceedings. They are not proceedings in which this Court can adjudicate on the cause of the disaster. The question of causation is obviously a difficult one, as shown by the fact that the Commissioner and the Chief Inspector of Air Accidents in his report came to different conclusions on it. But it is not this Court's concern now. This is not an appeal. Parties to hearings by Commissions of Inquiry have no rights of appeal against the reports. The reason is partly that the reports are, in a sense, inevitably inconclusive. Findings made by Commissioners are in the end only expressions of opinion. They would not even be admissible in evidence in legal proceedings as to the cause of a disaster. In themselves they do not alter the legal rights of the persons to whom they refer. Nevertheless they may greatly influence public and Government opinion and have a devastating effect on personal reputations; and in our judgment these are the major reasons why in appropriate proceedings the Courts must be ready if necessary, in relation to Commissions of Inquiry just as

to other public bodies and officials, to ensure that they keep within the limits of their lawful powers and comply with any applicable rules of natural justice.[14]

The question of corporate or individual liability remains untested in the courts: Criminal charges were not laid against the company or any personnel, and civil claims against the airline are in the process of settlement.[15] Since court proceedings on questions of liability are a remote possibility, it is almost certain that the causes of the crash and the blameworthiness of the actors involved will never be resolved beyond dispute. Recently, however, the position taken by the Royal Commission has been supported, and supported at length on substantial grounds, in *Impact Erebus*, a book written about the causes of the crash by Gordon Vette, a former top-ranking pilot with Air New Zealand.

Publicity and Counterpublicity

The Erebus crash was seen by the media as an unmitigated catastrophe. In New Zealand, it was regarded as a black day for the nation:

> The Antarctic air disaster will have gripped the heart of every New Zealander. Few areas of the country have not lost a citizen in the crash; hundreds of families are cruelly and suddenly bereaved. November 28, 1979, was indeed a day of tragedy in New Zealand history.[16]

Abroad, the story was front-page news, especially in Japan, the United States, and the other home lands of the tourists killed. (Nearly 200 media agencies beyond New Zealand requested reports from the airline about the crash.)[17]

Initially, much of the coverage of the fatal crash was sympathetic to Air New Zealand. Had the DC10 failed again? Had flight TE 901 been the victim of a sudden downdraft or volcanic force? Possibly the aircrew had been disoriented by a snow shower or a white-out. Perhaps there had been a pilot error in deciding to go down low. As details of the crash site emerged, however, a navigational error was suspected, and suspicion soon turned into hostile rumor when wide circulation was given to a false report that the last words of the pilot were "Where the hell are we?"[18] There was also a flurry about the absence of polar survival equipment on the Air New Zealand flight (by contrast, Qantas flights to the Antarctic carry such gear, even if, in the opinion of the Australian Flight Stewards Association, it is inadequate).[19]

By far the worst publicity was that generated by the Royal Commission. The onslaught began with the Report's unexpectedly severe findings, which were so purple as to make instant headlines. "'INCOMPETENT' PROCEDURES BLAMED FOR EREBUS CRASH" declaimed the *New Zealand Herald*; "LITANY OF LIES" cried *Time* magazine and the Melbourne *Age*; "AIR NEW ZEALAND 'COVERED UP CRASH BUNGLE'" intoned the *Canberra Times*.[20] As one columnist observed,

> Justice Mahon, a conservative jurist and eminent legal mind, has torn the lid off. His blistering statements have burned themselves into the consciousness of nearly all New Zealanders, leaving the expected fulminations of our politicians as pale shadows by comparison.[21]

Pale as the politicians' public statements turned out to be in comparison, there was nonetheless many a fulmination. The Leader of the Opposition, Bill Rowling, called for the sacking of the senior management of Air New Zealand, including the entire board of directors:

> There is no possible justification for them to retain their jobs even pending further investigation. Restructuring the airline at the highest level is essential.[22]

Another prominent politician questioned whether the Security Intelligence Service had been behind a burglary at the home of the deceased pilot of flight TE 901, Captain Jim Collins (an atlas used by Captain Collins to plot his path for flight TE 901 had been taken, but not a pearl necklace or diamond ring nearby), adding that "The whole thing is turning into a major Watergate scandal."[23]

More threatening than these political sallies were Justice Mahon's statements to the press when, having offered his resignation, he entered the lists of public debate. As well as reiterating many of the points made in his report, Mahon added a number of embellishments; the most incriminating, it may be speculated, was that instancing a document about navigational information supplied to Captain Collins which had been removed from an Air New Zealand file and replaced with another document bearing the same number (J2).[24]

Three books and a 50-minute television documentary about the Erebus disaster also have appeared,[25] and more adverse publicity could be in the making: The former Royal Commissioner has let it be known that he might write a book on the affair.

Although some public relations measures were taken by Air New Zealand, the company itself did not attempt any counteroffensive campaign in the media. However, the Court of Appeal decision had the effect of veiling the findings of the Royal Commission on the causes of the crash. Moreover, throughout the crisis, the company had the strong support of its leading shareholder, the Prime Minister and Minister of Finance, Robert Muldoon.

The public relations measures taken by Air New Zealand immediately after the crash included an advertisement expressing profound sympathy and concern, published throughout New Zealand. An internal briefing system was established to keep staff fully informed. Welfare was provided for victims' next-of-kin. The chief executive officer made himself available on a daily basis for press conferences. And the airline's advertising campaign (which had centered around the slogan "Nobody Does it Better") was terminated. The overall aim of these measures was to provide as "visual" and sensitive a response as possible. Not to do so, we were informed, would have been to risk the kind of hostility which American Airlines experienced when it remained "inscrutable" after the DC10 crash in Chicago.

When the Royal Commission handed down its report, the chief executive officer of Air New Zealand, Davis, issued a brief statement rejecting any allegations that his conduct had been inadequate or improper. A week later he announced his resignation, stressing that his purpose was "to remove a focus point from this current controversy and . . . hasten the recovery of the company";[26] in the words of his successor, it had been a "statesman-like" act. The media were not slow to treat the move as blood that had to be let.[27]

Air New Zealand's Board issued a series of press releases indicating the steps deemed necessary to resolve the crisis. "Extravagant conclusions" about the conduct or integrity of personnel were to be the subject of a legal challenge in the High Court.[28] Alleged administrative deficiencies would be investigated independently as a matter of urgency. A special committee would pursue the question of internal discipline when police inquiries had been completed. Personnel subject to allegations of inadequate or improper conduct would be assigned to other duties, in the interest of safety. Antarctic flights would be discontinued. Additional checks would be made of the computer flight planning system. Recommendations made in the Chippindale Report would be followed. And all sectors of the company's operations would be visited by a member of the Board to discuss the company's position and to provide reassurance that it would "not only survive but indeed come through the present ordeal a strengthened airline."[29]

That ordeal was later to be relieved by the decision of the Court of Appeal. The decision in itself did much to vindicate the reputation of Air New Zealand, Davis, and other key personnel.[30] Moreover, although the decision focused only on the findings in the Mahon Report that there had been a conspiratorial cover-up,[31] the furor that ensued when Davis attacked Justice Mahon's judicial competence distracted attention from the Royal Commission's findings as to the causes of the crash. As the Auckland *Star* commented editorially, the new sphere of controversy tended to eclipse the main conclusion of the Mahon Report:

> It is most unfortunate that a side-issue in Mr. Justice Mahon's Mt. Erebus disaster report has become the cause of controversy which threatens to obscure the real issue.
>
> The "orchestrated litany of lies" argument is of small significance beside the enormity of Mr. Justice Mahon's key finding that the single dominant and effective cause of a disaster which claimed 257 lives was the mistake made by Air New Zealand officials who programmed the DC10 to fly directly towards Mt. Erebus and omitted to tell the air crew.
>
> That finding has not been challenged. It is what remains, with all its dreadful implications, at the forefront of most New Zealanders' minds.
>
> Their concern is much more with the inefficient administrative procedures that led to the disaster than with the behavior of airline witnesses who appeared before the royal commission of inquiry.
>
> Mr. Justice Mahon's disappointment over the Appeal Court rebuff for his "litany of lies" remarks is understandable. But it is a great pity that the ensuing wrangle, with politicians at odds over what should now be done to clarify that aspect of the report, is being treated with such importance.[32]

Apart from the counterpublicity generated by the decision of the Court of Appeal, a number of influential persons came to Air New Zealand's aid. Chippindale defended the conclusions of his report with a 60-point critique of the Royal Commission's findings.[33] An anonymous "high legal authority" blamed Justice Mahon for using non-legalistic language and thereby causing an emotional public debate.[34] A retired U.S. Navy pilot with Antarctic experience claimed that 90 per cent of the blame for the crash lay with the pilot.[35] Air Marshal Sir Rochford Hughes, advisor on technical matters to counsel assisting the Royal Commission, expressed the opinion that the aircrew had been 10 per cent at fault, and implied that the Commissioner might have come to a similar conclusion had he been assisted by assessors with experience of polar aviation.[36] (Air New Zealand's reaction to these allocations of blame was to offer another: the company was 60 per cent to blame, the crew 40 per cent).[37] The company's main defender, however, was the Prime Minister, Muldoon.

Immediately prior to the release of the Mahon Report, Muldoon called upon everyone to rally around the airline; as one commentator observed, he was "'talking the market up' at a time when round the world the airline would be in very bad odor."[38] Soon after the Report was released, he criticized its "litany of lies" statement and related findings as unjustified.[39] Later, after Justice Mahon had entered the debate, Muldoon responded personally to the main points raised by the former Commissioner. For example, in relation to the allegedly sinister alteration to document J2, Muldoon stated that the airline had known all along that the document would be made public and that it had been altered for a proper purpose, namely "to ensure greater accuracy."[40] Some of these instances of counterpublicity were parried by Mahon,[41] but the strength of his remarks was attenuated by the fact that he now spoke at least partly as a judge in his own cause. Ultimately, however, the position taken by Mahon may be vindicated by the Privy Council when it decides the appeal now proceeding against the decision of the Court of Appeal. If so, the publicity surrounding the Erebus disaster will have only just begun.

Financial Impacts

Nightmarish as the Erebus crash was for Air New Zealand, the monetary impact was almost certainly small. The only financial loss attributable to the adverse publicity occasioned by the crash or by the Royal Commission was a possible slight loss of flight ticket sales.[42] We were told that, although it was impossible to quantify the impact (one indeterminacy was the parallel effect of the bad crash record of the DC10), and although there had been no noticeable move away from the company, "it had to have an impact somewhere," primarily a "48-hour blip" of hesitancy on the part of a few potential customers. Even if there was a change in consumer attitudes, the impact on sales could not be enormous because on many of the routes flown by Air New Zealand passengers have a limited choice of airline, if they wish to travel on certain days of the week.

All the evidence suggests that there was no substantial change in consumer attitudes. The crash had occurred on an unscheduled flight; the New Zealand public continued to recognize the airline as having one of the best safety records in normal operations. Within New Zealand, no attempt was made to boycott the airline. This was true even after the condemnatory findings of the Royal Commission. For instance, many Auckland travellers were reported to have told travel agents that they thought the airline had had a "raw deal" and that they wanted to "get behind" their national carrier.[43] More significantly, this estimate of consumer reaction was supported by the results of market research surveys commissioned by the airline shortly after both the crash and the publication of the Mahon Report. In January 1980, 73 per cent of a national sample of 2,000 persons responded that Air New Zealand was their first preference among airlines, a figure consistent with the average level for 1979, although below the peak reading of 77 per cent attained in November 1979 after an extensive advertising campaign. The conclusion drawn was that the accident "has little detrimental effect on New Zealanders' choice of airline." In May 1981, a similiar response was obtained. First preference for Air New Zealand was expressed by 72 per cent of a corresponding sample, and a follow-up question revealed that only 4 per cent of the respondents who preferred other airlines did so on the basis of "poor reputation." Despite the recent publicity over the Erebus disaster, it was concluded that "the public's confidence in the airline has not really been undermined."

Abroad, the reaction of consumers appears to have been business as usual. On the trans-Tasman run between Australia and New Zealand, the market share held by Air New Zealand has fairly constantly hovered around 55 per cent since 1978.[44] Moreover, in terms of passengers carried and passenger-kilometers flown on all international routes, Air New Zealand, unlike Qantas, increased its business in 1980 and 1981. The figures are as follows:[45]

	Air New Zealand	Qantas
Passengers carried in 1981	1,047,402	1,887,451
Passengers carried in 1980	1,006,225	1,974,894

Passenger-kilometers flown (millions) in 1981	4,531	15,282
Passenger-kilometers flown (millions) in 1980	4,430	16,478

In Qantas market research conducted in 1980 for the purpose of deciding upon a new corporate image campaign, 2,800 respondents were surveyed, supplemented by interviews and group discussions. It was found that Air New Zealand had not suffered significant consumer resistance as a result of the disaster: The typical response was that Air New Zealand was a "good little airline" that had been "unlucky" or "unfortunate." The major finding was that safety was not a significant determinant of consumer choice of airline: The data showed that consumers classify a large number of international airlines as "reputable companies" and passengers are equally happy with all of them in terms of safety.[46] Accordingly, Qantas decided not to base its new advertising campaign on the airline's impeccable safety record (immediately after the Erebus crash, Qantas had lost no time in telling the media that, unlike Air New Zealand, it carried polar survival gear on Antarctic flights).[47]

There were of course costs unrelated to the adverse publicity surrounding the disaster, the main items being damages claims, loss of the aircraft, cost of the recovery operation, legal expenses, and welfare assistance for relatives. Of these, the major items—damages and the plane—entailed no loss to Air New Zealand because insurance provided ample cover,[48] and insurance premiums over the past two years have actually decreased.

The losses stemming from the Erebus crash and its aftermath were relatively minor when compared with the financial difficulties surrounding the company's overall operations. An operating loss of US$35 million was reported for the year ending 31 March 1981. Moreover, the prospects immediately ahead for Air New Zealand are worrisome: In a recent report commissioned by the New Zealand Treasury, a team of U.S. aviation consultants has questioned the economics of the airline's recent switchover from DC10s to Boeing 747s.[49]

Non-Financial Impacts

The Erebus publicity suffered by Air New Zealand had a marked impact on prestige, morale, and ability to concentrate on normal tasks. The impact on corporate prestige was perceived as adverse in the extreme; it was "absolutely positive," we were told, "that the company's reputation had suffered immeasurably." To begin with, unlike many aircraft accidents in other parts of the world, the media had not treated this crash as a 24-hour wonder. Worse, the Mahon Report had added disaster to disaster by impugning the integrity of the company's top executives.

Individual prestige was therefore also bemirched. The worst affected were the chief executive officer, Davis,[50] and other personnel tarred by the Mahon Report "orchestrated litany of lies" allegation. Although the legal action taken by Air New Zealand against the conspiracy theory findings of the Mahon Commission succeeded, the decision of the Court of Appeal did not entirely repair the reputational damage. Apart from any residual effect of allegations once made, a finding of excess jurisdiction or breach of natural justice amounts in law to a procedural invalidation, not an acquittal.

Morale throughout the organization suffered seriously. It was reported to us that "the impact on 8,400 staff was quite dramatic." When news broke of the crash, the reaction was described in terms of depression and physical hurt, with employees even touching and cuddling each other for mutual comfort. This funereal reaction was attributable almost entirely to the catastrophic event rather than to adverse publicity, but as the crisis dragged on through the proceedings of the Royal Commission, adverse publicity became a major demoralizing factor. Accordingly, when Davis attacked Justice Mahon after the victory in the Court of Appeal, the Chairman of the Board publicly disowned these comments on the ground that they were inimical to morale and organizational recovery.[51]

Distraction was another non-financial impact attributable in significant part to adverse publicity. Much time of top management was spent responding to inquiries arising from the Royal Commission fracas. The acting chief executive summed up the personal impact by saying, "I don't know when I'll get time to run the company." The Board was also under siege: Apart from discussions among the Chairman and several politicians, Justice Mahon and other leading protagonists in the scandal, there was an investigation by the Prime Minister when he was pressured into making inquiries of his own.[52]

Reforms

A number of reforms resulted from the Erebus crisis and the consequent public demand for change. Within Air New Zealand, the chief executive resigned, attitudes toward safety were resensitized, and flight operating procedures were subjected to review. The Civil Aviation Division of the New Zealand Ministry of Transport, for its part, also underwent a shake-up, although in this case the chief executive survived. As for Royal Commissions of Inquiry, they had their wings clipped by the decision of the Court of Appeal, and statutory or administrative realignments may occur as well.

The decision of the Air New Zealand chief executive officer, Davis, to resign was not the product of internal corporate discipline but, we were informed, a voluntary act that had been accepted by the Board with great reluctance. Formally, this was a reform only in the sense of symbolic appeasement, but informally it served to highlight a new managerial rule: "Do not shred documents relating directly or indirectly to an accident but, where necessary as a matter of security, collect and safeguard them." Some have suggested that the resignation resulted in a beneficial change of leadership style, but this is a question beyond the ken of our study.[53]

No other personnel were subjected to disciplinary proceedings by Air New Zealand. The in-house inquiry proposed as a result of the Mahon Report was abandoned. The reason given by the Board of Directors was that it would be unfair to proceed against only two persons, especially since the police had decided to take no action (initially, 12 persons had been subject to the inquiry, but in the two years following the crash, six had left the company and four planned to leave soon).[54] We were told by insiders and by one executive who had left the company since the disaster that now there was more consciousness of safety problems within the organization, at least in flight operations and in other areas directly under the shadow of the disaster; "It makes you think again," said one top manager with feeling. It is impossible for us to assess the accuracy of these claims.

The picture as regards Air New Zealand's standard operating procedures remains incomplete. Recommendations made in the Chippindale Report have been followed (except for those which became irrelevant as a result of the company's decision to discontinue Antarctic flights); most notably, all flight plan entries into computers are independently checked immediately, and a word processor has been added to the flight operations division partly for this purpose.

The findings of the Mahon Commission were more far-ranging and adverse, the fundamental complaint being that too much reliance was placed on verbal communication, not only in the area of flight operations but also in management.[55] There was much resistance to these findings at Air New Zealand; in the words of one top manager we interviewed, "We did not need to make any changes [in relation to scheduled flights]. Our procedures were immaculate. The system was tried and proven over 40 years."

However, Air New Zealand did launch two inquiries, one by an International Air Transport Association committee (to report on the procedures of the flight operations division) and the other by a team of management consultants (to evaluate administration and communications systems throughout the airline). Both inquiries have made their reports but the findings are under confidential review.[56]

Will the results ever be subject to detailed public scrutiny? It has been said that

> Air New Zealand will be judged by the public at large on whether it has lived up to the social and behavioural standards expected today of a large public company—and this evaluation will be based on what happened, or did not happen, after the crash as much as before.[57]

However, as time passes by, the question of reform increasingly moves away from the spotlight and, in any event, public assessment of the merits of internal reforms will be governed by the nature and degree of the information the company decides to provide.

Rumblings of reform were also experienced by the Civil Aviation Division of the Ministry of Transport. Although the Division played a secondary role in the events leading to the crash, the Mahon Report was highly critical of its performance.[58] Moreover, the Commission had denounced the Director of Civil Aviation, Captain E. T. Kippenberger, for advancing the "palpably absurd" explanation that the crash may have been caused by some psychological disturbance simultaneously experienced by the pilot and co-pilot.[59] A review committee was established in the Department, and, although disagreement was expressed with many of the Royal Commission's findings, substantial administrative improvements were recommended in 12 areas.[60] Captain Kippenberger was never in real danger of being forced to resign, although some did clamor for his resignation.[61]

Finally, the Erebus crisis highlighted two weaknesses to which Royal Commissions of Inquiry are prone. To begin with, there is the risk of public accusations of crime being made without adequate opportunity to reply. This risk would be substantially reduced if, as decided by the Court of Appeal, the rules of natural justice were applied where there is a substantial danger of prejudicial publicity, and the possibility of providing more comprehensive protection by statute is in the wind.[62] Whether or not the decision of the Court of Appeal was correct on the facts of the case is another matter, and one which must await the decision of the Privy Council now pending on appeal.

Second, terms of reference can easily be skewed towards the causes of a disaster, without provision for follow-up inquiry into the adequacy of the preventive or curative measures adopted. With the benefit of hindsight, this seems a deficiency of the Erebus commission of inquiry. Had the adequacy of Air New Zealand's reform been included in the investigation, a forward-looking, constructive focus would have reduced sensationalist fixation upon the crash by putting the company's reactions on center stage.[63] Moreover, since the company's reactions were not the subject of inquiry, there is little public assurance today that those reactions have in fact been satisfactory.

CHAPTER 19

Summary of the
Case Studies

There is a sense in which the large corporation goes on forever; it marches "on its elephantine way almost indifferent to its succession of riders."[1] At worst, large corporations suffer periodic reincarnations; outright death in bankruptcy usually is reserved for smaller companies. Because of the regenerative capacities of major corporations, even the most severe impacts on them are relatively short-lived. Of course, deterrence does not depend on law breakers' suffering permanent adverse consequences. This is evident when we think how deterrence is supposed to work with common criminals: It is the hope of criminal justice policy that when individuals are sent to prison, this adversity can be put behind them at the end of the sentence and a fresh start made.

Accordingly, when in this summary we speak of significant adverse impacts, in all cases it is understood that the negative impact is temporary. Today, only a few of the companies that are the subjects of the case studies could be said to be still suffering as a result of their adverse publicity crisis. By the end of the decade, probably none of them will be.

Publicity and Counterpublicity

Many of the companies introduced substantial reforms in the wake of their adverse publicity crisis. However, not one of these reformers attracted favorable notice for its good deeds which in any way approached the intensity of the original poor publicity. While there were exceptions (e.g., the praise awarded Allied Chemical for its Toxic Risk Assessment Committee), the general reaction of the mass media was that good news is little or no news.

The General Motors, ITT, Lockheed, Ford emissions, BHP coke ovens, and J.P. Stevens case studies all illustrated in varying degrees how adverse publicity concerning one alleged wrongdoing can snowball into unfavorable coverage over other, unrelated, issues. Once a company gets into the public eye over one crisis, it becomes a favored target for indiscriminate muckraking.

All companies responded to the adverse publicity by explaining their side of the story, at least in terms of a written communication from management to employees. The great majority of the companies made a conscious decision *not* to run a counterpublicity campaign to ensure that their story was impressed upon the general public. The main reason given for this "hunkering down," as one executive described it, was the fear that adverse publicity over one crisis would spread and thereby bring other skeletons out of the closet. Most corporations, on advice from their public relations firms, decided to reduce the "time window" of their exposure. They would answer questions from the press, but they stopped short of actively generating their own publicity. The only genuine counterpublicity campaigns were run by J.P. Stevens, IBM, ITT, and Ford during the Pinto trial. In a more subtle way, James Hardie's change of image from James Hardie Asbestos to James Hardie Industries could be viewed as a counterpublicity campaign. Perhaps Allied Chemical could also be viewed as mounting a minor publicity effort since it placed an advertisement in the press to explain its side of the Kepone incident. General Motors' spying on Ralph Nader also was a counter of sorts.[2]

The most substantial counterpublicity campaign was run by ITT. And significantly, this was the company that succeeded in turning the adverse publicity to its long-term advantage. The only other company that could be viewed as having benefited in the long term from the heightened visibility resulting from the adverse publicity was Sharp.[3] ITT used public relations ju-jitsu to convert an adverse thrust into a new corporate image. ITT induced people to regard it as a humane, profitable, and technologically advanced company, as a good place to work, and as a good stock investment.

ITT's ju-jitsu must be kept in proper perspective. In no more than two of the 17 case studies could the adverse publicity be seen as rebounding to the advantage of the company—in Sharp's case by good luck, in ITT's by good management. But how many companies would be willing or able to spend the $10 million a year which ITT put into its unquestionably brilliant award-winning campaign?

It is a myth, therefore, that the typical response of corporations subjected to adverse publicity is to fight back aggressively in the media; they are more likely to issue bland denials or use more subtle counters such as ITT's image advertising. Many who read Mobil's aggressive anti-regulation advertisements in the United States have misinterpreted this as representing typical corporate public relations. As one newspaper pointed out, it is decidedly atypical: "In the staid ballroom of corporate dance, Mobil Corp. insists on doing the bump."[4]

Financial Impacts

Exploitation of adversity by competitors. In only one case (James Hardie) did we find even a minor example of competitors of the victims of the adverse publicity exploiting the problem in sales pitches to customers or advertising. As a Ford executive said of the reaction of General Motors and Chrysler to the Pinto publicity: "They were rooting for us on the footing that, but for the grace of God, there go I."[5]

Sales. In a number of the case studies (BHP coke ovens, BHP Appin Mine, Ford emissions, ITT, McDonnell Douglas, and Exxon) it can be fairly definitely asserted that the company lost no sales as a result of the adverse publicity. It is also likely that General Electric lost no sales because of the electrical equipment price-fixing conspiracy. Sharp and James Hardie both suffered notable losses of sales as a result of their adverse publicity, as did Ford from the Pinto crisis. J.P. Stevens could also be put in this category, although the setbacks were not so large a proportion of their business as with the other three companies. General Motors, Allied Chemical, Searle, IBM, and Air New Zealand suffered relatively minor losses of sales overall, while Lockheed probably suffered only from long delays in consummating sales.

Legal costs. For some companies the legal costs of fighting the allegations against them have been substantial (notably IBM, J.P. Stevens, General Electric, Air New Zealand, and Ford for its Pinto). In other cases (Allied Chemical, Ford emissions and Sharp), the fines themselves had non-trivial financial impacts. Such costs were not a result of adverse publicity except in so far as the adverse publicity resulted in the matters being brought to trial in the first place. Adverse publicity has played a more important role, however, in encouraging victims to sue for civil damages. This was certainly true of the General Motors, Allied Chemical, General Electric, IBM, and Ford Pinto cases. It is possible that James Hardie and BHP (over its coke ovens) will in the future suffer some civil damages as a result of affected workers being jolted into action by the adverse publicity. The Chilean government's breaking off of compensation negotiations with ITT over the nationalization of its Chilean telephone subsidiary could also be viewed as a rather unusual form of civil legal action prompted by adverse publicity.

Miscellaneous costs. Companies also suffered a variety of miscellaneous costs. In most cases, adverse publicity played a relatively small part in producing the impacts. The most significant of such miscellaneous costs were:

The costs of Ford's voluntary recall of the Pinto.

BHP's lost steel production as a result of both the coke ovens crisis and the Appin Mine disaster.

The lower prices that General Electric and IBM had to accept for certain of their product lines as a result of antitrust litigation against them.

The delay for Lockheed in renegotiating its recapitalization plans until the banks could see the outcome of its Consent Decree.

The cessation of Searle's research activities during the progress of the Food and Drug Administration and Senate investigations; and the bureaucratic obstruction, particularly in getting new drugs approved, arising from the deterioration of its relationship with the FDA.

The souring of worker-management relations at BHP as a result of the coke ovens crisis.

The massive cost of technological solutions to carcinogenic emissions at BHP and James Hardie.

The cost to Allied Chemical of tests for farmers and others who were worried about Kepone contamination.

The possibility of lost investment opportunities for Allied Chemical as a result of its new aversion to investing in highly toxic chemicals that could cause another disaster like Kepone.

Earnings overall. Taking all of the foregoing financial impacts into account, adverse publicity caused a notable setback to earnings, at least in the short term, in four cases: Ford (Pinto), Sharp,[6] James Hardie, and Searle. By a notable setback we mean that earnings would have been considerably higher without the adverse publicity. J.P. Stevens and General Electric might also be placed in this category, although we are not as sure about them. It is possible that in the longer term the initially adverse publicity could rebound to increase earnings for ITT, Sharp, and BHP (if the methane drainage program at the Appin Mine becomes profitable). While this is possible, we do not think it probable that the long-term benefits of the adverse publicity could ever come to exceed the short-term setbacks to earnings, except perhaps in the case of ITT. For the other eight companies, we would confidently assert that the diminution in earnings that could be attributed to adverse publicity in fact was minor—so small as not to be of any concern to investors.

The stockmarket. It is impossible to be certain that negative publicity had an adverse effect on the stock prices of any of the companies studied. However, in seven of the cases (Ford's Pinto, ITT, IBM, James Hardie, Searle, J.P. Stevens, and General Electric), our observations of stock prices and our discussions with analysts indicate that there was some identifiable adverse reaction of the market to the crisis. For two of those, however, (IBM and ITT), the adverse market reaction had no direct connection with the adverse publicity. With IBM, investor fears that the company could be broken up by the government, and not adverse publicity, were responsible for periodic downward pressures on IBM stock prices. With ITT, it was fear of nationalization of the corporation's Chilean assets without compensation that held prices down at critical times.

Even on this sample, which was selected as representing the most extreme manifestations of adverse corporate publicity, identifiable stockmarket reactions were evident in only a minority of cases. Yet what were the subjective perceptions of managers? Perhaps executives nervously interpret every downward flutter of the market as caused by the scandal. Since deterrence turns on the subjective perception of reality rather than the objective reality, this is an important question. Our data show the subjective perceptions of business executives concerning stockmarket impacts to be very much the same as the objective reality as we analyze it. Only with IBM, James Hardie, Searle, and Ford's Pinto was it felt that adverse publicity may have adversely affected stock prices, and then only in minor ways.

Non-Financial Impacts

In all but two of the case studies (ITT, BHP (Appin)) the executives interviewed reported that at the time of the crisis they felt that their corporate image had suffered because of the scandal. Moreover, to varying degrees they felt there to be a consequential decline in the prestige that senior management enjoyed in the community.[7] All the executives at ITT denied that such a drop in prestige had occurred, but only because the problem had been dealt with through their corporate image campaign. The executives also claimed that employee morale had not suffered, because the company had nipped the problem in the bud. While we find this hard to believe, there was no way for us to disprove the claim. All other companies claimed that employee morale had suffered, at least temporarily. The second case for which there was not a perceived diminution of corporate prestige was the Appin Mine disaster. Here the reason was that the Appin Mine was not identified in the public mind as being owned by BHP. The personal prestige of management of the mine certainly was perceived as having suffered, however.

A decline in employee morale might be assumed to have adverse financial consequences for the company. However, there are studies in organizational psychology which suggest that employee morale and productivity are not necessarily correlated.[8] Hence, the impact on morale has been classified as non-financial. Management tends to value employee morale for its own sake, with any improvement in productivity that follows being viewed as a happy bonus. Similarly, loss of prestige is also distinct from loss of money, although obviously such loss can have financial implications. Thus, IBM felt that it had faced some problems in recruiting talented graduates because of the image some people at some times had of the company as a ruthless monopolist.

In all of the cases, the distraction of top management from its normal responsibilities while people dealt with the crisis was reported as an important adverse impact. There was considerable psychological stress for senior managers in dealing with the media barrage. This too may have had financial consequences if top management executives missed lucrative investment or marketing opportunities during the period when they were preoccupied with the scandal. In all but two of the case studies (James Hardie and Ford on its emissions), the gruelling experience for senior management of being cross-examined by Senate committees, government prosecutors, coroners, or others at official inquiries was reported as a reason for wishing to avoid a recurrence. It is even possible that one suicide (at Lockheed) could be put down to the trauma of such public scrutiny.

With regard to non-financial impacts, therefore, we have a much more consistent picture of publicity stinging the company—through loss of corporate prestige, loss of prestige in the community for top management, trauma for executives in facing cross-examination about the scandal, distraction of top management from normal duties, and decline in employee morale. In addition, there were various more idiosyncratic impacts, notably loss of positions on other boards for J.P. Stevens directors, governments toppling in other parts of the world in the fallout from the Lockheed scandal, and some tension in trade relations between Australia and Japan over the Sharp prosecution.

Reforms

There is no case study in the book in which adverse publicity did not play some role in producing some corporate reform which, although perhaps in only a small way, would reduce the probability of a recurrence of the offense or wrongdoing alleged (and often other kinds of offense as well). In some case studies (most notably both BHP cases, ITT, and McDonnell Douglas) the reforms were fairly minor. In other cases (particularly General Motors, Exxon, and IBM) there were major reforms but adverse publicity played only a small part in fostering them. In most instances, however, adverse publicity played a significant role in prodding the company into change.

In eleven of the case studies (General Motors, General Electric, Allied Chemical, Sharp, both Ford cases, ITT, Lockheed, Exxon, IBM, and Searle) the place of compliance in the organization was strengthened either through increased staff, seniority, or added powers, or all three. In some instances, constituencies within the organization responsible for ensuring compliance with the law were given a great deal more clout after the crisis (e.g., at Allied).

233

In twelve cases (General Motors, General Electric, Allied Chemical, Sharp, both Ford cases, ITT, Lockheed, McDonnell Douglas, Exxon, IBM, and Searle) channels of communication from the bottom to the top of the organization were improved so that the chances of bad news about a law violation getting to top management and the Board were increased. This is an important protection against corporate crime. Once top management is tainted with the knowledge of illegality, it will be less likely to allow crime to continue on the assumption that junior scapegoats can be blamed. Being forced to know, the managers are forced to act to ensure that compliance systems are working.

Eight of the companies introduced policies by which key officers periodically provide written certification of compliance with certain company rules (Allied Chemical, Ford for emissions testing, ITT, Lockheed, McDonnell Douglas, Exxon, IBM, Searle). This type of forced accountability has advantages for compliance, particularly in countering buck-passing.[9] Eight companies introduced new training programs to ensure that their employees understood the laws that were the subject of the wrongdoing alleged (General Electric, Allied Chemical, Sharp, Lockheed, Exxon, James Hardie, Searle, and BHP with regard to its coke ovens).

In three of the case studies (James Hardie and both BHP cases), the most important reforms consisted of expensive technological changes. For J.P. Stevens, the major change was the company's yielding to the demands for unionization; reform occurred through the elimination of the fundamental cause of the crime rather than through rehabilitation as in the other cases. Allied Chemical and Searle introduced the unusual reform of incorporating compliance performance as one of the considerations in determining bonuses for executives. These two companies evidence another favorable outcome of their crises—they both won back the confidence they had lost with regulatory agencies by applying their expertise to assist regulators in drawing up new rules. The Environmental Protection Agency was laudatory of the assistance that Allied Chemical had given since the Kepone incident in designing new effluent standards, while Searle helped the FDA draft Good Laboratory Practices regulations for drug testing.

Three companies firmly disciplined middle managers who were believed to be responsible (General Electric, Sharp, Ford on emissions). For four others, the publicity contributed to the resignation or early retirement of the chief executive officer (Lockheed, Searle, J.P. Stevens, Air New Zealand).

While these lists go some way towards objectifying the pervasiveness of the reforms, the most important changes were qualitative and intangible. These were the changes in the culture of the organization, in the "climate of control," as in Lockheed, Exxon, Allied Chemical and James Hardie following their difficulties. For instance, instead of accepting audit committee reports without question as they once did, Lockheed directors now ask probing questions of the auditors and insist that they come back with more detail on crucial matters.

Reforms to tighten internal controls are of profound importance. Without such reforms the glare of publicity will at most prevent crime until the scandal runs out of steam. Lawrence Sherman concluded from his empirical study of corruption in four police departments that, "A punitive scandal may result in a short-term decline in corruption, but changes in internal control seem to be required to prevent a resurgence of corruption once the external 'heat' is off."[10] Sherman's work showed that the efficacy of scandal for preventing organizational crime does not depend on publicity directly affecting organizations' offenses so much as on a two-step process in which scandal produces reform of internal controls, and the new internal controls reduce crime. Moreover, his data show that a scandal arising from a relatively narrow form of crime can lead to controls that prevent many other types of corruption not involved in the precipitating events.

The present study has shown, beyond this, that a scandal involving a few companies in one country can ultimately result in reform in many companies in many countries. For example, the Foreign Corrupt Practices Act that followed the foreign bribery scandal in the United States transformed the internal accounting controls to detect slush funds which all major U.S. accounting firms demand of their clients. Because of the hegemony of the standards set by the Big Eight U.S. accounting firms throughout the world, Australian firms are now finding that they are being subjected to the same controls by their auditors.[11] In sum, short-term narrow-focus scandals *can* produce long-term broad reforms. Whether they will or not depends on the strengths of the new controls they produce. Beyond finding serendipitously that this can happen, we cannot state in how many of our cases it did happen since we did not systematically gather data on companies other than those subjected to the publicity. For example, we do not know how many airlines changed their safety procedures in light of the Mt. Erebus disaster, how many Australian companies tightened their advertising controls after the publicity given the Sharp case, or how many American companies wrote new antitrust policies after the heavy electrical equipment scandal.

Of course, not all of the reactions to the scandals in the companies studied could be interpreted as in the public interest. Some changes were designed to protect the company and its employees from further exposure rather than to protect the community. The precautions discussed in the BHP Appin, Ford Pinto, and J.P. Stevens cases to reduce the legal exposure of company officers in the event of a recurrence illustrate this, as may the decision by James Hardie to locate some of its asbestos manufacturing operations in Indonesia.

Some of the scandals led to worthwhile reforms outside the companies themselves. *Unsafe at Any Speed* was a major catalyst for the National Traffic and Motor Vehicle Safety Act of 1966. The foreign bribery crisis cleaned out nests of corruption in a number of foreign governments, brought legislative reforms to tackle corruption in Japan and some Arab countries, strengthened the will of the Securities and Exchange Commission to investigate international bribery among all Fortune 500 companies, brought the United States the Foreign Corrupt Practices Act of 1977, and gave the world through the United Nations an International Agreement on Illicit Payments. The Kepone incident ushered in the U.S. Toxic Substances Control Act of 1977. The Searle fiasco was in considerable measure responsible for the FDA's Good Laboratory Practices regulations to reduce drug-testing fraud. The Appin Mine disaster resulted in tougher enforcement of the New South Wales Coal Mines Regulation Act. Australia's asbestos scare gave it uniform and stringent asbestos regulations for the first time. The BHP coke ovens affair has not as yet brought about any legislative reform, but it has certainly given a little more backbone to the government of New South Wales in regulating occupational health. The Air New Zealand publicity contributed to a rethinking of the role of Royal Commissions themselves as well as causing a shake-up in the New Zealand Department of Civil Aviation. Finally, the James Hardie publicity not only fostered corporate and governmental reform, but union reform as well: The unions were pressured into taking a stronger interest in the health problems of asbestos workers.

Selection Bias in the Case Studies

As was emphasized in our Introduction, the case studies were not selected as representative of all instances where adverse publicity was directed against companies for violations of law. We will now consider the implications of some important ways in which the case studies were not typical. This will lead to an answer to the question: Would the conclusions have been different had different cases been selected? First, three types of *systematic bias* will be considered: (a) What if cases of low instead of high intensity publicity had been selected? (b) What if small companies had been studied instead of transnationals? (c) What if other types of offenses had been selected (e.g., tax evasion)? Second, *non-systematic bias* will be considered: For example, would the conclusion have been different if Westinghouse had agreed to interviews on the heavy electrical equipment price-fixing conspiracy instead of General Electric?

SYSTEMATIC SELECTION BIAS

Intensity of the adverse publicity. Cases were selected in an attempt to include the most severe adverse publicity assaults which could be found. In general, if impacts did not show up in these cases, they could not be expected to appear in less ferocious publicity attacks. Given that only a minority of these extreme cases evidence noticeable financial impacts, one would expect the financial consequences of less severe publicity to be almost invariably trivial. Further empirical work is needed to assess whether the strong non-financial and corporate reform impacts we have observed would result from adverse publicity of lower intensity.

Size of the company. Small firms, we suspect, would be more vulnerable to control by adverse publicity than the large ones we have studied. If they do not enjoy monopoly power, they cannot pass on financial impacts in higher prices to consumers. They have less flexibility and power to evade the consequences of a publicity onslaught. A multi-million dollar counterpublicity campaign à la ITT is out of the question, as is a $12 million James Hardie Research and Development program to develop a technological escape from the problem. Nor can small companies usually open a plant in Indonesia when the heat builds up at home. If they are not conglomerates, they cannot switch the emphasis in their investment from products sold directly to the public to sales to other corporations, as J.P. Stevens possibly did. Small companies do not have the head office staff to set up a special management group to handle the crisis while the rest of the management team gets on with the business of making profit, as did Allied Chemical with Kepone, Ford in the emissions case, or, to take the leading illustration, Proctor and Gamble in its handling of the tampons toxic shock crisis.[12]

On the other hand, what small companies can do more readily is to evade publicity by closing down the business and starting up again on the other side of town. Conglomerates can achieve the same functional result by going abroad or by staying where they are and changing the scandal-linked brand name. When Proctor and Gamble reenters the tampon market, it will not be under the "Rely" brand name. But the more important advantage that some small companies have, let us call these the "fly-by-night operators," is that they don't care about a poor reputation. They go into business with no intention of building a long-term future or cultivating a reputation among a clientele. Their goal is to operate on the fringe of the law for as long as they can get away with it and then move on. Such fly-by-night operations constitute only a tiny fraction of small businesses, but they account for a substantial proportion of the enforcement activities of regulatory agencies. Because of their lack of concern with a long-term reputation, adverse publicity is a limited weapon against them. But even so, publicity can be effective in shutting them down and thereby disrupting their predatory activities.

Small firms which sell all of their output directly to the public are uniquely susceptible to adverse publicity. One biting television program on fraud can finish a used car dealer. A public statement by a health official that a restaurant is infested with vermin can close down the business. There is plenty of anecdotal evidence to support these claims. Many small companies, and even medium-sized enterprises, have been bankrupted by regulatory agencies, who relied heavily on adverse publicity to do so.[13] Unorganized small producers can also be severely set back, without being actually bankrupted, by even minor adverse publicity outbursts. In the most notorious example, all American cranberry growers were devastated in 1959 when the Secretary of Health, Education and Welfare, Arthur Flemming, did no more than call a press conference to urge the public not to buy cranberries grown in Washington or Oregon because they might be contaminated with chemical weed-killer. Twenty one and a half million dollars worth of cranberries remained unsold across the country that Thanksgiving because of the press conference.[14] Had it been a single transnational company which had produced the contaminated product, corporate power would have been used to negotiate the terms and timing of the announcement as part of a package that might have included a voluntary recall associated with assurances that there was no need for alarm.

Nature of the alleged offenses. The case studies selected span a wide area of business regulation—fraud, occupational health and safety, labor relations, consumer protection, environmental protection, product safety, and antitrust regulation. We have not included any cases of tax violations, and given the evidence that tax offenses are not viewed as seriously as other corporate crimes,[15] adverse publicity could be expected to arouse less heat in this area. Similarly, complex securities frauds, because the public finds them difficult to understand, might be assumed to be unlikely to generate the organized resentment that would create heavy impacts. We doubt this, however. John Citizen may not understand the complexity of the transactions, but he grasps full well a bottom line that shows that the investing public has been duped of a million dollars.

NON-SYSTEMATIC SELECTION BIAS

There is an undeniable uniqueness about the case studies. While a severe program of internal discipline was the principal response of General Electric to the electrical equipment price-fixing scandal, Westinghouse, which was in the same boat, did not discipline any of its guilty executives. However, the important question is whether there is reason to believe that less severe impacts on average would have been found had different cases been included. By considering a few obvious omissions from the study, it will be shown that by selection of different cases which fit our sample guidelines, stronger impacts, if anything, might have been reported.

The Proctor and Gamble crisis over toxic shock syndrome caused by Rely tampons broke too late to be included in this study. If it had been included, the financial impacts would have been more clear than with any of our cases. The $75 million cost of the tampon recall was the major reason for the 36 per cent drop in company earnings for the quarter ending Setpember 30, 1980.[16] Had Johns-Manville been included as an asbestos case study instead of James Hardie, financial impacts many times greater would have been found because of the higher employee damages settlements granted by U.S. courts.[17] Hooker Chemical has reported far more severe problems with recruiting talented executives because of its image as a polluter than was noted by any of our companies.[18] And certainly none of them faced the campus recruitment difficulties of Dow Chemical, the maker of napalm, during the hectic days of student activism against the Vietnam war. None of our companies suffered the total devastation of corporate prestige that Distillers suffered over thalidomide: "Socially, particularly after thalidomide, it's much better to say that you work for Johnnie Walker than for the Distillers Company."[19]

None of our companies was so stung by the publicity as to run massive television advertising campaigns defending the quality of its products—as did Firestone to counter the adverse publicity over its tire recalls and McDonnell Douglas in regard to the DC10 engine safety problem. ITT did run an equally expensive corporate image campaign, but this did not even indirectly address the specific charges made against it. The way Firestone, McDonnell Douglas, and Proctor and Gamble were set back by their recent product safety crises leads us to a hypothesis advanced by a number of the executives we interviewed: *"Publicity hurts most when it challenges the integrity of a product."* The corollary is that publicity that attacks only the integrity of the sales tactics used in selling the product or the damage done to the environment in making it, does not hurt so much. Our own data support this hypothesis. The three companies which were most significantly affected on the stockmarket as a result of their adverse publicity crisis—Ford with the Pinto, James Hardie, and Searle—were all companies denounced because of the alleged dangers of their products.

The best assessment of the atypicality of our sample is available from the foreign bribery crisis, a scandal which has attracted more scholarly interest than all the other crises combined. Lockheed suffered more bad press than any other company involved in foreign bribery. It was not the worst company in terms of the amounts paid in bribes, but it was the company whose corruption caused the collapse of foreign governments. In spite of this, the impacts on Lockheed were not as severe as for many others. Lockheed did not have its Chairman jump to his death from atop a skyscraper apparently because he could not stand the shame, as did United Brands Chairman, Eli Black. Nor did the scandal cause any of the payoff recipients to commit suicide as did Japanese executive, Mitsushiro Shimada, following the Grumman bribery disclosures.[20]

None of the foreign bribery cases in our study involved substantial impacts on earnings or stock prices. This is consistent with the general picture which has emerged from other research. Neil Jacoby and his co-authors[21] considered investor reactions to foreign bribery disclosures by five companies and concluded that there was no significant selling of stock in response to the crisis. A similar analysis of eight foreign payments disclosures in the *Harvard Law Review*[22] showed only a small average adverse stockmarket reaction, which in each case persisted for about a week. Paul Griffin[23] conducted a systematic empirical study of stockmarket reactions to foreign bribery disclosures by 74 firms through comparisons with a control sample of firms of equivalent relative risk and similar asset size and industrial composition. The quasi-experiment covered a 17-week period surrounding the week in which each of the questionable payments were disclosed. Firms disclosing payments experienced a small decline in the value of their common shares. On average, less than half a per cent was wiped off share prices, and even this tiny impact was temporary. Within two to three weeks after the disclosure, security prices had reverted to normal levels. In other words the impact was so slight as to be imperceptible to analysts or to the firm's management, let alone to unsophisticated stockholders. Subsumed under the average impact for the 74 companies were a minority of companies for which there was a noticeable, though insubstantial, impact. Griffin's analysis showed that there was a considerably greater stockmarket reaction to: (a) the firms that made early disclosures (a leading example would be United Brands, whose stock dropped 40 per cent after its Chairman's suicide);[24] and (b) the firm which disclosed large rather than small dollar amounts in questionable payments.

In terms of the substantial effect of negative publicity on corporate reform, there is also no reason to assume that our case studies are atypical. Indeed, the impact of the foreign bribery scandal on McDonnell Douglas was less than for many other companies, who did not even disclose any questionable payments, such as General Dynamics, with whom we also spoke. We can draw this conclusion because we discussed with compliance personnel from all American companies we visited the impact of the foreign bribery scandal on them. All confirmed that the scandal transformed auditing and control procedures throughout American industry—the innocent as well as the guilty were pressed into reform. One joker in the pack appears to have been United Brands. Seymour Milstein, the company's Chairman, declined our request for an interview in these terms: "It has not been necessary for us to make substantial changes in our internal compliance systems and thus it seems to me that you should concentrate your efforts on other corporations whose problems have been more difficult."

The best evidence of the widespread nature of the foreign bribery shake-up is Donald Cressey and Charles Moore's study of *Corporation Codes of Ethical Conduct.*[25] Of the 119 codes included in their survey, 43 per cent were either drafted or revised in 1976, the year following the first nationwide publicity about corporate bribery.[26] Indeed, "twenty-nine of the codes explicitly state (and several more imply) that the code was either being issued or revised in response to the recent concern with corporate ethics growing from the Watergate and SEC investigations."[27] Even Australian companies have undertaken reforms in response to the U.S. foreign bribery scandal and the Foreign Corrupt Practices Act that came in its wake. Again, in the context of other research projects,[28] top management of Australian companies told us various ways in which this was so. The following communication was received from a senior manager in one of Australia's largest companies:

> The strongest support that internal audit has received in recent times has been the enactment in the U.S. of the Foreign Corrupt Practices Act of 1977. This Act, which I am sure you have studied, requires among other things that companies maintain a system of internal controls and that there are mechanisms in place to ensure that directors are able to assure themselves that regulations for which they are responsible are, in fact, being carried out.
>
> To meet any obligations under this Act, most U.S. companies have, on a cost/benefit basis, decided to strengthen their internal audit functions and ensure greater cooperation between the internal auditors and external auditors. This has meant that internal auditor organizations have had to look to increasing their standards of professional practice.

Thus, in considering whether our foreign bribery case studies are typical we have uncovered a clear illustration of a point made earlier: scandals can fuel industry-wide reform even across the whole economy as well as within the targets of the scandal.

SELECTION BIAS; SUMMARY

We have shown generally that (a) Had we chosen cases in which the publicity was less, the impacts could be expected to have been less; (b) Had we chosen small firms instead of massive transnationals, the impacts could be expected to have been greater on "reputable" firms but less on "fly-by-night" operators; (c) Had we chosen different examples of transnationals exposed to massive publicity, there is little reason to suspect that our findings would have been very different.

Conclusion

The data show that financial impacts of any significance occurred in only a small minority of the case studies. It was non-financial impacts that executives in all of the companies reported as the factors which truly hurt and which made them want to avoid a recurrence even if it cost a great deal of money to try to guarantee this. In short, at the level of subjective management perceptions, financial impacts were not a strong deterrent, while non-financial impacts—loss of corporate and individual prestige, decline in morale, distraction from getting on with the job, and humiliation in the witness box—were acutely felt.

We would not suggest that any of the companies studied did everything possible to reform themselves after the crisis. In many cases thoroughgoing reform was forsaken for piecemeal changes. Nevertheless, in *every* case there was some worthwhile reform. This is an arresting finding. There is not one empirical study of rehabilitation of human offenders which shows that some rehabilitation took place for every individual included in the study. Indeed, it is rare to find that intervention achieves a degree of rehabilitation for most, or even some, offenders.[29]

Equally significant is the demonstration in this study that convicting a corporation is not a necessary precondition to reform. Criminal convictions occurred only in five of the case studies, and even for two of these (Lockheed and General Electric) the most important reforms preceded conviction. When a company is struck by publicity concerning an alleged crime, it typically implements reform measures to persuade the government against following the publicity with a prosecution. This is also why the reforms are often more than cosmetic: The company cannot afford to have its reaction dismissed by a regulatory agency as window dressing; new policies or procedures must be capable of standing up to expert analysis as genuine improvements.

We are certainly not the first to document instances where corporate rehabilitation has resulted without imposition of conviction. Don Waldman,[30] in his valuable study of the impact of antitrust prosecution, showed that some of the most positive changes in the competitiveness of markets resulted from antitrust cases that the government lost. This is because when a company has the threat of divestiture or prosecution hanging over its head throughout the many years during which an antitrust case incubates, it generally improves its behavior. To be able to present itself to the court as other than a ruthless monopolist, it may pull down some of the barriers to entry into the industry which it had erected; it may cease retaliating (as by predatory pricing) against firms which try to compete; it may write a strict antitrust compliance code for its employees, as IBM did; and it may even actively recruit a competitor to the industry. The best illustration of this last reaction was the du Pont case,[31] when the company was acquitted in 1956 for monopolizing the cellophane market. The government defeat ended a nine-year court battle. During those nine years, du Pont improved its credentials as a competitor by recruiting the Olin corporation to enter the industry as a competing cellophane manufacturer. This move began on March 29, 1948, when, in anticipation of conviction as a cellophane monopolist, du Pont resolved that:

> . . . the Development Department in collaboration with the Rayon Department, be requested to ascertain promptly, and to report to the Executive Committee as to the possibility of interesting one or more concerns in going into the manufacture of cellophane cellulose film, and cellulose bands, on the basis of du Pont:
>   1. Furnishing its "know-how" (consisting of the best commercial practice at the time of the agreement with a new producer) and licenses under its pertinent U.S. patents, for a moderate fee;
>   2. Being willing to assist a new producer in a new plant project, on a moderate fee basis, as consultant, design contractor, subcontractor, or general contractor.[32]

Given that significant rehabilitation of the cellophane market took place even though the government lost its case, Waldman concluded: "It is apparent, therefore, that the effectiveness of antitrust policy cannot be measured simply in terms of government victories."[33] Similarly, the role of adverse publicity cannot be assessed simply in terms of the number of corporate violators it brings to justice. Our data suggest that informal publicity is an invaluable form of social control even when it leads to neither conviction of nor financial impact on the company.

Informal publicity is of course not the only mechanism for achieving reform without conviction. Sometimes corporations reform themselves to shake off the journalists snapping at their heels; on other occasions they do so to shake off a nagging inspector or a regulatory agency that keeps putting obstacles in the company's path; or reforms can be introduced, as in the du Pont case, to foil a prosecutor. This all means that there is a lot to be said for keeping after corporations. Public interest groups, regulatory agencies, and prosecutors can often right the wrongs that concern them without winning in court. However, publicity would have an important place in the development of a general theory of corporate crime control without conviction, because both regulatory agencies and prosecutors can be prodded into effective harassing tactics by the public pressure of publicity.

CHAPTER 20

Informal Publicity

Informal Social Control and Corporate Crime

Most of us obey the law most of the time because of informal social control—because we know others would think ill of us if we were criminals, because our family would be ashamed, because our socialization has taught us that criminal acts aren't "right." Crime rates are more responsive to the cultural processes of informal social control than to the deterrence, incapacitation, and rehabilitation that might follow from formal social control. Similarly, cultural forces affect rates of corporate offenses more profoundly than formal punishments; this is especially so given the infrequency with which white-collar criminals are brought to justice in our present criminal justice system. If we are serious about controlling corporate crime, the first priority should be to create a culture in which corporate crime is not tolerated. The informal processes of shaming unwanted conduct and of praising exemplary behavior need to be emphasized.

There are costs in encouraging the exposure which makes informal social control work, especially the risk of false accusations and intensive invasions of privacy. However, there are several reasons why, in the context of corporate crime, these costs lose much of the significance they otherwise have.

First, the stakes are higher with corporate crime. Corporations have an exploitative potential that goes far beyond individual opportunity or power.[1]

Second, companies of any size affect the public so much that it is entitled to know a great deal about their internal affairs.[2]

Third, corporations normally can cope better with false accusations against them than can individuals; while the wrongly scandalized individual might sit in a corner and have a nervous breakdown, a powerful corporation in a similar situation can fight back, if necessary by suing people, demanding retractions, or staging a morale- or prestige-boosting turnaround.[3]

Fourth, even when individuals are guilty of that which is rumored, stigma can create bigger problems than it solves. But stigma is not counterproductive in this way when directed at corporations and their personnel. With common criminals the stigmatizing process can push them further into a criminal self-conception. This is the contention of labelling theory, and one supported by some empirical evidence.[4] Arguments about enhancement of criminal self-conceptions cannot readily be applied to corporate offenders and those who act on their behalf. They are likely to regard themselves as unfairly maligned pillars of respectability, even in the face of extreme stigmatization. While one may meet people who have a self-conception as a thief, a safe-cracker, a prostitute, a pimp, a drug runner, or even a hit man, it is highly unusual to come across a company or executive with a self-conception as a corporate criminal. Moreover, while the young black offender can often enhance his status back on the street by having done some time, corporate offenders tend to experience shame and humiliation.[5] Corporations and their officers respond to bad publicity with moral indignation and denials, not assertions that "If you think I'm bad, I'll really show you how bad I can be": They need to defend their reputations before the general public, whereas the juvenile offender can slip easily into the ways of a delinquent street-corner society.

For the reasons outlined above, we view the benefits of an activist, participatory democracy, in which the powerful are forever facing challenges over alleged abuse of their power, as outweighing the costs of being unfairly maligned from time to time. However, the risk of injustice should be minimized, and later we take up the challenge of how this might be achieved.

Why Corporate Reputation Is Important

The large corporations studied in this book care greatly about their reputations. Adverse publicity is of concern not so much by reason of its financial impacts but because of a variety of non-financial effects, the most important of which is loss of corporate prestige. But why is corporate prestige or repute[6] important? Why should Henry Ford II bother to write to his employees a memo on "Standards of Corporate Conduct" that begins: "To succeed and even to survive, Ford Motor Company must have the trust and confidence of its many publics. A good reputation is a priceless asset. . . ."?[7]

Ford may be right in assuming that the prestige of the Ford Motor Company is important to a variety of publics. Customers may well be more inclined to buy Ford cars if they perceive Ford as a reputable company. Banks may be more willing to extend credit to see a reputable company through a rough period. Legislators may grant more credibility to representation from a prestigious corporation. Corporate prestige may attract better quality applicants for executive vacancies and may appeal more to investors. A study by Bozell and Jacobs Inc. surveyed the effect on company stock prices of more than 16,000 corporate image advertisements, as opposed to advertisements pushing sales of a particular product; corporate image advertising was found to contribute a modest though non-trivial four percent to the variability of a company's stock price.[8]

The advantages of corporate prestige provide some of the reasons for the explosion of corporate image advertising in the United States, Australia, and Great Britain.[9] Perhaps the most important change in the advertising industry over the past decade has been the growth of advertisements that try to communicate the benevolence, competence, and social value of a corporation at the expense of advertisements that push sales of a specific product.[10] But good repute is valued for more than its relevance to financial goals; it is valued for its own sake:

> The climate of opinion, and therefore the projection of the company as a moral, useful, and likeable member of society, which creates and sustains it, becomes (as it were) a *direct* objective of management. It does not contradict the purely business objectives as they are classically understood, but it is not simply subservient or intermediate to those objectives. It exists in its own right as an operational goal of prime importance.[11]

Business organizations are not unusual in seeking prestige for its own sake; universities, service groups, and football clubs do the same. One should never underestimate the importance to senior business executives (who, more often than not, are status-conscious people) of being perceived by their middle class peers as working for a prestigious company. And quite apart from these extrinsic rewards, for most people there is basic satisfaction in the feeling that they are working with a reputable team.

None of this is to deny the importance of *individual* responsibility and reputation to the social control of corporate crime. However, individual personnel often cannot be held responsible for corporate offenses, for a long string of reasons, practical and theoretical.[12] Thus, no one person may have been at fault for a disaster such as the Mt. Erebus crash, but organizational fault may nonetheless be present.[13] Even when particular personnel are culpable, moreover, loyalty, secrecy, and other organizational barriers typically make it difficult to obtain sufficient evidence of individual guilt.[14] There is thus little option but to proceed against corporations in most instances, at least as the law now stands.

Underlying the reputation of particular corporate or individual personnel is the good will of the general public toward the business community as a whole. Public opinion surveys show a dramatic decline during the 1970s in the proportion of the American populace who felt that business strikes a fair balance between profits and public interest.[15] An important motivation behind the rise of corporate image advertising is that business is troubled by this backlash. It is not an overstatement to say that many executives feel that, in protecting their own reputation, they are serving the noble purpose of defending the free enterprise system. This motiviation, however, is less salient than those related directly to the interests of the particular corporation.

In addition to the evidence presented by the case studies in this book, opinion surveys bear out the contention that corporations fear the sting of adverse publicity attacks on their reputations more than they fear the law itself.[16] A survey of 531 top and middle managers by the Opinion Research Corporation found that 92 percent of respondents did not believe that legislation would stop bribery of foreign officials; adverse publicity, by contrast, was thought to have some chance of achieving that goal.[17]

A *Harvard Business Review* survey of its readers[18] found that, for respondents who thought ethical standards in business had improved over the past 15 years, the three causal factors most often listed were:

Public disclosure; publicity; media coverage; better communication
(31%)

Increased public concern; public awareness, consciousness, and
scrutiny; better informed public; societal pressures   (20%)

Government regulation, legislation, and intervention; federal
courts   (10%)

To cap these attestations of corporate sensitivity to loss of prestige, it is worth recollecting the famous advice once given to Ford personnel by their then-president Arjay Miller: "Do that which you would feel comfortable explaining on television."[19]

The potential regulatory power of informal publicity has been hampered by a variety of obstacles. The more significant of these, together with suggestions as to how they might be overcome, are reviewed below under the following headings: consumer activism, investigative journalism, enforcement action, official inquiry, corporate disclosure, and international exposure.

Consumer Activism

It has become fashionable to dismiss muckraking as a vulgar and mischievous habit of the economically untrained.[20] Whatever the vulgarity or mischief-making, it is difficult to imagine consumer sovereignty working in the absence of rude awakenings. The hand of the marketplace is incapable of correcting invisible abuses, and making abuses plain to the general public usually requires the stimulus of shock.[21]

The doyen of contemporary muckrakers has been Ralph Nader.[22] The transformation of consumer consciousness that followed in the wake of *Unsafe at Any Speed* was reinforced by a series of successful campaigns in the ensuing years. Government agencies as well as corporations yielded significant reforms in concession to Nader's pen. For instance, Nader's Raiders issued a scathing report on the Federal Trade Commission in 1969.[23] Their castigation of the agency for weak antitrust and consumer protection enforcement prompted follow-up inquiries by the American Bar Association and by a Senate subcommittee.[24] Donna Randall has demonstrated in a systematic empirical study that the stringency of FTC enforcement dramatically increased following the Nader report.[25] There have been defeats mixed with the victories, however, and when we interviewed Nader he conceded that in the 1980s it is much more difficult for a consumer activist to effect substantial reform than it was in the 1960s when he rose to power. Corporations are more skilled in handling the assaults on them (witness ITT's ju-jitsu) and Ronald Reagan and other influential advocates of free-marketeering have rallied to their defense. The main obstacles in the path of the consumer movement, however, are lack of campaign funds and limited opportunity for effective legal redress.

Public interest groups notoriously lack the money necessary to wage effective campaigns against corporate wrongdoing. To be sure, there are notable exceptions (e.g., the well-financed campaign against J. P. Stevens), but as a general rule idealism is racked by budgetary starvation. What might be done to improve this situation?

One proposal is that public interest groups be given a percentage of fines against corporate offenders for the purpose of monitoring their subsequent behavior (e.g., part of a fine against a pharmaceutical company could be handed over to the Health Research Group).[26] This proposal would make the fine a stronger sanction by fostering a new breed of watchdog.[27] Given how companies hate to feed the mouths that bite them, subjective deterrence would be enhanced.

A predictable objection to this suggestion is that it is not the business of government to subsidize vigilantes, especially those who have an axe to grind. However, this complaint seems unfounded. The course of action encouraged would not be a substitute for justice but a dialectical aid to it, and hence akin to adversarial process, the approach to decision making hallowed in common law trials in the British tradition. In any event, the proposal could be modified to limit the provision of funds to specified functions of an advisory as opposed to combative nature (e.g., monitoring the news media for misleading advertisements).[28] Public interest groups might often be able to provide rapid, cheap surveillance; the fact that they are committed to a credo of consumer activism is no more an objection to their funding in such a capacity than is the faith of the Salvation Army to subsidies it receives for buttressing the welfare state.

Another promising reform would be to provide for *qui tam* suits allowing consumer groups to undertake private prosecution, and thereby to secure funds from any fine imposed.[29] *Qui tam* suits were relied upon heavily in England during the fourteenth and fifteenth centuries, the aim being to supplement a weak system of public enforcement by rewarding effective private prosecution. Anyone who violated statutory provisions subject to *qui tam* incurred an obligation to pay half of the penalty prescribed to an informer. The informer was entitled to recover that amount by a *qui tam* action, a civil action of debt. The practice was abused and acquired a bad name; it was restricted by a series of common informer statutes and eventually abolished in 1951. In the United States, *qui tam* suits are still available under some statutes, but their use over a broad range of regulation has been discouraged by the English experience.

251

There is, however, a groundswell of opinion that *qui tam* suits should be used more extensively as a means of assisting public enforcement agencies in the task of controlling corporate crime. Regulatory agency budgets are being slashed to the point where there no longer are sufficient resources to mount credible enforcement programs without private aid. Politically, there is a strong sentiment that power should be diffused more widely to individuals, whether the vision be possessive individualism or participatory democracy. Given these as well as other considerations, the President's Commission for a National Agenda for the Eighties has suggested that "Government might . . . encourage private lawsuits as a technique of preventing or redressing certain undesirable conduct in place of, or as a supplement to, intervention by a regulatory agency."[30]

A detailed statutory proposal for the modernization of *qui tam* actions has been advanced by Thomas Crumplar in the particular context of Securities and Exchange Commission enforcement. The basic thrust of this proposal is as follows:

> All persons would have the same right as the SEC to bring actions seeking the imposition of a newly created civil penalty for any violation of the securities laws. Such an action would be in the name of the United States and there could only be one such action for a particular alleged violation. Prior to proceeding further with the suit the private enforcer would have to give the SEC notice of his filing and substantially all the evidence in his possession regarding the alleged violation. The SEC would then have 60 days within which to: (1) preempt the private enforcer and bring suit itself; (2) ask the court to dismiss the private action; or (3) allow the private action to proceed. In case (3), the prosecution of the suit would be totally within the private party's control, except that he could not withdraw or settle without the consent of the SEC and the court.
>
> The chief incentives for bringing such a suit would be the payment to the successful private enforcer of his litigation costs plus an incentive award. A private enforcer preempted by the government would be awarded a finder's fee based on the value of the information he gave the United States. To prevent sloppily prosecuted or spurious suits a court would have the discretionary authority to require the plaintiff to pay the prevailing defendant his litigation expenses, for which it may also require the plaintiff to post bond.[31]

Crumplar's proposal could readily be generalized to cover a broad range of corporate regulation without at the same time encouraging a lawless régime of bounty hunters or "viperous vermin" (Sir

Edward Coke's description of common informers).[32] The evils which beset the old *qui tam* actions were due to inadequate governmental control over abuses of private prosecutorial power, abuses readily controlled by requiring that private prosecutions be brought to the attention of public enforcement agencies and, if necessary, dismissed, preempted, or otherwise supervised, subject to court approval.

Reviving *qui tam* suits in the way suggested would do more than merely provide a financial incentive for enforcement action by consumer groups—it would broaden the opportunity for collective legal redress. Class actions, public interest actions, and other remedies available to consumer groups are limited, in particular by class action requirements of notice and specificity of damages awards and, in the case of public interest remedies, by rules of standing.[33] These restrictions prevent class or public interest actions from realizing their potential as

> [an institutional] analogue to the mass demonstrations of the street [whose success] often hinges less on the ultimate outcome of the particular case than on the publicity, visibility and aroused popular reaction it evokes.[34]

An alternative way of enabling collectivist action against corporate wrongdoing, and thereby enhancing democratic participation in social control,[35] would be to allow consumers to make greater use of *qui tam* suits.

Qui tam procedure does not require that notice be given to all plaintiffs constituting the class represented, nor that damages be awardable for specific loss to identifiable victims. The action proceeds as a private prosecution for an offense, not as a civil claim for tortious or contractual remedy. Moreover, the status of the action as a private prosecution automatically confers standing upon citizens initiating suit. Accordingly, the device would allow consumers to mount a group action against corporate wrongdoers in circumstances where class or public interest litigation might otherwise be unavailable.[36]

Nothing in this should be taken to imply procedural free-for-all. Since unlimited resort to *qui tam* actions could conceivably overload the courts or duplicate the efforts of public enforcement agencies, there is cause for imposing some restraint.[37] Under Crumplar's proposal, a *qui tam* action could not proceed regardless of the risk of overload or duplication, but would be subject to a procedure enabling preemption or dismissal in cases where private prosecution would be inefficient. Thus, where prosecution is confined to serious cases as a matter of enforcement policy, *qui tam* actions would be subject to the same policy.[38] Moreover, rules governing pre-trial negotiations between enforcers and defendants could also be extended to persons proceeding by way of *qui tam*. In short, the object to be attained is not rampant prosecution or inquisition but sound deployment of private enforcement resources.

Administrative efficiency aside, it might be objected that a *qui tam* procedure presupposes the continued use of fines as a sanction against corporate offenders, whereas adequate deterrence or retribution requires resort to non-monetary forms of sentence (e.g., preventive orders, community service orders).[39] However, fines sufficient for the purpose of paying private enforcers could be used in combination with preventive orders and other alternatives to fines. Moreover, a sentence of community service could well be imposed upon a corporate offender in such a way as to require it to lend specific assistance to public interest groups (e.g., toxicological assistance to an environmental protection group for the purpose of monitoring the hazards of waste dumping).

Investigative Journalism

Investigative journalism is to democracy what predators are to the balance of nature: a corrective force, vigorous in attack and addicted to blood. As in nature, vigor and addiction can sometimes be counterproductive, but the corrective achievements of investigative journalists have surely vindicated their right to freedom of expression.

The success of investigative journalism in exposing and counteracting the dangers of collective evil has been much celebrated. Best known is Robert Woodward and Carl Bernstein's exposé in the *Washington Post* of the Watergate conspiracy.[40] This, after all, was the laser which enabled the U.S. body politic to remove an ominous cancer. The contributions of the media to control of corruption in government have also been extolled in Britain; as a prominent member of the Salmon Royal Commission remarked:

> Almost all the investigations that have led to prosecutions have been sparked off either by Private Eye [a satirical magazine] or by commercial television or by other branches of the media or by other unofficial bodies or individuals.[41]

Beyond the field of corruption, much has been done by the media to highlight corporate assaults upon life and limb and to provoke remedial or reformative action. Thus the *Sunday Times* Insight Team laid bare the unwillingness of the Distillers Company to compensate Thalidomide victims adequately and, in using the pressure of public opinion to promote settlement of claims, overcame the incapacity of the English legal system to provide adequate redress of mass personal injury claims.[42] Equally significant was the work of Michael Brown in bringing to light the dangers of Love Canal, an exposure which generated a massive public demand for preventive reform as well as for victim compensation.[43] Many further examples can readily be found, including Morton Mintz's probings into prescription drugs, Mark Dowie's exposure of the Pinto Papers, and Mike Muller's original alert about the baby-killing oversale of infant formula by multinationals operating in the Third World.[44] Conspicuous as the successes of investigative journalism are, however, they should not be allowed to distract attention from the excessive restraints on freedom of expression now imposed by the law of defamation and contempt of court.

The main impediment in the way of investigative journalism is the law of defamation. Although the U.S. courts have done much to restrict the scope of defamation and thereby maximize freedom of expression, the balance achieved is far from satisfactory because the law remains too restrictive in some respects and yet in others is too lenient.

The effect of *New York Times v. Sullivan*,[45] and *Time Inc. v. Hill*[46] is to restrict the scope of liability for defamation of public officials on matters of public interest.[47] Although these decisions allow considerable freedom of expression, they have been criticized as unduly chilling because, in the event of breach, damages awards are notoriously high.[48] As J. G. Fleming has observed

> A curious inflation has thus come to prevail by which damages for libel especially to public figures often far exceed awards for the most searing personal injuries; and this remains true whether they parade under the label of "punitive" or "aggravated" damages. In times of acute social stress, damage awards are frequently used by juries to wreak vengeance on political enemies, so well illustrated by the American experience of the Civil Rights struggle in the South which prompted the intervention of the United States Court in 1964 based on the First Amendment.[49]

Yet corporate targets of investigative journalism are also not given the protection they need, for two main reasons. First, to establish defamation it is necessary to prove negligence on the part of the defamer or, in the context of public figures, malice; this is a very demanding burden, especially if corporations are treated as public figures and hence put to proof of malice.[50] Second, corporations are entitled to recover damages only in relation to loss of goodwill as opposed to non-economic reputation; a corporation, it is said, "cannot experience pain and suffering, and it has no private life to shield."[51] The findings of the case studies in this book contradict the assumption upon which this limitation rests; corporations do value their non-economic reputation, and loss of reputation from adverse publicity can have adverse effects on morale within the organization. Just how significant an assault upon non-economic corporate repute can be is revealed by what the former chairman of McDonnell Douglas had to say about the possibility of the company's pleading guilty to racketeering under the Racketeer Influenced and Corrupt Organizations statute:[52]

> This [McDonnell Douglas] is my little baby, my little jewel. I cannot live with this settlement . . . . I can't see my baby clobbered this way. I can't live with it. I can't die with this . . . . I couldn't sleep last night—a deep inner psyche says fight it all the way; if we lose fight an appeal. That's where it stands. That's where Old Mac stands.[53]

Using a correction order rather than an award of damages as the usual remedy may be a better approach. The remedy of correction is available in France, Germany, Japan, and many Canadian provinces.[54] Article 623 of the Japanese Civil Code provides that, "If a person has injured the reputation of another, the court [may require] the former to take suitable measures for the restoration of the latter's reputation." More elaborate are the provisions of the draft Unfair Publication Act recently recommended by the Australian Law Reform Commission; one feature is a detailed specification of the factors a court should take into account before awarding damages for defamation rather than making a correction order.[55]

Were correction orders to be used as the main remedy for defamation, the weaknesses of the present law would be substantially overcome. First, the chilling effect now caused by the threat of large damages would be diminished: Damages would become the exception rather than the rule. Second, it would be possible to provide more extensive protection against defamation: Strict liability and liability for non-economic damage to corporate reputation may be inappropriate if the remedy for defamation is an award of damages;[56] but correction orders would enable a remedy whether or not the defamer was negligent or malicious, and whether or not the defamation impinged upon financial or non-financial corporate repute.[57]

Account also must be taken of the law of contempt. Until recently, the risk of liability in the United States for contempt by prejudicial publicity was virtually confined to cases of blatantly intentional prejudice.[58] Whereas English courts have strenuously sought to avoid "trial by newspaper" by prohibiting publicity deemed likely to prejudice fair trial,[59] U.S. courts have been restrained by the First Amendment's hatred of prior restraints upon freedom of expression; the scope of press comment has been maximized by relying upon defendant-oriented remedies (e.g., change of venue, as in Ford's Pinto trial) to avoid or minimize the effects of prejudice once caused.[60] Over the last decade, however, protective orders have increasingly been used to gag press comment, usually by the indirect method of holding *in camera* preliminary hearings or prohibiting witnesses from speaking to reporters.[61] Some of these orders have been struck down as unconstitutional, but a majority of the U.S. Supreme Court in *Nebraska Press Association v. Stuart*[62] conceded that, in an indeterminate range of cases, the risk of prejudicing the constitutional right to a fair trial can be so great as to outweigh the competing right of freedom of expression.[63] The degree of muzzling thereby permitted is limited, but nonetheless there is reason to question whether it is justified at all.

The value of freedom of expression in exposing and controlling corporate crime is difficult to deny. To begin with, the lesson of Watergate rings loud and clear:

> Think for a moment what would have happened in this American crisis had our history and Constitution reflected the British tradition in the area of press freedom. If this nation's courts adhered to the British rule, which forbids media comment on pending cases, none of the information that led to the President's downfall would have been released as early as it was, for fear of endangering the trial of several of the President's lieutenants and partners in crime. Under the British rule, either the case against the lieutenants would have been dismissed, a politically inconceivable step, or the public dissemination of the information would have been delayed, probably until after the President's second term, at which time the issue would have lost most of its newsworthiness.[64]

Much the same lesson has now been learned in England, even if against the judgment of its highest court. In the Thalidomide case,

257

Attorney-General v. Times Newspapers Ltd.,[65] the House of Lords upheld an injunction restraining the publication of a proposed *Sunday Times* article discussing whether the Distillers Company had been civilly negligent in failing to test the drug or to take it off the market when the risks became known. Subsequently, that decision was declared by the European Court of Human Rights to be contrary to Article 10 of the European Convention.[66] Although that declaration does not have the force of law, it is binding in practical effect. Moreover, the declaration has been influential at the level of statutory reform.[67]

Encouraging full media discussion of issues of corporate blameworthiness may also help to attune jurors to an unfamiliar wavelength of experience.[68] If Distillers Company had been prosecuted for reckless assault or manslaughter in relation to injuries or deaths resulting from the sale of Thalidomide, a critical issue would have been whether the company had taken an *unjustifiable* risk by introducing the drug in Britain without fully checking the safety data supplied by Chemie Grünenthal, the original manufacturer in Germany. Ordinary people on a jury could not be expected to decide that issue as an informed, experienced group of peers: even the lawyers representing the victims displayed an unsure grasp of the testing procedures then accepted as standard in the pharmaceutical industry.[69] Full press comment, including discussion of standards of care observed by other companies at home or abroad, would have more acclimatized jurors to the limits of corporate testing. Not to allow such acclimatization, it may be argued, is to defeat a traditional purpose of the jury system—to try defendants not only on the basis of the law and fact presented at trial, but also in light of the experience and common sense that jurors are supposed to have acquired outside the courtroom.[70]

More important, the application of criminal law to corporate persons is at such a primitive stage of development that many existing rules, procedural and substantive, are much in need of sustained critical scrutiny.[71] Ongoing case-by-case criticism in the press helps catalyze and shape reform, a social force illustrated by many of the case studies in this book (e.g., the influence of the Kepone case in galvanizing action for the Toxic Substances Control Act). To this it might be replied that there is enough opportunity for reformist press criticism after trial; but this objection fails to recognize the imperative of good timing. For instance, the thread of a scandal may be lost, as it was by the national press in its neglect of the belated *St. Louis Post Dispatch* revelations about McDonnell Douglas' contributions to Senator John C. Danforth.

Would freedom of expression be secured at too high a price if the press were allowed to comment in good faith about any matters pertinent to trial? In the case of individual defendants, gag orders, or even general prohibitions upon the publication of highly prejudicial information (e.g., confessions) may be justified on a limited basis, although it should be recognized that the empirical evidence as to the prejudicial influence on jurors is inconclusive.[72] However, in the case of corporate defendants, the lead time before corporate prosecutions is usually so long that prejudicial information is made public before gag orders or other prior restraints apply.[73] In the Pinto trial, for example, no American gag order nor English prior restraint would have been effective against the *Mother Jones* article or the pretrial adverse publicity generated by the previous civil case against Ford by the Pinto victim, Grimshaw. Moreover, if a fair trial of a corporate defendant did prove to be impossible, then damages, restitution, or injunctive relief are available as second-best solutions, provided civil liability can be established. By contrast, these solutions are inappropriate in the case of impecunious street criminals of no fixed abode. This way of looking at the problem of prejudice may seem unduly generous to corporations, but compromise solutions are already typical in practice. The vast majority of criminal proceedings against corporations result in consent orders or informal arrangements for compensatory, restitutive or injunctive relief.[74]

It remains to examine a different branch of contempt by prejudicial publicity—imposing unfair pressure upon litigants to forego their legal rights. This form of contempt does not exist in the United States, but it was endorsed by the House of Lords in the *Sunday Times* case.[75] Two members of the court, Lords Diplock and Simon, went so far as to say that an injuction on this ground could have been obtained against the earlier *Sunday Times* article, "Our Thalidomide Children: A Cause for National Shame," which criticized the Distillers Company for penny-pinching and dilatoriness in settling thalidomide damages claims, but stopped short of commenting on the legal issue of whether Distillers had committed the tort of negligence. Lord Diplock's position was this:

> The public mischief in allowing a litigant to be held up to public obloquy for availing himself in a court of justice of rights to which he is entitled under the law as it stands at the time, lies in the inhibiting effect which it might have upon all potential suitors if it were to become the common belief that to have recourse to the established courts of law for ascertainment and enforcement of their legal rights

and obligations would make them a legitimate target of public abuse. If laws are unjust they ought to be changed. . . . A campaign to change them should be directed to persuading parliament of the need, not to vilifying individual litigants for exercising their rights under the law as it stands. If a campaign directed to the latter object were to succeed in deterring litigants from enforcing their legal rights in courts of law which are under a constitutional duty to enforce them, the practical result would be to substitute government by the "media" for government by parliament in the particular field of legislation with which the campaign was concerned.[76]

The rhetoric of "government by media" stems from a legalistic bias. Morality often expects more of people or corporations than does the law.[77] One major reason is the delay, justified or not, in devising laws capable of working smoothly. Another is the desirability of promoting standards higher than those which can be achieved formally through law. Granted that the law cannot always reach the higher moral ground, it hardly follows that the media should be governed by the same incapacity.

Fortunately, a majority of the House of Lords in the *Sunday Times* case disagreed that the earlier article would have constituted contempt by unfair pressure: The article passed the test of "fair and temperate" criticism.[78] However, why should the media be subject to such a test at all? The relevant rationale, we are told, is to protect litigants from being pressured by hostile publicity into refraining from bringing or defending legal actions. However, fair and temperate *but adverse and highly incriminating* attacks may be just as likely as unfair and intemperate outbursts to encourage someone like Distillers not to stick to their legal guns. Indeed, since unfair outbursts are often defamatory and hence actionable, it is conceivable that steely-cold and accurate criticism represents more of a threat to freedom of litigation: Truth hurts. Denuded of a cogent rationale, the fair and temperate restraint endorsed by the House of Lords seems more effete judicial blandishment than justified rule of law.

Enforcement Action

Enforcement agencies use publicity for a number of regulatory purposes: to warn, educate, bring forth witnesses, advise victims of avenues of redress, and to sanction.[79] Of these, the last-mentioned is the most controversial, the main objection being that informal adverse publicity should not be used to punish corporations in the absence of fair trial. The key question that arises is whether it is possible to use the sanction of informal adverse publicity fairly without also destroying the advantages for which it is prized.

The sanction of informal adverse publicity is valued highly by enforcement agencies. In many cases the threat of adverse publicity is a more potent deterrent than the threat of fines or injunctive orders; fines or injunctions pale into insignificance when compared with financial, reputational, or emotional losses of the order res-tulting from the Food and Drug Administration publicity against Proctor and Gamble's Rely tampons or Bon Vivant's vichysoisse soup.[80] This potent threat gives enforcers an ace to play when, as is so often the case, the mode of enforcement is not formal trial and sentence but informal bargaining and settlement.

Valuable as informal publicity has proven to be as a sanction, the objection exists that there should not be punishment without fair trial.[81] Thus, the U.S. Equal Employment Opportunity Commission has been criticized for resorting to non-legal punishment when it issued an inflammatory news release in advance of the trial of American Telephone and Telegraph on charges of illegal discrimination; the releases stated that the agency's trial counsel regarded AT&T's alleged violations as "the most staggering and unbelievably overt [sex] discrimination I've ever encountered," and the company as being "in the dark ages."[82] The enforcement agency most criticized is the FDA, which has used informal adverse publicity blatantly to demonstrate the strength of its position in compliance negotiations.[83] The risk of injustice is well illustrated by the action taken by the FDA against International Medication Systems Ltd. (IMS).[84] When the company refused to recall certain drugs which had not been manufactured in accordance with the code of Good Manufacturing Practices, it was threatened with adverse publicity. Subsequently, when the company remained unbending, the FDA wrote to the nation's 7,000 hospitals warning against the use of IMS products on the ground that their sterility was compromised so as to present a "potential hazard to the public health." Later, the FDA's action was subjected to judicial review and reversed; the FDA was ordered to inform hospitals that "IMS was not shown to be guilty of violation of good manufacturing practices to the extent that its product represents a potential hazard to the public health."[85]

This risk of abuse, it may be said, should be kept in perspective. Regulatory agencies have many self-serving reasons for preventing unwarranted outbursts of publicity. Bureaucrats hate getting egg on their faces, and a large corporation vilified by an unfounded scare campaign can be counted upon to retaliate with complaints to Capitol Hill. Besides, a regulatory agency can afford to use adverse publicity in only a minority of the scandals it uncovers because of the problem of finite press interest in any one domain of regulation (it is for this reason that the FDA issues press releases fewer than 50 times a year).[86]

A way to reduce the number of scandals targeted for adverse publicity is to eliminate items most likely to backfire. Furthermore, even the most aggressive regulatory agencies depend on a cooperative attitude from industry to secure most of the compliance they get. The overwhelming majority of improvements (e.g., in consumer remedies or safety controls) do not come from enforcement action but from voluntary compliance with agency requests. To the extent that the agency acquires a reputation for unfairness through the abuse of its publicity power, the cooperative attitude it depends on will be jeopardized.

It may also be contended that unjust publicity is a relatively trivial problem compared with the reluctance shown by captive regulators to alert the public to suspected offenses;[87] a hundred true negative findings should outweigh a few false alarms, especially when the consequence of a failure to press a true negative test could be death while a false negative finding will cause only a sodden reputation or reparable financial loss. When added up, however, these contentions essentially amount to an apology for the status quo. They gloss over the risk of injustice and yet offer no solution to the problem of bureaucratic secrecy.

Another response to the risk of unjust informal publicity is to advocate more stringent controls upon administrative discretion. This is the tack taken by Ernest Gellhorn.[88] Gellhorn urges more extensive scope for judicial review, and recommends that enforcement agencies tighten their internal policies and procedures. Four main proposals are put forward. First, that unplanned, ill-considered outbursts of agency publicity should be curtailed by vesting authority to speak with the media in only one agency source. Second, that an agency should have clear policies on when adverse publicity is appropriate, and these should be reviewed periodically. Third, that agencies should consider having internal appeal procedures whereby outsiders wronged by unfair publicity can seek redress. Fourth, that

> Each agency should consider the feasibility of providing that where practicable, parties to be subjected to proposed adverse publicity be given advance notice and an opportunity to comment to the agency

upon the press announcement before its release. When an adverse disclosure is inaccurate or misleading, the agency should provide specific procedures for issuing a retraction, if requested, in the same manner (if feasible) in which the original publicity was disseminated.[89]

Commendable as these proposals are, they represent only one side of the coin. Standing alone, they would minimize the risk of injustice without fostering needed flexible and informal means of enforcement.

Lateral thinking is needed. Why not rely on voluntary rather than involuntary disclosure wherever possible? As a standard opening gambit in enforcement, corporate defendants could be given the opportunity to make a voluntary disclosure of the kind requested by the SEC in its campaign against foreign bribery.[90] In terms of technical design, this approach seems entirely feasible, although there is no denying that startup troubles have been experienced in the trial programs which have been mounted by the SEC, the Department of Justice, and other agencies.[91] The more fundamental question is one of broader policy. Are the advantages of a voluntary disclosure strategy outweighed by any significant disadvantages?

The prime advantage of voluntary disclosure is reduction of the costs of regulation to taxpayers. Voluntary disclosure can transfer a large part of the burden of enforcement to corporate defendants, thereby effecting substantial savings in agency time and investigative resources; it was this consideration more than any other which animated the SEC's strategy in the foreign bribery cases.[92] An added plus is the capacity of corporate disclosure to incriminate other defendants. Whether bribery, antitrust violations, or pollution, corporate offenses are so often common knowledge within an industry that inducing one offender to talk will usually produce evidence about others.[93] In the case of the Lockheed scandal, for instance, Lockheed's confession led to the downfall of numerous other companies involved in the payment of bribes, and numerous corrupt politicians were smoked out as well.

Voluntary disclosure also gives corporate offenders a chance to indicate what they propose to do to redeem themselves. It is thus more positive and forward-looking than the typical adverse publicity generated by enforcement agencies. This is important: As the experience of Allied Chemical after the Kepone crisis illustrates, corporations are capable of innovative responses in the wake of an offense; not to encourage this capacity is to forego a golden resource.[94]

Attractive as these advantages are, scepticism is inevitable. Won't corporations sit tight and refuse to cooperate? If they do cooperate, won't the price paid for that cooperation be undue lenience and inequality? And wouldn't a burst of voluntary disclosures become so boring as to dampen social antipathy towards corporate wrong-doing?[95] Let us consider these in turn.

Would corporate offenders refuse to cooperate? Many have criticized the SEC voluntary disclosure program on the ground that corporations have much to lose and little to gain.[96] The point may also be made that Ford's voluntary disclosure to the government of the emissions-testing fraud hardly occasioned clemency; rather, it produced $7 million in penalties. Nonetheless, these reactions reflect limitations of the voluntary disclosure technique as previously used; they do not destroy the concept. The incentives offered in the foreign bribery campaign or in the action against Ford for emissions-testing fraud may have been weak and unclear.

A much better scheme of incentives can readily be envisaged. It would be possible to spell out the degree of immunity or mitigation which full and satisfactory disclosure is to earn. For instance, there is much to be said for providing a discretionary power to confer immunity from criminal liability for an offense where a corporate offender (or indeed any type of offender) not only discloses full details of the offense, but also comes forward with a corrective program of restitution and prevention which is sufficiently praise-worthy to justify immunity. This particular form of incentive would be doubly advantageous. It would offer both a carrot (avoidance of criminal liability) and a Pogo stick (opportunity to bounce forward and win credit for an exemplary program of corrective action).

There also are the disincentives of involuntary adverse publicity for companies refusing voluntarily to disclose. Our proposal is to maximize the replacement of involuntary publicity (with all its problems of punishment without trial) by voluntary disclosure when-ever possible. However, it is important that regulatory agencies retain discretion to use involuntary publicity, subject to safeguards as discussed earlier, when the remedies volunteered are insufficient to protect the public.

If substantial incentives have to be offered to make voluntary disclosure work, would corporations be let off much too easily? And wouldn't it be blatantly inequitable to offer corporate offenders immunity from criminal liability when little mercy is shown towards street offenders? Understandable as these objections are, they are unpersuasive.

First, corporate offenders are usually subject to consent orders and other negotiated arrangements, an approach also based on compromise. To put the point another way, the objections in question do not take the existing reality as their starting point; they assume a command-and-sanction model of regulation, whereas negotiated settlement is the predominant model in practice.[97] It may readily be conceded that consent orders and the like are notorious avenues of *soft* compromise; August Bequai has protested,

> Who gets hurt in consent settlements? The SEC gets a notch in its gun. The law firm gets money, the public is happy because they read "fraud" in the newspaper and think criminality right away. The company neither admits nor denies anything. It's the perfect accommodation. And it's all one big charade.[98]

The main reason for such laxity, however, is the absence of rules for the game. A virtue of the recommended voluntary disclosure approach is that the incentives and the underlying policy of compromise need to be published before the idea can be successfully implemented; this is partly because corporations won't buy the deal otherwise,[99] and partly because regulators can't openly compromise criminal liability without telling the public what concessions are going to be won in return.

Second, getting to the bottom of a corporate offense is a laborious job which often swamps public investigators. Special regulatory techniques, including voluntary disclosure, are thus called for, just as special investigative techniques, including conferring immunity on informers, sometimes necessary to catch leaders in organized crime. More important, a well-conceived voluntary disclosure program would be structured to flush guilty corporate personnel from their organizational cover, thereby helping rather than hindering the equal application of criminal law to individual persons.

Finally, if voluntary disclosure were used generally, rather than sporadically as at present, would social antipathy towards corporate wrongdoing be dulled by overpublicity? There is little doubt that the more routine the sanction, the less the denunciation attached. A good example is provided by the U.S. Mine Safety and Health Act of 1977. Because the Act mandates the non-discretionary fining of every violation of a mandatory health and safety standard observed by an inspector, the sanction has become mundane for most mining companies, and attracts no interest from the mass media unless there is a disaster.[100] However, the use of voluntary disclosure as a routine tool of enforcement need not involve overpublication of the kind of information disclosed. Disclosures would be filed with the enforcement agency and made available as a matter of public record. It would then be up to media representatives or consumer activists to publicize whatever they choose. Conceivably, they might go overboard and publish too much but, as every publicist knows, to overpublish is to perish. To assist selection, enforcement agencies could provide running lists of the worst examples of corporate violation; for example, the Mine Safety and Health Administration (MHSA), realizing that day-to-day violations are not newsworthy, could release to the press each year the names of three or so coal mining companies with the worst violation rates.

To avoid undue negativism, the best examples of corporate compliance should also be listed; for instance, MSHA, in conjunction with the Mining Congress of America, now issues annual Sentinels of Safety Awards to coal and metalliferous mines with the best safety records. Given that the disclosures of all companies would be plainly on record for all to see, this approach would hardly breed abuse of administrative discretion. Added to this, a preventive remedy against such abuse would lie in the hands of corporations should they consider themselves to be at risk: The more virtuous the corrective program of action proposed, the less the chance of being either pilloried or unrewarded.

Official Inquiry

Official enquiries (e.g., congressional committees, royal commissions) have played an active role in exposing corporate illegality, for reasons selfish as well as public-minded. Political careers can be made by slaying corporate dragons (e.g., Senators Abraham Ribicoff and Warren Magnusson thrived on auto safety, Senators Estes Kefauver, Gaylord Nelson, and Edward Kennedy on abuses of power by pharmaceutical companies), and the press has a vested interest in reporting dragon-slayings:

> Investigations are a form of entertainment, even if they stir in the minds of some observers recollections of the Roman Amphitheater or of the public trials and executions of revolutionary régimes.[101]

Official enquiries into corporate illegality often occur as a second phase of social response, the first phase being exposure by investigative journalists or consumer groups, and the third phase, prosecution and/or reform. Nader's campaign against the Federal Trade

Commission illustrates this pattern as do the campaigns described in the ITT, Ford Pinto, General Motors, Allied Chemical, and BHP coke ovens case studies. Occasionally, the first phase is by-passed, as where standing committees, particularly of the American congressional type, generate their own exposés. For example, Senator William Proxmire's Subcommittee on Priorities and Economy in Government and Senator Frank Church's Multinational Corporations Subcommittee substantially created the foreign bribery scandal in the face of earlier press and public indifference. Whether as originators or regenerators of adverse publicity, official enquiries are often an indispensable step before prosecution and/or reform: Gradualism in the exposure of corporate wrongs is inevitable where, as is not uncommon, the facts are complex or difficult to prove.

Granted their undoubted value, official enquiries have been widely criticized for poaching on the domain of criminal investigation, and also for resorting to McCarthy-style smear tactics.[102] The Erwin Congressional committee investigating Watergate came under fire from President Richard Nixon for releasing prejudicial publicity prior to the criminal trial of those implicated.[103] To give another example, the Royal Commission looking into the Mt. Erebus disaster was held by the New Zealand Court of Appeal to have committed breaches of natural justice against Air New Zealand personnel by subjecting them to adverse suspicion without providing them with an opportunity to reply.[104]

Much can and should be done to minimize the risk of smear tactics. The Canadian Law Reform Commission has recommended that investigatory committees of enquiry should not report allegations of misconduct by any person until reasonable notice of the proposed allegations has been given, along with adequate opportunity to be heard in reply; this is in line with the example set by the New Jersey Commission of Investigation Act.[105] Likely targets of adverse publicity should also be given power to call and examine witnesses and, at the committee's discretion, to cross-examine witnesses.[106] Nonetheless, formal procedural protections would not prevent abuses at an informal level, including the following devious tactic practised by many a congressional committee:

Do not space hearings more than 24 or 48 hours apart when on a controversial subject. This gives the opposition too much opportunity to make all kinds of counter-charges and replies by issuing statements to the newspapers.[107]

Ploys of this kind raise the basic question of whether official enquiries spend too much time on retrospective scandal-mongering rather than on stimulating change. In the field of corporate regulation, as elsewhere, the objection is often heard that the main task of official enquiries should not be to do the investigative work of enforcement agencies, but to concentrate on matters relevant to legal, administrative, or other reform. To some extent this point is unjustified. For one thing, it underestimates the demand for extraordinary investigation where enforcement agencies lack the capacity, resolve, or independence needed to deal effectively with corporate defendants. Moreover, through public enquiries, self-regulation can be activated rather than merely praised as a virtue; as Francis Rourke has indicated,

> Publicity in itself may be a corrective, eliminating in some instances the need for legislation by bringing about a process of self-regulation by the group under scrutiny.[108]

However, the objection is justified in so far as it attacks official enquiries for never moving beyond past events when they should be examining the adequacy of corporate responses to the causes of a scandal.

The General Electric price-fixing case may be taken as an initial example. Valuable as the Kefauver hearings were in drawing public attention to the phenomenon of administered prices in the heavy electrical equipment industry, they made little contribution to the problem of devising effective and just systems of corporate compliance. Kefauver seemed bent on crucifying General Electric, Westinghouse, and their collaborators for what had happened, expressly in the hope that they would arise from the cross through making their internal compliance systems holy. Lengthy as the crusade was, however, scant inquiry was made into the reactions of General Electric and its fellow corporate conspirators. Was the action of Westinghouse in not disciplining guilty employees preferable to the radically more severe disciplinary action taken by General Electric? Did General Electric act appropriately in disciplining some but not all of the personnel conceded to have been implicated in the conspiracy? Was General Electric's compliance-auditing program sufficiently independent to achieve its intended function? The Kefauver hearings brought these questions to light but, in the end, left them in limbo.[109]

More remarkable was the inadequacy of the official enquiry into the Corvair controversy. The enquiry of the Senate Subcommittee on Executive Reorganization in 1966 dwelt upon General Motors' snooping into Nader's private life; as one critic rightly observed, "It was a great show, but it didn't make the cars any safer."[110] It was not until 1973, long after cessation of production of the Corvair, that the Senate Subcommittee reported on the question of safety, and even then it refrained from expressing any opinion upon the "ultimate safety" of the car; what mattered, so it was assumed, was whether General Motors had misled the Subcommittee during its earlier inquiry in 1966. These exercises of Congressional oversight were not only tangential but insensitive: They failed to address squarely the allegations made in *Unsafe at Any Speed* that General Motors was unjustifiably causing death and injury, allegations far more serious than any complaint of invasion of privacy or contemptible deceit. Even if it be conceded that these allegations raised issues of negligence and causation best decided by usual process of law, they also signalled at least one important question which called for broader public scrutiny: To what extent, if any, did the handling characteristics of the early-model Corvairs need to be modified in light of experience? If this question had been put fully and firmly to General Motors by a Congressional committee, and if the reactions of the company had been assessed in light of expert opinion from outside as well as from within the industry, consumers would have been better informed as to the handling characteristics of later as well as early-model Corvairs. At the same time, General Motors might have been cast less in the role of a villain answering for its sins, and more as a corporate leader expected to respond to the lessons of the past in ways minimizing the need for legislative intervention.[111]

A similar lack of official interest in scrutinizing corporate responses to highly publicized crises is apparent in the foreign bribery cases of the mid-1970s. Although several Congressional committees examined the events which triggered the scandal as well as the pros and cons of the Foreign Corrupt Practices Act that emerged, none looked at all deeply into the question of how the problem might best be handled as a matter of organizational self-control.[112] At the invitation of the SEC, Gulf Oil, Exxon and hundreds of other corporations prepared detailed reports indicating what they proposed to do by way of prevention or cure, yet these reports were never evaluated by any official tribunal. Rather, the task of outside scrutiny was relegated to the realm of academic commentary.[113]

Mention should also be made of the Air New Zealand and BHP Appin case studies. In the case of Air New Zealand, it may be recollected, the Royal Commission focused on the causes and circumstances of the Erebus crash, not the company's reactions to proposals that navigational and other procedures needed to be changed. Despite the scandal raised about those procedures, their revision has been left entirely to the company's discretion. That discretion may well be exercized adequately, but there is no indication to date that the outcome will be put to the test of public scrutiny. Nor has any such indication emerged after the Appin Mine disaster. The enquiry conducted by Judge Goran identified unsatisfactory organizational communications and defective procedures for ventilation changeovers as causes of the disaster. The response of management was to make a few changes in communications and ventilation procedures, but the adequacy of these changes has never been investigated by any commission of enquiry. Given the tumult and shouting which accompanied the enquiries into the events precipitating the Erebus and Appin disasters, the absence of follow-up in both cases was a perverse anticlimax.

If official enquiries are to focus more constructively upon the outcome of corporate scandals, the relevant empowering legislation should require that they follow up any findings or recommendations that invite a corporation to undertake disciplinary steps, procedural changes, compensatory or corrective measures, or other action.[114] A corporation subject to such a finding or recommendation should be under a statutory duty to prepare a detailed report indicating the nature of its response; that report should be mandated as the subject of assessment by the originating body of official enquiry. Official enquiries would then be structured in such a way as to minimize the danger of vindictive or mindless dragon-slaying, and to maximize the chance of reform. Politicians and other inquisitors of state would also be on public notice that they were expected to come up with helpful solutions.[115] Corporations would be spurred to act responsibly, and a good opportunity would be created for credit to be given publicly to those who deserve praise.[116]

Orienting official enquiries towards corporate reactions as well as to the initial source of scandal could conceivably destroy the theatricality which makes them popular among politicians.[117] However, theatricality need not be lost, for several reasons. First, corporate reactions to scandalous prior events hardly stand in isolation, but serve vividly to remind the public; to compensate the victims of Thalidomide is to revive the awful memory of their missing limbs. Second, irresponsible failures to cure or prevent industrial injury, pollution, and other harms in response to a scandal can be just as gripping as irresponsible failures at the time of the event;

in the Air New Zealand case study, for instance, the finding of the Mahon Commission that there had been a conspiratorial cover-up stole the limelight.[118] Third, spotlighting remedial or preventive responses would cast attention on what a corporation has done to get out of trouble; and since innovation is an idol of business, corporations may even gain favorable publicity. Fourth, the irony is that harm-causing acts by organizations are often less prone to scandal than subsequent managerial reactions: Many corporate offenses are the work of low or middle ranks, whereas questionable reactions to corporate offenses typically concern high managerial performance (consider e.g., the Appin Mine disaster: Top management was not involved in the communications breakdown at the mine, but the task of responsive reform fell squarely upon it).

Yet a cynic might contend that it is pointless to contemplate official enquiry into corporate responses to crisis because the very purpose of official enquiries is to use the smokescreen of scandal to maintain the appearance rather than the reality of effective social action. Thus, the *New York Times* saw nothing but mischief in Theodore Roosevelt's use of the Bureau of Corporations to publicize the evils of monopoly:

> It does not "bust the trusts" . . . . It will appease the public clamor against trusts, and it will do the trusts and combinations no harm. That is to say, it will fool the people, and that is the purpose of the Republican Congress.[119]

Given the limited degree of official inquiry into what corporations have actually done in response to scandals, political motivations remain suspect today.

Instead of retreating into cynicism, is it possible to provide an adequate guarantee that serious acts of corporate illegality will receive the public attention they deserve? A number of states in the United States have handled much the same problem with organized crime by setting up independent crime commissions, with full power to subpoena and examine witnesses, coupled with protection from liability for defamation.[120] A similar approach might well be adopted by establishing independent corporate crime and correction commissions.

Their brief would be essentially threefold. First, they would investigate acts of suspected corporate crime with a view to screening out cases where trial is unnecessary because the corporation concerned is prepared to undertake an agreed course of preventive or remedial action. This function would be the equivalent of pre-

271

trial diversion in individual criminal law. Second, in cases warranting trial, corporate crime and correction commissions would undertake the pre-trial investigation and review now performed by grand juries and preliminary judicial hearings.[121] Third, corporate crime and correction commissions would assess the adequacy of the preventive or curative reactions of a corporation, whether as agreed to by pre-trial settlement or as required by sentence upon conviction. In this capacity, they would do the type of work which might otherwise be performed by the probation service if that service were not overburdened with the supervision of individual defendants.

Pre-trial diversion would seem optimal as a means of reducing the costs of litigation and enforcing corporate rehabilitation; if so, it should be placed on an officially recognized and systematically operated basis. If pre-trial diversion is to be instituted, savings could also be made by combining it with the process of pre-trial investigation and review; a single-function mechanism, such as the grand jury, may be a procedural luxury we can no longer afford. As regards assessment of corporate measures of prevention or cure, there is a choice to be made among

    (a) having a weak, negligible checking system, as at present;

    (b) equipping the probation service to perform the task; or

    (c) developing a separate, specialized system for monitoring corporate compliance.

Alternative (a) may be rejected as wasteful of the resources committed to the prior stages of enforcement. As between alternatives (b) and (c), (c) would seem preferable because monitoring corporate compliance is more likely to require the appointment of experienced consultants than the deployment of probation officers with relatively little background in this field.

Corporate crime and correction commissions would not be counterproductive in one way that troubles organized crime commissions. To name less infamous organized crime figures in a crime commission report can signify that they have "arrived," an accolade that enhances the credibility of their threats. Since large corporations rarely depend on the threat of violence to achieve their ends, notoriety is unlikely to be seen by them as an asset.

Corporate Disclosure

Consumer groups, investigative journalists, enforcement agencies, official enquiries, and the general community can achieve informal social control of corporate crime only if they have adequate information about it. Access to pertinent corporate data, however, is hampered by unsatisfactory non-financial disclosure programs, by undue confidentiality of trade secrets, and by excessive emphasis on "mud-slinging."

Competition among companies is a poor wellspring of information about their questionable activities. When we began this research project, one of our tentative hypotheses was that competitor-initiated publicity might be exploited as a means of corporate control. However, as in the case of General Motors' reactions to the Ford Pinto trial, the response among competitors is typically one of sympathy, or perhaps relief at having been spared a similar ordeal. Moreover, the unwritten code of well-mannered business prohibits advertisement of a competitor's problems with the law, largely because companies see themselves as allied against government regulation. As in the case of any taboo, however, violations do occur behind the scenes: Although pharmaceutical companies will not instruct their sales representatives to tell doctors that a competitor has committed the offense of false advertising, they are not above squealing on an offender by slipping anonymous complaints to the FDA.

Another aspect of corporate life is the insulation from public scrutiny provided by the habit of regarding corporations as if they were entitled to much the same right of privacy as human persons. Ingrained as the idea of personifying corporations is, it conduces to overprotection by neglecting the public consequences of corporateness: Unlike individual persons, corporations function essentially as private governments, often with state-like spheres of influence and power.[122]

Accordingly, a British Government white paper on company law reform has stated categorically that companies have an obligation to disclose information impinging on the public interest:

> The bias must always be towards disclosure, with the burden of proof thrown on those who defend secrecy. The more people can see what is actually happening, the less likely they are to harbor general suspicions—and the less opportunity there is for concealing improper or even criminal activities. Openness in company affairs is the first principle in securing responsible behaviour.[123]

A similar position has also been taken by some corporations; behold Caterpillar Tractor's *Code of Worldwide Business Conduct*:

The basic reason for existence of any company is to serve the needs of people. In a free society, institutions flourish and businesses prosper only by customer acceptance of their products and services, and by public acceptance of their conduct.

Therefore, the public is entitled to a reasonable explanation of operations of a business, especially as those operations bear on the public interest. Larger economic size logically begets an increased responsibility for such public communications.[124]

Traditionally, the emphasis of legal requirements of corporate disclosure has been upon providing information for investors to make rational decisions.[125] Increasingly, however, it has been recognized that corporations have many other publics—notably consumers, employees, suppliers, and local communities—all of whom have a justifiable need to know about corporate intentions and capacities.[126] The information of most relevance to these publics is non-financial. Thus, the SEC has developed expanded material disclosure requirements that, in uncovering illegal acts of bribery and pollution, inform the public about matters of social as well as financial corporate performance.[127] Moreover, there has been considerable support for social audit programs which would require corporations to provide such information as industrial injury rates, effluent levels, number of environmental violations, and incidence of complaints about products.[128]

The SEC's expanded requirements of material disclosure have been widely criticized, mainly because the underlying policy of policing corporate conduct goes beyond what is needed for the limited purposes of investor protection.[129] Moreover, if the SEC is to police bribery and pollution, it is difficult to see why it should not also move into the precincts of automobile safety, occupational health, and adverse reactions to drugs.

A better approach would be to equip enforcement agencies with voluntary non-financial disclosure programs of the type previously recommended,[130] together with additional mandatory non-financial disclosure where needed (e.g., fiber-counts in stipulated areas of manufacturing plants where asbestos is used). The SEC would then be left to concentrate on its traditional specialized task of investor protection, a task inevitably neglected if it tackles the general field of corporate policing.[131] Second, reorienting the SEC's role toward investor protection could well bring about a greater emphasis upon disclosure of the procedural and other reform measures adopted by corporations after detection of an offense.[132] Rather than allowing a corporation to get away with confession and avoidance, the nature of its preventive reactions would be open to public examination. Moreover, it would thereby be possible to avoid the blatant lawlessness of allowing a specialized enforcement agency to assume a sweeping, legislatively undefined power of corporate regulation.[133] To the extent that a general means of corporate policing is necessary, the gap should be filled by creating an agency equipped with appropriate complementary or overriding powers, one possibility being a corporate crime and correction commission, as previously proposed.

The more ambitious proposal has often been made that corporations should be required to undertake a social audit detailing the total social costs and benefits of their operations and not merely the financial details traditionally checked by accountants.[134] Enticing as this idea may be, it attempts too much, too soon. For one thing, there is no agreement as to the standards which should govern full-scale social audits; as Christopher Stone has observed,

> Much of the value of a true audit . . . is that it has a set, prescribed structure, designed to display the answers to a series of questions which are the same for all companies. This the social auditors are nowhere near achieving. And it may well be beyond their grasp.[135]

For another, corporations typically have so many different kinds of social impacts that a total audit would doubtless dispirit auditors and readers alike.[136] In any event, to give currency to the concept of audit beyond the field of traditional accounting is to run a risk that important non-financial dimensions of compliance with the law will be obscured or driven out as a result of preoccupation with what can be reduced to numbers.[137]

Instead of chasing some amorphous, redundant, or counterproductive notion of social audit, it would seem much better to provide for additional mandatory disclosures where concealment is particularly likely to result in severe harm. Thus, corporations and their personnel are under no general duty to disclose serious product dangers of which they become aware (in 1979 a Bill was advanced for a new federal offense to cover this situation but, along with other proposals for revising the U.S. Criminal Code, it lapsed).[138] Given the degree of protection through mandatory disclosure lavished upon the investment community, this gap is doubly remarkable: Pintos allegedly incinerated people whereas bad investments occasion only financial loss.[139]

A second problem is the protection that trade secrets relating to corporate compliance now receive.[140] Corporations sometimes refuse to release information about useful preventive measures on the ground that rivals would thereby gain information of competitive advantage. For example, in the coke ovens case, BHP was impressed with the design of the coke ovens used in certain Japanese plants, but the Japanese were unwilling to make systematic emissions data available lest BHP be given vital clues about their advanced technology. Much more commonly, information is disclosed to regulatory agencies in the normal course of standard-setting, product-screening, or enforcement, and then treated as confidential by the agencies. The standard practice of the FDA is to deny access to testing data supplied for new drug applications, the view being that a new drug application "is personal to the manufacturer who makes it" (summaries, however, are provided); this practice flows from the terms of the Food, Drug and Cosmetic Act, which prohibits the revelation of testing data "concerning any method or process which as a trade secret is entitled to protection."[141]

From the standpoint of social control through informal publicity, the protection accorded to trade secrets is questionable on several grounds. First, the screening procedures for new drugs and other potentially dangerous products are kept behind a veil of trade secrecy which can cover up serious defects.[142] As McGarity and Shapiro have commented, the greater the number of those scrutinizing, the less the risk of error or fraud:

> An agency faces a difficult task in predicting the likely social consequences of a product's use solely on the basis of experimental testing data submitted by the product's proponent. Data are often scientifically inconclusive, permitting reasonable scientists to arrive at different interpretations. . . . In addition, test sponsors, because of their financial interest in agency approval, often will design and report studies in the light most favorable to their product. After a product is approved, agencies rarely have the time and resources to reevaluate the original test data in light of changing scientific evaluational criteria. Thus, questionable industry interpretations can remain undetected for years. In one case, fifteen years elapsed between the original regulatory decision to accept the manufacturer's interpretation that the pesticide "heptaclor" did not cause cancer in rats and later evaluation of the same data, buttressed by independent experimentation, finding strong evidence which indicated that "heptaclor" was very likely carcinogenic.[143]

Second, there is a risk of pro-industry bias where overworked agency personnel are allowed to arrive at decisions based on hidden material. Third, trade secrecy may operate to the detriment of public

276

confidence and agency morale, as McGarity and Shapiro have indicated by reference to the FDA experience:

> The FDA asserts that present secrecy policies prevent it from satisfactorily answering its critics, limiting public confidence in its judgments and causing deep resentment among FDA staff, who cannot reveal data that would help rebut public attacks against their decisions.[144]

Granted the need to protect trade secrets in order to preserve sufficient business incentive to innovate, the existing balance between public and proprietary interests leans too much toward the latter. An alternative approach would be to exempt health and safety testing data from trade secret protection, a compromise struck under recent U.S. statutes. Thus, under the Toxic Substances Control Act, health and safety studies of chemicals subject to the Act must be disclosed to the Environmental Protection Agency[145] and, under the Freedom of Information Act, they then become accessible to the public. To maintain an incentive for corporate innovation, provision is made for agency-assisted recouping of the costs of preparing health and safety data from those who subsequently make use of the data disclosed.[146] The resulting compromise between the public's need to know and the innovator's need for incentive is hardly perfect, but the balance struck would be superior to the trade secrecy bias illustrated by FDA drug approval procedures.[147] Above all, the raw data from drug-testing experiments submitted to the FDA would be available to anyone in the scientific community who wished to bring his or her critical faculties to bear on the quality of the research.

A third important conduit of corporate disclosure is whistle-blowing.[148] The usefulness of this approach is now widely recognized, to the point where a growing number of jurisdictions have statutory provisions which protect whistle-blowers against unfair dismissal and other abuses.[149] However, retaliatory tactics have made whistle-blowing a less effective tool of social control than it might be.[150]

As a means of corporate disclosure, "mud-slinging" has three serious limitations. First, recriminatory whistle-blowers are readily associated with informers, turncoats, saboteurs, and other low-life;[151] accordingly, they lack respectability and clout. Second, the bonds of loyalty and allegiance within organizations discourage attack: As Andrew Hacker has commented, the business code of cohesion resembles that of the FBI:

J. Edgar Hoover handed down an Iron Law to his subordinates: Never Embarrass the Bureau. Most corporations feel much the same way. It is not simply that embarrassments can lower public confidence in a company, with an accompanying decline in sales. For those at the top, the firm is much like a temple to which they pledged their careers. To defile its name, especially outside the precincts, approaches a profane act.[152]

Third, open communications within corporations may be inhibited should whistle-blowing to outsiders become a real threat; it is a truism of organizational theory that information sharing within an organization depends on trust and confidence between informant and recipient.[153]

If whistle-blowing is to work well as a means of corporate disclosure, a more constructive orientation is needed. As Charles Powers and David Vogel have argued,

> The task of ethical management is to have anticipated the pressures which would give rise to the concealed and harmful practice, and to have helped create patterns of communication within the organization so that whistle-blowing would not be necessary.[154]

Thus perceived, a sound strategy for whistle-blowing requires communication channels capable of bubbling up bad news and adequately resolving the issue which surfaces. The Exxon reforms in the wake of the Italian bribery episode are a good example of this strategy as are those of Allied Chemical in the aftermath of Kepone. This is not to imply that whistle-blowing should be kept in-house or that constructive internal resolution will always be possible. External whistle-blowing, and the right to blow the whistle, remain vital backstops, but sentencing and self-regulation should try to ensure that management receives and heeds complaints about suspected illegality.[155]

International Exposure

Given the very limited degree of formal social control that can be exercised over the activities of transnational corporations, the informal sanction of adverse publicity assumes extra significance. To date, international exposure has often proven effective as a substitute for formal regulation of transnational companies, but the amount of exposure possible is limited by parochial requirements of corporate disclosure, shortage of multijurisdictional investigative journalists, and non-access to any official international forum of complaint.

Countless public interest groups have been formed around the world, most of them drawing heavily on the Nader model.[156] This public interest movement is now entering a new phase of development with the internationalization of its activities—an internationalization of consumerism as a countervailing force against the inexorable internationalization of capital.

There has taken place the first successful international boycott of a company, namely that against Nestlé for its promotion of infant formula as a substitute for breast milk in the Third World.[157] INFACT (the Infant Formula Action Coalition) claims that Nestlé used a variety of unethical practices (including having sales representatives pose as nurses) to lure mothers in poor countries away from breast feeding, and that these practices had the effect of condemning many babies to death from malnutrition. In spite of a massive counterpublicity campaign by Nestlé,[158] the combination of the boycott and the adverse publicity eventually induced significant, though not total, reform. Nestlé announced a phase-out in 1978 of all mass media consumer advertising of infant formula. Improved warnings against nutritional misuse of the formula have been placed on labels, along with a suggestion that breast feeding is preferable. And in March 1982, Nestlé prepared "comprehensive policy guidelines" to bring itself into compliance for the first time with the World Health Organization's code on marketing infant formula.[159]

Another reform of note was that made by Abbott Laboratories. In 1975, an International Council of Infant Foods Industries (ICIFI) was formed by nine companies, including Abbott, as a response to the attack on their marketing practices by consumer groups. The council promulgated a voluntary code that marginally improved infant formula marketing practices. Pressure from INFACT and its associated church groups then resulted in Abbott Laboratories breaking ranks with the other eight transnationals and adopting a more stringent code than that of the ICIFI:

> The contrast between the codes provided leverage for critics to press ICIFI members to emulate the steps agreed to by Abbott. They included the limitation on direct consumer advertising, taking milk nurses out of uniform, and recognition that the potential market in developing countries is limited to the group of consumers defined by socio-economic characteristics. Abbott's willingness to take these steps

279

was influenced by its relatively low level of involvement in Third World markets, and by its extremely important stake in the United States market (55 percent of a $300 million market). For Abbott, it was prudent to defend its interests in the United States market by taking the "moral high road" in the controversy over infant formula use in the developing world.[160]

The tactics adopted by INFACT to pressure Abbott in this way are reminiscent of those used so effectively by the Amalgamated Clothing and Textile Workers Union in the J.P. Stevens campaign: divide and conquer by targeting the corporations that have the most tenuous interest in holding the line.

The growing internationalization of the consumer movement heralds the increased use of adverse publicity as an informal means of transnational control. In an era when strict control in the disposal of toxic wastes or banned pesticides in the United States can result in their being dumped in Third World countries which have neither government officials to enforce waste disposal laws nor local public interest groups to expose abuses, it is to be hoped that the international consumer movement will step into the breach by using adverse publicity transnationally as a sanction.[161] The internationalization of trade unionism may also be expected to burgeon, in which event publicity about occupational health and safety offenses will be less insular. Hopefully, it will thereby be possible to overcome dangerous ignorance due to the kind of protectionism displayed in the coke ovens case. Worthwhile as these developments would be, they will be slow in coming unless additional catalysts for international exposure are supplied.

One catalyst would be to expand the scope of mandatory corporate disclosure. Corporations could be required to disclose details of the practices of foreign subsidiaries or affiliates in areas (e.g., toxic waste disposal) where egregious departures from the standards of behavior required under local law are suspected in havens abroad, and where in the interest of international comity or self-repute, the home country is justified in maintaining an extraterritorial lookout for the transportation of offenses abroad. This strategy, already used successfully by the SEC against foreign bribery, could well be adopted in a variety of well-recognized trouble spots. For example, transnational data blockages are a notorious problem in the pharmaceutical industry. A health department in one country can approve a new drug for marketing without realizing that health authorities in another country had banned the same drug after their scientists discovered a danger associated with it. Physicians and patients can use drugs that they are told by the company have no side effects when that same company lists a variety of side effects in instructions for use in other parts of the world.[162] One safeguard against such double standards would be for individual countries to demand an international regulatory status document for each pharmaceutical product. This document would provide an up-to-date list of the countries in which the drug is approved, and the indications, contraindications, side effects and warnings which are required in each of those countries. This would be a useful resource to the consumer movement as well as to countries that cannot afford sophisticated information-gathering systems.

A potential limitation on more extensive corporate disclosure requirements is that some countries may erect barriers denying access to vital local information. Thus, the United Kingdom, Australia, and many other nations have enacted laws which deny the validity of U.S. orders seeking discovery of information relevant to antitrust or other suits.[163] Although these laws have so far been confined to protecting local sovereignty from the invasion of foreign judicial process, a parallel development is entirely conceivable should public embarrassment result from foreign mandatory disclosure laws. To anticipate this risk, however, is to confirm the value of such disclosure laws: the smoke of non-cooperation is usually a sign of fire. For example, in banning recognition of U.S. antitrust proceedings against the uranium cartel, the Australian government laid itself open to the suspicion that it was an accessory after the fact to price-fixing by Australian companies.

A second much-needed catalyst for international exposure is investigative journalism. The problem now is that domestic events preoccupy the attention of the media in those countries fortunate enough to have investigative journalists. One of the present authors has suggested that the United Nations set up an agency to sponsor a transnational media alert:

> The world could do with more Ralph Naders, more Bernsteins and Woodwards, but the problem is that such people are least likely to flourish where they are most needed. Uganda is yet to have its Ralph Nader. One interesting solution to transnational corruption would be for the United Nations to set up a anti-corruption agency. The sole responsibility of this agency would be to employ anti-corruption journalists in every country in the world. Such journalists would be free agents, snooping out stories and releasing them, free of charge, to the mass media of the country in which they operate. . . . Indeed, the United Nations anti-corruption agency could provide a front for

many newspapers to publish stories which they would not dare publish under the by-line of their own journalists. . . .

All of this is easier said than done. Idealistic people who were foolish enough to become anti-corruption journalists would have to expect to be the victims of considerable harassment and personal abuse. Those who were not idealistic could be expected to do very well as recipients of graft themselves. Getting informants from inside corporations to feed out information would not be easy.[164]

A further handicap is the lack of access of consumer and other groups to any official international forum of complaint. Some progress has been made in the draft United Nations Code of Conduct for Transnational Corporations. In its final form, the Code probably will include provisions on non-interference in internal political affairs, abstention from corrupt practices, transfer pricing, restrictive business practices, and environmental protection.[165] There is deep international dispute over the form of sanctions to be imposed for violations of the code and whether the imposition of such sanctions should be binding or non-binding on nations which ratify.[166] However, there would be value in even the weakest formulation of the code; nations, unions, or consumer groups could at least bring a complaint of violation before an international panel of experts for investigation, and the panel would have power to find against the corporation and publicize the finding. Adverse findings by an international tribunal would give impetus to boycotts (as launched against Nestlé) or to international trade union action against a flagrant occupational safety offender.[167] Remember too that consumers, unions, and even corporations in many undemocratic societies do not have access to the investigative tribunal that others take for granted. A hearing under a UN Code of Conduct for Transnational Corporations may be the only real opportunity for some consumers or workers to air grievances. Corporations accused of bad practices would be given an opportunity to reply or, if delinquent in the past, to indicate positively what they propose to do by way of correction; here, there is a lesson to be learnt from the experience of domestic official enquiries.

Conclusion

The use of informal publicity as a means of controlling corporate crime could be improved in many ways. The main improvements we have suggested are these:

282

(1) increased availability of *qui tam* suits for private prosecutions;
(2) modification of defamation laws to place more emphasis on correction orders, and relaxation of the law of contempt to allow good faith press comment on matters pertinent to trial;
(3) exploitation of immunized voluntary disclosure as a general strategy of corporate regulation;
(4) reorientation of official enquiries so as to require scrutiny of corporate reactions to events giving rise to scandal;
(5) imposition of mandatory corporate disclosure of risks of serious harms; and
(6) promotion of international exposure of irresponsible corporate practices through mandatory disclosure, investigative journalism, and an international forum of complaint.

Since the changes suggested would increase the degree of *informal* social control over corporate crime it may be argued that the law of the jungle would thereby spread too far. Given the desirability of enforceable guarantees of due process and equitable treatment, shouldn't the law be evolving towards greater, not less, reliance on *formal* social control?[168]

In suggesting and commending ways for improving the use of informal publicity as a sanction, we do not deny the advantage which formal social control has in being able to provide a superior guarantee of due process and equitable treatment. Indeed, it is this advantage as well as considerations of effective sentencing that lead us next to canvass the formal use of publicity as a sanction. Nevertheless, there is much to be said for increased reliance upon informal publicity as a means of controlling corporate crime.

There will never be the resources in the public sector for adequate public enforcement against corporate crime. Thus, sound policy must encourage private as well as public control. If legalistic purists find informal social control distasteful, they face the problem of carrying such a policy through to its logical conclusion. Should we, under the banner of due process, proscribe the name-calling of deviants, forbid gossip, and stop employers from firing employees they catch with their hands in the till? Few criminologists would disagree that it is not the societies with the most impressive criminal justice systems which have the lowest crime rates, but those with the most effective informal social control.[169] From this standpoint, public policy should be neither negative nor neutral towards informal social control, but should positively encourage popular participation in shaming and demanding reform. Checks and balances are needed, and we have made a number of recommendations accordingly (e.g., availability of correction orders on basis of strict liability for defamation of corporations; opportunity of right to reply to allegations made at official enquiries; improvement of safeguards surrounding immunized voluntary disclosure as a tool of corporate regulation).

It may be objected that there is a special danger in using adverse publicity to extend informal social control over corporate behavior: Corporations can respond by inflicting serious injustices upon personnel.[170] However, the question is not simply whether publicity attacks would result in indiscriminate internal sanctioning but whether the incidence of such indiscriminate sanctioning would markedly change. We doubt that it would: The more likely consequence is that the criteria for sanctioning would change. Personal success in business is largely a zero-sum game (one person's step down is another's step up), so that punishments and rewards issued under either financial or non-financial criteria result in roughly equal injustice. In companies that hire or promote according to profitability, people miss out unfairly because of erroneous assessments of their financial performance. Equally, in companies that promote or dismiss according to compliance performance, some are unjustly held back or fired because of incorrect determinations of culpability. By using the pressure of publicity to make compliance with the law a significant factor in private punishment and reward systems, we are unlikely to worsen the injustice inherent in such systems, but we are likely to improve law observance.

CHAPTER 21

Formal Publicity

Formal Publicity and Corporate Crime Control

Should greater use be made of adverse publicity as a formal sanction against corporate crime?[1] Publicity has considerable potential as a means of controlling corporate behavior, but many doubts arise as to the wisdom of using it formally as a sentence. The central aim of this chapter is to indicate what these doubts are and to assess whether they are justified. To begin with, however, we need to trace the ways in which formal publicity has been used to control corporate wrongdoing in the past. Broadly, formal publicity has been employed in three ways—as a punishment in criminal proceedings, as a penalty in quasi-criminal or administrative proceedings, and as a civil remedy.[2]

Since the abolition of the stocks, the formal use of publicity as a punishment has been rare.[3] In England, several Bread Acts during the first half of the nineteenth century enabled official publication of convictions for adulterating bread. Thus, section 10 of the Bread Act of 1822 provided as follows:

It shall be lawful for the Magistrate or Magistrates, Justice or Justices, before whom any such Offender or Offenders shall be convicted, to cause the Offender's Name, Place of Abode and Offense, to be published in some Newspaper which shall be printed or published in or near the City of London or the Liberty of Westminister, and to defray the Expense of publishing the same out of the Money to be forfeited— in case any shall be so forfeited as last mentioned, paid or recovered.[4]

According to Jeremy Bentham, it was quite common for magistrates to threaten offenders with advertisement upon a second conviction, and such publicity was regarded as being a more severe punishment than the statutory fine.[5] Despite this advantage, however, ignominious discrediting of offenders has fallen into disuse as a sanction.

A notable exception is the Australian Black Marketing Act of 1942, a statute in force until shortly after the end of Second World War.[6] Under this Act, details of conviction for the offense of black marketing were to be published in the *Commonwealth Gazette*. At the time of conviction, the court was required to order a notice or several notices of the conviction to be displayed at the offender's place of business continuously for not less than three months. The court was also required to decide the size, lettering, position, and content of such notices. Every notice was to be headed in bold letters, "Black Marketing Act 1942," and the entire notice was to be easily legible. If such a notice would not effectively draw the violation to the attention of persons dealing with the offender, a court could direct that a similar notice be displayed for three months on all business invoices, accounts and letterheads. In addition, the Attorney-General was authorized to direct newspaper publication or radio broadcasts of particulars relating to any black marketing offense.

Formal publicity has also been used as a penalty for administrative or quasi-criminal violations, especially by the U.S. Environmental Protection Agency. Thus, in *Southern Wholesale, Inc.*,[7] an action for illegally using leaded gasoline, a consent agreement required the defendant to prepare bumper stickers and posters advocating the use of unleaded gasoline, and to arrange for newspaper advertisements and radio announcements to like effect. Moreover, in *Highway Oil, Inc.*,[8] a similar action, the defendant was required to enliven Kansas City Royals baseball games by providing aircraft-towed banners bearing the messages "Unleaded Gas Makes Cents" and "Unleaded Gas Keeps the Air Clean."

As a civil remedy, formal publicity has frequently been used for the purposes of correction and prevention. Employers have often been required to post notices aimed at advising employees of unfair labor practices. In *NLRB v. J. P. Stevens & Co. Inc.*,[9] for example, J. P. Stevens was ordered to give notice by mail as well as by notice-board of anti-union violations to its employees in North and South Carolina. In the case of investor protection, remedial advice is also common. To give one example, in *SEC v. Heritage Trust Co*,[10] the defendant was required to send its shareholders copies of the court's decision, so that "investors may be fully and fairly informed as to the status of this case, possible legal remedies they may have, and its possible effect on their investment." Similarly, in the area of consumer protection, the U.S. Federal Trade Commission and the Food and Drug Administration have developed the remedy of corrective advertising, as applied in *ITT Continental Baking Co.*.[11] In this case, the makers of Profile bread, having deceptively advertised the weight-reducing potential of the product, consented to a cease and desist order requiring 25 percent of all advertising for one year to disclose that "Profile is not effective for weight reduction."

Given the reliance now placed on formal publicity as a civil remedy and, to a lesser extent, as a non-stigmatizing penalty, why not use formal publicity as a stigmatizing, prestige-lowering sentence in criminal proceedings? This was the approach recommended by the U.S. National Commission on Reform of Federal Criminal Laws (the Brown Commission) in a 1970 Study Draft. Section 405 of the Study Draft provided as follows:

> When an organization is convicted of an offense, the court may, in addition to or in lieu of imposing other authorized sanctions, . . . require the organization to give appropriate publicity to the conviction by notice to the class or classes of persons or sector of the public interested in or affected by the conviction, by advertising in designated areas or by designated media, or otherwise . . . .[12]

In the Final Report of the Commission, the above recommendation was watered down by stipulating that the publicity be transmitted only to "persons or classes of persons ostensibly harmed by the offense."[13] Ultimately, the proposal was dropped as a result of corporate pressure, but many have suggested that it should be revived.[14]

Publicity orders of the kind proposed by the Brown Commission offer three major advantages as a punishment against corporations. First, the present range of sanctions available against corporate offenders is very limited (fines and probation are the two main options); publicity orders would broaden the armory and thereby promote flexibility in sentencing. Second, the sanctions now available against corporations lack credibility as means of deterrence or retribution. Fines can often be passed on to consumers in higher prices, and probation is oriented more toward supervision than punishment.[15] By contrast, adverse publicity orders would jeopardize what we have found to be a vital part of organizational being—corporate prestige. Third, publicity orders would relate well to the general deterrent and educative aims of corporate criminal law. Unlike fines or probation, publicity orders of appropriate design would automatically convey information about the nature and sig-

287

nificance of corporate offenses, and the consequences of non-compliance.

Worthwhile as these advantages would be, major doubts surround the prospect of putting corporate offenders in the stocks. These doubts reduce to the following nine claims:

(1) Corporations cannot be stigmatized.

(2) Lowering a co oration's prestige raises formidable problems of persuasion n relation to formulation, transmission, and influence of the message.

(3) If corporations are seriously threatened by adverse publicity, they will resort to counterpublicity and other self-protective tactics.

(4) Formal publicity is unnecessary because serious corporate offenses will attract publicity informally via news or other media.

(5) It would be more effective to rely on preventive orders and other interventionist means of controlling corporate behavior.

(6) It would be more effective to direct adverse publicity at individual offenders within a corporation.

(7) Inducing consumers not to buy a defendant's products can be difficult or even impossible.

(8) Adverse publicity may have a significant deterrent and retributive impact on corporations, but only at the expense of distortion, spillovers, and other unwanted effects.

(9) The impact of punitive publicity is too uncertain to satisfy the demand of justice that punishment be proportionate to the offense committed.

Proponents of these views can be found in legal, government, and corporate circles. It will be argued that none of the objections withstands critical examination.

Corporations and Stigmatization

Can corporations be stigmatized? Conventional wisdom on corporate criminal law stresses that only individuals can be stigmatized.

At the outset, there is Herbert Packer's pessimism:

Of course, the only punishment that can be imposed on a corporation is a fine, apart from the stigma of conviction itself. How real that stigma is may be doubted. Sociologists of the Sutherland persuasion talk about corporate recidivists; but there is very little evidence to suggest that the stigma of criminality means anything very substantial in the life of a corporation. John Doe has friends and neighbors; a corporation has none. And the argument that the fact of criminal conviction may have an adverse effect on a corporation's economic position seems fanciful.[16]

Support for the viewpoint expressed by Packer is provided by Alan Dershowitz's study of newspaper coverage of the electrical equipment conspiracies:

> One can speculate that had no corporate executives been indicted, or had no prison sentences been imposed, even the newspapers which did publicize the recent case would have relegated the story to a small column on the financial page. Apparently therefore little moral opprobrium attaches to the convicted corporation except in the highly unusual case because few members of the general public are ever aware of such conviction. Moreover, even in the unusual case, like General Electric, the opprobrium is shunted away from the corporation and focused upon the convicted individuals. It is unlikely, therefore, that the threat of "tarnishing" moral opprobrium is significant to the [large] corporation in terms of profit diminution or effective deterrence.[17]

Recently, these views have been echoed in a *Harvard Law Review* encyclical on corporate crime.[18] Yet the position is vulnerable on six grounds.

First, assuming that Dershowitz's analysis of the newspaper coverage of the price-fixing conspiracies is totally accurate, which it is not, any conclusion that corporations cannot be stigmatized is unwarranted. The evidence presented by Dershowitz suggests only that the normal process of *informal* media reporting may have an insufficient stigmatizing effect. It has no bearing upon the potential impact of *formal* publicity sanctions, the purpose of which would be to *ensure* media coverage where informal processes do not.

Second, it is fanciful to suggest that corporate entities inherently lack the capacity to be stigmatized because they are fictitious beings, without friends and neighbors. The findings of our case studies confirm that corporate prestige and repute are highly valued within large organizations. Moreover, as our findings also indicate, the force of loyalty and collective sentiment can lead to soul-searching and loss of morale within organizations just as it can within the family of an individual convict. Were the position otherwise, one would hardly expect corporations themselves to sponsor so large an industry of corporate image-making. It is not uncommon for business to spend as much as \$1 billion per year on selling corporate images, as distinct from products and services.[19]

Third, it is short-sighted to assume that corporations can be punished only by cash fines or other non-stigmatizing means. It is true that equity fines can dilute the value of a company's stock, community service orders can require a corporate offender to use its skills and resources to perform a socially useful project, and punitive preventive orders can mandate particularly stringent organizational changes. But formal publicity sanctions would provide a quintessentially stigmatizing form of punishment.[20]

Fourth, as elaborated in a later section, it is a mistake to equate a company's economic position with the state of its reputation. The apple of prestige is different from the orange of assets.

Finally, although there is some force in the more subtle point raised by Dershowitz that opprobrium can be transferred from a corporation onto guilty individuals, this is a reflection of the limits of the present law rather than an eternal truth. At present, the law of corporate criminal liability is cast in such a way that the distinction between corporate and individual responsibility is often unclear. Corporate responsibility for wrongdoing now can be imposed without any finding as to the reasons that make resort to corporate as well as to individual punishment necessary. Were the law changed to require such a finding, however, the distinction between corporate and individual responsibility, together with the justification for assigning corporate responsibility, would become much clearer.[21] It is significant that, contrary to Dershowitz's account, the relationship between individual and corporate responsibility was in fact the subject of detailed discussion in a *New York Times* account of the conviction of General Electric and a number of its executives for price-fixing, and that several reasons for imposing corporate as well as individual responsibility (e.g., pressure to make profits) emerged clearly from that discussion.[22] The same type of inquiry should be undertaken formally by a court, and, where corporate responsibility is imposed, the reasons should be highlighted in any formal or informal publicity sanction that ensues.

Problems of Persuasion

Formal publicity sanctions are said to raise formidable problems of persuasion.[23] These problems are five-fold:

(1) the government is a poor propagandist;

(2) inducing a change in public attitudes is more difficult than inducing a change in product preferences;

(3) corporate offenses are typically bland and hence evoke little interest;

(4) government publicity may be drowned out because there is already too much noise about corporations in the communication channels of society; and

(5) the media may refuse to publish the information required to be disseminated under a formal publicity order.

The contention that the government is too poor a propagandist for formal publicity to work as a sanction has been forcefully put by John Coffee:

> It has trouble being persuasive; rarely is it pithy; never can it speak in the catchy slogans with which Madison Avenue mesmerizes us. At its best, the government sounds like the back pages of the *New York Times* ("good, gray and dull"); at its worst, its idea of communication is exemplified by the Federal Register. This soporific quality of governmental prose matters little when it is addressed (as it usually is) to lobbyists, bureaucrats, and lawyers. But to be effective, a publicity sanction must make the public pay attention. Those who have had success in reaching the public—e.g., the television networks and the advertising agencies—recognize H. L. Mencken's maxim as an iron law: No one ever lost money underestimating the intelligence of the American public.[24]

Although there is some force in this objection, it is more a caution than a shackle.

First, it is not obvious that a formal publicity sanction must be dull. If the defendant is asked to prepare the relevant message, and if the role of the court and the prosecution is to check and approve the message rather than to create it, the outcome need not be "Tombstone" advertising. For instance, brightline, racy, messages have been agreed to by defendants in EPA penal actions against illegal use of unleaded gas.[25] Moreover, the FDA policy for corrective drug advertising is that a corrective advertisement must use the same gimmick (be it even a photo of a scantily-clad female) as was used in the original misleading advertisement;[26] far from being "good, gray and dull," some FDA counterpublicity is "wicked, gaudy and beguiling".

Second, there is no need for a formal publicity sanction to captivate the general public in the way that television networks or newspapers must do to win ratings or hold circulation. If publicity is used to punish by lowering prestige, a sufficient punitive impact may well be inflicted by publicity directed only to business executives and "opinion leaders".[27] As put succinctly by one of Madison Avenue's media consultants, it is a mistake to think in terms of broadcasting rather than narrowcasting. "Nobody wants to reach everybody, but most advertisers think of broadcasting."[28] A message beamed to the coal mining industry in the *Mining Congress Journal* has more chance of reaching peer groups than one transmitted at random through a general newspaper; a complaint in the *Lancet* about a pharmaceutical company is likely to cause more waves in the medical profession than one published in the London *Times*.

Third, it is also misleading to look at the prospective consequences of publicity sanctions as if all that mattered was their impact on outsiders. What may matter far more is the impact of adverse publicity as perceived by corporate insiders.[29] Corporations conduct surveys of public opinion in the wake of a publicity crisis, but initially they may anxiously collect critical comments in the media. In all of our case studies, we were impressed by the way in which the companies were sensitized to adverse publicity by the so-called "morgue files" compiled by their news-clipping services; in the case of Ford, Lockheed, and Air New Zealand especially, even we as outsiders found the files depressing.

The difficulty has also been raised that we expect publicity sanctions to induce the public not merely to switch brands but to change attitudes, a novel requirement which goes beyond the demands of most commercial advertising.[30] This doubt rests on the following comparisons made by Paul Lazarsfeld and Robert Merton:

> Advertising is typically directed toward the canalizing of preexisting behavior patterns or attitudes. It seldom seeks to instil new attitudes or to create significantly new behavior patterns. "Advertising pays" because it generally deals with a simple psychological situation. For Americans who have been socialized in the use of a toothbrush, it makes relatively little difference which brand of toothbrush they use. Once the gross pattern of behavior or the generic attitude has been established, it can be canalized in one direction or another. Resistance is slight. But mass propaganda typically meets a more complex situation. It may seek objectives which are at odds with deep-lying attitudes. It may seek to reshape rather than to canalize current systems of values. And the successes of advertising may only highlight the failures of propaganda. Much of the current propaganda which is aimed at abolishing deepseated ethnic and racial prejudices, for example, seems to have had little effectiveness.[31]

Although a prestige-lowering instruction differs from an instruction to switch brands, it cannot be compared with attempts to conquer racial prejudice. We are not confronted with a need for the quantum leap required to resolve the problem of racial discrimination, but with the less exacting kind of attitudinal shifts that companies themselves seek to achieve by means of corporate image advertising.

A further objection is that corporate offenses are typically so bland as to make formal publicity sanctions of scant potential sting. Four considerations, however, suggest the opposite. First, although corporate offenses are often said to be "morally neutral," the considerable empirical evidence now available indicates that this is a misconception.[32] In one recent study of attitudes toward the seriousness of crimes, a national sample of 8,000 American respondents rated white-collar crimes causing injury to persons (e.g., lethal toxic waste pollution) as extremely serious.[33] Even in 1969, well before the heightened consciousness from Watergate, another national sample surveyed by Louis Harris showed moral antipathy as opposed to neutrality toward corporate crime. A manufacturer of unsafe automobiles was regarded as worse than a mugger (68% rating the manufacturer worse versus 22% against the mugger) and a businessman who illegally fixed prices was seen as worse than a burglar (54 per cent versus 28 per cent).[34] By contrast, tax offenses and false advertising do not appear to be regarded very seriously, but the attitudes of the public toward these and other examples of morally gray violations can no longer be regarded as typical of views about corporate crime.[35]

Second, outrage should not be postulated as the minimum criterion of public concern necessary for publicity to succeed as a sanction. As illustrated by our case studies, corporations flinch at public criticism even where the intensity of such criticism is far from overwhelming. Moreover, it is worth recollecting Harry Ball and Lawrence Friedman's observation in the context of antitrust laws that "grumbling acceptance . . . serves the purposes of the legal order perfectly well; wild enthusiasm is not necessary."[36]

Third, formal publicity sanctions could exploit the novelty or controversy of corporate crimes to make an impact. What better way to overcome traditional individualistic preoccupations about criminal responsibility than publicly to highlight the reasons in particular cases why it is insufficient to rely upon individual responsibility alone?[37]

Fourth, moral perceptions of offenses are not constant over time but are shaped by law, among other considerations. So-called "morally neutral" offenses may be perceived as relatively innocuous only because the public is unfamiliar with the circumstances and implications of violation. For example, there is some evidence that, following the Watergate media-fest, the U.S. public adopted a more punitive attitude toward white-collar crime.[38] By drawing public attention to the background and significance of particular violations, publicity sanctions would promote moral reflection about corporate offenses rather than allowing them to be kept from view.[39]

Another objection is that formal publicity sanctions would face the problem of an already saturated media unable to offer coherent and clear information:

> In the language of the communications theorist, there is too much noise in the channels for any message to be heard with clarity. Unkind words about corporations come from a multitude of sources today: Naderites, editorialists, television commentators, politicians facing election campaigns, etc. The result is that the currency is being devalued. Weak criticism tends to rob accurate censure of its expressive force. The criminal conviction of the corporation should be a unique event, but it loses its special force when the public constantly receives an implicit message that all corporations are corrupt or amoral.[40]

This objection requires substantial qualification. To begin with, the proposal at issue is not that adverse publicity be used as a formal sanction against corporations on every occasion where a corporation is convicted, but that it should be used selectively as one of a number of sentencing options. Second, enforcement agencies already seem well aware that publicity should be used sparingly; as one officer of the FDA has explained,

> There are several reasons why we try to restrict the number of times we seek publicity about something. The most basic one is that we want to reserve our efforts for those situations in which we really believe something should be brought to the public's attention. We know what happened to the boy who cried "adulterated" too often. He got himself and his message "adulterated." So, the issuance of too many public warnings would simply lessen the impact of a public warning about a serious health hazard.[41]

Third, formal publicity sanctions conceivably might reduce the problem of communication noise. An accurate and authoritative message transmitted under court order could provide a homing signal rather than merely another buzz. Above all, the objection at issue fails to discriminate between a publicity sanction aimed at the general public and a publicity sanction aimed primarily at a special interest or reference group, or at opinion leaders.[42] If a publicity sanction is used for the purpose of lowering prestige or inducing governmental intervention, as we recommend, the relevant targets are persons particularly capable of distinguishing a deep hiss from a light crackle or pop.

Finally, mention should be made of the possibility of the media refusing to publish information required to be disseminated under a formal publicity sanction. A number of people with whom we have spoken have raised this possibility, pointing to the experience of Mobil when the television networks denied access for its advertisements defending the U.S. oil industry.[43] The risk is unlikely to be significant because it would almost always be in the interest of the media to accept publicity sanction advertising, which would be paid for by the defendant at normal rates; certainly the FTC has not encountered this problem in its program of corrective advertising.[44] Mobil's difficulty arose because the advertisements it wanted to televise were highly critical of comments previously made by the television networks and clearly ideological. Likewise, one can understand the media's refusing to run an advertisement that is likely to result in another advertiser taking its advertising business elsewhere.[45] A comparable obstacle to formal publicity sanctions is likely to arise only where a newspaper or television station is owned by the corporate defendant or is itself the target of the sanction; if cooperation could not be secured in such a case, resort to other sanctions (e.g., fines, equity fines, community service orders, preventive orders) would be necessary.[46] Since access to private media would thus almost invariably be available, there would be no real need to resort to government newspapers or other state-run channels of communication.[47]

Counterpublicity

If formal publicity sanctions against corporations do in fact lower corporate prestige, won't corporations respond with counterpublicity or other self-defensive tactics? This is the standard claim:

> As recent Mobil Oil advertisements about the energy crisis should remind us, the corporation can fight back—and effectively. In addition, recent Supreme Court decisions upholding the corporation's first

amendment right to comment on public issues cloud the constitutional status of any attempt to restrict such corporate rebuttals.[48]

Moreover, some commentators have invoked parody, such as the following from Art Buchwald:

> We are now in the offices of the Deal, Rehobeth and Gluckstein advertising agency where they are making a presentation to J. B. Rabbit, president of LS & D Company, who has just been ordered by the FTC to spend a million dollars to inform the public that it was misled by claims that an LS & D coffee ground additive would give people 20 extra miles to the gallon. "First we need a catchy slogan. How's this: 'Anyone who put LS & D coffee grounds in his motor ought to have his head examined'?"
>
> "That's a good slogan?" "Wait, J. B. The FTC didn't say where we had to put the ads. We've worked out a media plan. One third for newspapers, one third for magazines and one third for television. We'll place full-page ads in the *New York Herald Tribune*, the *New York Journal American*, the *New York Sun*, the *New York World Telegram* and the *Long Island Daily Press*."
>
> "But those papers don't exist any more."
>
> "That's for the FTC to find out."
>
> "Where are you going to put the commercials?"
>
> "On the . . . Howard Cosell Variety Show."
>
> "Only in Bangladesh."[49]

There is no doubt that many instances of counterpublicity and other ploys can be found.[50] The very history of modern corporate public relations began in response to government criticism and the assaults of Upton Sinclair and other muckrakers. Numerous public relations campaigns have since been conducted by corporations in order to counter the effects of adverse publicity. The Standard Oil Trust and the great railroad combinations published in newspapers throughout the United States "huge advertisements attacking with envenomed bitterness the Administration's Policy." The infamous Carl Byoir and his associates launched major campaigns on behalf of the A & P chain stores in regard to tax laws and proposed antitrust suits, and on behalf of the Eastern railroads concerning possible legislation unfavorable to trucking companies. Freedom of expression, it cannot be denied, extends to corporate speech.[51]

Account should also be taken of other foreseeable tactics.[52] A corporation might resort to a massive sales campaign to distract attention from an offense. It is also conceivable that camouflage could be laid, for example by changing the name of the company or splitting a maligned enterprise into several shiny new divisions. Less obtrusively, corporate image advertising might be used as a prestige-protective investment in the event of public criticism at some future time.

Nor should any illusion be entertained about the lengths to which some defendants might go. Carl Byoir showed the way in his campaigns for A & P and other companies by making extensive use of *suppressio veri, suggestio falsi,* and by creating seemingly independent organizations in order to distribute purportedly authoritiative favorable publicity (the "third-party" technique).[53] Strategies of this kind have now become part of public relations' stock-in-trade. ITT's corrective advertising about Profile bread sought to make consumers believe that it was they who had misinterpreted the prior misleading advertisements:

> Hi, [celebrity's name] for Profile Bread. Like all mothers, I'm concerned about nutrition and balanced meals. So, I'd like to clear up any misunderstanding you may have about Profile Bread from its advertising or even its name. Does Profile have fewer calories than other breads? No. Profile has about the same per ounce as other breads. To be exact, Profile has seven fewer calories per slice. That's because Profile is sliced thinner. But eating Profile will not cause you to lose weight. A reduction of 7 calories is insignificant. It's total calories and balanced nutrition that count. And Profile can help you achieve a balanced meal because it provides protein and B vitamins as well as other nutrients. How does my family feel about Profile? Well, my husband likes Profile toast; the children love Profile sandwiches and I prefer Profile to any other bread. So you see, at our house, delicious taste makes Profile a family affair.[54]

Many examples can also be found of the third-party technique, one being Nestlé's promotion of "The Corporation Haters," an article in *Fortune* that vehemently attacked the activists pressing the infant formula boycott campaign.[55]

Yet would countertactics be as successful against formal publicity sanctions as has been speculated? Although corporations indulge in generalized image advertising, there is little incentive to launch a determined counterpublicity campaign against a formal publicity order. To begin with, there is sheer cost; public relations exercises of any intensity and imagination are hugely expensive.[56] Second, there is no guarantee of success in counterattack. On the contrary, there is a risk of attracting more adverse publicity; thus, when Mobil tried its hand at parody by publishing a spoof in response to a column by Russell Baker in the *New York Times,* it was exposed to further ridicule.[57] Third, formal court-ordered pronouncements of adjudicated guilt carry the prestige of law and hence normally have more credibility than rejoinders by newspaper reporters or corporate executives.

These points aside, our case studies suggest that counterpublicity is likely to be exceptional. All companies tried to explain their side of the story, but a large majority made a conscious decision *not* to resort to anything that could realistically be described as a counterpublicity campaign; the only genuine counterpublicity campaigns were those run by J. P. Stevens, IBM, ITT, and Ford in its defense at the Pinto trial. Moreover, only one counterpublicity campaign— that of ITT—was clearly successful,[58] and the total cost of the ITT campaign ran to eight figures. The main reason given by the companies for not launching counterpublicity attacks was the risk of further adverse publicity; it was better, according to the advice of public relations firms, to reduce the "time window" of exposure.

Although counterpublicity would seem a small threat, the law still might well respond to that possibility by giving corporate defendants a counterincentive. If corporate reactions to harm-causing acts or events were explicitly stressed by the court at the time of sentence, corporations would be faced publicly with two choices: to resist change and rebel against criticism with counterpublicity, or to respond constructively and gain credit officially for having done so.[59] This strategy is suggested by the turnaround towards compliance which Allied Chemical deliberately undertook in the wake of the Kepone crisis and for which it eventually gained some praise in the media.

Formal and Informal Publicity

Several of the corporate executives with whom we spoke were adamant that there was no need for a formal publicity sanction of the kind recommended by the Brown Commission.[60] In their opinion, serious corporate offenses almost invariably would attract publicity informally in the news media, and that was enough. However, because informal publicity can be selective, brief or inaccurate, formal publicity has a supplementary role to play.

One survey of the newspaper reports on the sentences handed down in the electric equipment cases showed that although the story made the news, most newspapers devoted substantially all their headline and column space to the executives who received prison sentences.[61] According to Dershowitz, who undertook this survey, "None of the newspapers emphasized that *corporations* were actually guilty of committing *crimes*" (as explained in the GE case study, however, this is a misleading assessment—at least the *New York Times* repeatedly referred to the company's liability for conspiracy).[62]

A similar survey, with like results, has been made by Sandra Evans and Richard Lundman of the newspaper accounts of another price-fixing scandal—the folding-carton conspiracies in the mid-1970s.[63] Of the 29 newspapers surveyed, only 16 covered corporate pleas and sentences. Of these 16, 4 named all 23 corporate defendants, 1 named 20, two named 12, one named five, five named one, and the remaining newspaper identified none. Moreover, only one newspaper used the word "crime" in its account. Despite the gravity of the prosecutions, the newspapers again had failed to provide a "frequent, prominent or criminally-oriented coverage."[64]

This points up precisely one of the advantages of formal over informal publicity. Some degree of publicity could be assured in cases otherwise likely to be neglected, by requiring corporate defendants to publish certain agreed-upon information about their crimes in specified media. In other words, a publicity vacuum could be avoided by coerced advertising, such as that used by the FTC for corrective advertising. Moreover, a detailed and accurate statement of the findings and disposition made in a case could be transmitted. A good illustration is the notice required under the remedial publicity order in *NLRB v. J. P. Stevens & Co. Inc.*[65] This notice detailed the nature of the injunctive relief granted against J. P. Stevens and recorded the denunciation of the company made by the U.S. Court of Appeals in its judgment:

> Stevens has acted in contempt of our Court decrees not once but twice, involving over thirty individual violations. . . .
> We do not take lightly the flouting of our orders not once, but twice. Nor can we view with equanimity the refusal of a large employer to abide by the law of the land and refrain from interfering with the rights of its employees. Should there be repetition of the Company's contemptuous conduct in the future, we are quite prepared to consider more drastic sanctions both for the Company and for the individual respondents than those ordered here. In short, we are determined that respondents shall comply with the provisions of the National Labor Relations Act and that the decrees of this court ordering them to do so shall be obeyed.

Formal orders would enable publicity to be placed in channels of communication superior to those that might be reached by informal publicity. This is suggested by the corrective advertising order made against STP Corporation in relation to false claims about the engine-saving virtues of its oil products.[66] The offending advertisements appeared in *Auto News, Car & Driver, Hot Rod, Popular Mechanics, Playboy, Road & Track, Scientific American,* and a number of other popular magazines. By contrast, the corrective advertisments appeared in *Business Week, Barron's, Forbes, Harvard Business Review, National Geographic, Newsweek,* the *Wall Street Journal,* and other opinion-leading publications. The FTC strategy was more to administer a shock to STP than to correct the false impressions previously created among consumers.[67] It does not follow that the publicity used by the FTC in the STP case "was an ineffective control mechanism":[68] The corrective advertising may have had a salutary deterrent or retributive effect on STP by lowering its prestige among those reading *Newsweek* and the other publications chosen by the FTC (admittedly, the FTC had no authority to use corrective advertising for punitive purposes, but that is not to deny the de facto punitive effect of what it required STP to do).[69] What the STP case indicates is the need not only to direct corrective advertising toward consumers previously misled, but also to exploit publicity formally as a punishment by directing it toward persons whose attitudes and opinions are relevant to corporate prestige.

Interventionist and Non-Interventionist Control

Why resort to publicity as a formal sanction when corporate crime might be controlled more effectively by directly regulating the internal affairs of corporations?

Over the last decade especially, interventionist regulation has often been suggested as the best route to corporate crime control. Christopher Stone has argued for a variety of preventive measures (e.g., mandatory injunctions) designed to rectify the inner workings of corporations that display lack of self-control.[70] The ideal commended is that

Instead of treating the corporation's inner processes as a "black box", to be influenced only indirectly through threats laid about the environment like traps, we need more straightforward "intrusions" into the corporation's decision structure and processes than society has yet undertaken.[71]

300

In regard to the Kepone crisis, for instance, Stone has argued that probation should have been used forcefully and intrusively to inquire into the organizational failings which led to the disaster, and that each of the corporations involved should then have been required to make its own recommendations for preventing a repetition. These recommendations might have included:

1. Alterations in the organization's pattern of operation, including the adoption of new standards for matters such as the monitoring of toxic-substance handling and the medical examination of employees.
2. Changes in personnel, including firings, suspensions, and hirings.
3. Establishment of new positions with specified tasks and responsibilities; in the case of Allied Chemical, liaisons with companies processing materials under contract.
4. Implementation of new information procedures designed to assure that appropriate data are adequately gathered and transmitted to corporate officers with the necessary authority.[72]

This approach focuses on defective structural arrangements within organizations, but the anatomy of corporate crime is more complex.[73] As Simeon Kriesberg has indicated, corporate crime may stem not only from defective standard operating procedures, but also from rational value maximizing (e.g., where illicit profits exceed the costs of possible fines and other consequences of conviction) and from bureaucratic politics (e.g., where an offense results from non-cooperation on the part of one organizational faction).[74] Where an offense results, even in part, from rational value maximizing or bureaucratic politics, insisting only upon rectification of defective operating procedures may be too limited a response. In terms of rational value maximization, it makes sense to attack the corporation's prestige by resorting to the sanction of adverse publicity. In terms of bureaucratic politics, adverse publicity might also be perceived as a threat to the secrecy which nurtures the growth of informal criminogenic coalitions.[75] In short, what is needed is not a single-minded interventionist strategy, but a many-sided approach with flexible use of a wide range of sentencing options; these should include not just mandatory injunctions but also adverse publicity and other possibilities.[76]

So little is known about the impact of sanctions against corporations that it is premature to depend heavily on any one kind. There is no substitute for experience in the field; as wide as possible a variety of sanctions against corporations should be available until we have a much larger pool of empirical information from which to refine policies of corporate crime control.

Publicity is hardly an interventionist sanction. It probes and prods, whereas a mandatory injunction dictates. At the same time, publicity is a far cry from the hands-off attitude of the fine. It can be used to direct the public spotlight into the black box of organizational control, and can highlight the need for particular disciplinary, structural, or other organizational action.[77] The *modus operandi* of its intrusion into corporate internal affairs is thus exploratory and agitative, a combination which complements intervention, addresses the weaknesses of non-intervention, and helps to keep corporations and regulators on their mettle.

Corporate and Individual Targets of Publicity

Would it not be more effective to direct adverse publicity at individual offenders rather than their corporate employers? This question cannot be answered simply in the affirmative or negative, but warrants a qualified response in three parts. First, cases often arise where, for reasons of efficacy or justice, individual criminal responsibility cannot be insisted upon; second, where individual criminal responsibility can be imposed effectively and justly, there is probably no need to publicize the fact formally as well as informally; and third, where individual criminal responsibility is not imposed, but a corporation is held responsible, pre-sentence or probationary orders should be available to generate and disclose information about the nature and extent of individual accountability for the offense subject to sentence.

Western legal systems are dominated by individualistic conceptions of fault and guilt. However, it is increasingly recognized that there are many situations where it is impractical, unjust, or impossible to assign individual responsibility for corporate crime. The task of investigating offenses committed on behalf of organizations can involve labyrinthian paths and hence prove beyond the bounds of practicality if the aim is to proceed against individual personnel; even the full-scale investigation conducted by the Federal Bureau of Investigation and the Justice Department in the electrical equipment conspiracies could not support a satisfactory case against all the personnel implicated. In other situations, the difficulty is not impracticality but injustice. It can be oppressive to proceed exclusively against individual personnel, especially minions,[78] where they have been exposed to extreme pressure to make profits, or where organizational resources, equipment, or operating procedures have been inadequate for the purposes of achieving compliance. An even clearer case in point is the so-called "structural crime" where efforts to impose individual responsibility on the basis of fault must fail because no one person (or conspiracy among persons) has intentionally, recklessly, or even negligently contributed to the corporate harmdoing, and yet where collective negligence is evident.[79]

Few better illustrations can be found than Air New Zealand's Mt. Erebus crash of a DC10. The main cause of the crash was the mistake made by several staff in programming the aircraft to fly directly towards Mt. Erebus without telling the aircrew; that mistake, so said a Royal Commission, was directly attributable "not so much to the persons who made it, but to the incompetent administrative airline procedures which made the mistake possible."[80]

Similarly, assuming that Pinto gas tanks created an unjustifiable risk of injury, it is doubtful whether any individual in Ford was really to blame:

> Was it the president or some other senior executive who never read the safety reports, but insisted on a cheap, profitable design? Or the lowly engineer who fashioned a design to the specification of others? Or, was it a middle executive in between who chose the only design, even if its defects were known to him, which complied with cost specifications imposed on him from a higher level?[81]

Granted such considerations, should adverse publicity be used formally against individual personnel where it is possible to hold them criminally responsible?

Where individual criminal responsibility can be imposed effectively and justly, it is probably unnecessary to resort to formal publicity orders. The conviction and sentencing of corporate executives almost invariably attracts widespread informal publicity. Moreover, the case for deploying adverse publicity formally against defendants is stronger in relation to corporations, largely because of the very limited range of sentencing options in our present corporate criminal law.[82]

The main question remains whether publicity should be directed at individual staff members after a corporation has been convicted given the inefficacy or injustice of trying to convict them as individuals. A concrete proposal to cover this situation, having its genesis in the McCloy report documenting Gulf Oil's slush funds and bribes, has been advanced by Coffee.[83] The McCloy report, prepared by outside counsel, triggered substantial procedural reforms at Gulf Oil and hastened the resignation of officials named in it. Furthermore, the revelations in the report were sufficiently interesting to be picked up by the press, and the report itself later became a paperback bestseller.[84] Taking this cue, Coffee has recommended that corporate offenders be required to employ outside counsel to prepare a McCloy-style report that names the key personnel involved and outlines in readable form what they did. Mandatory probationary or pre-sentence reports would be prepared "in considerable factual depth in the expectation that such studies will either find an audience in their own right or, more typically, provide the data base for investigative journalism."[85]

This proposal has substantial merit. First and foremost, it would enable critical public scrutiny of conduct beyond the reach of individual criminal law:

> Because courts and legislatures find vicarious criminal liability ethically troubling, the negligent official faces little threat that he will be the target of a criminal prosecution, even where his actions or inactions are a proximate cause of the corporation's offense. Similarly, the supervising official who "looks the other way" and tolerates misconduct by his subordinates is also likely to be effectively immune from the civil law's reach. Both, however, are within the reach of a publicity sanction. The mandated corporate self-study can focus both on active misconduct and on the passive negligence of senior officials.[86]

Moreover, the focus provided would promote deterrence in three useful ways:

> First, the manager suffers a loss of public and self-respect, which some research suggests is the most potent deterrent for the middle class potential offender. Second, adverse publicity substantially reduces the official's chances for future promotion or advancement within the firm. Competition for advancement is keen within almost all firms, and competitors of the culpable official can be relied upon to use adverse publicity about their rival to their own advantage. SEC proxy disclosure requirements may pose a further barrier to such an official's advancement. Finally, disclosure of the identity of the culpable official also invites a derivative suit by which any costs visited on the firm can be shifted (at least in part) to the individual.[87]

The strongest objection to this proposal is that it would be unjust to "[substitute] for a criminal trial, with all its procedural safeguards, a trial by a special counsel, like John McCloy, or by investigative journalists, like Woodward and Bernstein, or Mike Wallace."[88] However, this objection assumes that individual criminal law is the only legitimate social control over internal corporate misconduct. Internal corporate discipline operates largely as a private system of law, with its own rules of liability and standards of proof, many of which differ substantially from those pertinent under criminal law.[89] Provided that personnel subjected to the operation of internal discipline are given the right to answer charges made against them, and provided further that the restrictions upon prejudicial pre-trial publicity are complied with in relation to personnel subject to criminal charges, there is no warrant for keeping the outcome of internal disciplinary proceedings secret.

Indeed, there is positive merit in making the outcome of disciplinary enquiries public because in addition to imposing stigma, such reports may also clear the names of people suffering unwarranted stigma. Consider the report of the special tribunal established by the British Parliament to enquire into responsibility for the Aberfan disaster in which a waste tip owned by the National Coal Board washed down a valley killing 144 people.[90] Before this report was released we are told that "the tipping gang and its charge-hand (Mr. Leslie Davies) have all been bitterly reviled in Aberfan and treated as pariahs." However, the report in no uncertain terms cleared their names: " . . . We absolve them from all blame for the disaster . . . . The tip gang, including Mr. Davies, were . . . wholly untrained and quite incapable of observing the significance of what they saw." Instead, blame was placed on the National Coal Board and certain of its engineers for failing to have any policies on waste tip safety and in failing to monitor tip movements.

It is incorrect to assume that the proposal put forward by Coffee would *substitute* kangaroo-court justice for criminal trial. The proposal is not that criminal prosecutions of suspected corporate personnel be abandoned. Rather, it contemplates disclosure of internal disciplinary action in cases where, for the reasons quoted, corporate personnel are not subjected to criminal prosecution at that time. Doubtless, improvements can and should be made to the criminal process so as to enable the successful prosecution of a larger number of guilty personnel (above all, by provision of more staff for enforcement), but that is not to deny the value of publicity as a means for activating and enhancing a different sphere of regulation—internal corporate discipline.

Financial and Non-Financial Loss

Another claim is that formal publicity orders would be impractical due to the unlikelihood of discouraging consumers from buying a defendant's products or subscribing to its shares. It is contended that consumer behavior is rarely affected by adverse publicity. Mention has already been made of the views of Dershowitz and Packer to this effect;[91] much the same position has been endorsed by Leonard Leigh:

> As a general proposition, publicity and the stigma of conviction are likely to prove useful with respect to regulatory legislation, the purpose of which is to ensure adherence to proper standards, particularly with respect to foodstuffs, drugs, and other articles of consumption. Otherwise it is likely to go unnoticed. Yet to be effective, the stigma would have to be such that the corporation's clientele were much less ready to deal with it.[92]

These views seem to us incorrect.

To begin with, prestige cannot be equated with economic position. Although the theoretical literature on organizational behavior sometimes links prestige closely to financial standing, the orthodox view is that prestige is a goal highly valued in itself.[93] This is reflected in practice. Corporations pay large amounts to promote their public image, not merely for the purpose of financial aggrandisement, but in order to bolster their reputation.[94]

Is the prestige-lowering capacity of adverse publicity likely to be perceived as significant within an organization? The findings of our case studies support an affirmative answer. In all but two of 17 cases (ITT; BHP's Appin Mine disaster) the executives interviewed reported that the adverse publicity crisis had caused a perceived drop in corporate prestige. By contrast, in only three cases were sales affected at all severely. Moreover, it was felt at the same time that the individual prestige of senior management had been lowered.

Account should also be taken of the impact of adverse publicity on other non-financial areas of corporate sensitivity, notably morale and freedom from distraction and governmental intervention. The findings of our case studies support the hypothesis that adverse publicity is likely to have some potency as a non-financial sanction in these further respects.[95]

Even if formal publicity sanctions could be made to work, the attack continues, they would have unwanted side-effects, namely public fixation upon corporate deviance, excessive spillovers upon workers and consumers, and detraction from cool and sensitive regulation.[96]

The claim is often heard that adverse publicity is an extremist method of social control which distorts public perceptions of corporate deviance. A former editor of *Fortune* has criticized the lack of attention to the compliance side of business behavior in these terms:

> There is no guarantee—or even a probability—that if business conduct quickly improved the public would hear the news for years, if ever. Some scandals will always be available to observers who will not tackle the hard task of communicating business normality.[97]

More recently, a phalanx of books has been issued defending corporate capitalism against further assault.[98]

One response to this claim is to point out that it suffers itself from distortion. First, account must be taken of the good which results from publicity attacks. In all the cases studied in this book, some worthwhile reform resulted, and in many cases the changes were major (e.g., the Toxic Substances Control Act, as crystallized by the Kepone case). Second, blame can hardly be laid just at the door of critics—corporations themselves have frequently distorted reality by subjecting the public to a barrage of public relations newspeak.[99]

A further response is that a denunciatory publicity sanction should be used selectively in sentencing. Except in flagrant cases of violation, or where there is a poor record of non-compliance in the past, a corporate defendant should be given the opportunity to disclose what it has done by way of disciplinary or other reaction to the event giving rise to prosecution. A denunciatory publicity order would normally be appropriate only in the event of an inadequate corporate reaction, such as refusing to undertake satisfactory internal disciplinary action or failing to rectify poor standard operating procedures. Were adverse publicity held in reserve in this way, corporations would be given the chance to indicate what they have done to achieve satisfactory compliance. If they failed to show an adequate performance, any resulting ignominy

would be self-inflicted. If they come up with an exemplary performance, their virtue should be announced by the court as a reward.

Would formal publicity sanctions result in excessive spillovers
(e.g., employee layoffs, price increases)? The criticism has been
made that:

> Adverse publicity is something of a loose cannon; its exact impact
> cannot be reliably estimated nor is it controllable so that only the
> guilty are affected. Here, the recent Ford Pinto case supplies a par-
> adigm: although acquitted, Ford's ability to market the Pinto has
> obviously been impaired. The impact of reduced sales or the termi-
> nation of a product line once again falls disproportionately on workers
> at the bottom of the hierarchy. If we are willing to bear these costs
> (as sometimes we must), it seems easier to rely on even cash fines in
> preference to the wholly unpredictable impact of a legal stigma.[100]

Putting aside the issue of uncertainty, which is discussed in a later
section, this criticism seems unpersuasive.[101]

No one would dispute that, if the purpose of formal publicity
sanctions were to inflict monetary loss, it would be simpler to rely
on fines.[102] But the primary rationale for publicity as a sanction is
to inflict loss of prestige, a purpose beyond the capacity of fines.
This being so, the main intended impact of a publicity sanction—
loss of prestige—would be borne, not by workers, but by those
occupying more prestigious managerial ranks. Granted, the lowering
of prestige could also occasion a significant loss of sales. However,
as summarized in Chapter 19, the findings of our case studies
indicate that serious financial spillovers are likely to be the exception
rather than the rule. In any event, in cases where serious financial
spillovers are likely to occur (as in the Ford Pinto situation) it is
not at all obvious that the financial impact of a publicity sanction
would fall "disproportionately on workers at the bottom of the
hierarchy". Merely to say that a publicity sanction against a corporation would hit innocent people as well as guilty individuals is
to beg the issue: The same is true of *any* sanction imposed upon
a corporate entity.[103] (It is unnecessary here to question the util-
itarian and retributive footings upon which the punishment of
corporate entities has rested since at least the beginning of this
century. Individual desert cannot be an absolute principle in a
society where corporations are valued as a means of production
and distribution.)[104] The critical question is whether any overspills
impose a disproportionately heavy burden. In the context where
loss of sales is most likely to result from a formal publicity sanction—

dangerous products—the risk of imposing financial overspills on workers must be weighed up against the risk of concealing from consumers the dangers of a product which has given rise to the imposition of criminal liability upon its manufacturer; the impact of not reducing sales or terminating a product may fall lethally on consumers at the bottom of the production line.

It has also been urged that criminal publicity cannot compare with cool and sensitive regulation under civil procedures or negotiated compliance:

> The criminal process inherently involves adverse publicity, and, to this extent, some element of the punishment precedes the conviction. Publicity begins with the indictment, and an acquittal does not fully undo the damage. In contrast, the quieter, less public character of civil-law adjudication allows us to withhold the impact of adverse publicity until there has been a finding.
>
> Although a corporate defendant may be required to give notice of its conviction to victims, more serious problems emerge when the government itself seeks to broadcast the significance of the conviction outside the courtroom. In the frequent case where the defendant plea bargains and the government in return drops some of the charges in the indictment, it would seem improper for the government to discuss unproved and unadmitted allegations in its publicity efforts. Such an attempt would implicitly violate the plea bargain and would involve the government in possibly unconstitutional forms of stigmatization. Similar problems arise where officially prepared publicity describing the corporation's conduct alleges misbehavior by unindicted corporate officials. Restraint seems necessary in these circumstances, but it is likely to give a fragmentary, disjointed character to governmental efforts at publicity.[105]

However, this civil vs. criminal contrast seems much too overdrawn. The problem of prejudicial publicity is hardly confined to the criminal process; SEC allegations of civil violations are often accompanied by a barrage of adverse publicity prior to adjudication.[106] Besides, there is neither need nor justification in the criminal process for formal publicity sanctions to disclose unproved and unadmitted allegations, much less to allege misbehavior by unindicted officials. In the context of plea-bargaining and other forms of negotiated settlement, the threat of a formal publicity sanction would be used as a bargaining chip by enforcement officers in their negotiations with defendants; it would be available as an ultimate weapon should there be an unsatisfactory corporate response. It need not violate any constitutional or other protections. In regard to unindicted officials, formal publicity orders should not be used to allege criminal offenses, but to report the outcome of disciplinary enquiries undertaken by the corporate employer; this is Coffee's proposal, endorsed earlier.[107]

Uncertainty

Finally, there is the well-known concern that the impact of formal publicity sanctions is too uncertain to satisfy the demand of justice that punishment be proportionate to offense. This is often believed to be the strongest objection to the use of publicity as a formal sanction.

The standard reservation about such uncertainty may be summarized as follows.[108] A sanction implemented by publicity is a sanction that is indefinite in impact. Unlike the fine, no certain penalty is imposed at the time of conviction; sentence is determined later by the capricious jury of public opinion. Furthermore, the sentence can be mediated by counterpublicity. Control of the amount of publicity sanction imposed is thus removed from the hands of a court, and legislative upper and lower limits upon such publicity are difficult to set. Publicity sanctions are also uncertain because their impact will often vary according to the characteristics and circumstances of particular offenders. Some corporations will fear loss of corporate prestige more than others.[109] The view may be that no publicity is bad publicity; for example, in an Australian case, *Larmer v. Power Machinery Pty. Ltd.*,[110] the company's sales of electric welders increased by 15 per cent after the media published details of the conviction and fine it received for misleading advertising under the Trade Practices Act.[111]

These counter arguments rest on a false assumption, namely that the actual impact of a sanction in any case must be finite and proportionate to the relevant offense. This is not the criterion now applied in the criminal justice system. The most that is required to satisfy the principle of proportionality is formal proportionate quantification of sentence in advance, irrespective of the degree of actual impact upon an offender.[112]

In the present application of the principle of proportionality to imprisonment or fines, all that is measured is the length of term or amount of money. No attempt is made to achieve proportionality of actual impact upon the offender because the actual impact is not only difficult to measure but also infinitely various. Imprisonment for some may be a haven away from a miserable or dangerous existence; for others, it is worse than death. Likewise, a $1000 fine for indecency might take a penny-pinching pensioner to the brink of bankruptcy, but a bottom-pinching Rockefeller might laugh all the way to the bank.

It might be replied that the principle of proportionality, as now applied, at least requires the amount of punishment to be quantified, whereas quantification of formal publicity sanctions would not lie in the hands of a sentencing court. However, there is nothing in this point. As is apparent from the practice adopted in numerous corrective advertising orders and EPA penalty consent agreements, it is possible to quantify formal publicity orders in terms of media time or space, and cost.[113]

It might then be contended that the principle of proportionality requires that the impact of punishment be typically within a narrow band of variation: Imprisonment and fines, it could be argued, satisfy such a requirement, whereas the impact of formal publicity sanctions would cover a broader range because of the fickle nature of public opinion. This attempted distinction, however, depends on an empirical claim which goes far beyond the standard claim that publicity is merely uncertain in its impact. The claim is dubious.

The findings of our case studies suggest that the impact of adverse publicity on corporate prestige does not oscillate between extremes,[114] and sales and stock prices were seriously affected only in a minority of instances. Moreover, it is difficult to believe that fines do not vary widely in their impact; the $7 million paid by Ford in fines for emissions-testing fraud was not crippling at the time, but Ford executives pointed out to us that the impact upon their struggling company today would be quite different.[115]

The further rejoinder may be made that, as a matter of reform, the sentencing process is moving toward the ideal of proportionality of actual impact, and that the fine-tuning required to achieve this ideal could not readily be attained in the case of formal publicity sanctions. By contrast, the fine might seem more readily adjustable:

Although the impact of a fine may vary according to wealth, or be reduced where *D* compensates by increasing the price of its products, it is at least comparatively easy to take possible variations into consideration. In order to balance variations in wealth, fines could be based upon a percentage of *D*'s average annual turnover for the previous four or five years. The passing of fines on to consumers could be discouraged by an approach which requires the payment of a provisional fine, the final amount to be determined according to a percentage of *D*'s annual turnover for say two years after conviction.

311

Publicity sanctions do not offer similar opportunities for achieving an even impact.[116]

However, the difference ultimately seems minimal. The actual impact of fines would still be subject to current profitability, expected future profitability, access to loans, interest rates, monopoly status (and hence ability to pass a fine on to consumers), and other variables of fiscal sensitivity which, although critical, can be assessed only roughly in the sentencing process.[117] An approximate assessment of likely impact could also be made in the case of publicity sanctions; indeed, this type of assessment already is made where the impact of informal adverse publicity needs to be taken into account as a mitigating factor in sentencing.[118]

Conclusion

The potential advantages of formal publicity as a sanction against corporate offenders are widely recognized but inertia as well as skepticism about a variety of issues has blocked reform. In this chapter we have argued that the grounds upon which this skepticism is based are unpersuasive. Some objections are based upon false theoretical assumptions. Others neglect the possibilities of responsive reform. Above all, most depend on empirical claims which are inconsistent with the findings of the cases in this study.

We advance two recommendations. The first is that publication of the details about an offense be made available as a court-ordered sentence against corporate offenders. Second, pre-sentence or probation orders against corporate offenders should be used to require disclosure of organizational reforms and disciplinary action undertaken as a result of an offense.

Implementation of the first of these recommendations would require legislation along the lines proposed in 1970 by the U.S. National Commission on Reform of Federal Criminal Laws. To recapitulate, the Commission proposed the introduction of the following provision into the sentencing provisions of the U. S. Criminal Code:

When an organization is convicted of an offense, the court may, in addition to or in lieu of imposing other authorized sanctions, . . . require the organization to give appropriate publicity to the conviction by notice to the class or classes of persons or sector of the public interested in or affected by the conviction, by advertising in designated areas or by designated media, or otherwise . . . .[119]

This proposal is sufficiently broad to allow publication orders to be used in sentencing not only for punitive purposes but also as a remedy (e.g., corrective advertising, notification of prospective civil rights of action).[120] It is also couched so as to maximize flexibility of choice of media or content of message.[121] However, in stipulating that the publicity required be "to the conviction," the provision is too narrow. Power should exist to require a defendant to publish details of the organizational reforms or internal disciplinary action undertaken.

The second recommendation—that use be made of pre-sentence or probationary orders to provide McCloy-style reports—could be put into practice without enabling legislation, but it is likely to be neglected unless given statutory recognition.[122] Ideally, this sentencing option would be incorporated within a double-track legislative scheme of corporate disclosure (e.g., in a criminal code). The first track would be immunized voluntary disclosure, as proposed in Chapter 20, and the second would be mandatory disclosure, as recommended here. Corporate defendants could proceed along the first track and gain immunization, provided that (a) they are given this option by the prosecuting authorities, and (b) they decide to exercise the option and discharge their obligation under it by preparing and filing a satisfactory disclosure report. Defendants not proceeding along this first track would be subject to prosecution and, in the event of conviction, mandatory disclosure would be authorized as a possible sentence; the degree and type of disclosure required for satisfactory compliance would be the same as for immunized voluntary disclosure.

It would be a supreme feat of clairvoyance to specify the criteria that might eventually govern the application of the three different kinds of publicity sanction recommended—publication orders, immunized voluntary disclosure, and mandatory disclosure.[123] However, it is at least possible broadly to typify their operation. Publication orders would be warranted in egregious cases where emphatic stigmatizing is necessary for the purposes of specific or general deterrence, as in instances of repeated violations or failure despite clear warning to rectify poor operating procedures. By contrast, immunized voluntary disclosure would be particularly useful in complex cases where the costs of investigation and trial were enormous, or in circumstances where a corporation is trustworthy and indicates that it wishes to redeem itself by instituting an exemplary

313

program of corrective action. For their part, mandatory disclosure orders would cover a middle range of situations where the offense is not sufficiently egregious to justify strong public denunciation, but where immunized disclosure would be inappropriate because a conviction is needed to facilitate "coattail" civil suits, to define or to symbolize the type of harm proscribed by an offense, or to overcome intransigence on the part of a defendant. In practical terms, mandatory disclosure would be the most important. Many corporations may not be prepared to risk voluntary disclosure in exchange only for immunization from criminal liability (they would still be liable to civil suit, and individual personnel could even be placed in greater danger of criminal prosecution) and, in the event of conviction, mandatory disclosure would usually be less drastic than the imposition of an outrightly stigmatic publication order.

This is not to suggest that one or another of these three kinds of publicity sanction would be suitable in every case. On the contrary, to release a flood of scarlet letters would be misguided because corporate offenses and offenders are so diverse as to compel reliance on a disparate armory of sanctions; fines, preventive orders, and many other measures all have a significant role to play. But publicity sanctions, we contend, should be prominent in that armory.

APPENDIX A

Southern Wholesale, Inc., EPA
Docket No. CAA(211)–60 (1980)
(consent agreement)

8. Respondent shall place, within sixty (60) days of the issuance of the Final Order, four (4) one-quarter (¼) page advertisements describing the air quality and automobile maintenance benefits of unleaded gasoline in the *Charlotte Sunday*, Charlotte, North Carolina. These advertisements are to run consecutively, one per week over a four week period. . . . Respondent agrees to supply a copy of each advertisement to Complainant when each is run.

9. Respondent shall obtain within sixty (60) days of the issuance of the Final Order, forty (40) sixty (60) second radio announcements describing the air quality and automobile maintenance benefits of unleaded gasoline on both WSOC–AM and WIST–AM Radio. These radio announcements will be run over a month period during the morning and/or evening hours. . . .

Highway Oil Inc., EPA,
Docket No. CAA(211)–17 (1980)
(consent agreement)

4. Respondent shall, at cost to Respondent, purchase the following services:

At a cost of approximately four hundred dollars ($400) for each flight, for five (5) flights, on five (5) different dates, airplane-towed banners shall be towed so that the messages on them (as described below) can be seen by as many persons as is practical of those in attendance at the five 1980 Kansas City Royals baseball games referred to below. The messages to be towed are as follows (the messages are to be alternated, with one being towed on the first date and the other being towed on the following date, and so on):
   "UNLEADED GAS MAKES CENT$"
   "UNLEADED GAS KEEPS THE AIR CLEAN"
The characters shall be such that they may be easily seen and read by those attending the baseball games.
   The dates of the Kansas City Royals baseball games shall be chosen so that the banners reciting the above messages are calculated to be seen by as many persons as possible. The games selected for the flights shall be games that are scheduled to commence no later than 7:45 p.m. The flights shall commence no earlier than fifteen minutes before game time and, for night games, shall be completed before 9:00 p.m.

Notes

Chapter 1

1. Marshall B. Clinard and Peter C. Yeager, *Corporate Crime* (New York: Free Press, 1980), pp. 318–322.

2. By "crime" we mean misbehavior which constitutes an offense under existing law, whether the offense is penalized criminally or civilly (e.g., an OSHA violation not causing death is penalized civilly by fine). By "offense" we mean to include offenses which some observers would describe as *mala prohibita* as well as offenses *mala in se* (as to this unsatisfactory distinction, see Note, "The Distinction between Mala Prohibita and Mala in Se," *Columbia Law Review* 30 (1930): 74–86). By "corporate" crime we mean crime attributable to a corporate entity or any responsible individual persons acting on its behalf. For the purposes of this book it is unnecessary to attempt a fully armored definition of corporate crime: Our concern is not to assess the exact incidence of the phenomenon but to explore the use of publicity as a means of control. For this purpose, data on the impact of publicity on non-criminal deviance can be as useful as data from instances of proven corporate offenses. Accordingly, it would be pointless here to enter into the hoary debate about definition and measurement of corporate crime. Cf. Leonard Orland, "Reflections on Corporate Crime: Law in Search of Theory and Scholarship," *American Criminal Law Review* 17 (1980): 501–520, pp. 504–510. By "control" of corporate crime we mean to include control not only by formal command and sanction but also informally via disclosure effects as discussed in Note, "Disclosure as a Legislative Device," *Harvard Law Review* 76 (1963): 273–293.

3. Francis E. Rourke, *Secrecy and Publicity: Dilemmas of Democracy* (Baltimore: Johns Hopkins Press, 1961), ch. 6; Douglas M. Branson, "Progress in the Art of Social Accounting and Other Arguments for Disclosure on Corporate Social Responsibility," *Vanderbilt Law Review* 29 (1976): 539–683, p. 624.

4. Quoted in David Boulton, *The Grease Machine* (New York: Harper & Row, 1978), p. 253.

5. See generally Edwin H. Sutherland, *White Collar Crime* (New York: Dryden 1949), pp. 49–51; Gilbert Geis "Deterring Corporate Crime," in Ralph Nader and Mark J. Green, eds., *Corporate Power in America* (New York: Penguin, 1977): 182–197, pp. 185–192; Brent Fisse, "The Social Policy of Corporate Criminal Responsibility," *Adelaide Law Review* 8 (1978): 361–412, pp. 391–394.

6. Morton Mintz and Jerry S. Cohen, *America, Inc.—Who Owns and Operates the United States* (New York: Dial, 1971), p. xiv.

7. P. F. Strawson, "Freedom and Resentment," *Proceedings of the British Academy* 58 (1962): 187–211.

8. H. D. Lewis, "The Non-Moral Notion of Collective Responsibility," in Peter A. French, ed., *Individual and Collective Responsibility: The Massacre at My-Lai* (Cambridge, Mass.: Schenkman, 1972): 119–144, p. 143.

9. Thomas Donaldson, *Corporations and Morality* (Englewood Cliffs, N.J.: Prentice-Hall, 1982), ch. 2; Gerhard O.W. Mueller, "Mens Rea and the Corporation," *University of Pittsburgh Law Review* 19 (1957): 21–50. Cf. Peter A. French, "The Corporation as a Moral Person," *American Philosophical Quarterly* 16 (1979): 207–215; Peter A. French, *Collective and Corporate Responsibility* (New York: Columbia University Press, 1984).

10. John Braithwaite, *Corporate Crime in the Pharmaceutical Industry* (London: Routledge & Kegan Paul, 1983), chs. 2–4; Mark J. Green, Beverly C. Moore, Jr., and Bruce Wasserstein, *The Closed Enterprise System* (New York: Bantam, 1972), pp. 192–208.

11. John E. Conklin, *"Illegal but not Criminal": Business Crime in America* (Engelwood Cliffs, N.J.: Prentice-Hall, 1977), p. 132; Herbert L. Packer, *The Limits of the Criminal Sanction* (Stanford, Calif.: Stanford University Press, 1968), p. 362; U.S. National Commission on Reform of Federal Criminal Laws, *Study Draft* (Washington, D.C.: U.S. Government Printing Office, 1970), s. 405. Cf. Sanford H. Kadish, "Some Observations on the Use of Sanctions in Enforcing Economic Regulations," *University of Chicago Law Review* 30 (1963): 423–449, p. 434: "The only two practically available modes of imposing criminal sanctions upon the corporate defendant are through the stigma of conviction and the exaction of a fine."

12. See, e.g., Rourke, *Secrecy and Publicity*, ch. 6; Lawrence W. Sherman, *Scandal and Reform: Controlling Police Corruption* (Berkeley and Los Angeles, California: University of California Press, 1978); C. S. Morgan, *Regulation and the Management of Public Utilities* (Boston: Houghton Mifflin, 1923), 338–339; John C. Coffee, Jr., "'No Soul to Damn: No Body to Kick': An Unscandalized Inquiry into the Problem of Corporate Punishment," *Michigan Law Review* 79 (1981): 386–459, pp. 429–434; Jacqueline C. Wolff, "Voluntary Disclosure Programs," *Fordham Law Review* 47 (1979): 1057–1082; Ernest Gellhorn, "Adverse Publicity by Administrative Agencies," *Harvard Law Review* 86 (1973): 1380–1441; Brent Fisse, "The Use of Publicity as a Criminal Sanction against Business Corporations," *Melbourne University Law Review* 8 (1971): 107–150.

13. See e.g., Ross Cranston, *Regulating Business: Law and Consumer Agencies* (London: Macmillan, 1979), pp. 144–145.

14. M. David Ermann and Richard J. Lundman, *Corporate Deviance* (New York: Holt, Rinehart and Winston, 1982), pp. 139–144. See also Barry A. K. Rider and H. Leigh French, *The Regulation of Insider Trading* (London: Macmillan, 1979), pp. 424–426; Judson J. Wambold, "Prohibiting Foreign Bribes: Criminal Sanctions for Corporate Payments Abroad," *Cornell International Law Review* 10 (1977): 231–254, pp. 232, 250.

15. Packer, *The Limits of the Criminal Sanction*, p. 361. Note, however, the following passage, at p. 362:

> And then there is the unexploited sanction of publicity. If those who do business with the public were forced to expose the fact of their derelictions, through either labeling or advertising, a powerful deterrent to transgression might be added. Devices of this kind make conventional criminal sanctions pale by comparison. They suggest that thought needs to be given either to retreating from the criminal sanction in the economic regulatory sphere or to expanding its scope so as to achieve a better match between punishment and crime.

Is Packer conceding that corporations can be made to have neighbors?

16. Cf. Ermann and Lundman, *Corporate Deviance*, pp. 139–144.

17. See Note 2 above.

18. For a discussion of how qualitative data collection or corporate crime can proceed, see Braithwaite, *Corporate Crime in the Pharmaceutical Industry*.

19. See generally Howard Schwartz and Jerry Jacobs, *Qualitative Sociology* (New York: Free Press, 1979); John H. Jackson and Cyril P. Morgan, *Organization Theory* (Engelwood Cliffs, N.J.: Prentice-Hall, 1978), ch. 2. Michael Scriven, *Evaluation Thesaurus* (Point Reyes, Calif.: Edgepress, 1981), p. 126.

20. Sam T. Sieber, "The Integration of Fieldwork and Survey Methods," *American Journal of Sociology* 78 (1973): 1335–1359 (citation in original).

21. Matthew B. Miles, "Qualitative Data as an Attractive Nuisance: The Problem of Analysis," *Administrative Science Quarterly* 24 (1979): 590–601.

22. Ibid., p. 591.

23. Ibid., p. 590.

24. *Reliability* is the tendency of a given measurement procedure to elicit the same results each time it is applied under the same circumstances; *validity* is the degree to which a given measurement procedure measures what it purports to measure. If a factory that makes rulers erroneously produces a batch of 12-inch rulers that are all 13 inches long, then those rulers are reliable but invalid instruments of measurement.

25. Sam D. Sieber, *Project on Social Architecture in Education* (New York: Center for Policy Research, 1976), p. 1. See also John T. Dunlop, "Policy Decisions and Research in Economics and Industrial Relations," *Industrial and Labor Relations Review* 30 (1977): 275–282; John P. Dean, Robert L. Eichhorn, and Lois R. Dean, "Limitations and Advantages of Unstructured

Methods," in George J. McCall and J. L. Simmons, eds., *Issues in Participant Observation* (Reading, Mass.: Addison-Wesley, 1969).

26. This was not done for the Searle case study, data for which had been collected previously.

27. Miles, "Qualitative Data as an Attractive Nuisance," pp. 594–595.

28. See generally John Stuart Mill, *A System of Logic* 1 (London: Longmans, Green, Reader and Dyer, 3rd ed., 1875), pp. 451–464; Robert Ackermann, *Nondeductive Inference* (New York: Dover, 1966); C. I. Lewis, *An Analysis of Knowledge and Valuation* (La Salle, Ill.: Open Court, 1962), ch. 10.

29. Paradoxically, the very fact that human beings are free to make choices can be explained deterministically, as elaborated in David A. Kenny, *Correlation and Causality* (New York: Wiley, 1979), pp. 9–10:

> There may even be a biological basis for human freedom. The fuel of evolution, both biological and cultural, is variation. There can only be evolution if there are a set of different behaviors from which the environment selects. Perhaps nature programmed into the human brain something like a random number generator. This random number generator creates behavioral responses some of which are by chance adaptive. The organism then begins to learn which responses are adaptive to the situation. Culture, socialization, and values continually select from this pool of variable responses. For operant conditioning to work one needs a variable organism to shape. If human beings are fundamentally variable and, therefore, partially unknowable, then traditional social science has erred in presuming that human action is totally determined. Sadly, social science has taken only one track. It has emphasized control and constraint instead of emphasizing freedom and possibility.

30. French, "The Corporation as a Moral Person"; Thomas C. Schelling, "Command and Control," in James W. McKie, ed., *Social Responsibility and the Business Predicament* (Washington: D.C.: Brookings Institution, 1974): 79–108. Cf. Malcolm Warner, *Organizational Choice and Constraint: Approaches to the Sociology of Enterprise Behavior* (Farnborough: Saxon House, 1977).

31. John P. Dean and William F. Whyte, "How Do You Know If the Informant Is Telling the Truth," in McCall and Simmons, *Issues in Participant Observation*: 105–114.

32. Consider e.g., Paul A. Griffin, "Sensitive Foreign Payment Disclosures: The Securities Market Impact," in U.S. H.R. Committee on Interstate and Foreign Commerce, *Report of the Advisory Committee on Corporate Disclosure to the Securities and Exchange Commission*, 95th Cong., 1st Sess., 1977, pp. 694–743.

33. See Paul H. Cootner, *The Random Character of Stock Market Prices* (Cambridge, Mass.: MIT Press, 1964).

34. On the distinction between formal and informal publicity, see Fisse, "Publicity as a Criminal Sanction Against Business Corporations," p. 139.

Chapter 2

1. For a listing of many of the labor relations cases involving J.P. Stevens, see Amalgamated Clothing and Textile Workers Union, "J.P. Stevens Boycott Fact Sheets" (New York: May 1979).

2. Stevens Campaign News Service, "J.P. Stevens Charged in Georgia Spy Campaign" (New York: Amalgamated Clothing and Textile Workers Union, Aug. 27, 1979).

3. *New York Times*, 26 Jan. 1980, p. 36.

4. *New York Times*, 3 March 1980, p. D1.

5. "Pro Stevens Group Defeats U.S. Probe," *Greenville News/Greenville Piedmont*, 3 May 1980.

6. NLRB v. J.P. Stevens & Company, No. 210 (2d Cir. 1977), Decided 19 October 1977.

7. 80 LRRM 3127–3129 (1972).

8. U.S. Court of Appeals, Second Circuit No. 671—September Term 1976, Decided 31 August 1977.

9. Laina Savory, "Forced Off the Board: The ACTWU Corporate Campaign against J.P. Stevens," *Directors and Boards*, Summer 1979: 16–36, p. 22.

10. For another opinion that J.P. Stevens performed more poorly in sales than other leading textile companies during this period, see Frederick D. Sturdivant and Larry M. Robinson, *The Corporate Social Challenge: Cases and Commentaries* (Homewood, Ill.: Murin, 1981), pp. 17–18.

11. *New York Times*, 29 Dec. 1981, p. D4.

12. For the first three quarters of 1980, J.P. Stevens stock traded in the range $12.25–$16.50. For the fourth quarter the range was $15.00–$18.75.

13. See generally Ray Rogers, "How to Confront Corporations," *Business and Society Review* 38 (1981): 60–64.

14. Savory, "Forced Off the Board," p. 25.

15. Ibid., p. 26.

16. For the full press release, see Savory, "Forced Off the Board," p. 19.

17. *Wall Street Journal*, 20 Oct. 1980, p. 1.

18. Text of a speech by Ray Rogers to the Washington State Labor Council Convention, Aug. 28, 1978.

19. John Coffee has developed the anology of controlling corporate power through ju-jitsu rather than the direct confrontation of a sumo wrestler ("'No Soul To Damn: No Body to Kick': An Unscandalized Inquiry into the Problem of Corporate Punishment," *Michigan Law Review*, 79 (1981): 411).

20. *Los Angeles Times*, 26 Oct. 1980, p. 2.

21. See further Savory, "Forced Off the Board," p. 33.

22. NLRB v. Stevens.

Chapter 3

1. Ralph Nader, *Unsafe at Any Speed: The Designed-In Dangers of the American Automobile* (New York: Grossman, 1969).

2. Ibid., p. 9.

3. Ibid., p. 23.

4. Ibid., p. 38. See also J. Patrick Wright, *On a Clear Day You Can See General Motors* (New York: Avon, 1979), pp. 67–68.

5. Memorandum of Decision, Civil No. 771098 (1966, Superior Court of the State of California for the County of Los Angeles).

6. Ibid., pp. 43, 46.

7. Ibid., p. 64. We were informed by General Motors that tire pressures proved to be a factor in very few of the Corvair suits.

8. *Wall Street Journal*, 8 Sept. 1970.

9. 119 *Cong. Rec.*, 93d Cong., 1st Sess., 1973, S. 5897.

10. Ibid., S. 5896.

11. Ibid., SS. 5870–5903; *New York Times*, 16 March 1973, p. 81.

12. U. S. Department of Transportation, National Highway and Traffic Safety Administration, *Evaluation of the 1960–1963 Corvair Handling and Stability* (Washington, D.C.: U.S. Government Printing Office, 1972). See also 119 *Cong. Rec.*, 93d Cong., 1st Sess., 1973, S. 5870.

13. 119 *Cong. Rec.*, 93d Cong., 1st Sess., 1973, SS. 5884–5885.

14. Ibid., S. 5884.

15. *New York Times*, 16 March 1973, p. 81. See also *Washington Post*, 28 March 1973.

16. 120 *Cong. Rec.*, 93d Cong., 1st Sess., 1973, SS. 6060, 6075.

17. Ibid, S. 6061. See also *New York Times*, 25 October 1970, p. 43; *Washington Post*, 27 Sept. 1970.

18. See e.g., James Ridgeway, "Car Design and Public Safety," *New Republic* 151 (1) (1964): 9–11; *New York Times*, 30 Nov. 1965, p. 68; 23 March 1966, p. 1; and 25 Oct. 1970, p. 43; *Los Angeles Times*, 28 May 1971, p. 3; *New York Times*, 16 March 1972, p. 81; *Car and Driver*, Oct. 1964, p. 33, and Nov. 1961, p. 63.

19. *New York Times*, 23 March 1966, p. 32.

20. Conrad M. Cutliffe, Book Review of *Unsafe at Any Speed*, *Washington and Lee Law Review* 23 (1966): 445–447, p. 445.

21. James A. Henderson, Jr., Book Review of *Unsafe at Any Speed*, *Boston University Law Review* 46 (1966): 135–141, p. 140.

22. See generally, W.C. Whitford, "Strict Products Liability and the Automobile Industry," *Wisconsin Law Review* [1968]: 83–171.

23. See generally, Thomas Whiteside, *The Investigation of Ralph Nader* (New York: Arbor House, 1972); S. Prakash Sethi, *Up Against the Corporate Wall* (Engelwood Cliffs, N.J.: Prentice-Hall, 1971), p. 189; Robert L. Bishop and Jane Kilburn, "Penny Whistle or Public's Advocate?", *Public Relations Quarterly* 16(4) (1968): 7–24; Elinor Langer, "Auto Safety: Nader vs. General Motors," *Science* 152 (April 1966): 47–50.

24. *New York Times*, 6 March 1966; James Ridgeway, "The Dick," *New Republic* 154 (11) (1966): 11–13.
25. *New York Times*, 11 March 1966, p. 18.
26. Langer, "Auto Safety," p. 48.
27. *New York Times*, 23 March 1966, p. 1.
28. *New York Times*, 27 March 1966, section IV, p. 10.
29. *New York Times*, 23 March 1966, p. 1.
30. Ibid.
31. *Wall Street Journal*, 14 Aug. 1970, p. 4.
32. Langer, "Auto Safety," p. 49.
33. *Los Angeles Times*, 24 Sept. 1970.
34. Penelope E. Chart v. General Motors Corporation, 258 N.W. 2d 680 (1977, Sup. Ct. of Wisc.).
35. 15 U. S. C. §§ 1381–1431 (1976). See generally Langer, "Auto Safety"; Comment, "Federal Motor Vehicle Safety Legislation," *Ohio State Law Journal* 29 (1968): 177–216; Glen D. Nager, "Auto Recalls and the Pursuit of Safety," *Stanford Law Review* 33 (1981): 301–328.
36. Elizabeth Brenner Drew, "The Politics of Auto Safety," *Atlantic Monthly*, Oct. 1966: 95–102, p. 99.
37. Whiteside, *The Investigation of Ralph Nader*, pp. 14–15. General Motors later claimed that it had spent $193 million on safety in 1964: Drew, "The Politics of Auto Safety," p. 97.
38. See generally George F. Meeter, *The Holloman Story* (Albuquerque: University of New Mexico Press, 1967), pp. 91–99; John Paul Stapp, "Crash Inquiry Prevention," *Cincinnati Journal of Medicine* 39 (1958): 1–7; John Paul Stapp, "Human Tolerance Factors in Supersonic Escape," *Journal of Aviation Medicine* 28 (1957): 77–82; *Time*, Sept. 12, 1955, 80–82, 85–86. Since 1956 there has been an annual Stapp Car Crash Conference.
39. See also Christopher D. Stone, *Where the Law Ends: The Social Control of Corporate Behavior* (New York: Harper & Row, 1975), pp. 43–46.
40. Milton and Rose Friedman, *Free to Choose* (New York: Harcourt Brace Jovanovich, 1980), p. 192.
41. Kenneth J. Arrow, "Organizational Goals and Control Systems: Internal and External Considerations," in Lee E. Preston, ed., *Research in Corporate Social Performance and Policy* 1 (Greenwich, Conn.: JAI Press, 1978): 79–97, pp. 89–90.
42. Cf. General Motors, *Public Interest Report 1980* (Detroit, Mich.: GM 1980), p. 118:

Informed choice is not only the foundation of a free democracy, but the basis for a free and fair market system. With each choice—to buy or not to buy— customers "vote" for or against General Motors' products. General Motors and its competitors strive to win customers by advertising and otherwise informing their choices.

43. The $880,000 Corvair damages suit, Chart v. General Motors, arose from an accident in 1966, yet the litigation came to an end only in 1974.

Two jury verdicts in GM's favor were decided in 1965: *Time*, 20 Aug. 1965, 46–47 and 10 Sept. 1965, 37. (In the former case it was reported that "the jury wound up more impressed by the circumstances of the accident than by the configuration of the Corvair": *Time*, 20 Aug. 1965, p. 47.) Note also that many cases are settled out of court, thereby severely restricting feedback to the public: Henderson, Book Review, p. 139.

Chapter 4

1. John Monahan and Raymond W. Novaco, "Corporate Violence: A Psychological Analysis," in Paul Lipsitt and Bruce Sales, eds., *New Directions in Psycholegal Research* (New York: Van Nostrand, 1980): 3–25.

2. *New York Times*, 10 June 1978, p. 1.

3. Grimshaw v. Ford Motor Co., No. 197761 (Superior Court, Orange County, Ca., 1978).

4. Ind. Code, 35–42–1–5 (Supp. 1978).

5. See generally Comment, "Corporate Homicide: A New Assault on Corporate Decision-Making," *Notre Dame Law Review* 54 (1979): 911–924; Comment, "Corporate Criminal Liability for Homicide: The Controversy Flames Anew," *California Western Law Review* 17 (1981): 465–492; Comment, "Corporate Homicide: The Stark Realities of Artificial Beings and Legal Fictions," *Pepperdine Law Review* 8 (1981): 367–412.

6. *Chicago Tribune*, 14 March 1980.

7. Lee Strobel, *Reckless Homicide: Ford's Pinto Trial* (South Bend, Ind.: And Books, 1980), pp. 151–152.

8. *New York Times*, 4 April 1980, p. 8.

9. Strobel, *Reckless Homicide*, pp. 221, 223–225.

10. *New York Times*, 14 Feb. 1980, p. 20; *Wall Street Journal*, 14 March 1980, p. 7.

11. Strobel, *Reckless Homicide*, ch. 20.

12. Ibid., pp. 267–270.

13. See further Victoria Lynn Swigert and Ronald A. Farrell, "Corporate Homicide: Definitional Processes in the Creation of Diviance," *Law & Society Review* 15 (1980): 161–182.

14. Mark Dowie, "Pinto Madness," *Mother Jones*, Sept./Oct. 1977: 2–13.

15. E. S. Grush and C. S. Saunby, *Fatalities Associated with Crash-Induced Fires and Fuel Leakages* (internal document, Ford Motor Company, 1973).

16. Dowie, "Pinto Madness," p. 7. See also Strobel, *Reckless Homicide*, pp. 89–90.

17. Dowie, "Pinto Madness," p. 7.

18. Strobel, *Reckless Homicide*, pp. 19, 28.

19. See e.g., *National Times* (Australia), 27 Feb.–4 March 1978; Strobel, *Reckless Homicide*, p. 66.

20. *New York Times*, 4 May 1978, p. 22.

21. Strobel, *Reckless Homicide*, p. 23.

22. *Wall Street Journal,* 16 Jan. 1980.

23. Strobel, *Reckless Homicide.*

24. *Washington Star,* 13 March 1980.

25. *Los Angeles Times,* 8 Jan. 1980.

26. By contrast, in the electrical equipment conspiracies, corporate blameworthiness took second place to the jail sentences handed out to individual actors.

27. *Los Angeles Times,* 14 March 1980.

28. Ford Motor Company, Press Release, Aug. 29, 1977, p. 8. This release appears to have received little press coverage: see Swigert and Farrell, "Corporate Homicide," p. 175.

29. Strobel, *Reckless Homicide,* p. 217. See also *New York Times,* 21 Feb. 1980, p. 16.

30. *Chicago Tribune,* 26 Aug. 1978.

31. Bruce Mays, "Hans Zeisel: The Time of His Life," *Student Lawyer,* April 1980: 22–39, pp. 23, 37.

32. Strobel, *Reckless Homicide,* p. 104. An additional function was to offer selected news items for distribution to media unrepresented by a reporter at the trial: ibid., p. 120.

33. Strobel, *Reckless Homicide,* pp. 185, 203–212; *New York Times,* 20 Feb. 1980, p. 16.

34. *Los Angeles Times,* 14 March 1980.

35. *Detroit Free Press,* 14 March 1980; Malcolm E. Wheeler, "In Pinto's Wake, Criminal Trials Loom for More Manufacturers," *National Law Journal,* 6 Oct. 1981: 27–28 (first of five-part series). See also Richard A. Epstein, "Is Pinto a Criminal?," *Regulation,* March-April 1980: 15–21.

36. Irwin Ross, "How Lawless are Big Companies?," *Fortune,* 1 Dec. 1980: 56–64.

37. *Advertising Age,* 7 April 1980. Ford used car prices were also severely affected: *Houston Post,* 15 Sept. 1978.

38. *Advertising Age,* 7 April 1980.

39. Ibid.

40. *New York Times,* 17 Feb. 1980, section IV, p. E9.

41. *New York Times,* 10 June 1979, p. 26. See also Strobel, *Reckless Homicide,* p. 41.

42. Yarborough v. Ford Motor Co., Civil No. 80 CI 409 (Dist. Ct., 45th Judicial District, Texas, 1980).

43. *Indianapolis News,* 15 March 1980. See also John B. Schnapp, *Corporate Strategies of Automotive Manufacturers* (Lexington, Mass: Lexington Books, 1979), p. 48.

44. Cf. Christopher D. Stone, *Where the Law Ends: The Social Control of Corporate Behavior* (New York: Harper & Row, 1975), pp. 39–40.

45. *Wall Street Journal,* 1 Oct. 1979, pp. 1, 39; *New York Times,* 10 June 1979, p. 26.

46. Strobel, *Reckless Homicide,* pp. 40–41.

47. *Washington Post*, 26 Aug. 1978; Walter Guzzardi, Jr., "Ford: The Road Ahead," *Fortune*, 11 Sept. 1978: 36–48, p. 42.

48. Strobel, *Reckless Homicide*, p. 41.

49. *New York Times*, 10 June, 1979, p. 26.

50. Guzzardi, "Ford: The Road Ahead," p. 42.

51. *Houston Post*, 25 Sept. 1978.

52. H. R. 7040 (1980); U. S. H. R., Subcommittee on Crime of the Committee on the Judiciary, *Corporate Crime*, 96th Cong., 2nd Sess., 1980. See also *New York Times*, 16 March 1980, section IV, p. 20.

53. Cf. W. Allen Spurgeon and Terence P. Fagan, "Criminal Liability for Life-Endangering Corporate Conduct," *Journal of Criminal Law & Criminology* 72 (1981): 400–433.

54. Strobel, *Reckless Homicide*, p. 79.

55. Ford, *Policy Document F-1* (Dearborn, Mich.: Ford, 1979).

56. But note that the Pinto case was one of several instanced in support of a federal bill requiring corporate managers to disclose the existence of life-threatening defects to the relevant enforcement agency: Subcommittee on Crime, *Corporate Crime*, pp. 8–11. See also *New York Times*, 16 March 1980, section IV, p. 20.

57. *Buffalo Evening News*, 14 March 1980.

58. See generally Hugh Dalziel Duncan, *Symbols in Society* (New York: Oxford University Press, 1968).

59. See generally Stephen J. Schulhofer, "Harm and Punishment: A Critique of Emphasis on the Results of Conduct in the Criminal Law," *University of Pennsylvania Law Review* 122 (1974): 1497–1607; Christopher D. Stone, "The Place of Enterprise Liability in the Control of Corporate Conduct," *Yale Law Journal* 90 (1980): 1–77, pp. 36–45.

60. Guido Calabresi, *The Costs of Accidents: A Legal and Economic Analysis* (New Haven, Conn.: Yale University Press, 1970), p. 256.

61. See generally Jonathan D. Glover, *Causing Death and Saving Lives* (New York: Penguin, 1977); Richard T. DeGeorge, "Ethical Responsibilities of Engineers in Large Organizations," *Business & Professional Ethics Journal* 1 (1981): 1–14 Rachel Dardis and Claudia Zent, "The Economics of the Pinto Recall," *Journal of Consumer Affairs* 16 (1982): 261–277.

Chapter 5

1. 42 U.S.C. §7521 (1976). See generally Richard B. Stewart, "Regulation, Innovation and Administrative Law," *California Law Review* 69 (1981): 1256–1377, pp. 1302–1305; James E. Krier and Edmund Ursin, *Pollution and Policy: A Case Essay on California and Federal Experience with Motor Vehicle Air Pollution 1940–1975* (Berkeley and Los Angeles: University of California Press, 1977).

2. *Wall Street Journal*, 13 June 1972, p. 10.

3. Ibid.

4. *New York Times*, 14 Feb. 1973, p. 1.

5. Civil No. 39659, U. S. Dist. Ct. (Eastern Dist. of Mich., 1973).

6. *New York Times*, 23 May 1972, p. 1; 3 June 1972, p. 1; 14 Feb. 1973, p. 1.

7. *New York Times*, 14 Feb. 1973, p. 1. See generally Nicholas P. Chopey, "Will Detroit Go Honda?," *Chemical Engineering*, 30 April 1973: 38–40.

8. *Wall Street Journal*, 6 June 1972, p. 2; 13 June 1972, p. 10; 21 Sept. 1972, p. 2; 14 Feb. 1973, p. 4.

9. *Wall Street Journal*, 13 June 1972, p. 10.

10. *Wall Street Journal*, 8 Nov. 1979, p. 34.

11. *Wall Street Journal*, 21 Sept. 1972, p. 2; *New York Times*, 24 May 1972, p. 17.

12. *New York Times*, 14 Feb. 1973, p. 1.

13. *Wall Street Journal*, 13 Sept. 1972, p. 3.

14. *New York Times*, 28 May 1972, section IV, p. 5.

15. *Wall Street Journal*, 16 Feb. 1973, p. 14.

16. See Ch. 6.

17. *New York Times*, 23 May 1972, p. 1.

18. *New York Times*, 28 May 1972, section IV, p. 5.

19. *Wall Street Journal*, 8 June 1972, p. 2.

20. Ibid.; *New York Times*, 6 June 1972, p. 49.

21. *Wall Street Journal*, 8 June 1972, p. 2.

22. *Wall Street Journal*, 13 June 1972, p. 10.

23. It may also be noted that Henry Ford II in a public lecture only a few years previously had stressed the importance of emission-free cars: Henry Ford II, *The Human Environment and Business* (New York: Weybright & Talley, 1970), pp. 56–59.

24. Lee Strobel, *Reckless Homicide: Ford's Pinto Trial* (South Bend, Ind.: And Books, 1980), pp. 218–220.

25. Ibid., p. 259.

26. Ibid., p. 220.

27. See generally Tom Nugent, "The Pollution of Bureaucracy," *Nation*, 1 Nov. 1975: 434–436.

28. *Wall Street Journal*, 13 June 1972, p. 10.

29. *Wall Street Journal*, 14 Feb. 1973, p. 4.

30. *New York Times*, 6 June 1972, p. 49; 3 June 1972, p. 1.

31. Cf. *Wall Street Journal*, 8 Nov. 1979, p. 34.

32. See further *Wall Street Journal*, 8 June 1972, p. 2.

33. See Walter Guzzardi, Jr., "Ford: The Road Ahead," *Fortune*, 11 Sept. 1978: 36–48, p. 44 (Ford alleged to have bribed an Indonesian general in order to win a telecommunications contract; allegation later investigated by the Justice Department, no charges being brought).

34. See generally Donald A. Jensen, "An Industry Viewpoint," *Journal of the Air Pollution Control Association* 23 (1973):838; Nugent, "The Pollution of Bureaucracy"; Stewart, "Regulation, Innovation and Administrative Law."

35. *Wall Street Journal*, 16 Feb. 1973, p. 14; *New York Times*, 18 Feb. 1973, section IV, p. 4; Guzzardi, "Ford: The Road Ahead," p. 38.

36. See Chopey, "Will Detroit Go Honda?"; John B. Schnapp, *Corporate Strategies of the Automobile Manufacturers* (Lexington, Mass.: Lexington Books, 1979), pp. 73–75.

Chapter 6

1. See generally S. Prakash Sethi, *Allied Chemical and the Kepone Controversy* (Richardson, Texas: University of Texas at Dallas, Center for Research in Business and Social Policy, 1980); Richard E. Wokutch and Robert J. Litschert, "Life Science Products Company," in Kenneth W. Olm, F. J. Brewerton, Susan R. Whisnant, Francis J. Bridges, eds., *Management Decisions and Organizational Policy* (Boston: Allyn & Bacon, 3rd ed., 1981): 377–392.

2. Matthew R. Goode, *Criminal Conspiracy in Canada* (Toronto: Carswell, 1976), pp. 109–137.

3. William Goldfarb, "Health Hazards in the Environment: the Interface of Science and Law," *Environmental Law* 8 (1978): 645–662, pp. 658–660.

4. United States v. Allied Chemical Corporation, Sentencing Transcript, CR-76-0129-R (Oct. 5, 1976, U. S. Dist. Ct., Eastern Dist. of Va., Richmond Div.).

5. Christopher D. Stone, "A Slap on the Wrist for the Kepone Mob," *Business and Society Review* 22 (Summer, 1977): 4–11, p. 8.

6. The suspicion lingers on: *Wall Street Journal*, 8 July 1980. Section 2, p. 25.

7. Frances S. Sterrett and Caroline A. Boss, "Careless Kepone," *Environment* 19 (March, 1977): 30–36; Robert J. Huggett and Michael E. Bender, "Kepone in the James River," *Environmental Science & Technology* (August 1980): 918–923.

8. A ban still applies, but only to species that accumulate Kepone in their tissues.

9. *Time*, 22 Sept. 1980; Environmental Protection Agency, *Mitigation Feasibility for the Kepone-Contaminated Hopewell/James River Areas*, NTIS Report PB-286 084 (Washington, D.C.: U. S. Government Printing Office, 1978), p. 12. One official estimated that dredging and removing two inches of mud and sediment from the bottom of the James would create a landfill 30 feet deep and 30 miles long: *Wall Street Journal*, 29 Sept. 1976.

10. *New York Times*, 6 Oct. 1976, p. 1.

11. See Ch. 5.

12. *Los Angeles Times*, 11 Dec. 1977. See also Stone, "A Slap on the Wrist for the Kepone Mob," p. 8.

13. "Kepone and the Toxic Control Bill," *Wall Street Journal*, 29 Sept. 1976, p. 24; "Allied Chemical Enters No Contest Plea for 940 Counts in Federal Kepone Case," *Wall Street Journal*, 20 Aug. 1976, p. 2; "Indictments

Said Likely in Kepone Study Involving Life Science, Allied Chemical," *Wall Street Journal*, 5 April 1976, p. 11; "Chemical Firm's Story Underscores Problems of Cleaning Up Plants," *Wall Street Journal*, 2 Dec. 1976, p. 1.

14. See especially "How Kepone Became a Name for Environmental Disaster," *Washington Star*, 20 Sept. 1976.

15. CBS, *Sixty Minutes* 8(2), Dec. 14, 1975.

16. U. S. Senate, *Kepone Contamination, Hearings before the Subcommittee on Agricultural Research and General Legislation of the Committee on Agriculture and Forestry*, 94th Cong., 2nd Sess., 1976; U. S. H. R., *Oversight Hearings on the Occupational Safety and Health Act: Occupational Safety Hazards, Hearings before the Subcommittee on Manpower, Compensation, and Health and Safety of the Committee on Education and Labor*, 94th Cong., 2nd Sess., 1976.

17. *Washington Post*, 24 Jan. 1976.

18. 15 U.S.C. §§2601 et seq. See generally K. Gaynor, "Toxic Substances Control Act," *Vanderbilt Law Review* 30 (1977): 1149–1195.

19. In addition to the measures specified below, Allied Chemical made an inaugural grant to the *Harvard Environmental Law Review*, established in 1977. It also advised its personnel routinely by broadsheet as to the company's view of the matter (e.g., "The Facts about Kepone," *Today* 6(1), Jan. 1976). Subsequently, the corporation changed its name to Allied Corporation (*Wall Street Journal*, 12 Feb. 1981), but as a result of diversification, not Kepone.

20. *Washington Post*, 2 Jan. 1976, p. 1.

21. *Washington Post*, 7 Oct. 1976; Marvin H. Zim, "Allied Chemical's $20-Million Ordeal with Kepone," *Fortune*, 11 Sept. 1978: 82–91, pp. 83–84; Allied Chemical Corporation, *Annual Report 1976* (Morristown, N.J.: Allied, 1976), p. 8.

22. *Wall Street Journal*, 10 May 1976, p. 8.

23. *New York Times*, 17 Oct. 1976, p. F5.

24. Allied Chemical Corporation, *Allied Chemical Corporation and the Kepone Problem* (Morristown, N.J.: Allied, 1978).

25. Zim, "Allied Chemical's $20-Million Ordeal."

26. Allied Chemical Corporation, *Annual Report 1975* (Morristown, N.J.: Allied, 1975), p. 38.

27. Allied Chemical Corporation, *Annual Report 1976*, p. 38; *Annual Report 1977* (Morristown, N.J.: Allied, 1977), p. 42.

28. *Washington Star*, 25 Sept. 1976.

29. Zim, "Allied Chemical's $20-Million Ordeal," p. 88; *Wall Street Journal*, 14 Oct. 1977, p. 5. Allied has not issued a figure, except to say that the total cost of criminal and civil liability has been less than $30 million (the criminal fine imposed was $13.25 million).

30. *Washington Post*, 26 June 1976.

31. Allied Chemical, *Allied Chemical Corporation and the Kepone Problem*, pp. 33–34.

32. Zim, "Allied Chemical's $20-Million Ordeal," p. 83.

33. *Wall Street Journal*, 30 July 1981, p. 46.

34. See further Zim, "Allied Chemical's $20-Million Ordeal," p. 83.

35. Ibid., p. 91.

36. See further Allied Chemical, *Allied Chemical Corporation and the Kepone Problem*, pp. 34–36. Note also SEC v. Allied Chem. Corp., Civil Action No. 77–0373 (D.D.C., filed March 4, 1977). Under this decree Allied Chemical agreed to take such action as the company determined to be "necessary and proper" and to "maintain policies, practices and procedures to apprise its management of material environmental risk areas and material environmental uncertainties in connection with its business." Ibid., p. 2.

37. Thomas C. Hayes, "Complying with E.P.A. Rules," *New York Times*, 16 Jan. 1980, p. D1.

38. Ibid.

39. See further Zim, "Allied Chemical's $20-Million Ordeal," pp. 83–84.

40. Letter to authors, 12 Aug. 1981, also pointing out that assessment of many environmental hazards is presently impossible. See further Arthur D. Little Center for Environmental Assurance, *Managing for Environmental Assurance* (1981).

41. Not one third of executive *pay*, as stated in Hayes, "Complying with E.P.A. Rules."

42. Arthur D. Little, *Managing for Environmental Assurance*, p. 6.

43. See Goldfarb, "Health Hazards in the Environment," p. 659. However, Allied has advised us that "we recognize that [review short of supervision of the operations of supply contractors] might waive protection that might otherwise be available under the rule of non-liability, but believe this to be the appropriate course of action": letter to authors, 13 Oct. 1981.

44. Letter to authors, 19 June 1981.

45. Interview with J. Miller, Head, Enforcement Section, EPA, Nov. 1980.

46. Hayes, "Complying with E.P.A. Rules."

47. *New York Times*, 28 Jan. 1980, p. A16.

48. 15 U.S.C. §§2601 et seq.

49. *Wall Street Journal*, 29 Sept. 1976, p. 24.

50. *Washington Post*, 12 Feb. 1976.

51. Stone, "A Slap on the Wrist for the Kepone Mob," pp. 9–10; Christopher D. Stone, "The Place of Enterprise Liability in the Control of Corporate Conduct," *Yale Law Journal* 90 (1980): 1–77, pp. 65–76.

Chapter 7

1. E.g., S.A. Henry, "Cancer of the Scrotum in Relation to Occupation," *Oxford Medical Publications*, 1946: 40–48.

2. M. Kawai and K. Harada, "Epidemiologic Study of Occupational Lung Cancer," *Archives of Environmental Health* 14 (1967): 859–864; D.D. Ried and C. Buck, "Cancer in Coking Plant Workers," *British Journal of*

Industrial Medicine 13 (1956): 265–269; William J. Lloyd, "Long Term Mortality Study of Steelworkers, Part V: Respiratory Cancer in Coke Plant Workers," *Journal of Occupational Medicine* 13 (1971): 53–68; Hiroyuki Sakabe, Kenzaburo Tsuchiya, Noburu Takebura, Shigeru Nomura, et al., "Lung Cancer among Coke Oven Workers: A Report to Labour Standard Bureau, Ministry of Labour, Japan," *Industrial Health* 13 (1975): 57–69.

3. E.g., R. Doll, R.E.W. Fisher, E.J. Gammon, W. Gunn, et al., "Mortality of Gasworkers with Special Reference to Cancers of the Lung and Bladder, Chronic Bronchitis and Pneumoconiosis," *British Journal of Industrial Medicine* 22 (1965): 1–12.

4. U.S. Occupational Safety and Health Administration, "Exposure to Coke Oven Emissions: Occupational Safety and Health Standards," *Federal Register* 41 (206), Oct. 22, 1976, p. 46744. See also American Iron & Steel Institute v. OSHA, 577 F.2d 825 (1978) where the OSHA coke oven emissions standard of 0.15 mg. of benzene-soluble particulate was upheld by the Court of Appeals, Third Circuit.

5. The Company made the following comment in response:

There are very few US batteries with water-sealed standpipe caps. Moreover, there are batteries in the USA which today still involve manual removal of charging lids. Many US batteries, even some of their newest batteries, do not have mechanical door cleaners on machines and yet the inference is that, compared to the US situation, Australia (BHP) is behind and deficient in this area because we choose not to agree with some USA decisions and regulations. This view ignores the areas where we have adopted other remedies.

6. The company's response to this sentence in the draft we sent them for comment was as follows:

This is a true statement but again gives no perspective. We do not deny that there are instances where such very high figures have been recorded. However, they are the infrequent exception rather than the rule. As is the case with the American and other overseas coke ovens, an emission level of 0.15 mg/m³ is routinely not met in many areas but it is rare indeed for an exposure level to be 100 times the level. Moreover, in many cases where very high values have been reported we have doubts as to the validity of the result in that unrepresentative readings can be easily generated by holding a sample filter over an emission source. There have been numerous occasions when this practice has been detected.

Legally enforceable limits in America have not, at this point in time, resulted in compliance by American batteries, as is the simplistic inference implicit in the text. The nature of the problem and the stringency of the standard, notwithstanding the engineering and work practice controls specified by the OSHA regulations, have meant that the standard is currently unattainable in a number of areas on all batteries throughout the world for which we are privy to information.

7. Vaclav Masek, Jach Zdenek, and Jiri Kandas, "Content of 3, 4 Benzo(a)pyrene in the Working Clothes and Underwear of Workers at a Pitch Coking Plant," *Journal of Occupational Medicine* 14 (7) (1972): 548–551.

8. The company denies that its attitude was "intransigent":

> That there were claims by the union for changes, which the Company did not accept, is not disputed. Whether any fairminded person examining what was claimed, what was agreed to, and what effects might reasonably be expected from not agreeing to all the unions' claims, would conclude that the Company's attitude was intransigent is debatable! Certainly Bauer J. in his recent judgment, effectively concluded that some of the unions' claims were not reasonable.

9. Steel Works (Broken Hill Proprietary Company Limited) Award and Another Award, Industrial Commission of New South Wales 355 (26 November 1981).

10. *Australian*, 11 Sept. 1980.

11. *Illawarra Mercury*, 6 Sept. 1980.

12. *Illawarra Mercury*, 12 Oct. 1979.

13. *The Metal Worker*, Sept. 1980.

14. *Sydney Morning Herald*, 13 Oct. 1979.

15. *Illawarra Mercury*, 13 Oct. 1979.

16. Ibid.

17. *Illawarra Mercury*, 23 Sept. 1978.

18. *Illawarra Mercury*, 12 Sept. 1980.

19. N.S.W. Legislative Assembly, *Hansard*, 23 Oct. 1980, p. 2087.

20. Cf. *Australian Financial Review*, 24 July 1981.

21. The expenditure on new doors is the major new capital investment, which the company points out was beginning to take shape before the industrial campaign:

> The decision to install new doors had nothing to do with an industrial campaign. The trials with Ikio doors were begun in 1976. It was the Company's intention all along to employ these doors subject only to the doors proving suitable. The initial design did not.

22. Notification under S.25A by Australian Iron and Steel Pty. Limited of a Dispute with the Amalgamated Metalworkers and Shipwrights Union and Ors Re Claim for Two Lockers for Each Employee and Other Claims— Coke Ovens Department, Compulsory Conference 281, Industrial Commission of New South Wales, 4 June 1981.

23. BHP offered this response:

> In many cases, e.g. water-sealed standpipe caps, the engineering reforms were completed prior to the commencement of significant data collection. We have no doubt that these steps have "measurably improved" the situation but because statistics were not kept during the period prior to the steps being taken we cannot statistically evidence our conclusion.

24. *Sydney Morning Herald*, 17 Oct. 1979.
25. Compulsory Conference 281, transcript.
26. Steel Works Award, p. 86.
27. Commonwealth of Australia, House of Representatives Standing Committee on Environment and Conservation, *Hazardous Chemicals: Second Report on the Inquiry into Hazardous Chemicals* (Canberra: Australian Government Publishing Service, 1982), pp. 120–123.

Chapter 8

1. Judge A.J. Goran, *Explosion at Appin Colliery on 24th July, 1979, Report of an Inquiry by the Court of Coal Mines Regulation, New South Wales* (undated).
2. Report of Inquest before J. Hiatt, Stipendiary Magistrate, Campbelltown Coroner's Court, 19 Dec. 1980.
3. Goran Report, p. 67.
4. Inquest Report, p. 33.
5. Ibid.
6. Ibid., p. 46.
7. Ibid., p. 13.
8. Ibid., p. 14.
9. Goran Report, p. 86.
10. *Sydney Morning Herald*, 4 Dec. 1979, p. 12.
11. Inquest Report, p. 18. In its comments on our draft, BHP further pointed out:

Reference is made in the reports as to the installation of a Corex mine monitoring system which had partly been installed at the time of the explosion. This system involved continuous monitoring of airways throughout the mine with computerized recordings produced on the mine surface and involved an overall cost of $250,000. The installation of such a device is itself indicative of "management's" concern to monitor accurately gas levels and does not support the allegation that management was supporting flagrant violations of gas levels.

12. Goran Report, p. 90.
13. Ibid., p. 78.
14. Ibid., p. 79. Subsequently, BHP had this to say in commenting on our draft:

While it is acknowledged with hindsight that communication in the desired manner may not have reached as far as it should have, there is no question that considerable efforts were made on the part of the Manager and UnderManager-In-Charge to acquaint the officials under their immediate charge with the proposed ventilation changeover.

15. See also the discussion in Andrew Hopkins, "Crime Without Punishment: The Appin Mine Disaster," *Australian Quarterly*, Summer 1981: 455–466.

16. Of course there is no reason why prosecutions could not have been launched for violations even though those violations were not responsible for the disaster: However, we were told that Judge Goran was concerned about the diffuse and confused nature of responsibility for the violations and desired to avoid anyone being scapegoated for the disaster. Clearly, to recommend prosecution of any individual for an offense that was not the cause of the disaster would run a risk that in the public mind this individual would be unfairly stigmatized for causing the disaster. Further, Hopkins ("Crime Without Punishment," p. 457) reports that Judge Goran recommended against prosecution of the corporation in a confidential letter to the Minister for Mines because of the Judge's distaste for vicarious liability in such cases. On the question of corporate fault for homicide in industrial accidents where the exact causal sequence cannot be specified with certainty, see People v. Warner-Lambert Co., 434 N.Y.S. Ct. App. 159 (1980).

17. Goran Report, pp. 23, 29.

18. Ibid., p. 24.

19. In its comments on our draft, BHP was at pains to point out that it had made considerable investments in methane drainage prior to this further prodding:

> Investigation into the methane drainage had been carried out by the Company for many years prior to the explosion and in fact at the time of the explosion, Japanese and British consultants had completed their inspections and were in the process of formulating reports. The British recommendations were subsequently implemented, in addition to other measures which also have since been taken. Gas recovered from drainage is being discharged to atmosphere and as yet the Company has not been able to justify expenditure to utilise the gas commercially.

20. J.J. Breslin and R.J. Anderson, *Observations on Current American, British and West German Underground Coal Mining Practices* (Columbus, Ohio: Battelle Memorial Institute, 1976), p. 113.

21. *Illawarra Mercury*, 28 Feb. 1980.

22. "Goran Inquiry Recommendations," *Australian Coal Miner*, Aug. and Sept. 1980: 21–22, 39–43.

23. New South Wales Coal Mines Regulation Act, 1982, s. 141.

24. R.D.G. Reed, "Differences Between the 1912 Coal Mines Regulation Act and the New Proposed Act," *Australian Coal Miner*, June 1981: 44–48.

25. *Australian Financial Review*, 5 April 1981, p. 37.

26. Address by N.S.W. Minister for Mineral Resources to the Colliery Managers' Association (University of New South Wales, Sydney, 9 May 1981).

Chapter 9

1. Samuel S. Epstein, *The Politics of Cancer* (San Francisco: Sierra Club Books, 1978); U.S.H.R., Subcomm. on Compensation, Health and Safety of the Comm. on Education and Labor, *Asbestos-Related Occupational Diseases,* 95th Cong., 2nd Sess., 1979; Erman and Lundman, *Corporate Deviance* pp. 68–69.

2. Jean A. O'Hare, "Asbestos Litigation: The Dust Is Yet to Settle," *Fordham Urban Law Journal* 7 (1978): 55–91.

3. Timothy Hall, *The Ugly Face of Australian Business* (Sydney: Harper & Row, 1980), p. 30.

4. 17–19 November, 1977. See also *The Age,* 1 February 1978; *Canberra Times,* 14 November 1978; *Daily Telegraph,* 28 July 1978; *Australian Financial Review,* 16 October 1978; *National Times,* 10–15 October 1977.

5. James Hardie, Interhouse Memo from H.A. Hudson, Manager, Factory Operations, to all Factory Managers, March 1976.

6. William J. Nicholson, "Case Study 1: Asbestos—the TLV Approach," *Annals of the New York Academy of Sciences* 271 (1976): 152–65.

7. New York Academy of Sciences, *Cancer and the Worker* (New York: (N.Y.A.S., 1977).

8. Australian Broadcasting Commission, *Asbestos: Work as a Health Hazard* (Sydney: A.B.C., 1978), p. 97.

9. For example, see the company flyer to its employees of March 28, 1979, "Setting the Record Straight".

10. *Wall Street Journal,* 3 March 1981, p. 18.

11. Hall, *Ugly Face of Australian Business,* p. 34.

12. *Rydge's,* Sept. 1979, p. 55.

13. See, in particular, Federated Miscellaneous Workers Union of Australia, *An Assessment of the Occupational Hygiene Programme at James Hardie & Co. Ltd. Asbestos Plants in Victoria, New South Wales and South Australia, 1980–1981* (Melbourne: F.M.W.U.A., 1981). This comprehensive report concluded, among other things, that:

> The dust generation equipment is probably the best in the country. To my knowledge, Hardies are the only organization in Australia undertaking any experimental, as opposed to workplace, sampling/counting research . . . .I am impressed by the objectivity of the senior hygiene staff. I see them as good scientists with a definite interest in encouraging good hygiene practice based on scientific principles. (p. 53)

14. The South Australian government tests reported in the Miscellaneous Workers Union report (ibid., pp. 236–249) mentioned in Note 13, above, are also tentatively suggestive of improvement in recent years.

15. However, a policy draft is being considered by management.

16. Federated Miscellaneous Workers Union, *Occupational Hygiene at James Hardie,* p. 7.

17. See Barry J. Castleman, "The Export of Hazardous Factories to Developing Nations," *International Journal of Health Services* 9 (1979): 569–606; Barry J. Castleman, "More on the International Asbestos Business," *International Journal of Health Services* 11 (1981): 339–340.

18. Australian Broadcasting Commission, *Asbestos*, p. 5. For an account of Australian asbestos regulation prior to 1978, see Neil Gunningham, "Asbestos Hazards and Legal Regulation," *Legal Service Bulletin* 3 (1978): 46–49.

Chapter 10

1. *Financial Review*, 31 Dec. 1974, p. 1. See further V. G. Venturini, *Malpractice: The Administration of the Murphy Trade Practices Act* (Sydney: Non Mollare, 1980), pp. 336–339.

2. Sharp once claimed that the figure was US$27,000 but the solicitor denied this: *National Times*, 14–19 July 1975, p. 43.

3. Hartnell v. Sharp Corporation of Australia Pty. Ltd. 5 A. L. R. 493 (1975).

4. Ibid., pp. 498–499.

5. Ibid., p. 496.

6. See also *Australian*, 17 April 1975, p. 3; *Advertiser*, 17 April 1975, p. 10; *Canberra Times*, 17 April 1975, p. 6; *Financial Review*, 17 April 1975, p. 1.

7. *Sydney Morning Herald*, 17 April 1975, p. 1.

8. *Age*, 17 April 1975, p. 1.

9. *National Times*, 18–19 July 1975, pp. 42–43.

10. *Broadcasting and Television Advertising, Marketing and Media Weekly*, 24 April 1975, p. 8. However, given that Sharp was not a member of the Australian Association of National Advertisers, which made the comment, this reaction may have been sour grapes. See also "Sharp 'Lucky'," *Canberra Times*, 18 April 1975.

11. For example, *Financial Review*, 22 and 29 Oct. 1975.

12. *Nihon Keizai Shimbun*, 17 April 1975, p. 8; *Asahi Shimbun*, 17 April 1975, p. 8.

13. Rodney Clark, *The Japanese Company* (New Haven: Yale University Press, 1979), p. 54.

14. *Financial Review*, 17 April 1975, p. 8.

15. *National Times*, 14–19 July 1975, p. 42.

16. Compare the gloomy prognostication about the impact of adverse publicity on sales in *Rydge's*, Sept. 1975, p. 116.

17. Andrew Hopkins, *The Impact of Prosecutions under the Trade Practices Act* (Canberra, Australian Institute of Criminology, 1978), p. 6.

18. *National Times*, 14–19 July 1975, p. 43.

19. See generally Clark, *The Japanese Company*, pp. 244–245.

20. *National Times*, 14–19 July 1975, p. 42.

21. See further Clark, *The Japanese Company*, chs. 5–6.

22. See further Hopkins, *The Impact of Prosecutions under the Trade Practices Act*, pp. 4–5.

23. As Hopkins (ibid., p. 5) has maintained, "Sharp's failure was a failure to involve the appropriate technically qualified people in checking the advertising copy before publication." Note also the opinion of the solicitor then representing Sharp that "An administration was allowed to evolve which was heavy on selling talent but which saw advertising only as a selling tool and not as an administrative responsibility. Accurate records were not kept of key meetings, a vital letter was completely mislaid, the technical department was clearly never in proper liaison with the advertising department." *National Times*, 14–19 July 1975, p. 43.

24. *Adbrief*, 18 April 1975.

25. Hopkins, *The Impact of Prosecutions under the Trade Practices Act*, pp. 5–6.

26. Simeon M. Kriesberg, "Decisionmaking Models and the Control of Corporate Crime," *Yale Law Journal* 85 (1976): 1091–1129, pp. 1103–1105; Graham T. Allison, *Essence of Decision: Explaining the Cuban Missile Crisis* (Boston: Little, Brown, 1971), ch. 5.

Chapter 11

1. Anthony Sampson, *Sovereign State: The Secret History of ITT* (London: Hodder & Stoughton, 1973), p. 237.

2. George Lardner, Jr., "Suit Against Police Discloses '75 ITT Spying," *Washington Post*, 9 Oct. 1980, pp. A26–27.

3. Ibid.

4. *Wall Street Journal*, 21 Aug. 1978, p. 5.

5. *Washington Post*, 8 March 1979, p. A3.

6. See David Menkhous, "Graymail: Constitutional Immunity from Justice?," *Harvard Journal on Legislation* 18 (1978): 389–427.

7. *Washington Post*, 18 Feb. 1979, p. C7.

8. Ibid.

9. Suzanne Weaver, while not doubting that the White House did attempt to influence the Justice Department, contends that the latter did not decide to drop the ITT case for corrupt political reasons: *The Decision to Prosecute: Organization and Public Policy in the Antitrust Division* (Cambridge, Mass.: MIT Press, 1977).

10. Sampson, *Sovereign State*, p. 210.

11. Ibid., p. 238.

12. *Advertising Campaign Report Newsletter: ITT* (New York, Sept. 1979), p. 3.

13. See also Bill Abrams, "How ITT Shells Out $10 Million or So a Year to Polish Reputation," *Wall Street Journal*, 2 April 1982, pp. 1, 16; Robert Lamb, William G. Armstrong, Jr., and Karolyn R. Morigi, *Business,*

Media and the Law: The Troubled Confluence (New York: New York University Press, 1980), p. 68.

14. Sampson, *Sovereign State*, p. 254.

15. Robert Sobel, *ITT: The Management of Opportunity* (New York: Times Books, 1982), p. 349.

16. For a more detailed account of the reforms see ITT, *Supplementary Report of the Special Review Committee of the Board of Directors* (New York: ITT, March 9, 1982), pp. 90–101.

17. *Wall Street Journal*, 30 Nov. 1981, p. 31.

18. ITT, *Report of the Special Review Committee of the Board of Directors* (New York: ITT, January 11, 1978); ITT, *Supplementary Report.*

19. ITT, *Supplementary Report*, p. 97.

20. Ibid., p. 54.

Chapter 12

1. See John Braithwaite, *Corporate Crime in the Pharmaceutical Industry* (London: Routledge & Kegan Paul, 1983), ch. 3.

2. U.S. Senate, Subcommittee on Health of the Committee on Labor and Public Welfare, *Preclinical and Clinical Testing by the Pharmaceutical Industry, 1976*, 94th Cong., 2nd Sess., 1976, part II, p. 9.

3. Ibid., pp. 13–14.

4. Ibid., p. 15.

5. Ibid., p. 35.

6. Ibid., p. 39.

7. Ibid., p. 41.

8. Ibid., part III, p. 4.

9. *Wall Street Journal*, 9 April 1976, p. 30.

10. *Washington Post*, 20 July 1976, p. A2.

11. *Washington Post*, 11 July 1975, p. 3.

12. *Chicago Tribune*, 12 July 1976, p. 2.

13. See 43 Fed. Reg. 60,013 (1978); 21 C.F.R. § 58 (1981).

Chapter 13

1. Lockheed Corporation, *Report of the Special Review Committee of the Board of Directors* (Burbank, Calif.: Lockheed, May 16, 1977), p. 14.

2. Ibid., p. 17.

3. David Boulton, *The Grease Machine* (New York: Harper & Row, 1978), pp. 6–19.

4. One Lockheed executive responded to this passage in the draft by defending Arthur Young:

Arthur Young is described as deciding "It was time for self-preservation." That characterization may be a bit of an unfair twist to Arthur Young's position.

They were concerned with certifying financial results in accordance with accepted accounting and auditing practices and procedures when there was some indication that they had not had the benefit of full disclosure. They were not attempting to "shrug off all responsibility." . . . Rather, it was a normal response by Arthur Young, as independent auditors, to disclosures about certain Lockheed practices of which they had not been previously informed or which had been misrepresented to them.

5. Boulton, *Grease Machine*, p. 19.

6. Securities and Exchange Commission v. Lockheed Aircraft Corporation, Daniel J. Haughton, A.C. Kotchian, Civil Action No. 76, 0611, Complaint for Permanent Injunction and Certain Ancillary Relief (U.S. District Court for the District of Columbia, April 13, 1976).

7. Securities and Exchange Commission v. Lockheed Aircraft Corporation, Daniel J. Haughton, A.C. Kotchian, Civil Action No. 76, 0611, Final Judgments of Permanent Injunction and Certain Ancillary Relief (U.S. District Court for the District of Columbia, April 13, 1976).

8. Lockheed, *Report of Special Review Committee*, p. 13.

9. Federal Trade Commission, Docket No. C-2942, Lockheed Corporation, Decision and Order, December 2, 1978.

10. Federal Trade Commission, Docket No. C-2942, Lockheed Corporation, Complaint, December 2, 1978.

11. U.S. v. Lockheed, 79–00270 (U.S. District Court for the District of Columbia, July 1, 1979).

12. Under U.S.C. §1058.

13. Under U.S.C. §1343.

14. Under U.S.C. §1343.

15. This is a reference to the fact that one of Lockheed's largest operating companies is in Georgia.

16. In fact the logo has since been changed but the reason given by the company was that "it simply did not have a modern look."

17. Boulton, *Grease Machine*, p. 102.

18. *Los Angeles Times*, 4 April 1980, section 1, p. 3.

19. *Wall Street Journal*, 1 May 1980, p. 48.

20. *Washington Post*, 6 Feb. 1977, pp. H1, H3.

21. See James E. Post, *Corporate Behavior and Social Change* (Reston, Va.: Reston Publishing, 1978), pp. 202–213.

22. *Washington Post*, 6 Feb. 1977, pp. H1, H3.

23. *Wall Street Journal*, 6 Nov. 1981, p. 39; 27 Jan. 1982, p. 30; *Australian Financial Review*, 9 June 1982.

24. Mark Green, Alice Tepper Marlin, Victor Kamber, and Jules Burnstein, *The Case for a Corporate Democracy Act of 1980* (Washington, D.C.: Public Citizen's Congress Watch, 1980).

25. *New York Times*, 4 May 1979, section 4, p. E3.

26. See *Washington Star*, 22 April 1976. Clarence Walton, for example, says: "Lockheed's misadventures nearly shoved Italy to the Communist camp and *did* materially influence the fall of a government in Japan. . . ."

Walton, ed., *The Ethics of Corporate Conduct* (Englewood Cliffs, N.J.: Prentice-Hall, 1977), pp. 3–4.

27. *New York Times*, 16 June 1978, p. 1.

28. *Wall Street Journal*, 21 Sept. 1979.

29. Boulton, *The Grease Machine*, p. 269.

30. *Wall Street Journal*, 15 June 1981, p. 27.

31. L. Kraar, "How Lockheed Got Back Its Wings," *Fortune*, Oct. 1977: 199–210.

32. Lockheed Corporation, *Corporate Report to Lockheed Employees* (Burbank, Calif.: Lockheed, May 26, 1977).

33. Boulton, *Grease Machine*, p. 269.

34. Ibid., p. 276.

35. Lockheed, *Report of Special Review Committee*, p. 18.

36. Because "unusual financial transactions" are defined very broadly, and because reporting anything which might be questionable is a self-protective means of passing the buck to head office, corporate staff often receive reports of very petty irregularities.

37. Lockheed, *Report of Special Review Committee*, p. 24.

38. A Lockheed executive who commented on our draft felt that we had overstated the case here:

> There is a statement that there are problems recruiting outside directors, with the implication that the difficulty resulted from Lockheed's "checkered reputation." You overstate the case. For the past seven or eight years most American corporations have had that problem, not because of company reputations but because of increased litigation by shareholders and enforcement actions of government agencies against officers and directors in a wide variety of areas, such as environmental concerns, mergers and acquisitions, general management deficiencies, and fiduciary responsibility under employee benefit laws. The specter of foreign payment problems for persons considering directorships was really short-lived, being overshadowed by the multitude of those other considerations.

39. Lockheed Corporation, *Management Policy Statement: International Consultants* (Burbank, Calif.: Lockheed, as revised June 19, 1980).

40. Lockheed, *Report of Special Review Committee*, p. 16.

41. Translation supplied to authors by General Counsel's office, General Dynamics.

42. Royal Decree No. M/14 of 1977.

43. Ibid., at p. 6 of English translation.

44. See also *Japan Business Law Journal* 2 (1981), p. 309.

45. For example, agents who passed bribes, if eliminated, can, in many industries, be replaced by an independent layer in the distribution network.

Chapter 14

1. McDonnell Douglas, 10K form on file at SEC, 1975.
2. Marshall B. Clinard and Peter C. Yeager, *Corporate Crime* (New York: Free Press, 1980), p. 168.
3. U.S. v. McDonnell Douglas Corporation, John C. Brizendine, Charles M. Forsyth, James S. McDonnell III, and Sherman Pruitt, Jr., 79–00516 (U.S. District Court for the District of Columbia, November 9, 1979).
4. For example, *St. Louis Post Dispatch*, 26 June 1981, p. 1.
5. *Washington Post*, 3 July 1981, p. A2.
6. *New York Times*, 31 Aug. 1980, p. 2.
7. One Lockheed defense attorney, a former CIA employee, stated that in addition to the CIA, the State and Defense Departments had known that Lockheed was making foreign payoffs: Pawel Horoszowski, *Economic Special Opportunity Conduct and Crime* (Lexington, Mass.: Lexington Books, 1980), pp. 114–115.
8. *McDonnell Douglas Standards of Business Ethics and Conduct* (St. Louis, Mo.: McDonnell Douglas, 1980), p. 5.
9. *Corporate Control Procedure, Marketing/Sales Independent Contractors Including Consultants/Agents/Representatives* (St. Louis, Mo.: McDonnell Douglas, Oct. 6 1980).

Chapter 15

1. Edward D. Herlihy and Theodore A. Levine, "Corporate Crisis: The Overseas Payment Problem," *Law and Policy in International Business* 8 (1976): 552, citing SEC Registration Statement Form S-7, Exxon Corp., Commission File No. 2–54, 661, September 25, 1975, pp. 29–30.
2. For example, Gall v. Exxon Corp., 418 F. Supp. 508 (S.D.N.Y. 1976), *complaint dismissed*, No. 75 Civ. 3682 (S.D.N.Y. January 17, 1977).
3. Exxon denied this in its response to the draft of this chapter: "We are not aware of any Exxon payments to third world officials to secure drilling and prospecting rights."
4. Exxon Corporation, *Determination and Report of the Special Committee on Litigation* (New York: Exxon, Jan. 23, 1976), pp. 13–14.
5. Of course one reason for asserting such control is to avoid the publicity of further scandals. But as we shall see below, there are other reasons as well—for example, protecting the corporation from financial manipulations that serve the interests of the subsidiary or its executives but not the interests of the organization as a whole.
6. William Clifford and John Braithwaite, *Cost-Effective Business Regulation* (Canberra: Australian Institute of Criminology, 1981), p. 30.
7. Ibid., p. 34.
8. Exxon Corporation, *Business Ethics Policy Compliance Program* (New York: Exxon, March 13, 1978).

9. Exxon, *Report of Special Committee on Litigation.*

10. Exxon Corporation, *Policy Statement, Financial Controls—Internal Auditing* (New York: Exxon, July 23, 1973).

11. Clifford and Braithwaite, *Cost-Effective Regulation*, pp. 24–25.

12. *Wall Street Journal*, 14 April 1976, p. 3. In relation to Exxon itself, see, "Political Slush Fund Hid Other Spending, Cost Exxon Millions," *Wall Street Journal*, 14 Nov. 1975, p. 1. The Firestone slush fund provides a more spectacular illustration of a mix of embezzlement and bribery:

> One week after he resigned as vice chairman and principal financial officer of the Firestone Tire and Rubber Co. in May 1976, 62-year-old Robert P. Beasley was identified by the Securities and Exchange Commission as the administrator of an illegal $1.1 million political slush fund maintained by the company. Last week, a Federal grand jury in New York charged that Beasley had carried the illegal scheme one step further: instead of doling out all of the money to politicians, the jury said, he siphoned off the lion's share for himself. In a 40-count indictment, the jury said that Beasley diverted most of the money to buy securities or repay the principal of interest on personal loans. Shortly before his retirement, Beasley returned $206,101 to the company treasury. An additional $330,000 from the fund, collected between 1970 and 1973, apparently went to politicians, and Firestone has sued Beasley for $625,000 still unaccounted for. Beasley had no comment on the Federal charges, but he said earlier that he was a "fall-guy" for other company executives, including retired chairman, Raymond C. Firestone. *Newsweek*, November 7, 1977, p. 84. (Beasley was subsequently sentenced to four years in prison.)

In early 1976 Iran's Prime Minister Amir Abbas Hoveyda claimed that in at least two foreign bribery cases:

> It seemed that certain operatives of these companies pocketed the money themselves and told the shareholders that it had been paid out to some Iranians as bribes. Some crumbs may have been distributed to Iranians, but the meat went back overseas. Donald R. Cressey and Charles A. Moore, *Corporation Codes of Ethical Conduct* (New York: Report to Peat, Marwick and Mitchell Foundation, 1980), p. 68.

Chapter 16

1. See generally John Herling, *The Great Price Conspiracy* (Washington, D.C.: Luce, 1962); Clarence C. Walton and Frederick W. Cleveland, Jr., *Corporations on Trial: The Electrical Cases* (Belmont, Calif.: Wadsworth, 1964); Gilbert Geis, "The Heavy Electrical Equipment Antitrust Cases of 1961," in Gilbert Geis and Robert F. Meier, eds., *White-Collar Crime: Offenses in Business, Politics and the Professions* (New York: Free Press, 1977): 117–132.

2. Herling, *The Great Price Conspiracy*, ch. 9; Richard Austin Smith, *Corporations in Crisis* (New York: Doubleday, 1963), pp. 110–111, 125–126.

3. Charles A. Bane, *The Electrical Equipment Conspiracy: The Treble Damage Actions* (New York: Federal Legal Publications, 1973), pp. 1–6.

4. Bane, *The Electrical Equipment Conspiracy*, pp. 9–10. As regards *nolo contendere* see generally John J. Flynn, "Criminal Sanctions under State and Federal Antitrust Laws," *Texas Law Review* 45 (1967): 1301–1334, pp. 1325–1329.

5. Bane, *The Electrical Equipment Conspiracy*, pp. 11–12; Geis and Meier, *White-Collar Crime*, p. 119.

6. *New York Times*, 12 Feb. 1961, section IV, p. 6.

7. *New York Times*, 7 Feb. 1961, p. 26.

8. Ibid.

9. See also Herling, *The Great Price Conspiracy*, pp. 256, 289–291.

10. *Wall Street Journal*, 7 Feb. 1961, p. 2.

11. *New York Times*, 7 Feb. 1961, p. 1.

12. *Life*, 24 Feb. 1961, p. 30.

13. Copy on file.

14. *New York Times*, 30 April 1961, section IV, p. 10. See further Herling, *The Great Price Conspiracy*, ch. 15.

15. U. S. Senate, *Administered Prices, Pts. 27 & 28, Hearings before the Subcommittee on Antitrust and Monopoly of the Committee on the Judiciary*, 87th Cong., 2nd Sess., 1961; Estes Kefauver, *In a Few Hands: Monopoly Power in America* (New York: Pantheon, 1965), p. ix.

16. *New York Times*, 21 April 1961, p. 20; 26 April 1961, p. 1; 4 May 1961, p. 21; 21 May 1961, p. 43; 6 June 1961, p. 1.

17. U. S. Senate, *Administered Prices*, p. 16974, but cf. p. 17672.

18. Herling, *The Great Price Conspiracy*; Walton and Cleveland, *Corporations on Trial*; John G. Fuller, *The Gentlemen Conspirators* (New York: Grove, 1962); Richard Austin Smith, "The Incredible Electrical Conspiracy," *Fortune*, April 1961: 132–137; May 1961: 161–164.

19. E.g., Joseph Goldstein, Alan M. Dershowitz, and Richard D. Schwartz, *Criminal Law: Theory and Process* (New York: Free Press, 1974), pp. 937–940.

20. *New York Times*, 8 Feb. 1961, p. 16.

21. Ibid.

22. Ibid.

23. U. S. Senate, *Administered Prices*, pp. 16829, 16840, 16891, 16960, 17003, 17009–17014.

24. *Nation*, 18 Feb. 1961: 129.

25. Herling, *The Great Price Conspiracy*, p. 309.

26. *Los Angeles Times*, 31 Oct. 1961.

27. *Value Line Survey*, 13 March 1961.

28. Alan M. Dershowitz, "Increasing Community Control over Corporate Crime: A Problem in the Law of Sanctions," *Yale Law Journal* 71 (1961): 280–306, p. 289.

29. *New York Times*, 16 June 1961, p. 1; Herling, *The Great Price Conspiracy*, p. 303.

30. Cf. Malcolm R. Burns, "The Competitive Effects of Trust-Busting: A Portfolio Analysis," *Journal of Political Economy* 85 (1977): 717–739.

31. Fuller, *The Gentlemen Conspirators*, p. 165.

32. *New York Times*, 30 April 1964, p. 47. See also Bane, *The Electrical Equipment Conspiracy*, p. 251.

33. *New York Times*, 30 April 1964, p. 47.

34. *New York Times*, 12 Feb. 1961, section IV, p. 6.

35. *New York Times*, 30 April 1961, section IV, p. 10.

36. Dershowitz, "Increasing Community Control over Corporate Crime," p. 289.

37. See e.g., *New York Times*, 7 Feb. 1961, p. 1; *Los Angeles Times*, 7 Feb. 1961; *New York Times*, 8 Feb. 1961, p. 1. See also Herling, *The Gentleman Conspirators*, p. 115.

38. *New York Times*, 12 Feb. 1961, section IV, p. 6.

39. *New York Times*, 7 Feb. 1961, p. 1; 8 Feb. 1961, p. 1.

40. *New York Times*, 30 April 1961, section IV, p. 10.

41. See e.g., *New York Times*, 12 Feb. 1961, section IV, p. 6.

42. Herling, *The Great Price Conspiracy*, pp. 296–297; Walton and Cleveland, *Corporations on Trial*, p. 103.

43. E.g., General Electric, *Interim Report—The Recent Settlement of the Electrical Industry Antitrust Cases* (Fairfield, Conn.: General Electric, Dec. 14, 1960), p. 6.

44. See also U. S. Senate, *Administered Prices*, p. 17674.

45. *Sharon Herald*, 14 Feb. 1961.

46. U. S. Senate, *Administered Prices*, pp. 17707, 17770; *New York Times*, 26 April 1961, p. 1.

47. *New York Times*, 28 Feb. 1961, p. 1. See also Herling, *The Great Price Conspiracy*, pp. 257–258.

48. See especially GE's statement immediately after sentencing: *New York Times*, 8 Feb. 1961, p. 16.

49. Walton and Cleveland, pp. 117–124.

50. Fuller, *The Gentleman Conspirators*, p. 223.

51. S. 2254, H.R. 8138, 87th Cong., 1st Sess. (1961).

52. U. S. Senate, *Legislation to Strengthen Penalties under the Antitrust Laws, Hearings before the Subcommittee on Antitrust and Monopoly of the Committee on the Judiciary*, 87th Cong., 1st Sess., 1961. Cf. Yamashita v. Styer, 327 U. S. 1 (1946). One much less controversial reform was the passage of legislation for civil investigative demands to avoid the necessity for grand jury investigation: 15 U.S.C. §§1311–1314 (1976).

53. Herling, *The Great Price Conspiracy*, p. 278; Smith, *Corporations in Crisis*, p. 97.

54. Geis and Meier, *White-Collar Crime*, p. 140.

55. See further John Braithwaite, *Corporate Crime in the Pharmaceutical Industry* (London: Routledge & Kegan Paul, 1983), ch. 5.

56. Walton and Cleveland, *Corporations on Trial*, pp. 96–101.

57. U. S. Senate, *Administered Prices*, pp. 17671–17672.

58. Walton and Cleveland, *Corporations on Trial*, p. 103.

59. *New York Times*, 14 Feb. 1961, p. 36.

60. Walton and Cleveland, *Corporations on Trial*, p. 106.

61. General Electric, *Interim Report*, p. 4.

62. Glanville Williams, *Criminal Law* (London: Sweet & Maxwell, 1978), ch. 3.

63. Brent Fisse, "The Social Policy of Corporate Criminal Responsibility," *Adelaide Law Review* 8 (1978): 361–412, p. 397.

64. U. S. Senate, *Administered Prices*, p. 17288.

65. See Bane, *The Electrical Equipment Conspiracy*, chs. 1–3. However, General Electric was protected to a limited extent by attorney-client privilege and grand jury secrecy: ibid., ch. 10.

66. Ralph Cordiner, GE chairman, quoted in Walton and Cleveland, *Corporations on Trial*, p. 97. See also U. S. Senate, *Administered Prices*, p. 17674.

67. General Electric, *Policy on Compliance with the Antitrust Laws* (Fairfield, Conn.: General Electric, 1970), p. 3.

68. U. S. Senate, *Administered Prices*, pp. 16790, 16872.

69. Ibid., p. 17672. General Electric was also required by a consent decree to supply for the next 20 years a copy of the consent decree to each member of its board of directors, to all present and future officers of the company, and to department heads, and to set up a program to instruct key domestic management employees on the application, meaning, and effects of the terms of the decree.

70. See Geis and Meier, *White-Collar Crime*, p. 128.

71. U. S. Senate, *Administered Prices*, p. 17672.

72. Richard A. Whiting, "Antitrust and the Corporate Executive," *Virginia Law Review* 48 (1962): 1–49, p. 18; James A. Waters, "Catch 20.5: Corporate Morality as an Organizational Phenomenon," *Organizational Dynamics* 6 (Spring, 1978): 3–19, pp. 6–7.

73. General Electric, *Interim Report*, p. 5.

74. See generally "Developments in The Law—Corporate Crime: Regulating Corporate Behavior through Criminal Sanctions," *Harvard Law Review* 92 (1979): 1229–1375, pp. 1298–1301.

75. But see Robert J. Hoerner, "Misprision of Antitrust Felony," *Cleveland State Law Review* 28 (1979): 529–563 (canvassing the possibility of non-disclosure amounting to the offense of misprision of a felony).

76. U. S. Senate, *Administered Prices*, p. 17672. The new auditing rules were as follows:

Whenever any major price change has been made with respect to a product line or a major part thereof, it shall be the responsibility of the Department General Manager to have a report made and retained in the Department's files (for a period to be specified from time to time by the General Counsel) describing the change and the business reasons involved. Each such report shall have attached to it a certification of the Department General Manager, and any other employee responsible for the change or for recommending the change, that the pricing decision has been independently arrived at and is in no way related to any implied or expressed agreement or understanding with competitors. Determination of what constitute "major price changes" and "major parts of a product line" shall be made by the Department General Manager after consultation with his Division General Manager.

77. U. S. Senate, *Administered Prices*, p. 17672. The new rules for annual review provided that:

It is the basic responsibility of each manager at least annually to ask directly of each employee reporting to him any specific questions concerning the subject matter of, and compliance with, this Policy which may seem appropriate in the light of the duties of the particular employee. Each manager, should, by thoughtful questioning, tailored to the particular circumstances affecting each individual's work, encourage free and meaningful communication by employees. It is one objective of this procedure to develop at an early stage information on any areas of operations which are generating doubts among our own people *before* such doubts arise outside the Company. Where an individual employee has doubts or suspicions, these should be promptly and fully disclosed, leaving to higher management and the General Counsel's Office the responsibility for deciding whether such doubts or suspicions justify further inquiry.

78. U. S. Senate, *Administered Prices*, p. 17770.

79. Bane, *The Electrical Equipment Conspiracy*, pp. 385–387. See also David F. Lean, Jonathan D. Ogur, and Robert P. Rogers, *Competition and Collusion in Electrical Equipment Markets: An Economic Assessment* (Washington, D.C.: U.S. Government Printing Office, 1982).

80. Cf. Waters, "Catch 20.5," pp. 8–9.

81. Cf. John C. Coffee Jr., "Beyond the Shut-Eyed Sentry: Toward a Theoretical View of Corporate Misconduct and an Effective Legal Response," *Virginia Law Review* 63 (1977): 1100–1278, pp. 1189–1190.

Chapter 17

1. IBM, *IBM Business Conduct Guidelines (G.506–0001–4)* (Armonk, N.Y.: IBM, 1977).

2. *Wall Street Journal*, 19 May 1982, p. 27.

3. *Wall Street Journal*, 27 Jan. 1981, p. 6.

4. *Newsweek*, Feb. 9, 1981: 4.

5. *Wall Street Journal*, 12 Nov. 1981, p. 33.

6. *Wall Street Journal*, 3 April 1981, p. 27.

7. *Wall Street Journal*, 2 April 1982, p. 3.

8. *New York Times*, 31 March 1982, pp. A1, D6.

9. *New York Times*, 10 March 1982, p. D9.

10. *Wall Street Journal*, 31 March 1982, p. 1.

11. *New York Times*, 22 March 1982, p. D2.

12. See e.g., *Standard & Poor's Standard NYSE Stock Reports* 45 (244) (December 20, 1978), §17.

13. Within two weeks of the stopping of the case, a slight improvement in IBM stock was evident. IBM added five points, to close on January 22, 1982, at 62½, during a period when the Dow-Jones Industrial Average was steady. In the following two months, while the recession savaged stockmarkets badly, IBM was one of the stocks which held up well. This was in spite of an announcement of a 12% drop in earnings for the fourth quarter of 1981. Interestingly, however, after Judge Edelstein criticized the Justice Department dismissal of the case, IBM fell 3⅜ to 58½ in very active trading.

14. *Wall Street Journal*, 12 Jan. 1982, pp. 3, 14.

15. IBM, *Report to IBM Stockholders, Annual Meeting, April 28, 1980* (Armonk, N.Y.: IBM, 1980).

16. *Newsweek*, August 24, 1981: 45.

17. Robert Sobel, *IBM: Colossus in Transition* (New York: Times Books, 1981), p. 262.

18. IBM, *Business Conduct Guidelines*.

19. Nancy Foy, *The IBM World* (London: Eyre Methuen, 1974), pp. 151–152.

20. IBM, *Business Conduct Guidelines*, p. 29.

21. Ibid., p. 18.

22. Ibid., p. 29.

23. Ibid., p. 21.

24. Ibid., p. 26.

25. At IBM's request, the four following examples paraphrase the actual wording in this "IBM Internal Use Only" document.

26. *Wall Street Journal*, 12 Nov. 1981, p. 33.

27. Katherine Davis Fishman, *The Computer Establishment* (New York: Harper & Row, 1981), p. 148.

28. IBM, *Data Processing Division Public Sector Marketing Guidelines* (Armonk, N.Y.: 1980).

29. Ibid.

30. For a discussion of this problem, see George Getschow, "Some Middle Managers Cut Corners to Achieve High Corporate Goals," *Wall Street Journal*, 8 Nov. 1979.

31. In fact, the "contention system" applies to all areas of IBM business, not just corporate policies. It occurs in product development, technology, and the other IBM activities.

32. Don E. Waldman, *Antitrust Action and Market Structure* (Lexington, Mass.: Lexington Books, 1978); Don E. Waldman, "Economic Benefits in the IBM, AT&T, and Xerox Cases: Government Antitrust Policy in the '70s," *Antitrust Law and Economics Review* 12 (1979): 75–92.

33. If Waldman's research had been conducted several years later we wonder whether he would have qualified his conclusions, since it is doubtful that IBM's marketing practices were much constrained in the few years

before the dropping of the case in 1982. By 1979, most analysts seemed convinced that IBM was so sure of prevailing that impacts on the case were barely considered in pricing and other competitive decisions.

34. Waldman, *Antitrust Action*, pp. 132–142.

35. *Standard and Poor's Industry Surveys*, July 1979.

36. Waldman, "Economic Benefits," p. 79.

37. Ibid., p. 80.

38. Ibid.

39. And one can only speculate whether Apple, Commodore, and Tandy would have emerged with their clear early leads over IBM in microcomputers had they been hanging back in fear of takeover by the giant or of a latter-day operation SMASH.

40. *New York Times*, 10 Jan. 1982, p. 16.

41. Ibid. By August 1982, many in the financial community were arguing that IBM's pricing policies had already become more aggressive at least in part because of dismissal of the government case. See Andrew Pollack, "IBM's Aggressive Pricing," *New York Times*, 9 Aug. 1982, pp. D1, D7.

42. IBM has not made a significant acquisition since the government suit was launched in 1969.

43. For a discussion, see Tamer Lewin, "Dismissing Antitrust Suits," *New York Times*, 1 June 1982, p. D2.

Chapter 18

1. New Zealand Office of Air Accident Investigation, *Aircraft Accident Report No. 79–139* (Wellington: Ministry of Transport, 1980), para. 3–37.

2. N. Z., *Report of the Royal Commission to Inquire into the Crash on Mount Erebus, Antarctica, of a DC10 Aircraft Operated by Air New Zealand Limited* (Wellington: N. Z. Government Printer, 1981), paras. 224–225.

3. Ibid., para. 393. Note also para. 364: "System failures within the structure of the Flight Operations Division was the originating and decisive cause of this disaster".

4. Ibid., para. 54.

5. Ibid., para. 363.

6. Ibid., para. 377.

7. Ibid., p. 167.

8. See text and reference at Note 26, below.

9. The Airline Pilots Association threatened to consider calling a strike if Air New Zealand attempted to overturn the findings of the Royal Commission that pilot error had not caused the crash: *The Australian*, 2–3 May 1981.

10. *New Zealand Herald*, 23 Dec. 1981. The allegations in issue were various, but all related essentially to the Commission's findings that there had been a conspiratorial cover-up.

11. Ibid.

12. *New Zealand Herald*, 26 Dec. 1981.

13. *New Zealand Herald*, 25 May 1982; *Reform*, 1982, p. 57.

14. C. A. 95/81 (Wellington: N. Z. Government Printer, 1982), p. 3. Although it is not our place to pass judgment on the findings of the Chippindale and Mahon reports (conceivably, the disaster was caused by both pilot error and misnavigation from headquarters), it is unfortunate that the majority of the Court of Appeal should juxtapose the conclusions of the two reports in such a manner as to imply that they are more or less of equal authority: The Royal Commission was established not merely to give a second opinion, but to enable a more independent and detailed inquiry that the Departmental investigation could be expected to provide. See further *Star Weekender* (Auckland), 6 Feb. 1982; Gordon Vette, *Impact Erebus* (Auckland: Hodder and Stoughton, 1983), pp. 299–347.

15. The possibility of laying criminal charges against two persons was reviewed by the Crown Law Office: *New Zealand Herald*, 5 Sept. 1981; *Dominion*, 7 Sept. 1981. A Labour politician also raised the possibility of charging the company and implicated staff with manslaughter as well as offenses relating to the administration of justice: *New Zealand Herald*, 30 April 1981. As to the possibility of charges against Air New Zealand, it should be noted that the company is not legally an instrumentality enjoying the shield of the Crown but a limited liability company in which the government holds all the shares. However, under N.Z. law a company is not subject to liability for manslaughter: R v. Murray Wright Ltd. [1970] N.Z.L.R. 476. The need for further official inquiry has also been suggested: *Auckland Star*, 21 Jan. 1982; *New Zealand Herald*, 28 Jan. 1982.

16. *Timaru Herald*, 30 Nov. 1979.

17. See e.g., *Japan Times*, 29 Nov. 1979; *Mainichi Daily News*, 30 Nov. 1979; *Chicago Tribune*, 29 Nov. 1979; *Detroit News*, 28 Nov. 1979; *Sydney Morning Herald*, 30 Nov. 1979; *The Sun* (Sydney), 29 Nov. 1979.

18. *Japan Times*, 30 Nov. 1979; *New York Times*, 11 Dec. 1979 (early suspicion of navigational error); Ken Hickson, *Flight 901 to Erebus* (Christchurch: Whitcoulls, 1980), p. 107 (false rumor).

19. *The Australian*, 30 Nov. 1979; *The Dominion* (Wellington), 4 Dec. 1979; *The Herald* (Melbourne), 29 Nov. 1979. See further Michael Guy, *White-Out!* (Martinborough, N.Z.: Alister Taylor, 1980), pp. 36–38.

20. *New Zealand Herald*, 28 April 1981; *Time*, May 11, 1981; *Age* (Melbourne), 28 April 1981; *Canberra Times*, 28 April 1981.

21. *Southland Farmer* (Invercargill), 18 May 1981.

22. *The Australian*, 29 April 1981.

23. *Sunday News* (Auckland), 17 May 1981.

24. *New Zealand Herald*, 7 Jan. 1982. For other media statements by Justice Mahon see *New Zealand Herald*, 2, 14 and 29 Jan., and 4 Feb. 1982.

25. Hickson, *Flight 901 to Erebus*; Guy, *White-Out!*; Vette, *Impact Erebus*; Stewart Macpherson, "Deathflight 901" (television documentary, 1981).

26. *New Zealand Herald*, 5 May 1981. The view has been expressed that the chairman of the Board of Directors should have resigned: Noel Holmes, *To Fly a Desk: Sir Geoffrey Roberts, Father of Air New Zealand* (Auckland: Reed, 1982), p. 189.

27. *New Zealand Herald*, 5 May 1981; *Otago Daily Times*, 5 May 1981; *Wanganui Chronicle*, 5 May 1981.

28. Air New Zealand, Press Release, April 28, 1981.

29. Air New Zealand, Press Release, May 2, 1981.

30. There was also an element of sympathy for Davis when Justice Mahon "dropped a bombshell" with a public statement that in the Report "he carefully abstained from any finding" against Davis vis-à-vis his finding that there had been an "orchestrated litany of lies": *New Zealand Herald*, 24 Dec. 1981.

31. But see text and reference at Note 40.

32. *Auckland Star*, 11 Jan. 1982. See also *New Zealand Herald*, 23 Dec. 1981.

33. *New Zealand Herald*, 29 Jan. 1982. For a critical review of Chippindale's response, see John MacDonald, "Vital Questions Will Never Be Answered," *Star Weekender* (Auckland), 6 Feb. 1982; Vette, *Impact Erebus*, pp. 299–347.

34. *Hawera Star*, 15 May 1981.

35. *Waikato Times*, 5 May 1981. See also "Garbage in, Garbage out," *Flight International* 119 (3760) (1981): 1587.

36. *New Zealand Herald*, 2 Feb. 1982.

37. *New Zealand Herald*, 23 Jan. 1982; *New Zealand Herald*, 3 Feb. 1982.

38. *National Business Review*, May 4, 1981, p. 9. See also *Daily Telegraph* (Sydney), 29 April 1981.

39. *New Zealand Herald*, 30 April and 1 May 1981; *Southland Farmer* (Invercargill), 18 May 1981.

40. *New Zealand Herald*, 16 Jan. 1982. See also *New Zealand Herald*, 29 Dec. 1981, 16 Jan. and 2 Feb. 1982.

41. *New Zealand Herald*, 29 Jan. 1982. See also *New Zealand Herald*, 2 and 4 Feb. 1982.

42. *Press* (Christchurch), 30 Nov. 1979 (concern voiced about reaction of consumers abroad).

43. *Southland Times* (Invercargill), 15 May 1981. See further Guy, *White-Out!*, p. 233.

44. Interview with Market Research Manager, Qantas, Sept. 1981.

45. Air New Zealand, *Annual Report 1981* (Auckland, N.Z.: Air New Zealand, 1981), pp. 28–29; Qantas Airways, *Annual Report 1981* (Sydney: Qantas, 1981), pp. 56–57.

46. See reference at Note 44, above.

47. *Dominion* (Wellington), 4 Dec. 1979. There was no requirement in law that such gear be carried.

48. As one economist observed, most airlines are insured against the worst possible eventuality ("which would be something like a 747 full of

American lawyers crashing into one full of American doctors"): *N. Z. Economic News Bulletin*, May 4, 1981. For one history of the civil claims see Guy, *White-Out!*, ch. 12.

49. *New Zealand Herald*, 27 April 1982. Cf. Air New Zealand, *Annual Report 1981*, p. 6–7.

50. Apart from the slur on his own name, his daughter reportedly suffered the embarrassment of being in a first-year law class that was required to study the adverse comments made against her father in the Mahon Report: *New Zealand Herald*, 24 May 1981.

51. *New Zealand Herald*, 29 Dec. 1981. See also *New Zealand Herald*, 7 Jan. 1982.

52. *New Zealand Herald*, 29 April 1981 and 23 Jan. 1982. Answers were provided in a 17-page letter dated June 3, 1981; this document remains confidential.

53. Davis's style has been described as "autocratic" and "hubristic": *Report of the Royal Commission*, para. 373; *Otago Daily Times*, 5 May 1981. As to management philosophy and risk management, see Hickson, *Flight 901 to Erebus*, pp. 256–258.

54. *New Zealand Herald*, 26 Dec. 1981.

55. *Report of the Royal Commission*, paras. 365–366.

56. *New Zealand Herald*, 20 July 1981 (receipt of IATA report). In a letter dated Sept. 30, 1982, we were advised by Air New Zealand that our interest in the inquiries is noted but "these were in-house matters which have been kept in that context."

57. Cf. Tony Black, "The Erebus Inquiry," *New Zealand Law Journal* (1981): 188–190, p. 190.

58. *Report of the Royal Commission*, paras. 378–384. Note also *Aircraft Accident Report No. 79–139*, para. 3–30; Holmes, *To Fly a Desk*, pp. 187–189.

59. *Report of the Royal Commission*, para. 289(g). In a recent letter to the authors, the Ministry of Transport has expressed the following reservations about this passage in the text:

We have some qualms about the fairness of your statements. The actual passage in the transcript from which Mr. Mahon makes his criticism shows that it was a *suggestion* of Mahon's put to Captain Kippenberger in cross-examination and to which he (Kippenberger) replied "He (the co-pilot) may have been suffering from the same thing." It is *quite wrong* to suggest (as Mahon does) that this was Captain Kippenberger's major thesis.

60. N. Z., *Review of Civil Aviation Division in the light of Reports by the Royal Commission of Inquiry and the Chief Inspector of Accidents on the Crash of a DC10 Aircraft on Mount Erebus, Antarctica* (Wellington: State Services Commission and Ministry of Transport, 1981).

61. *New Zealand Herald*, 5 May 1981.

62. Tony Black, "Commissions, Witness and Counsel," *New Zealand Law Journal* (1981): 17–19, pp. 17–18. See generally Leonard Arthur Hallett,

Royal Commissions and Boards of Inquiry (Sydney: Law Book Co., 1982), ch. 10.

63. Cf. U.S., *Report of the President's Commission on the Accident at Three Mile Island* (Washington, D.C.: U. S. Government Printing Office, 1979), pp. 61–67. In a recent letter to the authors from the Ministry of Transport the following comment is made upon this passage:

> This does not provide the full picture. One of the terms of reference was "(j) Any other facts or matters arising out of the crash that, in the interests of public safety, should be known to the authorities charged with the administration of civil aviation in order that appropriate measures may be taken for the safety of persons engaged in aviation or carried as passengers in aircraft." The Commissioner failed to make any recommendations under this heading and consequently the focus was shifted to the causes rather than to what could be done to make aviation safer.

In our opinion, however, such a term of reference does not go far enough: explicit reference should be made to the adequacy or otherwise of a corporation's reactions to a commission's recommendations.

Chapter 19

1. Kenneth E. Boulding, *The Organizational Revolution* (Chicago: Quadrangle, 1968), p. 139.

2. Air New Zealand could not be said to have run a counterpublicity campaign. However, the Prime Minister of New Zealand and others could be regarded as having done so on the company's behalf.

3. Another example of an Australian Trade Practices Act prosecution for misleading advertising's actually increasing sales for the convicted company was the Power Machinery case. See Andrew Hopkins, *The Impact of Prosecution under the Trade Practices Act* (Canberra: Australian Institute of Criminology, 1978), p. 12.

4. *Sunday News Journal* (Wilmington), 10 January 1982.

5. Conversely, companies under public attack generally tend not to defend themselves by dragging other companies down with them. For example, when Firestone was under siege in the late 1970s over the safety of its radial tires, the company "decided to defend the 500 on its own merits and not by raising questions about the quality of another company's tires." Intercollegiate Case Clearing House, *Corporation v. Environment: The Case of the Firestone 500 Radial* (Cambridge, Mass.: Sloan School of Management, Massachusetts Institute of Technology), p. 17.

6. The notable setback to earnings was only for Sharp Australia.

7. Community prestige should be interpreted here broadly as including respect from the executive's own families, a dimension continually affirmed as important in our interviews. For example, in a roundtable discussion with six General Motors executives, we were told that the Chairman's

advice had once been: "You ought not to do anything that you don't want your mother to read about in the newspapers."

8. Charles P. Ramsden, "Performance, Satisfaction, Effort," *Personnel Administration and Public Personnel Review* 1 (1972): 4–8; Albert R. Martin, "Morale and Productivity: A Review of the Literature," *Public Personnel Review* 30 (1969): 42–44; Robert L. Kahn, "Productivity and Job Satisfaction," in Timothy W. Costello and Sheldon S. Zalkind, eds., *Psychology in Administration* (Englewoods Cliffs, N.J.: Prentice-Hall, 1963): 98–105.

9. Christopher D. Stone, *Where the Law Ends: The Social Control of Corporate Behavior* (New York: Harper & Row, 1975), pp. 203–206; John Braithwaite, *Corporate Crime in the Pharmaceutical Industry* (London: Routledge & Kegan Paul, 1983), ch. 9.

10. Lawrence W. Sherman, *Scandal and Reform: Controlling Police Corruption* (Berkeley and Los Angeles: University of California Press, 1978), pp. 252–253.

11. See further text following Note 28 below.

12. *Wall Street Journal*, 17 Nov. 1980.

13. Phillip G. Schrag recounts how Detective, a publicly traded company which was defrauding consumers, was bankrupted in the aftermath of a direct action campaign, which included adverse publicity, by the New York City Department of Consumer Affairs: "On Her Majesty's Secret Service: Protecting the Consumer in New York City," *Yale Law Journal* 80 (1971): 1529–603. Industrial Bio-Test, one of the largest contract testing laboratories in the U.S., was bankrupted by the FDA after allegations had been made against it of fudging data on the safety testing of drugs. Pharmaceutical companies ceased giving their toxicology testing contracts to IBT after the FDA warned them that data submitted to the agency that had been collected by IBT would be subjected to a special audit. Braithwaite, *Corporate Crime in the Pharmaceutical Industry*, ch. 3. In another FDA case, the agency forced a recall of Bon Vivant vichyssoise. The company was bankrupted even though only one of its products was contaminated with botulism: Ernest Gellhorn, "Adverse Publicity by Administrative Agencies," *Harvard Law Review* 86 (1973): 1381, 1413; Richard S. Morey, "Publicity as a Regulatory Tool," *Food, Drug and Cosmetic Law Journal* 30 (1975): 469–477.

14. Gellhorn, "Adverse Publicity," pp. 1408–1409.

15. Peter Rossi, Emily Waite, Christine E. Bose, and Richard E. Berk, "The Seriousness of Crimes: Normative Structure and Individual Differences," *American Sociological Review* 39 (1974): 224–237; Marvin Wolfgang, *National Survey of Crime Severity Final National Level Geometric Means and Ratio Scores by Offense Stimuli Items* (Philadelphia: University of Pennsylvania, 1980); Francis T. Cullen, Bruce G. Link and Craig W. Polanzi, "The Seriousness of Crime Revisited: Have Attitudes toward White-Collar Crime Changed?" *Criminology* 20 (1982): 83–102.

16. *Wall Street Journal*, 29 Oct. 1980.

17. *Wall Street Journal*, 3 March 1981, 9 June 1982.

18. *Wall Street Journal*, 17 Oct. 1980.

19. Wally Olins, *The Corporate Personality* (London: Design Council, 1978), p. 121. A corporation which has suffered much more loss of corporate prestige than any of the companies in our study is Nestlé over the infant formula scandal. That scandal has also produced substantial reform recently: "Nestlé Announces Change in Its Infant Formula Policies," *Multinational Monitor*, April 1982, p. 10; *New York Times*, 2 May 1982, p. 8, and 5 May 1982, p. C17; James E. Post and Edward Baer, "Demarketing Infant Formula: Consumer Products in the Developing World," *Journal of Contemporary Business* 7 (1980): 17–35.

20. *New York Times*, 25 March 1979, section I, p. 7.

21. Neil Jacoby, Peter Nehemkis, and Richard Eells, *Bribery and Extortion in World Business: A Study of Corporate Political Payments Abroad* (New York: Macmillan, 1977), p. 56.

22. Note, "Disclosure of Payments to Foreign Government Officials under the Securities Act," *Harvard Law Review* 89 (1976): 1855.

23. Paul A. Griffin, "Sensitive Foreign Payment Disclosures: The Securities Market Impact," in *Report of the Advisory Committee on Corporate Disclosure to the Securities and Exchange Commission* (Washington, D.C.: U.S. Government Printing Office, 1977).

24. Harry V. Ball and Lawrence M. Friedman, "Criminal Sanctions in Enforcement of Economic Legislation," in John Johnson and Jack Douglas, eds., *Crime at the Top: Deviance in Business and the Professions* (Philadelphia: Lippincott, 1978), p. 334.

25. Donald R. Cressey and Charles A. Moore, *Corporation Codes of Ethical Conduct* (New York: Report to Peat, Marwick and Mitchell Foundation, 1980).

26. Ibid., p. 5. A General Accounting Office survey of almost 200 large American companies found that further reforms were made in 75% of the companies following the Foreign Corrupt Practices Act. These included strengthening codes of conduct, tougher internal audit staff, improved internal control documentation, and greater independence for board audit committees. Seventy percent of respondents believed that the Act effectively reduced questionable foreign payments. General Accounting Office, *Impact of Foreign Corrupt Practices Act on U.S. Business* (Washington D.C.: U. S. Government Printing Office, 1981), pp. 6–12.

27. Ibid., pp. 15–16.

28. E.g., William Clifford and John Braithwaite, *Cost-Effective Business Regulation: Views from the Australian Business Elite* (Canberra: Australian Institute of Criminology, 1981).

29. See the classic review by Douglas Lipton, Robert Martinson, and Judith Wilks, *The Effectiveness of Correctional Treatment: A Survey of Evaluation Studies* (New York: Praeger, 1975).

30. Don E. Waldman, *Antitrust Action and Market Structure* (Lexington, Mass.: Lexington Books, 1978).

31. U.S. v. E.J. du Pont de Nemours & Co., 351 U.S. 377 (1956).

32. Waldman, *Antitrust Action*, p. 36.
33. Ibid., p. 40.

Chapter 20

1. See generally Phillip I. Blumberg, *The Megacorporation in American Society: The Scope of Corporate Power* (Englewood Cliffs, N.J.: Prentice-Hall, 1975); Andrew Hacker, ed., *The Corporation Take-Over* (New York: Harper & Row, 1964); Ralph Nader and Mark J. Green, eds., *Corporate Power in America* (New York: Penguin, 1977); Robin Marris, ed., *The Corporate Society* (London: Macmillan, 1974); Jeffrey H. Reiman, *The Rich Get Richer and the Poor Get Prison: Ideology, Class, and Criminal Justice* (New York: Wiley, 1979).

2. The U.S. Supreme Court has held that "corporations can claim no equality with individuals in the enjoyment of a right to privacy. . . . They are endowed with public attributes. They have a collective impact on society, from which they derive the privilege of acting as artificial entities": United States v. Morton Salt Co., 338 U. S. 632, 652 (1950). See also Howard Simons and Joseph A. Califano, Jr., *The Media and Business* (New York: Vintage, 1979), pp. xi–xii, xx–xxiii.

3. Most of the companies studied in this book decided against counter-publicity. They were not too devastated to fight back, but other ways of tackling the problem were seen as better aligned with the company's interests.

4. As to labelling theory see Edwin Lemert, *Social Pathology* (New York: McGraw-Hill, 1951); Howard S. Becker, *Outsiders: Studies in the Sociology of Deviance* (New York: Free Press, 1963); Irving Goffman, *Stigma* (Englewood Cliffs, N.J.: Prentice-Hall, 1963); Charles W. Wright and Susan C. Randall, "Contrasting Conceptions of Deviance in Sociology: Functionalism and Labelling Theory," *British Journal of Criminology* 18 (1978): 217–231. For empirical evidence see Donald J. West and David P. Farrington, *The Delinquent Way of Life* (London: Heinemann, 1977). Note, however, that corporate and individual offenders may possibly have more in common when it comes to sainthood, the opposite of stigma: cf. Albert K. Cohen, *The Elasticity of Evil* (Oxford, U.K.: Basil Blackwell, 1974), pp. 32–39.

5. Marshall B. Clinard, *The Black Market: A Study of White-Collar Crime* (New York: Rinehart, 1952); Gilbert Geis, "The Heavy Electrical Equipment Antitrust Cases of 1961," in Marshall B. Clinard and Richard Quinney, eds., *Criminal Behavior Systems* (New York: Holt, Rinehart and Winston, 1967); Kenneth Mann, Stanton Wheeler, and Austin Sarat, "Sentencing the White-Collar Criminal," *American Criminal Law Review* 17 (1980): 479–500.

6. Prestige and repute may have slightly different connotations, prestige being favorable regard based more on status, repute favorable regard based

more on propriety. The difference is so slight, however, that we use the words interchangeably.

7. Henry Ford II, *Policy Letter C–3, Standards of Corporate Conduct* (Detroit: Ford Motor Company, 1976), p. 1.

8. Nancy Yashihara, "$1 Billion Spent on Identity: Companies Push Image of Selves, Not Products," *Los Angeles Times*, 10 May 1981, pp. 1, 17.

9. See Roy Birch, "Corporate Advertising: Why, How and When," *Advertising Quarterly* 57(5) (1978): 5–9.

10. Robert Lamb, William G. Armstrong, Jr., and Karolyn R. Morigi, *Business, Media and the Law* (New York: New York University Press, 1980), pp. 66–69; *Los Angeles Times*, 10 May 1981, p. 1.

11. Charles Channon, "Corporations and the Politics of Perception," *Advertising Quarterly* 60(2) (1981): 12–15, p. 13. See also Wally Olins, *The Corporate Personality: An Inquiry into the Nature of Corporate Identity* (New York: Mayflower Books, 1978); Russell B. Stevenson, Jr., "Corporations and Social Responsibility: In Search of the Corporate Soul," *George Washington Law Review* 12 (1974): 709–736, p. 724; *Wall Street Journal*, 20 July 1982, p. 56; and text and references below at Note 93, Ch. 21.

12. See Brent Fisse, "The Social policy of Corporate Criminal Responsibility," *Adelaide Law Review* 8 (1978): 361–412, pp. 371–382.

13. N. Z., *Report of the Royal Commission to Inquire into the Crash on Mount Erebus, Antarctica, of a DC10 Aircraft Operated by Air New Zealand Limited* (Wellington: N. Z. Government Printer, 1981), para. 393.

14. Fisse, "Social Policy of Corporate Criminal Responsibility," pp. 371–373.

15. Thomas J. Stanley and Larry M. Robinson, "Opinions on Consumer Issues: A Review of Recent Studies of Executives and Consumers," *Journal of Consumer Affairs* 14 (1980): 207–220; Herman Nickel, "The Corporation Haters," *Fortune*, June 16, 1980, p. 126.

16. Fear of adverse publicity and fear of the law are not mutually exclusive, but they can be responded to independently in an opinion survey.

17. Opinion Research Corporation, *Executive Attitudes toward Morality in Business* (Princeton, N.J.: Opinion Research Corporation, 1975). See also F. T. Allen, "Corporate Morality: Executive Responsibility," *Atlanta Economic Review* 9 (1976): 8–11.

18. S. N. Brenner and E. A. Molender, "Is the Ethics of Business Changing?" *Harvard Business Review*, Jan.–Feb. 1977; 59–70.

19. Quoted in W. J. Byron, "The Meaning of Ethics in Business," *Business Horizons*, Dec. 1977: 31–34, p. 34.

20. See Milton Friedman and Rose Friedman, *Free to Choose* (New York: Harcourt Brace Jovanovich, 1980), ch. 7. For more balanced accounts, see Harry H. Stein, "American Muckrakers and Muckraking: The 50-Year Scholarship," *Journalism Quarterly* 56 (1979): 9–17; Gilbert Geis and Herbert Edelhertz, "Criminal Law and Consumer Fraud: A Sociolegal View," *American Criminal Law Review* 11 (1973): 989–1010.

21. Mark V. Nadel, *Corporations and Political Accountbility* (Lexington, Mass.: Lexington Books, 1976), pp. 252–253; M. David Ermann and Richard J. Lundman, *Corporate Deviance* (New York: Holt, Rinehart and Winston, 1982), p. 137; Kenneth J. Arrow, "Organizational Goals and Control Systems: Internal and External Considerations," in Lee E. Preston, ed., *Research in Corporate Social Performance and Policy* 1 (Greenwich, Conn.: JAI Press, 1978): 79–97, pp. 88–90; Richard M. Cooper, "Freedom of Choice in the Real World," *Food Drug Cosmetic Law Journal* 34 (1979): 612–624.

22. See generally Robert F. Buckhorn, *Nader: The People's Lawyer* (Englewood Cliffs, N.J.: Prentice-Hall, 1972); Charles McCarry, *Citizen Nader* (New York: Saturday Review Press, 1972).

23. Edward Finch Cox, Robert C. Fellmeth, and John E. Schulz, *The Nader Report on the Federal Trade Commission* (New York: Baron, 1969).

24. American Bar Association, *Report of the ABA Commission to Study the Federal Trade Commission* (Chicago: ABA, 1969); U.S. Senate, Comm. on Commerce, *Magnusson-Moss Warranty—Federal Trade Commission Improvement Act*, S. Rep. No. 93–151, 93d Cong., 1st Sess., 1973.

25. Donna M. Randall, "The Social Control of Big Business," unpublished paper delivered at American Society of Criminology Annual Meeting, San Francisco, Nov. 1980. See also Earl W. Kintner and Christopher Smith, "The Emergence of the Federal Trade Commission as a Formidable Consumer Protection Agency," *Mercer Law Review* 26 (1975): 651–688.

26. Ralph Nader advanced this proposal informally during his Australian lecture tour in 1980.

27. Cf. Delaware Citizens for Clean Air Inc. v. Stauffer Chemical Co., 367 F. Supp. 1040, 1047–1048 (1973).

28. See e.g., "Developments in the Law—Deceptive Advertising," *Harvard Law Review* 80 (1967): 1005–1163, pp. 1143–1144.

29. See generally Dan D. Pitzer, "The Qui Tam Doctrine: A Comparative Analysis of Its Application in the United States and the British Commonwealth," *Texas International Law Journal* 7 (1972): 415–440; Robert W. Fischer, Jr., "*Qui Tam* Actions: The Role of the Private Citizen in Law Enforcement," *University of California at Los Angeles Law Review* 20 (1973): 778–803; U. S., Staff of Conservation and Natural Resources Subcomm. of the House Comm. on Government Operations, *Qui Tam Actions and the 1899 Refuse Act: Citizen Lawsuits against Polluters of the Nation's Waterways*, 91st Cong., 2nd Sess., 1970; Gary S. Becker and George J. Stigler, "Law Enforcement, Malfeasance, and Compensation of Enforcers," *Journal of Legal Studies* 3 (1974): 1–18; William M. Landes and Richard A. Posner, "The Private Enforcement of Law," *Journal of Legal Studies* 4 (1975): 1–46. *Qui tam* actions should be distinguished from mere reimbursement of litigation costs, as provided for in e.g., 42 U.S.C. § 7604(d) (1980 Supp.); H. R. 7010, 96th Cong., 3rd Sess. (1980), § 605. See further *Wall Street Journal*, 29 Nov. 1971, p. 1 and 28 Jan. 1982, p. 48.

30. U.S., President's Commission for a National Agenda for the Eighties, *A National Agenda for the Eighties* (Washington, D. C.: U. S. Government Printing Office, 1980), p. 109.

31. Thomas C. Crumplar, "An Alternative to Public and Victim Enforcement of the Federal Securities and Antitrust Laws: Citizen Enforcement," *Harvard Journal on Legislation* 13 (1975): 76–124, pp. 102–103. But see Andrew Sidman, "The Outmoded Concept of Private Prosecution," *American University Law Review* 25 (1976): 754–794.

32. Edward Coke, *The Third Part of the Institutes of the Laws of England* (London: Clarke, 1809), section 194. See also Robert Nozick, *Anarchy, State, and Utopia* (New York: Basic Books, 1974), ch. 2.

33. As to class actions and their limitations, see generally "Developments in the Law: Class Actions," *Harvard Law Review* 89 (1976): 1318–1644. As to rules of standing, see generally Kenneth E. Scott, "Standing in the Supreme Court—A Functional Analysis," *Harvard Law Review* 86 (1973): 645–692; Joseph Vining, *Legal Identity: The Coming of Age of Public Law* (New Haven: Yale University Press, 1978).

34. James E. Starrs, "The Consumer Class Action—Part II," *Boston University Law Review* 49 (1969): 407–513, p. 408.

35. Cf. Zenon Bankowski and Geoff Mungham, *Images of Law* (London: Routledge & Kegan Paul, 1976), p. xiii ("law is an imperial code, it emasculates man by offering the solution of his problem to 'experts'; it reflects the professionalized society. The only way out is for men to seize their lives and transform themselves and the world."). See also Sidney Kraus and Dennis Davis, *The Effects of Mass Communication on Political Behavior* (University Park: Pennsylvania State University Press, 1976), pp. 288–289 (importance of transactional as opposed to communicator-dominated model of communication).

36. This is not to say that *qui tam* suits would cover the ground entirely (they would not apply to torts or breaches of contract) but statutory offenses would usually be available to provide a basis for *qui tam* actions under appropriate specific or general enabling provisions.

37. See Fischer, "*Qui Tam* Actions," p. 799; Kenneth W. Dam, "Class Actions: Efficiency, Compensation, Deterrence, and Conflict of Interest," *Journal of Legal Studies* 4 (1975): 47–73, pp. 68–70. Cf. Pitzer, "The Qui Tam Doctrine," p. 439; *Wall Street Journal*, 29 Nov. 1971, p. 1.

38. Crumplar, "Citizen Enforcement," pp. 116–118.

39. See James Geraghty, "Structural Crime and Institutional Rehabilitation: A New Approach to Corporate Sentencing," *Yale Law Journal* 89 (1979): 353–375; Stephen A. Yoder, "Criminal Sanctions for Corporate Illegality," *Journal of Criminal Law & Criminology* 69 (1978): 40–58; Brent Fisse, "Community Service as a Sanction against Corporations," *Wisconsin Law Review* (1981): 970–1017.

40. Carl Bernstein and Robert Woodward, *All the President's Men* (New York: Simon & Schuster, 1974). See also Troy A. Zimmer, "The Impact

of Watergate on the Public's Trust in People and Confidence in the Mass Media," *Social Science Quarterly* 59 (1979): 743–751.

41. Mrs. Ward Jackson in *Report of Royal Commission on Standards of Conduct in Public Life* (London: Her Majesty's Stationery Office, 1976), p. 119.

42. See Harvey Teff and Colin R. Munro, *Thalidomide: The Legal Aftermath* (Farnborough: Saxon House, 1976), pp. 27–64; Phillip Knightley, Harold Evans, Elaine Potter, and Marjorie Wallace, *Suffer the Children: The Story of Thalidomide* (New York: Viking, 1979), chs. 9–14.

43. Michael Brown, *Laying Waste: The Poisoning of America by Toxic Chemicals* (New York: Pocket Books, 1979).

44. Morton Mintz, *By Prescription Only* (Boston: Houghton-Mifflin, 1967); Mark Dowie, "Pinto Madness," *Mother Jones*, Sept./Oct. 1977: 2–13; Mike Muller, *The Baby Killers* (London: War on Want, 1974).

45. 376 U.S. 254 (1964).

46. 385 U.S. 374 (1967).

47. See generally Harold L. Nelson and Dwight L. Teeter, *Law of Mass Communications* (Mineola, N.Y.: Foundation Press, 3rd ed., 1978), ch. 4; Lee J. Levine, "The Editorial Function and the Gertz Public Figure Standard," *Yale Law Journal* 87 (1978): 1723–1751; David A. Anderson, "Libel and Press Self-Censorship," *Texas Law Review* 53 (1975): 422–481.

48. See J. G. Fleming, "Retraction and Reply: Alternative Remedies for Defamation," *University of British Columbia Law Review* 12 (1978): 15–31; Australia, Law Reform Commission, *Report No. 11, Unfair Publication: Defamation and Privacy* (Canberra: Australian Government Publishing Service, 1979), para. 257; Stuart Taylor Jr., "Post Libel Verdict Worries the Press," *New York Times*, Aug. 1, 1982, p. 20. A recent example is the $2.02 million verdict against the Washington *Post* in favor of Mobil President William P. Tavoulareas and his son: *Time*, Aug. 9, 1982, p. 43. Note, however, that defendants have a strong record of success in appeals against liability for defamation: Marc A. Franklin, "Suing Media for Libel: A Litigation Study," *American Bar Foundation Research Journal* (1981): 797–831. It should also be noted that in Gertz v. Robert Welch Inc., 418 U.S. 323 (1974), the Supreme Court restricted damages recoverability to actual as opposed to presumed injury to reputation.

49. Fleming, "Retraction and Reply," pp. 15–16.

50. See Martin Marietta Corp. v. Evening Star Newspaper Co., 417 F. Supp. 947 (1976); Patricia Nassif Fetzer, "The Corporate Defamation Figure as First Amendment "Public Figure," *Iowa Law Review* 68 (1982):35–86; Nessa E. Moll, "In Search of the Corporate Private Figure: Defamation of the Corporation," *Hofstra Law Review* 6 (1978): 339–360; George E. Stevens, "Private Enterprise and Public Reputation: Defamation and the Corporate Plaintiff," *American Business Law Journal* (1974): 281–293; Note, "Libel and the Corporate Plaintiff," *Columbia Law Review* 69 (1969): 1496–1513.

51. Moll, "In Search of the Corporate Private Figure," p. 339.

52. 18 U.S.C. §§ 1961–1968 (1976).

53. From prosecutor's transcript of meeting with McDonnell, Justice Department, Washington, D.C., Sept. 26, 1980.

54. We are indebted to the survey reported in Law Reform Commission, *Unfair Publication*, paras. 254–255.

55. Law Reform Commission, *Unfair Publication*, pp. 216–217, clause 28. See also James H. Hulme, "Vindicating Reputation: An Alternative to Damages as a Remedy for Defamation," *American University Law Review* 30 (1981): 375–414. Cp. AAFCO Heating & Air Conditioning Co. v. Northwest Publications, Inc., 321 N.E. 2d 580, 587 (1974); Nelson and Teeter, *Law of Mass Communications*, pp. 156–157.

56. See Kenneth T. Roth, "In Defense of Fault in Defamation Law," *Yale Law Journal* 88 (1979): 1735–1751.

57. Cf. Law Reform Commission, *Unfair Publication*, para. 94, recommending that correction orders be available to corporations, but unpersuasively dismissing the significance of non-financial corporate reputation.

58. Alfred Friendly and Ronald L. Goldfarb, *Crime and Publicity: The Impact of News on the Administration of Justice* (New York: Vintage, 1968), p. 251. See generally Nelson and Teeter, *Law of Mass Communications*, ch. 8.

59. See C. J. Miller, *Contempt of Court* (London: Elek, 1976), ch. 6; Zelman Cowen, "Some Observations on the Law of Criminal Contempt," *University of Western Australia Law Review* 7 (1965): 1–39; Ernest D. Giglio, "Free Press—Fair Trial in Britain and America," *Journal of Criminal Justice* 10 (1982): 341–358; Louis L. Jaffe, "Trial by Newspaper," *New York University Law Review* 40 (1965): 504–524.

60. United States v. Abbott Laborabories, 505 F. 2d 565 (1974). See also Franklin Zimring, "'Free Press—Fair Trial' Revisited: Defendant-Centered Remedies as a Publicity Policy," *University of Chicago Law Review* 33 (1966): 512–530. Cf. American Bar Association, Advisory Committee on Fair Trial and Free Press, *Standards Relating to Fair Trial and Free Press* (New York: A.B.A., 1966).

61. See Nelson and Teeter, *Law of Mass Communications*, pp. 255, 291–304; Dov Apfel, "Gag Orders, Exclusionary Orders, and Protective Orders," *American University Law Review* 29 (1980): 439–484.

62. 427 U.S. 539 (1976).

63. See further Benno C. Schmidt, Jr., "Nebraska Press Association: An Expansion of Freedom and Contraction of Theory," *Stanford Law Review* 29 (1977): 431–476; Note, "Protective Orders against the Press and the Inherent Powers of the Courts," *Yale Law Journal* 87 (1977): 342–371; *New York Times*, 18 May 1982, p. A17.

64. John Kaplan, "Of Babies and Bathwater," *Stanford Law Review* 29 (1977): 621–626, p. 622. See also Zechariah Chafee, *Government and Mass Communications* (Hamden, Conn.: Archon Books, 1965), pp. 432–433.

65. [1974] A. C. 273. See further Knightley et al, *Suffer the Children*, ch. 16; M. Rosen, *The Sunday Times Thalidomide Case: Contempt of Court and*

Freedom of the Press (London: British Institute of Human Rights, 1979); Nathanson, "The Sunday Times Case: Freedom of the Press and Contempt of Court under English Law and the European Human Rights Convention," *Kentucky Law Journal* 68 (1980): 971–1025.

66. "European Court of Human Rights: Judgment in Sunday Times Case," *International Legal Materials* 18 (1979): 931–962.

67. See Contempt of Court Act, 1981 (U.K.), s. 5. See also Great Britain, *Report of the Committee on Contempt of Court* (London: Her Majesty's Stationery Office, Command 5794, 1974), paras. 143–145; South Australia, Criminal Law and Penal Methods Reform Committee, *Fourth Report, The Substantive Criminal Law* (Adelaide: South Australian Government Printer, 1978), para. 3.9. But see G. B., *Contempt of Court* (London: Her Majesty's Stationery Office, Command 7145, 1978), pp. 9–10.

68. See generally Thomas Donaldson, *Corporations and Morality* (Englewood Cliffs, N.J.: Prentice-Hall, 1982), pp. 125–156.

69. See Knightley et al., *Suffer the Children*, ch. 10.

70. Special juries, composed of persons experienced in matters of business and regulation, might be used to minimize the problem, but this possibility raises problems of elitism and practicality. See generally W. R. Cornish, *The Jury* (Harmondsworth: Penguin, 1971), pp. 197–201; South Australia, Criminal Law and Penal Methods Reform Committee, *Third Report, Court Procedure and Evidence* (Adelaide: South Australian Government Printer, 1976), para. 6.11.

71. See "Developments in the Law—Corporate Crime: Regulating Corporate Behavior through Criminal Sanctions," *Harvard Law Review* 92 (1979): 1227–1375; Simeon M. Kriesberg, "Decisionmaking Models and the Control of Corporate Crime," *Yale Law Journal* 85 (1976): 1091–1129; Criminal Law and Penal Methods Reform Committee, *Fourth Report*, paras. 5.5–5.10.

72. See Rita J. Simon, "Does the Court's Decision in *Nebraska Press Association* Fit the Research Evidence on the Impact on Jurors of News Coverage?," *Stanford Law Review* 29 (1977): 519–528; "Nebraska Press Association," pp. 443–451; *Age* (Melbourne), 1 July 1982.

73. Friendly and Goldfarb, *Crime and Publicity*, pp. 167–168; Charles Garry and Dennis Riordan, "Gag Orders: *Cui Bono?*," *Stanford Law Review* 29 (1977): 575–590, p. 577. See also Knightley et al., *Suffer the Children*, pp. 225–226.

74. See Marshall B. Clinard and Peter C. Yeager, *Corporate Crime* (New York: Free Press, 1980), pp. 87–89; Albert J. Reiss, Jr., and Albert D. Biderman, *Data Sources on White-Collar Law-Breaking* (Washington, D.C.: National Institute of Justice, 1980), pp. 274–298; Miriam S. Saxon, *White-Collar Crime: The Problem and the Federal Response*, Report No. 80–84 EPW (Washington, D.C.: Congressional Research Service, Library of Congress, 1980), pp. 54–55.

75. Attorney-General v. Times Newspapers Ltd., [1974] A.C. 273. See further Miller, *Contempt of Court*, pp. 133–136.

76. [1974] A.C. 273, 313.

77. Consider e.g., W. H. Walsh, "Pride, Shame and Responsibility," *Philosophical Quarterly* 20 (1970): 1–13, p. 13. The *Sunday Times* campaign against Distillers pivoted upon this point: see Knightley et al., *Suffer the Children*, p. 180.

78. [1974] A.C. 273, 295, 306, 326.

79. See Ernest Gellhorn, "Adverse Publicity by Administrative Agencies," *Harvard Law Review* 86 (1973): 1380–1441, pp. 1382–1383. Enforcement agencies may use publicity for these purposes where illegality is suspected but there are no reasonable grounds for laying charges. See e.g., Japan, Federal Trade Commission, *Anti-Monopoly Policy of Japan* (Tokyo: Federal Trade Commission, 1982), p. 2: In cases where the leading enterprises including the largest one in a highly concentrated industry have raised the prices of goods or services by a similar amount or similar rate within a period of three months, the FTC may request reports on the reason for the price increases. The reports filed are to be made public in the FTC's annual report which is to be submitted to the Diet. It is expected that this reporting and disclosure system will have the effect of preventing enterprises from undue and agreed-upon price hikes.

80. *Wall Street Journal*, 3 Nov. 1980, p. 1 (Rely Tampon); Gellhorn, "Adverse Publicity," p. 1413 (Bon Vivant).

81. See Note, "Disparaging Publicity by Federal Agencies," *Columbia Law Review* 67 (1967): 1512–1528; Robinson B. Lacy, "Adverse Publicity and SEC Enforcement Procedure," *Fordham Law Review* 46 (1977): 435–458, p. 458; Catherine A. Olsen, "Corporate Liberty Rights in Reputation," *Boston University Law Review* 61 (1981):1271–1274.

82. EEOC Newsletter, Aug. 1971, part 2, p. 3, quoted in Gellhorn, "Adverse Publicity," p. 1401.

83. Thomas J. Austern, "Is Government By Exhortation Desirable?", *Food Drug Cosmetic Law Journal* 22 (1967): 647–654; Richard S. Morey, "FDA Publicity aganist Consumer Products—A Time for Statutory Revitalization?", *Business Lawyer* 30 (1974): 165–178.

84. United States v. International Medication Systems Ltd., No. 73–626—WPG (C.D. Cal., June 27, 1973), discussed in Morey, "FDA Publicity Against Consumer Products," pp. 172–174.

85. Morey, "FDA Publicity," p. 173.

86. Wayne L. Pines, "Regulatory Letters, Publicity and Recalls," *Food Drug Cosmetic Law Journal* 31 (1976): 352–359, p. 354.

87. Consider e.g., James S. Turner, *The Chemical Feast* (New York: Grossman, 1970), ch. 2.

88. See reference in Note 79 above.

89. Gellhorn, "Adverse Publicity," pp. 1431–1432.

90. See U.S. SEC, *Report of the Securities and Exchange Commission on Questionable and Illegal Foreign Payments Submitted to the Senate Committee on Banking, Housing and Urban Affairs*, 94th Cong., 2nd Sess., 1976, pp. 6–7; Deborah A. DeMott, "Reweaving the Corporate Veil: Management Struc-

ture and the Control of Corporate Information," in Deborah A. DeMott, ed., *Corporations at the Crossroads: Governance and Reform* (New York: McGraw-Hill, 1980), pp. 308–311. The disclosures contemplated would involve waiver of attorney-client privilege. Cf. Note, "Corporate Self-Investigations under the Foreign Corrupt Practices Act," *University of Chicago Law Review* 47 (1980): 803–823.

91. See Jacqueline C. Wolff, "Voluntary Disclosure Programs," *Fordham Law Review* 47 (1979): 1057–1082, pp. 1058–1061.

92. See SEC, *Report on Questionable and Illegal Foreign Payments*, pp. 6–7. Interview with Stanley Sporkin, former Director of Enforcement, SEC, Nov. 1981.

93. Wolff, "Voluntary Disclosure Programs," pp. 1064–1065. See also Ermann and Lundman, *Corporate Deviance*, p. 91.

94. See Fisse, "Community Service as a Sanction Against Corporations," pp. 990–1003.

95. Cf. John C. Coffee, Jr., "'No Soul to Damn: No Body to Kick': An Unscandalized Inquiry into the Problem of Corporate Punishment," *Michigan Law Review* 79 (1981): 386–459, pp. 426–427; *Wall Street Journal*, 9 July 1976, p. 1.

96. See Wolff, "Voluntary Disclosure Programs," p. 1060.

97. It may also be noted that disclosure as recommended is consistent with the recent trend toward public notification of consent agreements: See e.g., Note "The ITT Dividend: Reform of Department of Justice Consent Decree Procedures," *Columbia Law Review* 73 (1973): 594–634.

98. August Bequai, "Why the SEC's Enforcer Is in over His Head," *Business Week*, 11 Oct. 1976: 70–76, p. 70. This is not to deny the potential deterrent or preventive value of mitigation of sentence, within limits: See generally Leslie Sebba, "Mitigation of Sentence in Order to Deter," *Monash University Law Review* 6 (1980): 268–293.

99. Wolff, "Voluntary Disclosure Programs," pp. 1059–1060. Stanley Sporkin, former SEC Director of Enforcement, regarded a formal guarantee as unnecessary because "the rules of the game were widely known": interview Nov. 1981. *Sed quaere.*

100. See John Braithwaite, *To Punish or Persuade: Enforcement of Coal Mine Safety* (manuscript in preparation).

101. Francis E. Rourke, *Secrecy and Publicity: Dilemmas of Democracy* (Baltimore: Johns Hopkins Press, 1961), p. 118.

102. See Alan Barth, *Government by Investigation* (New York: Viking, 1955), pp. 81–111; James Hamilton, *The Power to Probe: A Study of Congressional Investigations* (New York: Random House, 1976), ch. 4; G. B., *Report of Royal Commission on Tribunals of Inquiry* (London: Her Majesty's Stationery Office, Command 3121, 1966), paras. 6–21; David R. Mummery, "Due Process and Inquisitions," *Law Quarterly Review* 97 (1981): 287–333; Tony Black, "Commissions, Witness and Counsel," *New Zealand Law Journal* (1981): 17–19; Note, "The Distinction Between Informing and Prosecu-

torial Investigations: A Functional Analysis for 'Star Chamber' Proceedings," *Yale Law Journal* 72 (1963): 1227–1242.

103. Hamilton, *The Power to Probe*, p. 141.

104. New Zealand Court of Appeal, 95/81 (1981).

105. New Jersey Statutes Annotated 52: 9 M–4; Canada, Law Reform Commission, *Report 13, Advisory and Investigatory Commissions* (Ottawa: Information Canada, 1979), pp. 38–39.

106. Law Reform Commission, *Advisory and Investigatory Commissions*, pp. 39–40. Cf. Hannah v. Larche, 363 U. S. 420 (1969).

107. Douglas Cater, *The Fourth Branch of the Government* (Boston: Houghton Mifflin, 1959), p. 59.

108. Rourke, *Secrecy and Publicity*, p. 119.

109. Cf. W. Wallace Kirkpatrick, "The Adequacy of Internal Corporate Controls," *Annals of the American Academy of Political and Social Science* 343 (1962): 75–83.

110. Elinor Langer, "Auto Safety: Nader vs. General Motors," *Science* 152 (1966): 47–50, p. 49.

111. Cf. Daniel P. Moynihan, "The War against the Automobile," *Public Interest* (1966, No. 3): 10–26, pp. 13–17.

112. Consider SEC, *Report on Questionable and Illegal Foreign Payments*, pp. 44–48; U.S. H.R., Committee on Interstate and Foreign Commerce, *SEC Voluntary Compliance Program on Corporate Disclosure: Staff Study by The Subcommittee on Oversight and Investigations*, 94th Cong., 2nd Sess., 1976.

113. See e.g., DeMott, "Reweaving the Corporate Veil"; John C. Coffee, Jr., "Beyond the Shut-Eyed Sentry: Toward a Theoretical View of Corporate Misconduct and an Effective Legal Response," *Virginia Law Review* 63 (1977): 1099–1278.

114. Cf. U. S., *Report of the President's Commission on the Accident at Three Mile Island* (Washington D.C.: U. S. Government Printing Office, 1979), p. 1 (example of constructively oriented terms of reference); H. R., Committee on Interstate and Foreign Commerce, *SEC Voluntary Compliance Program*, p. 13 (finding that "Corporate declarations of cessation of illegal or questionable activities are insufficient absent thorough follow-up investigation by the Commission").

115. Cf. Fred L. Polak, *The Image of the Future: Enlightening the Past, Orienting the Present, Forecasting the Future* 1 and 2 (New York: Oceana Publications, 1961); Wendell Bell and James A. Mau, eds., *The Sociology of the Future* (New York: Russell Sage Foundation, 1971); Walter Kaufman, *Without Guilt and Justice: From Decidophobia to Autonomy* (New York: Dell, 1973); Philippe Nonet and Philip Selznick, *Law and Society in Transition: Toward Responsive Law* (New York: Harper & Row, 1978), pp. 92–94.

116. Cf. Simons and Califano, *The Media and Business*, pp. xi, xiii.

117. Cf. James L. Peacock, *Consciousness and Change: Symbolic Anthropology in Evolutionary Perspective* (Oxford: Basil Blackwell, 1975), pp. 136–137.

118. If shame is to be used sparingly, as urged in Al Katz, "Dangerousness: A Theoretical Reconstruction of the Criminal Law—Part II,"

Buffalo Law Review 21 (1972): 603–640, pp. 620–621, it may often be essential to hold it in reserve until corporate reactions have been assessed.

119. *New York Times*, 13 Feb. 1903, p. 8.

120. Notably New Jersey, New York, Illinois, Hawaii, and Pennsylvania. See e.g., New Jersey Statutes Annotated 52: 9 M–1 et seq.

121. This is suggested, for example, by the informal screening process in the Appin Mine disaster when, at the request of the Minister for Mines, Judge Goran was asked to advise on the question whether grounds for prosecution arose from his report; see Andrew Hopkins, "Crime Without Punishment: The Appin Mine Disaster," *Australian Quarterly*, Summer 1981, pp. 455–466, p. 457. Rules for coordination would be necessary to avoid duplication of investigative effort and excessive hardship to defendants at the pre-trial stage of corporate criminal process. Cf. "Developments in the Law—Corporate Crime," pp. 1311–1340.

122. As regards personification of corporations, see Thurman Arnold, *The Folklore of Capitalism* (New Haven: Yale University Press, 1937), ch. 8. As regards corporations as private governments see Grant McConnell, *Private Power and American Democracy* (New York: Knopf, 1966); Sanford A. Lakoff and Daniel Rich, *Private Government* (Glenview, Ill.: Scott, Foresman, 1973); Nadel, *Corporations and Political Accountability*, ch. 5.

123. G. B., Department of Trade and Industry, *Company Law Reform* (London: Her Majesty's Stationery Office, Command 5391, 1973), para. 10.

124. Caterpillar Tractor Company, *A Code of Worldwide Business Conduct* (Peoria, Ill.: Caterpillar Tractor Co., 1977), p. 9.

125. See Thomas J. Schoenbaum, "The Relationship between Corporate Disclosure and Corporate Responsibility," *Fordham Law Review* 40 (1972): 565–594.

126. See generally George A. Steiner, *Business and Society* (New York: Random House, 2nd ed., 1974); Simons and Califano, *The Media and Business*, pp. xvii–xvii; Stevenson, "Corporations and Social Responsibility," p. 726; Russell B. Stevenson, Jr., *Corporations and Information: Secrecy, Access, and Disclosure* (Baltimore: Johns Hopkins Press, 1980), chs. 9–11.

127. See A. A. Sommer, Jr., "The Impact of the SEC on Corporate Governance," in DeMott, *Corporations at the Crossroads*, pp. 177–215. However, under the Reagan administration, the trend is being reversed: see *New York Times*, 21 April 1982, p. D1.

128. See e.g., Frederick D. Sturdivant and Larry M. Robinson, *The Corporate Social Challenge* (Homewood, Ill.: Irwin, 1981), pp. 145–150; Clark C. Abt, *The Social Audit for Management* (New York: Amacom, 1977); David Imberg and Peter MacMahon, "Company Law Reform," *Social Audit* 1 (2) (1973): 3–17.

129. See U.S. SEC, *Staff Report on Corporate Accountability*, for Senate Committee on Banking, Housing and Urban Affairs, 96th Cong., 2nd Sess., 1980, pp. 227–327; U.S. H.R., Committee on Interstate and Foreign Commerce, *Report of the Advisory Committee on Corporate Disclosure to the*

Securities and Exchange Commission, 95th Cong., 1st Sess., 1977, chs. 7–8; Homer Kripke, *The SEC and Securities Disclosure: Regulation in Search of a Purpose* (New York: Law and Business, 1979), p. 275; Roberta S. Karmel, *Regulation by Prosecution* (New York: Simon & Schuster, 1982); Lamb, Armstrong, and Morigi, *Business, Media and the Law*, p. 86; Note, "Disclosure of Payments to Foreign Government Officials under the Securities Acts," *Harvard Law Review* 89 (1976): 1848–1870; *Business Week*, 27 Nov. 1978: 86–92. But see Simon M. Lorne, Book Review of Kripke, *The SEC and Securities Disclosure, University of Pennsylvania Law Review* 128 (1980): 1261–1273.

130. See text at Notes 90–100 above.

131. See Note, "Foreign Bribes and the Securities Acts Disclosure Requirements," *Michigan Law Review* 74 (1976): 1222–1242, pp. 1241–1242.

132. See Douglas M. Branson, "Progress in the Art of Social Accounting and Other Arguments for Disclosure on Corporate Social Responsibility," *Vanderbilt Law Review* 29 (1976): 539–683, p. 675; Coffee, "Beyond the Shut-Eyed Sentry," pp. 1265–1266; Eric D. Roiter, "Illegal Corporate Practices and the Disclosure Requirements of the Federal Securities Laws," *Fordham Law Review* 50 (1982): 781–813. Consider also Lawrence W. Sherman, *Scandal and Reform: Controlling Police Corruption* (Berkeley and Los Angeles: University of California Press, 1978), ch. 9.

133. Cf. Coffee, "Beyond the Shut-Eyed Sentry," p. 1252.

134. See e.g., Ralph W. Estes, "A Comprehensive Corporate Social Reporting Model," in Lee J. Seidler and Lynn L. Siedler, *Social Accounting: Theory, Issues and Cases* (Los Angeles: Melville, 1975): 185–204.

135. Christopher D. Stone, *Where the Law Ends: The Social Control of Corporate Behavior* (New York: Harper & Row, 1975), p. 244.

136. Consider e.g., Ralph K. Winter, *Government and the Corporation* (Washington, D. C.: American Enterprise Institute for Public Policy Research, 1978), pp. 53–56.

137. See Kenneth E. Boulding, *The Organizational Revolution: A Study in the Ethics of Economic Organization* (Chicago: Quadrangle Books, 1968), pp. 131, 135–36; Hugh Stretton, *The Political Sciences* (London: Routledge & Kegan Paul, 1969), pp. 404–410. It was for this reason that Allied Chemical decided not to use the term "audit" to describe the non-financial compliance measures it introduced after the Kepone crisis.

138. H. R. 4973, 96th Cong., 1st Sess., 1979; H. R. 7040, 96th Cong., 2nd Sess., 1980. See further U. S. H. R., Subcommittee on Crime of the Committee of the Judiciary, *Corporate Crime*, 96th Cong., 2nd Sess., 1980; John Conyers, Jr., "Corporate and White-Collar Crime: A View by the Chairman of the House Subcommittee on Crime," *American Criminal Law Review* 17 (1980): 287–300, pp. 293–297; W. Allen Spurgeon and Terence P. Fagan, "Criminal Liability for Life-Endangering Corporate Conduct," *Journal of Criminal Law & Criminology* 72 (1981): 400–433; John W. Hanley, "Monsanto's 'Early Warning' System," *Harvard Business Review* 59(6) (1981):

107–120. There is, however, entrenched resistance to disclosure of hazardous risks: See e.g., *New York Times*, 15 March 1982, p. 1.

139. Cf. H. R. 7010, 96th Cong., 2nd Sess., 1980, §201 (proposed Corporate Democracy Act, annual report disclosure provision of which extends to very limited range of injury-causing activities). By contrast, §508(a), would impose an obligation on corporate officers similar to that contemplated under H. R. 4973, 96th Cong., 1st Sess., 1979, as discussed above.

140. See generally Kent Greenawalt and Eli Noam, "Confidentiality Claims of Business Organizations," in Harvey J. Goldschmid, ed., *Business Disclosure: Government's Need to Know* (New York: McGraw-Hill, 1979), pp. 378–412; Stevenson, *Corporations and Information*, ch. 2.

141. 21 U.S.C. §331(j) (1976). However, where corporate conduct or information involves illegality, the right to secrecy may be defeated as a matter of public interest. See Guthrie v. Harkness, 199 U. S. 148, 157–59 (1905); Allied Mills Industries Pty. Ltd. v. Trade Practices Commission, 34 A.L.R. 105 (1981). For reviews of the law and practice in this area, see Dorothy Glancy, "Disclosure of Trade Secrets under the US Freedom of Information Act," *European Industrial Property Review* 2 (1981): 38–44; Thomas O. McGarity and Sidney A. Shapiro, "The Trade Secret Status of Health and Safety Testing Information: Reforming Agency Disclosure Policies," *Harvard Law Review* 93 (1980): 837–888; Roger P. Gilson, Jr., "Administrative Disclosure of Private Business Records under the Freedom of Information Act," *Syracuse Law Review* 28 (1977): 923–980; Paula R. Latovick, "Protection for Trade Secrets under the Toxic Substances Control Act of 1976," *Journal of Law Reform* 13 (1980): 329–365; Susan Hileman Malone, "The Corporate Dilemma in 'Reverse' FOIA Suits: Chrysler Corp. v. Schlesinger," *University of Pittsburgh Law Review* 40 (1978): 93–119; *Business Week*, 1 March 1982: 34.

142. See e.g., Consumer Products Safety Commission v. GTE Sylvania Inc., 445 U. S. 902 (1980) (suppression of safety information about television sets); Samuel S. Epstein, "Polluted Data," *The Sciences*, July/Aug. 1978: 16–21, p. 20 (alleged suppression by Allied Chemical of studies indicating carcinogenicity of Kepone).

143. McGarity and Shapiro, "Trade Secret Status of Health and Safety Testing Information," pp. 840–841.

144. Ibid., p. 844.

145. 15 U.S.C. §2613(c) (1976). See generally Latovick, "Toxic Substances Trade Secret Protection."

146. 15 U.S.C. §2604(h)(2)(B) (1976).

147. See McGarity & Shapiro, "Trade Secret Status of Health and Safety Testing Information," pp. 876–888. However, moves are afoot to curtail the scope of the Freedom of Information Act in its application to corporate information held by administrative agencies: See *New York Times*, 16 Oct. 1981, p. A 22; *Wall Street Journal*, 15 Dec. 1981, p. 33; and 21 May 1982, p. 7.

148. See generally Ralph Nader, Peter J. Petkas, and Kate Blackwell, eds., *Whistle Blowing* (New York: Grossman, 1972); Alan F. Westin, ed., *Whistle-Blowing! Loyalty and Dissent in the Corporation* (New York: McGraw-Hill, 1981).

149. See Ermann and Lundman, *Corporate Deviance*, p. 166. See also H. R. 7010, 96th Cong., 2nd Sess., 1980, §401.

150. The mud-slinging dimension comes to the fore in the two leading anthologies, Nader, Petkas, and Blackwell, *Whistle Blowing*, and Westin, *Whistle-Blowing!*

151. See Ermann and Lundman, *Corporate Deviance*, p. 168; *Wall Street Journal*, 2 May 1976, p. 1. But see Norman Bowie, *Business Ethics* (Englewood Cliffs, N.J.: Prentice-Hall, 1982), p. 142.

152. Alan F. Westin and Stephan Salisbury, eds., *Individual Rights in the Corporation* (New York: Pantheon, 1980), p. 88.

153. See further Coffee, "Beyond the Shut-Eyed Sentry," p. 1265. Note that internal whistle-blowing systems, as at Exxon, may also be prone to interpersonal breakdowns in trust and cooperation within the corporation, but the whistle blower who complains publicly "betrays" the corporation as well as colleagues.

154. Quoted in Bowie, *Business Ethics*, p. 144.

155. Contrast e.g., David W. Ewing, *Freedom inside the Organization* (New York: McGraw-Hill, 1977), ch. 9 (focus only on employee bill of rights). Preventive orders could be made available as a sentencing option for this purpose; see generally Stone, *Where the Law Ends*, ch. 16; Brent Fisse, "Responsibility, Prevention, and Corporate Crime," *New Zealand Universities Law Review* 5 (1973): 250–279.

156. See e.g., Rainer Hellmann, *Transnational Control of Multinational Corporations* (New York: Praeger, 1977), p. 113; *Wall Street Journal*, 28 Aug. 1981, p. 24 (Poland spawns consumer movement).

157. Other companies were also involved. See generally S. Prakash Sethi and James E. Post, "Public Consquences of Private Action: The Marketing of Infant Formula in Less Developed Countries," *California Management Review* 21 (1979): 35–48.

158. See Douglas Johnson, "A Glimpse at Nestlé's Anti-Boycott Strategy," *Business and Society Review* 37 (Spring, 1981): 65–67.

159. *Multinational Monitor*, April 1982: 10. Nestlé has also financed a committee, headed by Senator Edmund Muskie, to monitor its marketing practices on infant formula: *New York Times*, 5 May 1982, p. C17.

160. James E. Post and Edward Baer, "Demarketing Infant Formula: Consumer Products in the Developing World," *Journal of Contemporary Business* 7 (1980): 17–35.

161. See e.g., Mark Dowie, "The Corporate Crime of the Century," *Mother Jones*, Nov. 1970: 23–49; David Weir and Mark Schapiro, "Pesticide Pollution Goes Multinational," *Business and Society Review* 37 (Spring, 1981): 47–53; *Wall Street Journal*, 8 April 1980, p. 1.

162. See generally Milton Silverman, *The Drugging of the Americas* (Berkeley and Los Angeles: University of California Press, 1976); Milton Silverman, Philip R. Lee, and Mia Lydecker, *Prescriptions for Death: The Drugging of the Third World* (Berkeley and Los Angeles: University of California Press, 1982).

163. Protection of Trading Interests Act, 1980 (United Kingdom); Foreign Proceedings (Prohibition of Certain Evidence) Act, 1976 (Australia); Foreign Antitrust Judgments (Restriction of Enforcement) Act, 1979 (Australia); Business Records Protection Act, 1947 (Canada). See generally Note, "Ordering Production of Documents from Abroad in Violation of Foreign Law," *University of Chicago Law Review* 31 (1964): 791–810; Note, "Foreign Nondisclosure Laws and Domestic Discovery Orders in Antitrust Litigation," *Yale Law Journal* 88 (1979): 612–628; Gillian Triggs, "Extraterritorial Reach of United States Anti-Trust Legislation: The International Law Implications of the Westinghouse Allegations of a Uranium Producers' Cartel," *Melbourne University Law Review* 12 (1979): 250–283.

164. John Braithwaite, "Transnational Corporations and Corruption: Towards Some International Solutions," *International Journal of the Sociology of Law* 7 (1979): 125–142, pp. 128–139.

165. U. N. Economic and Social Council, Commission on Transnational Corporations, *Transnational Corporations: Codes of Conduct* (New York: U. N. E/C. 10/AC. 2/8, 1978). See also U. N. Economic and Social Council, Commission on Transnational Corporations, "Intergovernmental Working Group Report on the Formulation of a Code of Conduct," *International Legal Materials* 16 (1977): 709–723.

166. For a pessimistic view re international regulation and an optimistic view re regional regulation, see Hellmann, *Transnational Control of Multinational Corporations*, pp. 119–126.

167. Perceived as a significant threat in George W. Coombe, Jr., "Multinational Codes of Conduct," *Business Lawyer* 36 (Nov., 1980): 11–43, p. 25; *The Economist*, Oct. 8, 1977: 89.

168. Cf. Robert C. Clark, "The Interdisciplinary Study of Legal Evolution," *Yale Law Journal* 90 (1981): 1238–1274. But see Lawrence M. Friedman, *The Legal System: A Social Science Perspective* (New York: Russell Sage Foundation, 1979), pp. 287–290. The value of formal control by law, however, should not be exaggerated, given both the limited access of plaintiffs or complainants to the system and the restricted intake of violators. See e.g., Bruce Wasserstein and Mark J. Green, *With Justice for Some* (Boston: Beacon Press, 1972). There is also a case for minimizing resort to law, on the ground that negotiation and mediation are more effective and less drastic. See e.g., Note, "Rethinking Regulation: Negotiation as an Alternative to Traditional Rulemaking," *Harvard Law Review* 94 (1981): 1876–1891.

169. See Marshall B. Clinard, *Cities with Little Crime: The Case of Switzerland* (Cambridge: Cambridge University Press, 1978); William Clifford, *Crime Control in Japan* (Lexington, Mass.: Lexington Books, 1976), pp. 7–12. As

Jane Jacobs has expounded in *The Death and Life of Great American Cities* (Harmondsworth: Penguin, 1965), p. 41:

> The first thing to understand is that the public peace—the sidewalk and street peace—of cities is not kept primarily by the police, necessary as police are. It is kept primarily by an intricate, almost unconscious, network of voluntary controls and standards among the people themselves, and enforced by the people themselves. In some city areas—older public housing projects and streets with very high population turnover are often conspicuous examples—the keeping of public sidewalk law and order is left almost entirely to the police and special guards. Such places are jungles.

170. See e.g., Robert Lindsey, "Ex-Boss Contends He's Scapegoat in Lockheed Scandal," *Chicago Tribune*, 11 July 1977.

Chapter 21

1. See generally Marshall B. Clinard and Peter C. Yeager, *Corporate Crime* (New York: Free Press, 1980), pp. 318–322; Francis E. Rourke, *Secrecy and Publicity: Dilemmas of Democracy* (Baltimore: Johns Hopkins Press, 1961), ch. 6.

2. It is unnecessary for present purposes to tackle the vexed problem of specifying the distinctive features of punishment, penalties, and remedies. The important question is not the name of a regulatory practice but whether it is justifiable, an issue governed by how its advantages and disadvantages compare with those of practices with different rules of implementation: See John Griffiths, "The Limits of Criminal Law Scholarship," *Yale Law Journal* 79 (1970): 1388–1474, pp. 1410–1411. See generally Note, "'Corrective Advertising' Orders of the Federal Trade Commission," *Harvard Law Review* 85 (1971): 477–506, pp. 499–501; Note, "Toward a Constitutional Definition of Punishment," *Columbia Law Review* 80 (1980): 1667–1685.

3. See further Brent Fisse, "The Use of Publicity as a Criminal Sanction against Business Corporations," *Melbourne University Law Review* 8 (1971): 107–150, pp. 110–117.

4. 3 Geo. IV c. cvi (1822). Similar provisions were: 55 Geo. III c. xcix (1815), s. 3; 6 & 7 Will. IV c. 37 (1836), ss. 8, 12; 1 & 2 Vict. c. 28 (1838), ss. 7, 11.

5. *The Works of Jeremy Bentham* 1, ed., John Bowring (London: Simpkin, Marshall, 1843), p. 460.

6. For U. S. examples, see Clinard and Yaeger, *Corporate Crime*, p. 320, n. 18.

7. Environmental Protection Agency, Docket No. CAA (211)—60 (1981) (consent agreeement). The relevant terms of the consent agreement are set out in Appendix A. See also Sears Roebuck & Co. Inc., EPA, Docket No. CAA (211)—44 (1980); Harry Smith, Jr. d/b/a Refinery Fresh Service

Station, EPA, Docket No. CAA (211)—142 (1980); Swan Oil Company, EPA, Docket No. CAA (211)—185 (1980); Yellow Cab Company, EPA, Docket No. CAA (211)—133 (1980).

8. EPA, Docket No. CAA (211)—17 (1980) (consent agreement). The relevant terms of the consent agreement are set out in Appendix B.

9. D. L. R. (BNA) 10–31–77 El (1977). See also J. P. Stevens & Co., Inc., v. NLRB, 380 F.2d 292, 304–305 (1967).

10. 402 F. Supp. 744, 752 (1975).

11. 79 F. T. C. 248 (1971). See also Warner-Lambert Co., 86 F. T. C. 1398 (1975). See generally George Eric Rosden and Peter Eric Rosden, *The Law of Advertising* 1 (New York: Bender, 1976), ch. 9; Note, "'Corrective Advertising' Orders;" Note, "*Warner-Lambert Co. v. FTC*: Corrective Advertising Gives Listerine a Taste of its Own Medicine," *Northwestern University Law Review* 73 (1978): 957–979.

12. U. S., National Commission on Reform of Federal Criminal Laws, *Study Draft* 1 (Washington, D.C.: U. S. Government Printing Office, 1970), s. 405. Adverse publicity sanctions were included in many of the legislative bills which ensued. See e.g., S.1, 94th Cong. 1st Sess., 1975, §2004; H. R. 10850, 94th Cong. 1st Sess., 1975, §2004; H. R. 3907, 94th Cong. 1st Sess., 1975, §2004; H. R. 333, 94th Cong., 1st Sess., 1975, §3007.

13. U. S. National Commission on Reform of Federal Criminal Laws, *Final Report* (Washington, D.C.: U. S. Government Printing Office, 1971) s. 3007.

14. Interview with Louis B. Schwartz, Director of the National Commission on Reform of Federal Criminal Laws, Nov. 1980. See also John E. Conklin, *"Illegal but not Criminal": Business Crime in America* (Englewood Cliffs, N.J.: Prentice-Hall, 1977), pp. 132–133; Simeon M. Kriesberg, "Decisionmaking Models and the Control of Corporate Crime;" *Yale Law Journal* 85 (1976): 1091–1121, p. 1108.

15. As to the limitations of fines, see Christopher D. Stone, *Where the Law Ends: The Social Control of Corporate Behavior* (New York: Harper & Row, 1975), ch. 6. As to the punitive possibility of probation, see James A. Geraghty, "Structural Crime and Institutional Rehabilitation: A New Approach to Corporate Sentencing," *Yale Law Journal* 89 (1979): 353–375.

16. Herbert L. Packer, *The Limits of the Criminal Sanction* (Stanford, Calif.: Stanford University Press, 1968), p. 361.

17. Alan M. Dershowitz, "Increasing Community Control over Corporate Crime," *Yale Law Journal* 71 (1961): 281–306, p. 289.

18. "Developments in the Law—Corporate Crime: Regulating Corporate Behavior through Criminal Sanctions," *Harvard Law Review* 92 (1979): 1227–1375, pp. 1365–1366.

19. See *Los Angeles Times*, 10 May 1981, p. 1; *Wall Street Journal*, 2 April 1982, p. 1.

20. See further John C. Coffee, Jr., "'No Soul to Damn: No Body to Kick': An Unscandalized Inquiry into the Problem of Corporate Punishment," *Michigan Law Review* 79 (1981): 386–459, pp. 413–424 (equity

fines); Brent Fisse, "Community Service as a Sanction against Corporations," *Wisconsin Law Review* (1981): 970–1017; Geraghty, "Structural Crime and Institutional Rehabilitation"; Stephen A. Yoder, "Criminal Sanctions for Corporate Illegality," *Journal of Criminal Law and Criminology* 69 (1978): 40–58.

21. See further Brent Fisse, "Criminal Law and Consumer Protection," in A. J. Duggan and L. W. Darvall, eds., *Consumer Protection Law and Theory* (Sydney: Law Book Co., 1980): 182–199, pp. 182–184.

22. See Anthony Lewis, "Trust Case Raises Big Questions," *New York Times*, 12 Feb. 1961, section IV, p. 6.

23. See Coffee, "'No Soul to Damn: No Body to Kick'," pp. 425–427; Fisse, "Publicity as a Criminal Sanction against Business Corporations," pp. 126–133.

24. Coffee, "'No Soul to Damn: No Body to Kick'," pp. 425–426. See also Harold Wilensky, *Organizational Intelligence: Knowledge and Policy in Government and Industry* (New York: Basic Books, 1969), pp. 147–151.

25. See references in Notes 7–8 above. It may also be noted that formal publicity would appeal to materialistic self-interest if used to punish an offender by providing the notice necessary for a class-action suit by the victims of the offense.

26. See John Braithwaite, *Corporate Crime in the Pharmaceutical Industry* (London: Routledge & Kegan Paul, 1983), ch. 6.

27. Fisse, "Publicity as a Criminal Sanction against Business Corporations," p. 143. See also Ira M. Millstein and Salem M. Katsh, *The Limits of Corporate Power* (New York: Macmillan, 1981), ch. 6.

28. *New York Times*, 8 Oct. 1981, p. D16.

29. It is a mistake to equate punitive publicity orders with remedial corrective advertising orders. The former are concerned primarily with the impact on defendants, the latter primarily with the impact on victims. It follows that the findings of such studies as Robert F. Dyer and Phillip G. Kuehl, "A Longitudinal Study of Corrective Advertising," *Journal of Marketing Research* 15 (Feb. 1978): 39–48, are inconclusive re punitive efficacy.

30. Fisse, "Publicity as a Criminal Sanction against Business Corporations," p. 129.

31. Paul F. Lazarsfeld and Robert K. Merton, "Requisite Conditions for Propaganda Success," in Reo Millard Christenson and Robert O. McWilliams, *Voice of the People* (New York: McGraw-Hill, 1962): 340–343, pp. 341–342.

32. For statements of the objection, see Coffee, "'No Soul to Damn: No Body to Kick'," pp. 426–427; Fisse, "Publicity as a Criminal Sanction against Business Corporations," pp. 131–133. The evidence as to public attitudes is reviewed at length in John Braithwaite, "Challenging Just Deserts: Punishing White-Collar Criminals," *Journal of Criminal Law & Criminology* 73 (1982): 1301–1341, pp. 1309–1316. Cf. Sanford H. Kadish, "Some Observations on the Use of Criminal Sanctions in Enforcing Eco-

nomic Regulations," *University of Chicago Law Review* 30 (1963): 423–449 (non-empirical support of "moral neutrality" thesis).

33. Marvin Wolfgang, *National Survey of Crime Severity: Final National Level Geometric Means and Ratio Scores by Offense Stimuli Items* (Philadelphia: University of Pennsylvania, unpublished manuscript).

34. "Changing Morality: The Two Americas; A Time—Louis Harris Poll," *Time*, June 26, 1969: 93.

35. See Braithwaite, "Challenging Just Deserts," pp. 1309–1316.

36. Harry V. Ball and Lawrence M. Friedman, "The Use of Criminal Sanctions in the Enforcement of Economic Legislation: A Sociological View," *Stanford Law Review* 17 (1965): 197–223, p. 209. Cf. Coffee, "'No Soul to Damn: No Body to Kick'," pp. 426–427.

37. See further Brent Fisse, "The Social Policy of Corporate Criminal Responsibility," *Adelaide Law Review* 8 (1978): 361–412, pp. 371–382.

38. See Braithwaite, "Challenging Just Deserts,"pp. 1309–1316; and particularly Francis T. Cullen, Bruce G. Link, and Craig W. Polanzi, "The Seriousness of Crime Revisited: Have Attitudes toward White-Collar Crime Changed?," *Criminology* 20 (1982): 83–102.

39. This is suggested by the way in which moral opinion developed during the Pinto trial: See Victoria Lynn Swigert and Ronald A. Farrell, "Corporate Homicide: Definitional Processes in the Creation of Deviance," *Law and Society Review* 15 (1980): 161–182. As to the educative impact of law, see generally Judith N. Shklar, *Legalism* (Cambridge, Mass.: Harvard University Press, 1964), pp. 120–121; Hugh Dalziel Duncan, *Symbols in Society* (New York: Oxford University Press, 1968), pp. 236–248; Sidney Kraus and Dennis Davis, *The Effects of Mass Communication on Political Behavior* (University Park: Pennsylvania State Press, 1976); Jonathan Glover, *Responsibility* (London: Routledge & Kegan Paul, 1970), pp. 155–160; Stanley I. Benn, "Freedom and Persuasion," *Australasian Journal of Philosophy* 45 (1967): 259–275; Tibor Scitovsky, "Ignorance as a Source of Oligopoly Power," *American Economic Review, Papers and Proceedings*, 40(2) (1950): 48–53; Franklin Zimring and Gordon Hawkins, "The Legal Threat as an Instrument of Social Change," *Journal of Social Issues* 27(2) (1971): 33–48; Alfred E. McCormick, Jr., "Rule Enforcement and Moral Indignation: Some Observations on the Effects of Criminal Antitrust Convictions upon Societal Reaction Processes," *Social Problems* 25(1) (1977): 30–39.

40. Coffee, "'No Soul to Damn: No Body to Kick'," p. 426.

41. Wayne L, Pines, "Regulatory Letters, Publicity and Recalls," *Food Drug Cosmetic Law Journal* 31 (1976): 352–359, p. 354.

42. See further Fisse, "Publicity as a Criminal Sanction against Business Corporations," pp. 142–144.

43. See *Chicago Tribune*, 5 Feb. 1980; *Los Angeles Times*, 31 Jan. 1980.

44. Interview with Robert Pitofsky, former FTC commissioner, June 1982. Almost invariably, FTC corrective advertising is agreed to by consent order, the one exception to date being the Listerine case, Warner-Lambert Co., 86 F. T. C. 1398 (1975). See further Robert Pitofsky, "Beyond Nader:

Consumer Protection and the Regulation of Advertising," *Harvard Law Review* 90 (1977): 661–701, pp. 700–701.

45. See Canada, *Report of the Royal Commission on Corporate Concentration* (Ottawa: Information Canada, 1978), p. 348. Cf. Philip W. Moore, "What's Good for the Country is Good for GM," *Washington Monthly*, Dec. 1970: 10–18, p. 14 (example of alleged cancellation of $80,000 of newspaper advertising by General Motors because of coverage given to "consumer matters").

46. As to business subversion of the media, see Bernard Rubin, *Big Business and the Mass Media* (Lexington, Mass.: Lexington Books, 1977), p. 13; S. Prakash Sethi, *Up Against the Corporate Wall* (Englewood Cliffs, N.J.: Prentice-Hall, 1977), pp. 427–452. On sanctions, see references in Note 20 above. The alternative of compelling the media to publish a message specified by court order would seem unconstitutional: Miami Herald Publishing Co. v. Tornillo, 418 U. S. 241, 257 (1974). See generally David B. Gaebler, "First Amendment Protection Against Government Compelled Expression and Association," *Boston College Law Review* 23 (1982): 995–1023.

47. Cf. Fisse, "Publicity as a Business Sanction against Corporations," pp. 147–148.

48. Coffee, "'No Soul to Damn: No Body to Kick'," p. 426. See also S. Prakash Sethi, *Advocacy Advertising and Large Corporations* (Lexington, Mass.: Lexington Books, 1977); William B. Waegel, M. David Ermann, and Alan M. Horowitz, "Organizational Responses to Imputations of Deviance," *Sociological Quarterly* 22 (1981): 43–55; Maria Shao, "Concerns Seeking Credibility Put Scientists in Spotlight," *Wall Street Journal*, 22 Sept. 1981, p. 29.

49. *Washington Post*, 19 Feb. 1978, quoted in M. David Ermann & Richard J. Lundman, *Corporate Deviance* (New York: Holt, Rinehart and Winston, 1982), p. 141.

50. See Fisse, "Publicity as a Criminal Sanction against Business Corporations," pp. 133–135.

51. Virginia State Board of Pharmacy v. Virginia Citizens Consumer Council, Inc., 425 U. S. 748 (1976) (commercial speech protected by First Amendment); First National Bank of Boston v. Bellotti, 435 U. S. 765 (1978) (traditional First Amendment protection extends to corporate persons). See further Herbert Schmertz, *Corporations and the First Amendment* (New York: Amacom, 1978); Edward L. Barrett, Jr., "'The Uncharted Area'—Commercial Speech and the First Amendment," *University of California at Davis Law Review* 13 (1980): 175–209; William Patton and Randall Bartlett, "Corporate 'Persons' and Freedom of Speech: The Political Impact of Legal Mythology," *Wisconsin Law Review* (1981): 494–512.

52. See generally *Wall Street Journal*, 2 April 1982, pp. 1, 16 (image advertising as advance protection); *Rydge's Journal*, Feb. 1980: 22–25 (saturation-selling); *New York Times*, 1 Nov. 1981, p. F6 (namesmanship); *Wall Street Journal*, 28 Oct. 1981, p. 33 (spinoff subsidiaries to improve image);

M. David Ermann, "The Operative Goals of Corporate Philanthropy: Contributions to the Public Broadcasting Service, 1972–1976," *Social Problems* 25(5) (1978): 504–514.

53. See Jean Begeman, "Psychological Warfare: A & P Brand," *New Republic*, Nov. 14, 1949: 11–13; Note, "Appeals to the Electorate by Private Businesses: Injury to Competitors and the Right to Petition," *Yale Law Journal* 70 (1960): 135–150, p. 138.

54. ITT Continental Baking Co., 79 F. T. C. 248 (1971).

55. See Douglas Johnson, "A Glimpse at Nestle's Anti-Boycott Strategy," *Business and Society Review* 37 (Spring 1980): 65–67.

56. See e.g., *Wall Street Journal*, 2 April 1982, p. 1.

57. *Wall Street Journal*, 21 Dec. 1981, p. 23. Note also the suspension of advertising by Mitsubishi and Hitachi after being accused of stealing trade secrets from IBM: *Wall Street Journal*, 1 July 1982, p. 22.

58. It is possible that counterpublicity contributed somewhat to the dropping of the antitrust suit against IBM. See further Ch. 17, above.

59. Cf. the view typically expressed in business that good works attract little public recognition. See e.g., Howard Simons and Joseph A. Califano, Jr., eds., *The Media and Business* (New York: Vintage Books, 1979), pp. xiv-xv.

60. See Note 12 above.

61. Dershowitz, "Increasing Community Control over Corporate Crime," pp. 288–289.

62. Ibid., p. 298. Cf. Lewis, "Trust Case Raises Big Questions"; and see further Ch. 16, above.

63. Sandra S. Evans and Richard Lundman, "Newspaper Coverage of Corporate Price-Fixing: A Replication," unpublished manuscript.

64. Ibid.

65. D. L. R. (BNA) 10–31–77 E1 (1977).

66. Federal Trade Commission Docket No. C-2777 (1978). We are indebted in what follows to Ermann and Lundman, *Corporate Deviance*, pp. 139–141, for their critique of this case.

67. Ermann and Lundman, *Corporate Deviance*, 141.

68. Ibid.

69. A criticism frequently levelled at FTC corrective advertising is that it is punitive as opposed to remedial: See e.g., Note, "Corrective Advertising: Panacea or Punishment," *Duquesne Law Review* 17 (1978): 169–187.

70. Stone, *Where the Law Ends*, part 4. See also Lawrence W. Sherman, *Scandal and Reform: Controlling Police Corruption* (Berkeley and Los Angeles: University of California Press, 1978), ch. 9 (scandal has short-term impact but internal reforms are of dominant significance in the longer term).

71. Stone, *Where the Law Ends*, p. 121.

72. Christopher D. Stone, "A Slap on the Wrist for the Kepone Mob," *Business and Society Review* 22 (1977): 4–11, p. 11.

73. See further Christopher D. Stone, "The Place of Enterprise Liability in the Control of Corporate Conduct," *Yale Law Journal* 90 (1980): 1–77,

pp. 7–28; Deborah A. deMott, "Reweaving the Corporate Veil: Management Structure and the Control of Corporate Information," in Deborah A. deMott, ed., *Corporations at the Crossroads: Governance and Reform* (New York: McGraw-Hill Book Company, 1980); 279–324.

74. Kriesberg, "Decisionmaking Models and the Control of Corporate Crime."

75. We are indebted to John Byrne for this point.

76. See references at Note 20 above. See also John C. Coffee, Jr., "Beyond the Shut-Eyed Sentry: Toward a Theoretical View of Corporate Misconduct and an Effective Legal Response," *Virginia Law Review* 63 (1977): 1099–1278.

77. Cf. Coffee, "'No Soul to Damn: No Body to Kick'," pp. 429–34; Fisse, "Publicity as a Criminal Sanction against Business Corporations," p. 121.

78. As to the tendency of responsibility for white-collar crime to be passed downward in the power structure, see generally John Braithwaite, "Paradoxes of Class Bias in Criminal Justice," in Harold Pepinsky, ed., *Rethinking Criminology* (Beverly Hills, Calif.: Sage, 1982): 70–75.

79. See Fisse, "Social Policy of Corporate Criminal Responsibility," pp. 373–376.

80. N.Z., *Report of the Royal Commission to Inquire into the Crash on Mount Erebus, Antarctica, of a DC10 Aircraft Operated by Air New Zealand Limited* (Wellington: N.Z. Govt. Printer, 1981), para. 393.

81. John C. Coffee, Jr., "Making the Punishment Fit the Corporation: The Problems of Finding an Optimal Corporation Criminal Sanction," *Northern Illinois University Law Review* 1 (1980): 1–36, 48–55, p. 52.

82. See references at Note 20 above.

83. Coffee, "'No Soul to Damn: No Body to Kick'," pp. 429–434. See also South Australia, Criminal Law and Penal Methods Reform Committee, *Fourth Report, The Substantive Criminal Law* (Adelaide: South Australian Government Printer, 1978), pp. 361–362 (proposal that internal discipline orders be available as a sentence against corporate offenders).

84. John J. McCloy, *The Great Oil Spill* (New York: Chelsea House, 1976).

85. Coffee, "'No Soul to Damn: No Body to Kick'," p. 431.

86. Ibid., p. 433–434.

87. Ibid., p. 433.

88. Mark Crane, "Commentary: The Due Process Considerations in the Imposition of Corporate Liability," *Northern Illinois Law Review* 1 (1980): 39–48, p. 42.

89. The prescription and enforcement of internal disciplinary obligations depend on contract of employment, at least traditionally. See Lawrence E. Blades, "Employment at Will vs. Individual Freedom: On Limiting the Abusive Exercise of Employer Power," *Columbia Law Review* 67 (1967): 1404–1435.

90. *Report of the Tribunal to Inquire Into the Disaster at Aberfan on October 21st, 1966* (London: Her Majesty's Stationery Office, 1966), p. 93.

91. See text and references at Notes 16–17 above. See also Coffee, "'No Soul to Damn: No Body to Kick'," p. 429.

92. L. H. Leigh, *The Criminal Liability of Corporations in English Law* (London: Weidenfeld & Nicholson, 1969), p. 160.

93. Wally Olins, *The Corporate Personality: An Inquiry into the Nature of Corporate Identity* (New York: Mayflower Books, 1978): A. A. Berle, *The 20th Century Capitalist Revolution* (New York: Harcourt, Brace, 1954), pp. 90–91; Earl Frank Cheit, ed., *The Business Establishment* (New York: Wiley, 1964), pp. 184, 188, 191; George Katona, *Psychological Analysis of Economic Behavior* (New York: McGraw-Hill, 1951), p. 204; Irwin Ross, *The Image Merchants* (Garden City, N.Y.: Doubleday, 1959), pp. 266–67; Charles Channon, "Corporations and the Politics of Perception," *Advertising Quarterly* 60 (2) (1981): 12–15; Russell B. Stevenson, Jr., "Corporations and Social Responsibility: In Search of the Corporate Soul," *George Washington Law Review* 12 (1974): 709–736, p. 724. For a different view, see Albert T. Lauterbach, *Men, Motives and Money* (Ithaca, N.Y.: Cornell University Press, 2nd ed., 1959), p. 227.

94. See references at Note 19 above. See also *Wall Street Journal*, 2 July 1982, p. 22.

95. Consider also the impact of adverse publicity on the goodwill the community feels toward business as a whole. See text and references at Note 15, Ch. 20.

96. There are other less significant possible disadvantages as well (e.g., loss of possible money from fines for future enforcement; risk of encouraging some to find ways to break law as a result of discovering facts about offenses and the way they are committed, investigated, or punished). See Fisse, "Publicity as a Criminal Sanction against Business Corporations," pp. 141–142, 145. See also Henry Mintzberg, *The Structuring of Organizations* (Englewood, Cliffs, N.J.: Prentice-Hall, 1979), p. 427 (risk of excessive centralization of power within corporations).

97. Max Ways, "A Plea for Perspective," in Clarence Walton, ed., *The Ethics of Corporate Conduct* (Englewood Cliffs, N.J.: Prentice-Hall, Inc., 1977); 102–126, p. 113. We do not endorse Ways' concept of "business normality" as a valid criterion of analysis; on the contrary, we reject it as vacuous.

98. See e.g., Ralph K. Winter, *Government and the Corporation* (Washington, D.C.: American Enterprise Institute for Public Policy Research, 1978); Irving Kristol, *Two Cheers for Capitalism* (New York: Basic Books, 1978); M. Bruce Johnson, ed., *The Attack on Corporate America: The Corporate Issues Sourcebook* (New York: McGraw-Hill, 1978).

99. Douglas M. Branson, "Progress in the Art of Social Accounting and Other Arguments for Disclosure on Corporate Social Responsibility," *Vanderbilt Law Review* 29 (1976): 529–683, pp. 657–658.

100. Coffee, "'No Soul to Damn: No Body to Kick'," pp. 427–428.

101. The impact of the Pinto adverse publicity on sales is discussed in Ch. 4.

102. See Fisse, "Publicity as a Criminal Sanction against Business Corporations," pp. 117–118.

103. The equity fine, as proposed by Coffee, is the paradigm case because it is aimed directly at devaluing the shares of all shareholders. See "'No Soul to Damn: No Body to Kick'," pp. 413–424.

104. See David Miller, *Social Justice* (Oxford: Clarendon Press, 1976), pp. 291–299.

105. Coffee, "'No Soul to Damn: No Body to Kick'," pp. 428–429.

106. See e.g., SEC v. International Telephone and Telegraph Corporation, SEC, Civil No. 78/0807, where ITT filed a motion to seal a complaint about foreign bribes to be filed by the agency (the company claimed that details of foreign bribes were trade secrets, and that disclosure to the public would cause irreparable injury). The motion ultimately failed. Appeal No. 78-0807 (U. S. Court of Appeals, 1978).

107. See text and references at Notes 83–89 above.

108. See further Fisse, "Publicity as a Criminal Sanction against Business Corporations," pp. 139–141.

109. Rourke, *Secrecy and Publicity*, pp. 240–242.

110. 14 A. L. R. 243 (1977).

111. Andrew Hopkins, *The Impact of Prosecutions under the Trade Practices Act* (Canberra: Australian Institute of Criminology, 1978), p. 12. See also Ross Cranston, *Regulating Business: Law and Consumer Agencies* (London: Macmillan, 1979), pp. 144–145.

112. Under the Eighth Amendment far less is required: Rummell v. Estelle, 445 U.S. 263 (1980) (formally proportionate sentence not required under Eighth Amendment except in capital cases and "unique factual circumstances"). Cf. Note, "'Corrective Advertising' Orders," pp. 501–503 (discussion of proportionality in remedial context). Note also that proportionality is not necessarily an absolute principle. It may be qualified by considerations of practicality, exemplary punishment, uncertainty as an aid to deterrence, and voluntary assumption of risk.

113. See e.g., reference at Note 11 above and Appendices A and B.

114. To this it may be objected that all the cases we have studied were extreme and hence the proposition in the text is what one might expect. However, we advocate the use of adverse publicity as a formal sanction only in extreme cases. Moreover, although the cases we selected for study were extreme, they were far from uniformly extreme.

115. See Ch. 5. See also Ch. 10 (vagaries of financial recovery at Sharp).

116. Fisse, "Publicity as a Criminal Sanction against Business Corporations," p. 140.

117. See e.g., Hartnell v. Sharp Corporation of Australia Pty. Ltd., 5 A. L. R. 493 (1975); TPC v. Pye Industries Sales Pty. Ltd. (No. 2), A. T. P. R. 40-089 (1978); United States v. ITT Continental Baking Co.,

420 U. S. 223 (1975); R. v. Rolex Watch Company of Canada Limited, 53 C.C.C. (2d) 445, 451 (1980).

118. See e.g., Eva v. Southern Motors Box Hill Pty. Ltd., 16 A. L. R. 428, 437 (1977).

119. See references at Note 12 above.

120. Publication orders could thus be used: (a) as a punishment and remedy combined, as in cases where punitive as opposed to merely remedial corrective advertising is warranted; or (b) as a remedy alone in cases where punishment is not warranted but where it is expedient to use the criminal process to dispense a remedy.

121. See section on "Problems of Persuasion," above.

122. Cf. Coffee, "'No Soul to Damn: No Body to Kick'," pp. 457–459. Note also the argument that judicial use of probation to fashion new forms of sentences is an undemocratic impingement on the legislative prerogative. See "Reflections on White-Collar Sentencing," *Yale Law Journal* 86 (1977): 589–664, pp. 626–629, 636–637.

123. Rough and ready as the sentencing of individual offenders is, the sentencing of corporate offenders is at an even more primitive stage of development. Among many other prospective sources of complexity in sentencing, the corporate criminal justice system has yet to confront the problems of choice which arise if publicity orders and other sanctions are available against corporate defendants as alternatives to the fine.

Index

Index

Coal Mines Regulation Act (N.S.W.), 91, 92, 99, 100, 236
Coatsworth, John H., 126
Code of Worldwide Business Conduct (Caterpillar Tractor), 273
Coffee, John C., Jr., 23 n.19, 303–304, 305, 310
Coke ovens, 4, 78–88, 267, 276
Coke, Sir Edward, 253
Collins, Captain Jim, 217
Colonial Sugar Refinery Ltd. (CSR) (Aust'l), 101
Commerce Department (U.S.), 191
Commission of Investigation Act (N.J.), 267
Commonwealth Gazette (Aust'l), 286
Communication breakdowns, 55–56, 60–62, 72–73, 93, 98, 117, 138, 156, 168–169, 194–196, 213–214, 234, 271, 277–278
Community service orders, 295
Compensation, out of court settlement, 81–82
Competitors, exploitation of adverse publicity, 47, 48, 59, 152, 201, 212, 229, 273. *See also* Sales impact of adverse publicity
Compliance. *See* Auditing; Corporate regulation; Corporations, internal discipline; Corporations, internal controls; Culture, corporate; Deterrence; Formal publicity as a sanction; Incentives; Informal publicity as a sanction; Reform, corporate; Social audit
Compliance with the Environmental Laws (Allied Chemical), 74
Computer Automation Corporation, 211
Connor, John J., 71
Conspiracy, criminal, 63, 162
Consumers: activism, 3; boycott, 14, 16–17; choice, 37–39, 53–54; groups, 39, 251–253. *See also* Corporate disclosure; Health Research Group; Infant Formula Action Coalition; Nader, Ralph, 253–254
Contempt, of court, 13, 16, 257–260
Control Data Corporation, 198–199
Conway, Virgil E., 20–21
Copp, Harvey, 56
Cordiner, Ralph, 184, 188, 191, 194
Corporate communications, bubbling up, 74, 194–196. *See also* Communications breakdowns

Corporate crime: definition, 1 n.2; social impact, 1–2, 183. *See also* Corporate offenses; Responsibility, individual and corporate
Corporate crime commissions, 271–272
Corporate Crime in the Pharmaceutical Industry (Braithwaite), 8
Corporate decision-making, 37, 122–123, 301. *See also* Corporate reactions to crises
Corporate disclosure, 263, 272–279. *See also* Mandatory disclosure; Voluntary disclosure
Corporate image, 19–20, 47, 50, 59, 66–67, 106, 108, 117, 128–130, 201, 222, 232, 248–249, 306; image advertising, 66–67, 293. *See also* Adverse publicity; Corporate reactions to crises; Counterpublicity; Prestige, corporate; Reputation, loss of as sanction
Corporate offenses, 1–2, 239, 293–294; risktaking offenses, 51–52, 53–54
Corporate prestige. *See* Prestige, corporate
Corporate reactions to crises: absence of praise for good reactions, 227; cover-up, 214–215; hunkering down, 66, 228; lack of official scrutiny of, 225–226, 268–270; self-protective steps, 25, 53, 61–62, 99, 210, 236; task force approach, 60, 69. *See also* Incentives; Technological fixes; Voluntary disclosure
Corporate reform. *See* Reform, corporate
Corporate regulation. *See* Corporate offenses; Corporations, sanctions against; Criminal liability, corporate; Criminal liability, individual; Damages; Enforcement, and corporate regulation; Extraterritorial limits of corporate regulation; Formal publicity, as a sanction; Extraterritorial limits of corporate regulation; Incentives; Informal publicity, as a sanction; Mandatory injunctions; Punishment; Reform, corporate; Reputation, loss of as sanction; Responsibility, individual and corporate; Sentencing; Standard operating procedures; Training programs
Corporate reputation. *See* Prestige, corporate

Index